T0344234

Renaissance Magic and the Return of the Golden Age

The Occult Tradition and Marlowe, Jonson, and Shakespeare

John S. Mebane

University of
Nebraska Press
Lincoln & London

Acknowledgments for the use of previously
published material appear on page xv.
Copyright © 1989 by the University
of Nebraska Press

First paperback printing: 1992

Library of Congress
Cataloging-in-Publication Data
Mebane, John S., 1946-
Renaissance magic and the
return of the Golden Age : the occult
tradition and Marlowe, Jonson, and
Shakespeare / John S. Mebane.
.p. cm.
Bibliography: p.
Includes index.
ISBN 0-8032-3133-4 (alk. paper)
ISBN 0-8032-8179-X (pbk.)
1. English drama - Early modern and
Elizabethan, 1500-1600 - History and criticism.
2. English drama - 17th century -
History and criticism. 3. Occultism
in literature. 4. Magic in literature.
5. Golden age (Mythology) in
literature. 6. Marlowe, Christopher,
1564-1593. Doctor Faustus.
7. Jonson, Ben, 1573?-1637. Alchemist.
8. Shakespeare, William, 1564-1616.
Tempest. 9. Renaissance - England. I. Title.
PR658.03M43 1989
822'.3'0937 - dc19 88-22068
CIP

⊗

To the memory of my parents,
John Harrison Mebane
and
Hannah Price Kallam Mebane

Contents

Illustrations

This study is founded on the premise that literature, history, and philosophy must forge interrelationships which are symbiotic rather than predatory. One of its major purposes is to construct for Renaissance plays on magic a more detailed and genuinely illuminating historical context than has previously been provided; at the same time, I have avoided treating the plays purely as historical allegories or simple ideological statements, seeking instead to explore the dramatists' responses to historical and philosophical currents in a manner which enhances our awareness of the plays' artistic sophistication. Christopher Marlowe, Ben Jonson, and William Shakespeare were thoroughly familiar with the symbolic importance of occult philosophy in the intellectual history of their own era, and the opening chapters provide information which deepens our understanding of the moral, philosophical, social, and political issues to which the playwrights were responding. Simultaneously, the earlier chapters are ends in themselves, and the book as a whole traces a historical movement from its roots in civic humanism through a process of radical development in the Hermetic/Cabalist tradition to its culmination in the birth of science and in attempts to promote radical social and religious reform. In addition to seeking to enhance our appreciation of Renaissance plays in purely aesthetic terms, the study as a whole is intended to reassess our current understanding of ethical and philosophical issues which are central to the Renaissance and which have contributed to the development of modern values and institutions.

A complete theoretical defense of my attempt to reconstruct the mental outlook, values, and emotions of Renaissance philosophers and playwrights, as well as their manipulation of reader or audience response, is obviously far beyond the scope of this preface. I would like to emphasize, however, that in general I concur with the central arguments of Wayne Booth's sagacious book *Critical Understanding: The Powers and Limits of Pluralism.* I would, perhaps, go somewhat further than Booth in stressing that different kinds of critical endeavor may be valid, even when they seem to arrive at conflicting, rather than complementary, interpretations of the same texts. This is not to assert that all interpretations are of equal standing, nor to abandon entirely the quest for a degree of objectivity; it is simply to admit that knowledge is contingent upon the contexts in which interpretation occurs, and there are practical as well as theoretical reasons why none of us can claim to have arrived at certainty. One of the central challenges of contemporary humanistic study is the problem of maintaining a generous tolerance while, at the same time, respecting canons of evidence and striving to refine our criteria of truth. As I reflect upon this study after its completion, I feel the need to emphasize in this preface that the rival interpretations which I have discussed in most detail in this book—including those whose theoretical assumptions differ from my own—are typically those which I have found to be the most challenging possible alternatives to the readings presented in the following chapters. Because of the scope of the study it has been difficult to represent in the notes the full range of opinion on the texts and problems which I have discussed, and I have therefore included in the Bibliography a number of additional important studies.

While I cannot accept entirely E. D. Hirsch's assertion that the only valid critical endeavor is the attempt to reconstruct the meaning intended by the author, there is nonetheless a great deal in the work of Hirsch, Booth, and others which suggests that there are sound methodologies for making an informed inquiry concerning what an author may have wished to communicate. In the present study my own interests have frequently centered upon the manner in which various authors—philosophers and scientists, as well as dramatists—have struggled to express their own visions and/or to affirm their own values while responding to the constraints imposed by their audiences, by censorship, and by numerous other factors. In some cases, as in the study of Jonson's masques (which are sometimes annotated in detail by the author himself), we have access to a wealth of materials which enable us to make such an inquiry an educated one. In the case of other works, such as Marlowe's *Dr. Faustus*, the inquiry must be somewhat more speculative, but may still be informed by evidence. While I have found no single methodology which provides the sole key to all texts, the study is unified by the conviction that Renaissance authors, as John Wallace has convincingly argued, typically expected their audiences to apply to their own situations the principles implied by the authors' works.[1] Historical research may best illuminate those principles and hence intensify our awareness of a work's relevance to our own lives.

I also agree with Professor Hirsch that one can strive with some degree of success to distinguish between one's intepretation of texts and one's ethical, political, or aesthetic evaluations (*Validity*, 139–63; *Aims*, 1–13, 95–158). One of the healthiest developments in recent criticism is that value judgments of many different kinds are more frequently being made explict, rather than manifesting themselves only in an indirect and unacknowledged fashion, and I have striven in the following chapters to distinguish clearly between my explications of a text and my assessments of its value. The works which I have discussed in the earlier chapters were selected in large part because they were documents of the first importance in the development of the Renaissance occult tradition, and they were among those which were most influential in sixteenth- and seventeenth-century England. The plays and masques by Marlowe, Jonson, and Shakespeare were chosen because they are, in my judgment, the most artistically sophisticated works on occult philosophy in the English Renaissance, and each of them has, in addition, a unique social, historical, or philosophical interest. *Dr. Faustus* dramatizes with exquisite poignancy the emotional and intellectual conflicts of those who sought to liberate themselves from excessive authoritarianism and oppressive orthodoxy. Jonson's *Alchemist* and in some instances his court masques, while striving to affirm traditional social and political values, are among the first literary texts to endeavor to assimilate into poetry the clear-sighted objectivity and the rejection of mysticism which contributed to Baconian science, and Jonson's ambivalent treatment of symbolism, as well as his combination of traditional, moderate humanism with the new assault upon "enthusiasm," make him a transitional figure of the first importance. *The Tempest*, perhaps the most intricate of these works from a purely aesthetic standpoint, offers a paradoxical and yet coherent compromise between the intensified quest for liberation and the traditional belief that self-fulfillment derives from participation in a larger community. Moreover, Shakespeare's play asserts on a variety of levels and with remarkably ingenious artistic strategies the hope that art may at times make possible a genuine communion between the artist and his or her audience, and, in doing so, endeavor to reform human life. The validity of such a vision of the possibilities of art cannot, of course, be proven, but it may, as I have attempted to convey in my final chapter, be experienced. This book is in part an effort to realize the possibility of such communion.

Although this study has expanded and changed substantially over the years, it has its origins in a doctoral dissertation directed by Professor Frank Manley of Emory University. For his tolerance and guidance, and, most of all, his example of integrity, I am deeply grateful. Professors Harry Rusche and the late Carl Bain read the original dissertation and made valuable suggestions. John Wallace made it possible for me to spend a summer at the University of Chicago, and he read a draft of the manuscript in its entirety and made important recommendations. Gordon O'Brien, Barbara Traister, and Carolyn Moser have also read the manuscript with great care and made helpful suggestions. Dennis Dougherty proofread the manuscript and saved me from a number of errors and inconsistencies. My colleagues at the University of Alabama in Huntsville have provided help and encouragement in many forms: Jane Kromm provided valuable assistance with the illustrations; H. E. Francis, Liza Davis, Bill Munson, and Richard Moore have read portions of the study and made helpful comments; and I am grateful to Carter Martin for his expressions of confidence in my work.

For stimulating and guiding my interests in the study of literature, history, philosophy, and religion, I am especially grateful to Neal Prater, Jim Skinner, Allen King, David Morefield, and Lewis Hay of Presbyterian College, and to Larry Ingle, now of the University of Tennessee at Chattanooga. My interest in some of the specific aspects of Renaissance intellectual history which are discussed here was intensified by a course in the Regiment of Princes tradition which was taught at Emory by John Bugge.

My research could not have been completed without the generous cooperation of the Folger Shakespeare Library, The Beinecke Rare Book and Manuscript Library of Yale University, Yale Medical Library, the New York Public Library, the Memorial Library of the University of Wisconsin, the University of Chicago Libraries, Woodruff Library of Emory University (especially the staff of Special Collections and of the Reference Department), the Troy State University System libraries, and the library of the University of Alabama in Huntsville. Among the many librarians who performed tasks beyond their normal duties are Harriet Venable, Greta Boers, and Del Williams. Portions of my research were supported by grants from Troy State University and the University of Alabama in Huntsville.

Portions of this book have previously been published in different form: part of Chapter 7 as "Renaissance Magic and the Return of the Golden Age: Utopianism and Religious Enthusiasm in *The Alchemist*," in *Renaissance Drama X: Comedy,* ed. Leonard Barkan (Evanston, Ill.: Northwestern University Press, 1979), 117–39; a portion of Chapter 4 as "Skepticism and Radical Reform in Cornelius Agrippa's *On the Uncertainty and Vanity of the Arts and Sciences,*" *Renaissance Papers 1987* (Durham, N.C.: Southeastern Renaissance Conference), 1–10; and brief sections of Chapters 6 and 9 as part of "Metadrama and the Visionary Imagination in *Dr. Faustus* and *The Tempest,*" *South Atlantic Review* 53, no. 2 (May 1988): 25–45. I gratefully acknowledge permission from Northwestern University Press, the Southeastern Renaissance Conference, and the South Atlantic Modern Language Association to reprint the material here in revised form.

My wife, Carol, and my children—David, Alan, and Hannah— have supported my work in countless ways, including tolerating my absence from home at times when I should have been there. Elizabeth Mebane brought comfort and emotional support to my family at a time when we most needed it.

The most profound debt is acknowledged in the dedication.

A Note on Texts,
Translations, and Illustrations

Translations are my own unless I note otherwise. I have normally
provided English versions in the text, and in those instances in which
problems of translation are an important issue, or in which major
questions of interpretation might arise, I have provided quotations
in the original language in a note or in parentheses. In other cases I
provide a reference to the original rather than a full quotation.

In quoting from old-spelling texts I have shortened long *s* and
silently expanded some contractions. I have also expanded speech
prefixes in plays.

The illustrations, which appear as a single chronological group-
ing following p. 110, serve two purposes. First, figures 1–6 provide
contrasting images which underscore the diversity of attitudes
toward science, magic, and magicians in the Renaissance and seventeenth century. Second, figures 4 and 7–9 illustrate differing responses to magic as represented in works by Marlowe, Jonson, and
Shakespeare. As I explain further in Chapter 5, the title page to Robert Recorde's *Castle of Knowledge* (fig. 1) suggests that knowledge can
grant human beings a degree of control over their destinies, releasing them from their bondage to Fortune. The title page to John Dee's
Monas Hieroglyphica (fig. 3) and Rembrandt's *Faust* (fig. 5) provide
impressive representations of the mystical symbols of the cosmos
which were utilized by alchemists and magicians such as Dee himself
(fig. 2) and which Ben Jonson satirized in *The Alchemist* and elsewhere. In contrast, the engraving on the title page to Marlowe's *Dr.
Faustus* (fig. 4) embodies a somewhat cruder conception of the magician as conjurer. Bruegel's *The Alchemists* (fig. 6) parallels Ben Jonson's masterful dramatic satire, while the Prospero of John Gilbert's

engraving (fig. 9) appears as the dignified master of the depraved Caliban. William Hamilton's illustration to *The Winter's Tale* (fig. 7) is a fine rendition of a scene in which a statue is apparently brought to life, as in the Hermetic *Asclepius;* my discussion of this scene in Chapter 9 stresses Shakespeare's comparison between art and magic, as well as his largely positive response to the occult tradition. Finally, the frontispiece to the Rowe edition of *The Tempest* (fig. 8) suggests that the ostensibly frightening aspects of Prospero's art are, in reality, sheer fantasy.

Chapter One

Renaissance Magic
and the Return
of the Golden Age

The twentieth century has seen vigorous challenges to the traditional view of the Renaissance as a time when Western civilization rejected the otherworldliness and asceticism of the Middle Ages and asserted the dignity, freedom, and power of the individual. One of the benefits of this controversy is that we have been reminded that periods of history are much more diverse than our generalizations sometimes make them appear to be.[1] It is difficult to prove that any period of history was dominated entirely by a quintessential "spirit of the age" which influenced virtually all important thinkers; the Renaissance, in particular, was a period of diverse activities and intense conflicts, of clashes of ideas and values which lend themselves to dramatic treatment. If we acknowledge, however, that progressive or radical forces were firmly opposed by conservative and reactionary ones during the fourteenth, fifteenth, sixteenth, and early seventeenth centuries, we may retain, with important qualifications, our conception of the Renaissance as a time when a significant number of artists, humanists, poets, philosophers, and scientists placed a new emphasis upon human freedom and asserted a new acceptance, in both the secular and the religious spheres, of self-assertiveness and ambition. One of the most potent symbols in Renaissance thought and literature of this new conception of human nature was magic.

Renaissance studies have been transformed and in many ways revitalized by the recent controversies concerning the nature and significance of the occult tradition which flourished throughout Europe during the sixteenth and early seventeenth centuries. In her seminal work *Giordano Bruno and the Hermetic Tradition,* Frances Yates aggressively maintained that the Hermetic philosophy and the magic often associated with it were central to the Renaissance, stimulating the period's most fervent hopes for reformation and promoting a view of the divinity and power of humanity which far surpassed that of Renaissance humanism, which Yates regarded in *Giordano Bruno* as an essentially conservative force. Further, Yates maintained that the practical magic developed by Marsilio Ficino, Pico della Mirandola, Cornelius Agrippa, Giordano Bruno, and others stimulated the growth of modern science by advancing the attitude that the exercise of human control over nature was an appropriate development of humankind's God-given creative potential. In *The Occult Philosophy in the Elizabethan Age,* Yates asserted that Hermetic/Cabalist philosophy was the dominant force behind movements for reform in sixteenth-century England, and she interpreted much of the literature of the period as engaged in the debate over Christian Cabala and natural magic. Peter French, R.J.W. Evans, and others have sought to confirm and extend many aspects of Yates's theories, and important studies by Christopher Hill, Paolo Rossi, Allen Debus, and others have provided independent evidence that magic helped to stimulate genuine science.[2]

Charles Trinkaus, however, has challenged Yates's assertion that occult philosophy was the source of the new optimism about human nature, arguing that patristic theology exerted a prior and more important influence upon Italian humanists and philosophers. Wayne Shumaker, Andrew Weiner, and others have questioned the extent to which magic was central to the English Renaissance, and Yates's interpretations of specific literary works have often been regarded as excessively esoteric and sometimes reductive. In addition, numerous scholars are currently engaged in a wide-ranging and stimulating controversy concerning the relationship between Renaissance occult philosophy and modern science. In a review of recent studies on the subject, Brian Vickers, although he stresses that additional research is needed, goes so far as to assert that Yates's theory concerning the influence of occult philosophy upon the development of genuine science is "almost wholly unfounded." William G. Craven, in *Giovanni Pico della Mirandola, Symbol of His Age: Modern Interpretations of a Renaissance Philosopher,* has argued that Pico della Mirandola, whose philosophy Yates saw as fundamental in asserting that humankind should exert control over both the natural world and its own destiny, was in reality more orthodox than subversive, more interested in contemplation than action. Professor Craven concludes his study by asserting that nineteenth- and twentieth-century researchers have misinterpreted Pico because their interpretive hypotheses have been founded upon erroneous assumptions: the desire to exalt the Renaissance as a time when modern values were founded has misled most modern scholars, Craven argues, to perceive a greater emphasis upon human dignity, freedom, and power in Pico and in the period as a whole than actually existed.[3]

In the initial chapters of this study I shall reexamine the role of Neoplatonism and Hermetic/Cabalist magic in the Renaissance, focusing in particular upon two areas of controversy: (1) the recent debates concerning the relationship between the occult tradition and Renaissance humanism, and (2) the extent to which Renaissance magic may have contributed to the emergence of genuine science. My thesis is that philosophical occultism carried to its logical extreme the humanists' affirmation of the power of human beings to control both their own personalities and the world around them. In the late sixteenth and early seventeenth centuries, magic became the most powerful manifestation of the growing conviction that humankind should act out its potential in the free exercise of its powers on the social and natural environment; moreover, those who explored "natural magic" often asserted that the quest for truth should not be limited by traditional religious, political, or intellectual authorities. Although Rossi, Vickers, and others are correct to emphasize that occult philosophy is fundamentally different from or even inimical to genuine science in many respects, transitional figures such as Thomas Rainold, John Dee, and many of the English Paracelsians cannot be categorized purely and simply as "occult philosophers" or "scientists"; and even more advanced and methodologically sophisticated researchers, including Francis Bacon, were influenced by the occultists' dream of a renovation of knowledge and by their assertion that human beings can command and perfect nature. In later chapters I propose to show that Christopher Marlowe, Ben Jonson, and William Shakespeare were consciously aware that philosophical occultism had given impetus to the burgeoning enthusiasm of the period about humanity and its powers. The primary evidence of this awareness is the explicit use within the literary works themselves of images and ideas which appear in the treatises of occult philosophers such as those which I shall examine in Chapters 2–6; in the cases of

Marlowe and Jonson, we have the additional corroborating evidence of allusions to specific magicians, as well as documentary evidence of the authors' reading and/or personal acquaintance with authors on both sides of the controversies over magic and witchcraft. *Dr. Faustus, The Alchemist,* and *The Tempest* give us not only their authors' responses to the activities of contemporary conjurers or con-artists, or to purely literary traditions, but their reactions to the Renaissance assertion that human beings are creatures of infinite potential. Each of these three playwrights was thoroughly familiar with the philosophical, social, and political implications of Hermetic/Cabalist magic, as well as with the claims of particular occult philosophers, and a study of these plays in the context of the controversies concerning magic, science, and the renewal of human knowledge and human society can illuminate both philosophical and aesthetic dimensions of the works which we cannot otherwise appreciate.

As we reflect upon the Renaissance and its relationship to our own culture, it is well to remember that even Jacob Burckhardt, whose *Civilization of the Renaissance in Italy* established the terms of nineteenth- and twentieth-century debate about the period, was ambivalent concerning the value of modern individualism. Although he believed that the Renaissance had liberated us from superstition and repression and had established a magnificent ideal of human perfection, he also wrote at length of the amorality of certain expressions of personal independence and power. He argued that political disunity and uncertainty in Italy, combined with freedom from imperial control, had created an environment in which personal power was respected more than legitimate authority. Indeed, so frequently did the state itself appear to be without divine sanction or other legitimate foundation that it finally appeared to be a purely human creation, and Machiavelli's belief that the end justified the means became typical of the period. Individual princes, aware of the fundamental insecurity of their government, sought to conquer neighboring principalities in order to make themselves more secure. The terrifying consequences of the political situation in Italy are best described in Burckhardt's own terms:

> As a result of this outward danger an inward ferment was in ceaseless activity; and the effect of the situation on the character of the ruler was generally of the most sinister kind. Abso-

lute power, with its temptations to luxury and unbridled selfishness, and the perils to which he was exposed from enemies
and conspirators, turned him almost inevitably into a tyrant in
the worst sense of the word. Well for him if he could trust his
nearest relations! But where all was illegitimate there could be
no regular law of inheritance, either with regard to succession
or to the division of the ruler's property; and consequently the
heir, if incompetent or a minor, was liable in the interest of the
family itself to be supplanted by an uncle or cousin of more
resolute character. The acknowledgment or exclusion of the
bastards was a fruitful source of contest; and most of these
families in consequence were plagued with a crowd of discon-
tented and vindictive kinsmen. This circumstance gave rise to
continual outbreaks of treason and to frightful scenes of domestic bloodshed. Sometimes the pretenders lived abroad in
exile, and, like the Visconti who practised the fisherman's craft
on the Lake of Garda, viewed the situation with patient indif-
ference. When asked by a messenger of his rival when and
how he thought of returning to Milan he gave the reply: "By
the same means as those by which I was expelled, but not till
his crimes have outweighed my own." (Burckhardt, 1:28–29)

The documents and legends which fascinated Burckhardt were
also among the most popular literary sources of English Renaissance
dramatists; the bloody tale of the murder of the Duchess of Malfi is
one of the centerpieces of Burckhardt's chapter on "Morality" as well
as of Renaissance theater, and *The Tempest* is only one of dozens of
English plays which deal with Italian political intrigue. English history provided sufficient analogues to the tales which came from Italy
to establish the relevance of the stories to the English playgoer, and
despite the relative stability of Elizabeth's reign there was considerable fear that a problem of succession could resurrect the chaos of
the Wars of the Roses. The amoral assertion of Machiavellian *virtù*
was never as widely accepted in England as Burckhardt tells us it
was in Italy, but it captured the imagination of several major artists
and intellectuals, including Christopher Marlowe. Marlowe's plays,
which initiated the great period of popular theater in England, struck
a chord in their audiences because they focused upon issues which
were of vital concern to reflective Englishmen: the nature and limits

of individual power, the status of traditional institutions and authorities, and the proper relationship between the individual and the
community. The symbolic issues which the Renaissance stage utilized most frequently to dramatize these problems were Machiavelli-
anism, revenge, and magic.

Magic was popular among English Renaissance playwrights and
their audiences for a wide variety of reasons. The perennial allure of
the unknown and the forbidden, as well as the opportunity for spectacular stage business, no doubt contributed to the success of plays
on the occult, and there were several literary and dramatic traditions
which playwrights drew upon.[4] Purely literary traditions, however,
do not entirely explain why plays on magic suddenly became of vital
concern in the 1580s and continued to be such a compelling subject
on the stage until the 1620s, when interest in plays on sorcery and
witchcraft gradually declined. A. W. Ward once attributed the beginning of the trend to Giordano Bruno's visit to Oxford in 1583, but
the interest in plays about magic also correlates directly with a resurgence of pamphlet literature on alchemy and other Hermetic subjects, as well as with an increase in the number of works published
on mathematics, applied science, and Paracelsian medicine; it also
coincides with an upsurge in trials for witchcraft.[5] The late sixteenth
and early seventeenth centuries in England witnessed the culmination of an intense struggle between those who maintained the continuing validity of traditional sources of knowledge and those who
asserted that inherited beliefs must be tested and, if necessary, rejected. The climax of the struggle was Francis Bacon's ultimately
successful call for a renewal of human knowledge based upon an
appeal to experience, but during Bacon's own lifetime only a handful
of Englishmen could distinguish clearly between controlled experimentation and the claims of Paracelsians or Hermeticists that
genuine knowledge of nature was a combination of experience and
divine revelation. A bewildering array of natural philosophies
claimed people's allegiance, and clearly implicit in every stage of the
debate was the sometimes exhilarating, sometimes profoundly disquieting fact that the limits of human knowledge and power had not
been finally established.

Magicians in the Hermetic and Paracelsian traditions appealed
to God for aid and enlightenment, and they emphasized that their
own knowledge and abilities were derived from a higher power, but

at the same time they acted on the belief that humanity, also, is in part divine and therefore capable of controlling at least the lower spheres of the cosmos. Compared to modern scientists, Renaissance magicians operated within a cosmological framework which seems fantastic, and which had to be rejected before genuine science could evolve. Nonetheless, in daring to believe that the human mind could guide and command the creative forces of nature, they asserted important attitudes and values which eventually contributed to the evolution of genuine science. Hermetic magicians and Paracelsians often proclaimed the overthrow of the traditional authorities which had imposed strict limits upon the search for truth; together with the mechanical artisans with whom they frequently allied themselves, they are among Bacon's immediate predecessors in emphasizing experience, rather than mere citation of Galen or Aristotle, as the appropriate test of assertions about nature. Perhaps most importantly, they predicted that the imminent renewal of all of human knowledge would bring with it the reform of human society and of human nature itself.

Such attitudes were accepted by numerous important and influential thinkers, but they were condemned by many, and frequently even a pious magus like John Dee was called upon to defend himself against charges that he was in league with the devil. The followers of Pico della Mirandola, Cornelius Agrippa, or Paracelsus attempted to distinguish between their own intellectual magic and Satanic witchcraft or common superstition, but orthodox churchmen and conservative intellectuals regarded virtually all attempts to alter nature or to dissent from the authorized versions of natural philosophy as sinful. A belief that one possessed occult wisdom was seen by the orthodox as an illusion stimulated by excessive pride and manipulated by the Father of Lies. Whereas those who accepted magic tended to believe that human nature was perfectible and that human beings had the right—indeed, the responsibility—to reshape the world around them, more traditional thinkers, drawing upon well-established Christian doctrine, condemned the occult arts as damnable. The magicians themselves proclaimed that they were motivated by piety and love, and that their purposes were consonant with those of the natural order itself; their adversaries accused them of a simple lust for power.

In order to illuminate fully the symbolic value of magic in Renaissance thought and literature and to recreate for the modern reader the detailed understanding of occult philosophy which was enjoyed by Marlowe, Jonson, and Shakespeare, I shall trace Renaissance occultism back to its roots in Florentine Neoplatonism, exploring its relation to the widespread feeling among Renaissance humanists and philosophers that they were living in an age of spiritual, cultural, and political rebirth. Subsequently we shall consider the careers of the Elizabethans who carried on the Hermetic/Cabalist tradition and whose radical conception of human nature was a major source of the exciting literary and scientific activity of the late sixteenth and early seventeenth centuries in England.

HUMANISM, NEOPLATONISM, AND OCCULT PHILOSOPHY

Any study of the central issues in Renaissance intellectual history must come to terms with the varied definitions of the term *humanism.* In its broadest sense, *humanism* refers to any school of thought or set of attitudes which is concerned primarily with human problems, values, and capabilities. Often it implies, in addition, an emphasis upon practical wisdom and social reform, as opposed to abstract philosophy or speculation. Within the field of Renaissance studies the term refers to the historical movement which promoted a new understanding of the Greek and Roman classics, and which reasserted the importance of literature, moral philosophy, and rhetoric as essential subjects in the education of competent citizens and political leaders. Beyond these basic generalizations, there are divergent viewpoints concerning the nature and scope of Renaissance humanism. Two of the most influential conceptions of the movement are those developed by Eugenio Garin and Paul Kristeller.

Professor Garin has argued that humanism promoted confidence in humankind's creative power. Humanists popularized the belief that their own era was a time of renewal, and they asserted that humanity was largely in control of its own destiny. Garin concedes that most humanists were not systematic philosophers, but he maintains that the movement was nonetheless of crucial significance for the development of both philosophy and science because it promoted modern critical habits of mind. Of utmost importance was the historical perspective which enabled the humanist to see a text of

Aristotle or Cicero not as a timeless authority, but as a human creation composed under the limitations of a given culture. Classical art, literature, and philosophy were to be appraised and evaluated critically, but they also were highly valued as sources of ideals and of practical advice on a wide variety of topics, from morality and politics to civic planning and architecture. Although humanists initially regarded insight into problems of ethics and politics as more valuable than knowledge of nature, eventually their insistence upon the critical reevaluation of traditional authorities, their rediscovery of relatively neglected or unknown scientific texts, their assertion of human control over our environment, and their general sense of the renewal of knowledge were decisive factors in creating an atmosphere conducive to scientific discovery. Rhetoric—at the center of humanistic education—was valued as a tool of moral and political persuasion; Petrarch asserted that harmonious words expressed the essence of a harmonious soul, and oratory thus uplifted and refined the personality. Later humanists such as Ermalao Barbaro, Garin suggests, regrettably permitted rhetoric to degenerate at times into merely decorative or persuasive speech, devoid of ethical value and divorced from reality, so that even a philosopher like Pico della Mirandola, who had been profoundly influenced by humanism, would find occasion to criticize the tendency to separate words and things, to pursue grace of expression more fervently than truth.[6]

Paul Kristeller differs from Garin primarily by limiting his use of the term *humanist* fairly strictly to the scholar and/or teacher of the disciplines which Renaissance usage itself termed the *studia humanitatis:* grammar, rhetoric, history, poetry, and moral philosophy. He emphasizes that logic, mathematics, metaphysics, science, law, and medicine were not included in this group of disciplines, and he therefore objects to the tendency "to identify Renaissance humanism with the philosophy, the science, or the learning of the period as a whole."[7] Moreover, he is reluctant to regard humanism as a coherent school of thought promoting any unified philosophy. Kristeller's definition of humanism has been widely adopted, and consequently recent studies have often excluded from the humanist movement those Renaissance scholars and intellectuals whose major interests were in magic and science, metaphysics, or other fields.[8]

While Garin and Kristeller differ in the extent to which they see humanism as a unified movement or a philosophical tendency, I am inclined to view many of their disagreements as a matter of emphasis and definition. Kristeller agrees with Garin that humanism promoted an emphasis upon the value of humankind, a judgment which he sees as implicit in the program of the *studia humanitatis* itself.[9] He objects to Garin's description of humanism as a "philosophical movement" not only because Garin includes disciplines such as logic or economics as within the humanists' sphere, but also because the two scholars adopt different conceptions of philosophy: Kristeller limits the term to the discipline which is concerned with technical problems in logic, metaphysics, epistemology, ethics, and aesthetics, whereas Garin suggests that philosophy can be "understood as an unceasing exploration and taken to be a critical consciousness of the mind's activities, of its human measure and its limitations as well as its potentialities" (*Italian Humanism*, 222). Kristeller does not refer to Ficino or Pico as "humanists," but he emphasizes that they were strongly influenced by humanism, as were many other philosophers, scientists, and theologians. Despite their differences, Kristeller and Garin are in substantial agreement concerning many aspects of humanism and its influence, and the works of both scholars can help us to appreciate the ways in which humanism was a progressive force in the period, rather than an essentially conservative one.

In this study I shall adopt the definition of humanism which has been developed by Professor Kristeller, but at the same time I wish to emphasize the influence of humanism beyond strict disciplinary boundaries. We must also recognize that humanists were individuals whose interests may not have been narrowly confined to philology and rhetoric. Few of us would deny the title of humanist to John Colet, but we must concede that he was engrossed in certain types of philosophy and theology which Erasmus found of little value. Similarly, I cannot see why we should regard Reuchlin's scholarship in Judaic studies as essentially opposed to humanism simply because Erasmus probably would not have approved of Reuchlin's fascination with the Cabala. Some individuals in the Renaissance were intensely concerned with both humanism and philosophy (occult or otherwise), whereas others embraced one and opposed the other.

One of the attitudes cultivated by the humanists which occult philosophers developed in a more radical fashion was the ideal of self-perfection. The hope for regeneration has been the heart of Christianity in all ages, but in the Renaissance the traditional idea that we are made in the image of God and can attain complete self-realization by restoring that image to its prelapsarian purity was transformed and revitalized by the increasing optimism about human nature and by the humanists' glorification of a wide range of creative activities. Although they never entirely denied the human need for divine grace, Renaissance humanists and philosophers tended much more than their medieval predecessors to grant the individual soul a degree of self-sufficiency in shaping its own nature and destiny. Petrarch began to move in this direction by emphasizing that one's inner life is a constant process of moral and spiritual self-creation.[10] Marsilio Ficino, who founded the tradition of Renaissance Hermeticism, went a step further than his humanist predecessor by asserting that the initial impulse which turns the soul toward God comes not through an act of grace, as Augustine tells us, but from a free decision of the individual soul itself.[11] Pico della Mirandola's development of the attitude is probably the most widely known: through grace God created humanity in His own image, but it remains for individuals to realize, through free creative acts, the potential which God has given them.[12] The concept of the self as a work of art, an idea which became central to Renaissance culture, expresses the tendency of the period to allow "art," in the broad sense of "human creative activity," to compete with divine grace as the shaping force in human life and destiny. Many writers controlled this dangerous tendency by asserting that divine grace grants power to human art, but the balance between the powers of God and the powers of humanity was precarious: there was increasing fascination with the tantalizing possibility, articulated in England by Marlowe's tragic heroes, that humanity alone might be fully responsible for its own psychological development and its own history.

Renaissance humanists often asserted that the regeneration of the individual soul can—indeed, must—result in the reformation of the external world. They emphasized that we should strive to imitate God and to become co-workers with Him, and they reinterpreted this traditional doctrine so as to grant human beings greater control over their worldly circumstances than medieval theologians had normally allowed.[13] To realize our divine potential we must, like God, exercise our powers in creative acts through which we reproduce in the external world the perfection we have come to see within our own minds. The belief that we can assist God in perfecting His creation manifested itself in numerous areas of Renaissance thought and culture. The civic humanists regarded humanity as the agent through whom God's eternal law is revealed in human society, and they used this doctrine as theoretical support for a program of social and political reform. Poets, painters, and sculptors strove to embody the transcendent forms they perceived in subjective visions in symbolic idealizations of the human form and of the natural world.[14] Artist and humanist alike believed that creative power sprang from a subjective process of self-purification and enlightenment, and both were attempting, in different ways and within acknowledged limits, to restore a corrupted world to a state of perfection. The crucial difference between the magician and other Renaissance "artists" (to use the term in its broadest sense) is that the occultists accepted no limits whatsoever: they proclaimed that the human mind could unite itself fully—and in this life—with the mind of its Creator, and in Postel, Paracelsus, Bruno, and others we shall encounter occult philosophers who proclaimed that God had chosen them personally to eliminate all traces of corruption from human society.

Optimism with regard to humanity's ability to repair the Fall lay behind much of the popular rhetoric of the return of the Golden Age. As Harry Levin has shown us in *The Myth of the Golden Age in the Renaissance,* the fifteenth and sixteenth centuries restored the legend of a lost Golden Era to a position of genuine prominence in art and literature, and readers of the classics began to identify the pagan Golden Age with the Christian Eden. It was typically described as a time and place in which selfish appetites, particularly lust and greed, had not yet corrupted the human will. Both men and women acted out of spontaneous love and friendship, and the restraint of external laws was unnecessary. The human race lived as one great family; all goods, in many versions of the myth, were held in common, and there was no social hierarchy. Humankind was in intimate accord with nature, whose bounty provided sustenance with only a minimum of human effort. Classical authors sometimes asserted that men and women had been companions of the gods, sharing their wisdom and powers, or that ancient heroes had been demigods themselves. As Professor Levin emphasizes, both pagan and Christian authors disagreed among themselves about certain aspects of our unfallen condition: some preferred monogamy to free love, fruitful labor to total leisure. But what remained essential in every version of the myth was a vision of the potential of the human mind and will, a potential which many Renaissance thinkers began to believe could be regained.

In most periods of history the myth of the Golden Era is used negatively, to define the faults of the present age, but in the Renaissance it was often used positively, to point to the accomplishments of the present and the possibilities of the immediate future.[15] Ficino described his own time as a "golden century" which had "brought back to light the liberal arts, which were all but extinguished: grammar, poetry, oratory, painting, sculpture, architecture, music, the ancient chanting of songs to the Orphic lyre."[16] The theme of "The Golden Age Restored" was a favorite in courtly entertainments and civic pageantry from the time of the Medici in Florence through the reigns of Elizabeth and James I in England. When Lorenzo de Medici's son became Pope Leo X, the celebration in Florence included a symbolic representation of the birth of a new era: "From the center of the car rose a great globe in the form of the world," an observer recorded, "upon which a man lay prostrate on his face as if dead, his armor all rusted, and from the open fissure of whose sundered back emerged a small boy all naked and gilded, representing the revival of the golden age and the end of the iron age, which expired and was reborn through the election of the pope" (Levin, *Golden Age*, 39–40). Such ingenuity hardly surpasses that of Ben Jonson and Inigo Jones, who collaborated on a series of Jacobean court masques which celebrated the power of the government of James I to transform the Iron Age into a Golden Era of virtue and justice. *The Golden Age Restored*, presented at the English court in 1615, presents the descent from heaven of Pallas Athena, who banishes warfare and corruption and recalls Astraea, the goddess of justice, to a renewed reign on earth. Frequently Jonson's masques suggest that moral reform results from the leadership of monarchs and courtiers whose natural virtues have been perfected by humanistic education, religion, and moral self-discipline.[17]

It would be easy enough to dismiss all instances of such spectacular praise as mere flattery. If we examine closely the careers of the artists and intellectuals who offer such homage, however, we often find that their work springs from genuine confidence in a ruler or a system of government and from sincere hopes for social and cultural progress. Erasmus tells us that one can sometimes exert a benevolent influence upon a ruler by praising him. Three years after Pope Leo X's coronation, for example, Erasmus wrote to the pontiff to congratulate him for accomplishing precisely what had been expected: Leo's promotion of peace, his improvement of piety, and his patronage of arts and letters had already begun to transform an age of corruption into one of gold.[18] But the letter is not simply blandishment, designed to win favor from the great patron for Erasmus himself; it is a serious effort to confirm and encourage certain enlightened policies which Erasmus felt that the pope had already initiated. A well-known personal letter sent from Erasmus to Wolfgang Capito on February 26, 1517, testifies to his sincerity:

> It is not part of my nature, most learned Wolfgang, to be excessively fond of life. . . . But at the present moment I could almost wish to be young again, for no other reason but this, that I anticipate the near approach of a golden age; so clearly do we see the minds of princes, as if changed by inspiration, devoting all their energies to the pursuit of peace. The chief movers in this matter are Pope Leo, and Francis, King of France. . . .
>
> Therefore, when I see that the highest sovereigns of Europe, Francis of France, Charles, the King Catholic, Henry of England and the Emperor Maximilian have set all their warlike preparations aside, and established peace upon solid, and, as I trust adamantine foundations, I am led to a confident hope, that not only morality and Christian piety, but also a genuine and purer literature may come to renewed life or greater splendor.[19]

The fact that these letters were written on the eve of decades of religious warfare gives them a certain poignancy. Yet the conflicts of the sixteenth century seem to have intensified the widespread hopes for a reformed and united Christendom, rather than extinguishing them. The ideals implied by the myth of the Golden Era continued to inspire programs of social reform, and humanists continued to proclaim that the knowledge and powers which had been lost through the Fall could be regained at least partially through education. Treatises in the "regiment of princes" tradition detailed the manner in which humanistic education and religion combined to produce, as Castiglione's Signor Ottaviano puts it, "that virtue which perhaps among all human things is the greatest and rarest, that is, the manner and method of right rule: which of itself alone would suffice to make men happy and to bring back once again to earth that Golden Age which is recorded to have existed once upon a time when Saturn ruled."[20] Initially most humanists hoped that reforms would be brought about by enlightened monarchs and magistrates, but the idea that the individual can be perfected by education and by a communion with God of which all human souls are capable bore within it the seeds of an attack upon the established hierarchies of church and state. Eventually it helped to produce revolutionaries such as John Milton, in whose life and work the influences of humanism, radical Protestantism, and Hermetic occultism are intermingled. In 1644 Milton wrote that "the end then of Learning is to repair the ruines of our first Parents by regaining to know God aright, and out of that knowledge to love him, to imitate him, to be like him, as we may the neerest by possessing our souls of true vertue, which being united to the heavenly grace of faith makes up the highest perfection."[21] A few paragraphs later in Milton's essay we learn what the practical consequences of "Learning to know God aright" are, as he defines "a compleat and generous Education" as "that which fits a man to perform justly, skilfully, and magnanimously all the offices both private and publick of Peace and War" ("Of Education," 4:280). The two definitions of education do not conflict, for the love of God did not find its complete fulfillment, for Milton or for others in the humanist tradition, in contemplative isolation. Enlightenment is genuine only if it issues in virtuous action.

After the Reformation, humanism sometimes combined, as in Milton, with more radical currents, but in general the earlier humanists were the moderates among those who believed that spiritual rebirth must result in the regeneration of society. A much more radical influence is the tradition of Christian millenarianism, which extends back through the Middle Ages and in some instances has roots in ancient Gnosticism. Revolutionary sects such as the Amaurians, the Brethren of the Free Spirit, and the Anabaptists drew upon ideas which have been traced back to ancient Neoplatonism and the mystery religions, and adherents of some of the sects were spiritual alchemists.[22] They tended to exalt personal, subjective inspiration above external religious authority, and in some cases they even asserted the possibility of the full Incarnation of God in an individual initiate. Members of several dissenting religious groups claimed to have attained a spiritual perfection and innocence equivalent to that of the Garden of Eden. These mystical sects at times exerted important social and political influence, as they demanded the dissolution of existing institutions and prophesied that the millennium was imminent.

This mystical tradition is an important factor in the reformist and revolutionary currents of the Renaissance and the seventeenth century, but its radical character distinguishes it clearly from the reform movements promoted by most of the humanists. The mystical cults generally drew their support from the lower social and economic classes or from other groups who, for various reasons, were denied a meaningful place in the existing hierarchy. Humanism, in contrast, affected the educated classes. Humanists such as Thomas More, who possessed considerable social and political influence, desired a closer communion with God, on the one hand, and a life lived in the world, yet transformed by a sense of moral and religious purpose, on the other.[23] They sought the reform of existing institutions, not their overthrow, and they usually retained a healthy awareness of their limitations. More's *Utopia,* for example, implies some very startling proposals for the improvement of society, yet it also suggests the humanist's awareness of the limits which political reality and human weakness impose upon the reformer. In book 1 of *Utopia* More suggests that educated counselors cannot perfect a government, even though they may initiate some genuine improvements: "For it is impossible that all should be well," More tells us wryly in one key section, "unless all men were good, a situation which I do not expect for a great many years to come!" (*Utopia,* 101). One of the purposes of much humanist literature, including *Utopia,* is to remind us that mortal creatures cannot free themselves entirely from moral and spiritual infirmities. But no such sense of limitation is present in the more revolutionary, mystical tradition: its leaders often claimed that as agents of God they could do no wrong, and their aim was to overthrow totally the existing order and initiate a new age in which the human community would become socially and spiritually flawless.

In Florentine Neoplatonism there was a complex interaction among humanism, scholasticism, and the Neoplatonic and Gnostic philosophies which had influenced the radical sects. The resulting compound was the intellectual foundation of the occult tradition which spread throughout Europe and to which Marlowe, Jonson, and Shakespeare responded. The Neoplatonists retained much of the method and vocabulary of scholasticism, but they also absorbed from the humanists their intense concern with the dignity and freedom of humanity, their appreciation of the beauty of this world, and their celebration of the uniqueness and the creative powers of the individual. The Neoplatonists attempted to reconcile these attitudes with traditional Christian philosophy by emphasizing God's immanence in the created world and His incarnation in humanity. Whereas in the dominant medieval philosophies the value of individual earthly creatures was derived from their participation in a transcendent universal, Ficino tended to bring the universal to earth, to see it as immanent in the concrete particulars of the created world. God is immediately present, in other words, in the "forms" or "souls" of natural objects, and our love for the beauty of those forms is a particularization of our love of God. Our desire to reproduce or even to perfect that beauty in our own creations is a manifestation of our longing to be like Him. Similarly, human social and political reforms were regarded by Ficino and his followers as the means through which God's providential plans are brought into being in worldly history.[24] The Neoplatonists exalted contemplation much more than most of the humanists did, and in general they were more intensely involved in abstract speculation; still, they were eager to celebrate human cultural and political achievements, and the descent from contemplation to action receives prominent consideration in their philosophy.

In 1463 Cosimo de' Medici requested that Ficino postpone his translation of Plato in order to render into Latin the Greek texts known as the *Corpus Hermeticum.* These Gnostic texts had probably been composed between 100 and 300 A. D., but they were attributed to an ancient sage named Hermes Trismegistus who was reputed to have been a predecessor of Plato. Once disseminated in Ficino's translation, the Hermetic writings helped to stimulate a conception of humanity which is far more radical than that which we see in Petrarch, Erasmus, or Ben Jonson. The Hermetic books which Ficino gathered under the title *Pimander* contain an account of the creation, fall, and redemption of humankind which in many ways resembles the Christian scheme, but which asserts that prelapsarian Humanity possessed godlike creative powers and was closely akin to the Son of God, the Logos who created the visible world. Through love of the natural world, Humanity experiences the descent into the realm of matter and forgets its divine origin, but the effects of this Fall can be overcome in a regenerative experience which restores divine knowledge and power.[25] In the *Asclepius,* which was known in a Latin version during the Middle Ages, Hermes Trismegistus proclaims that the power of human beings to perform magic is a sign of this inherent divinity. The *Asclepius* also predicts a transformation of the world in which nature will be totally perfected, all evil destroyed, and the ancient religion of the One God restored on earth.[26] The Arabic *Picatrix,* which Ficino probably used as a source for his own works on magic, contains an account of a Utopian city constructed by Hermes Trismegistus in which occult arts figure prominently.[27] Hermeticism could often lead to otherworldliness and a withdrawal from social and political affairs, but the Utopian and apocalyptic elements in the Hermetic and pseudo-Hermetic literature could also stimulate political activism of various sorts, including actual revolution. Ficino himself was concerned with purifying the soul; he was fascinated by the idea that the human personality could regain its lost magical powers, but he was not likely to connect the regeneration of humanity with radical social, political, or religious reform. Giordano Bruno, Thomas Campanella, and many of the Paracelsians, as we shall see, responded quite differently.

Although Ficino is often fairly cautious in discussing heterodox ideas from pagan sources, one can certainly see the influence of the Hermetic view of the soul in his works. In his *Theologia Platonica de immortalitate animorum* he defends not only the soul's immortality, but also its essential divinity and grandeur. One indication of the human soul's nobility, Ficino argues, is humankind's unlimited creative power; another is our insatiable longing for the infinite. We cannot be satisfied with any finite truth or limited achievement: we can find peace only in union with God. "The human Soul transcends each finite thing, because whatever finite truth or goodness you might offer to it, the intellect can think more, and the will can strive further."[28] All human ambition springs ultimately from our impulse to become Godlike:

We have already spoken of how humanity emulates all of God's works through various arts and thus, as the image of God, brings forth all things. We have also said that human beings always strive to rule both themselves and all other creatures, both humans and beasts, and that they cannot bear any form of servitude. Even if they are forced to serve, they hate their master, for to be a slave is contrary to human nature. . . . The sense of shame and of honor, peculiar only to the human race, signifies that something of inexpressible majesty lies within us, something which it would be a sin to defile, and which is worthy of the deepest reverence. . . . The immeasurable magnificence of our soul may be seen from this, that humankind will not be satisfied with the power of command over this entire world if we learn, having conquered this one, that another world remains which we have not yet conquered. . . . Thus human beings wish no superior and no equal, and we will not suffer anything to remain excluded from our command. . . . This status belongs to God alone; therefore humanity seeks a divine condition.[29]

This impulse to reach for infinity is hardly compatible with the sense of human limitations which we find in More or Erasmus, and several scholars have suggested that humanism and the occult tradition are fundamentally opposed. In *Giordano Bruno and the Hermetic Tradition* (159–68) Frances Yates underscored Erasmus' opposition to magic and to abstract philosophy in general, and she argued that the interests of those humanists involved with the study of Latin classical texts were "entirely different" from those of the scholars and philosophers who were influenced primarily by the Greek texts of Plato, the Neoplatonists, and the "ancient theologians" such as Hermes or Orpheus. The "Latin" humanists were preoccupied with the practical affairs of human society, and they disapproved of what they regarded as grandiose speculations concerning humanity's magical powers. The very style of their writings, Yates continues, reflects their affirmation of rational order and decorum, as well as an acceptance of human limits. In contrast, the predominantly Greek spirit of the Neoplatonists is more extreme in its enthusiasm about human aspirations, and much more likely to express itself in unrestrained emotional terms. By the time she had written *The Occult*

Philosophy in the Elizabethan Age Yates had modified her view of the relation between humanism and occultism, but her earlier work remains influential. In addition, Hiram Haydn, Charles Nauert, Charles Zika, and others have emphasized that the humanists affirmed rationality and tended to be conservatives or moderates, whereas the occultists, who claimed to rely on intuition, believed that they could transcend the limitations which were accepted by the humanists, as well as by traditional scholastic philosophers.[30]

These generalizations contain some truth, but in two important respects they need to be modified. First, we should concede that they do not apply to all individuals. It is true that Erasmus disapproved of occultism, just as Paracelsus and Giordano Bruno assailed the conservative, orthodox, and socially powerful among the grammarians. It is also accurate to say that some occult philosophers sought absolute knowledge through divine revelation because they grew impatient with the limitations of human reason, just as some of them became political or religious radicals because they were dissatisfied with a limited program of social reform. But there are many eclectic thinkers in whose minds various aspects of humanism, Neoplatonism, and Hermetic/Cabalist occultism interact freely: Ficino, Pico, Reuchlin, Colet, Spenser, and Milton are among the most prominent examples, and one is tempted to add to this list the name of William Shakespeare, whose arch-magician Prospero describes his mastery of "the liberal arts" as a stepping stone to "secret studies" (*Tempest,* I.ii.73, 77). In the following sections on Ficino and Pico we shall find that for the founders of the occult tradition in the Renaissance there was a natural progression through the humanistic disciplines and scholastic philosophy to a more advanced stage of knowledge and wisdom, one based upon divine revelation. This progression was accepted by Cornelius Agrippa in his *Occult Philosophy,* although he subsequently rejects traditional education in *The Uncertainty and Vanity of Arts and Sciences.* Paracelsus, on the other hand, consistently claims (with a certain unconscious irony) that his reliance upon experience and divine revelation is more pious and humble than an assertion of the claims of reason. By no means did those who proclaimed the superiority of revelation always denigrate formal education or rationality, but this was certainly the case in some instances, especially among the Paracelsians.

Secondly, I would emphasize that in general, occult philosophy is not so much the opposite of the humanism of Petrarch or Erasmus as it is the radical extension of certain humanist attitudes.[31] The emphasis which many of the humanists placed on freedom and self-determination, their belief that we can repair the effects of the Fall through knowledge, and their emphasis upon our similarity to God and our role as an instrument of the divine will all receive a philosophical foundation in Renaissance Neoplatonism and are carried to their logical extreme in Neoplatonic magic. We can clarify precisely how this radicalization takes place by looking more closely at the position of *magia* in the philosophies of Marsilio Ficino and Giovanni Pico della Mirandola.

Chapter Two

Art and Magic in
the Philosophy of
Marsilio Ficino

Most discussions of Ficino's theory and practice of magic have centered, naturally enough, on *De vita coelitus comparanda* (*On Life Connected with the Heavens*), the third book of *De vita libri tres*.[1] This work
is an important source for detailed information about actual magical
procedures, but in order to understand how magic became a radical
extension of the humanists' vision of humankind, we must try to
appreciate the position of magic in Ficino's entire philosophy, especially his *Theologia Platonica*. The importance of humanity in Ficino's
philosophical system derives from our central position in the universe; as perceivers or "interpreters" of nature, as artists, and, finally,
as magicians, it is the sacred privilege of humankind to unite the
intelligible and the physical aspects of the cosmos and thus to play a
role in perfecting the created world. We can fully comprehend Ficino's celebration of humanity, then, only within the context of his
doctrine of the unity and perfection of the cosmos.

Ficino conceives of the coherence of the universe in terms of
the mediation of opposites. Platonic Forms or Ideas, which are aspects of God's own essence,[2] are vivifying forces which unite with
their opposite, matter, through the mediation of the rational soul.
Through this union the "seeds" or beginnings of forms which exist
in matter are brought to life. The full realization and perfection of
any creature is thus its full participation in the Idea which governs
it.[3] Humanity is the center of the cosmos and the mediator between
the eternal and the temporal worlds because we occupy the lowest
position in the hierarchy of souls and the highest station in the series
of bodies (Kristeller, *PMF,* 385–89). In addition, as microcosm and

as the living image of God, humanity contains, in principle, all things, and we participate in the knowledge and powers of the entire universal hierarchy. The human Mind (*Mens*), for example, the intuitive faculty which is the highest of the three parts of the individual soul, is part of the series of minds which emanates from God. It thus participates in the Divine Mind and contains innate Ideas which apparently are closely related to those which form the basis of physical nature. The lowest part of the human soul, the *Idolum,* consists of the fantasy, sense, and the nutritive power. It animates the body and links the soul to the order of nature. Between the *Mens* and the *Idolum* is the *Ratio* (Reason), which can move freely between higher and lower.[4]

Ficino combines this view of humanity as both microcosm and center of the universe with an interesting and important interpretation of the Incarnation. Christ, as the universal *Humanitas,* includes and is present in individual human beings in the same way that other universals include their embodiments. He is the *primum* of the genus "Humanity" in Whom all of us participate. The Savior thus mediates not only between God and humanity, but also, *through human knowledge and action,* between God and all of the lower levels of the cosmos: human beings, because they participate in Christ, can help in various ways to effect the redemption of the fallen world. One way in which this occurs is through human perception and contemplation; the divine Ideas are reflected more perfectly in the human Mind than they are in the external world, and when we perceive natural objects and unite them in our Minds to their archetypes, we effect, in a sense, the unity and perfection of the cosmos:

The Soul of [a human being], which is affected by the individual impulses of individual bodies through its earthly body, receives these images of the Ideas maculated by the matter of the universe through perception, but collects them through fantasy, cleans and refines them through reason, and connects them at last with the universal Ideas of the mind [*Mens*]. So the celestial ray that had descended to the lowest things returns to the higher beings, because the images of Ideas, formerly dispersed in matter, are collected in the fantasy, and, formerly impure, they are purified in reason, and formerly particular, they are lifted in the mind [*Mens*] to universality. In this way the Soul of [humankind] restores the world that had already been shaken [*iam labefactatum restituit mundum*].[5]

Elsewhere Ficino indicates that the love of humankind for both higher and lower realms leads us to unite the extremes of form and matter not only in thought, but also in creative action. We do so by means of the "innumerable arts" through which we demonstrate our similarity to the divine Creator. Unlike the lower animals, we are not limited to the practice of a single art to which our species is subject; instead, since the human soul contains the powers of all of the species, we can choose to perform whatever creative activity we please. Moreover, since parts of the human soul transcend the physical world, we not only imitate nature, we compete with it or even excel it. It is here that the Renaissance Neoplatonist departs from the Aristotelian tradition, which had limited humankind to the imitation of nature, and asserts a vision of humanity which is a necessary part of an atmosphere conducive to the birth of science:

> Human arts make by themselves whatever nature herself makes, as if we were not the servants of nature, but her rivals. Thus did Zeuxis paint grapes in such a manner that birds flew to them. . . . Praxiteles in a certain temple of the Indians formed a Venus of marble so beautiful that it scarcely could be preserved safe and pure from the lustful glances of those passing by. Archytas Tarentinus made a dove out of wood with his knowledge of mathematics, set it in motion, and breathed a spirit into it so that it flew [*libravit, inflavit spiritu adeo ut volaret*]. The Egyptians, as Hermes tells us, constructed statues of the gods which spoke and walked. Archimedes of Syracuse made a model of the heavens out of bronze in which all seven planets completed their movements as truly as in the skies. . . . I pass over the pyramids of the Egyptians, the buildings and the workshops in metal and glass of the Greeks and the Romans. *In fine, humankind imitates all the works of divine nature, and the works of lower nature we perfect, reform, and amend.*[6]

Ficino's reference to the animation of Egyptian statues is an allusion to the passage in *Asclepius* in which we are told that the ancient priests drew spirits (*daemones*) into the statues of the gods by sympathetic magic.[7] Ficino was fascinated by this legend, and he alludes to it continually in his works. In the passage just quoted he is presenting such magic as the pinnacle of humanity's creative powers and as proof of the human soul's divinity and immortality.

Before he elaborates further on magic, Ficino first praises the lower arts, beginning with the technology through which we provide for our basic physical needs. In order to provide for the body, delight the senses, and exercise the reason, we master the elements and the lower animals. Our providential care and Godlike mastery of all which is beneath us make us God's viceroys and prove once again our divine nature. Humankind is due even greater praise for our creation of civil order than for the domestic arts, for in the creation of government we imitate the heavenly kingdom. In mathematics, music, and architecture, in exploring the inner workings of nature, and in poetry and oratory we reveal our participation in the Godhead (*Theologia*, 2:224–26). The culmination of Ficino's proof of humankind's divinity, however, is his treatment of how the human soul becomes one with God and receives the power to perform such feats of magic as the alchemical transformation of species, which "is called a miraculous work not because it is beyond the capacity of our soul, when it becomes an instrument of God, but because, since it is difficult and is rarely done, it occasions wonder." Individuals who have purified their souls and become thoroughly dedicated to God have also received the power to "gather the clouds together in rain, drive away fogs, cure the diseases of human bodies," and perform other feats of magic which are recorded by many Platonists and attested by "ancient theologians" such as Hermes and Orpheus (*Theologia*, 2:229). The alchemical transformation of lower species into higher ones is, in particular, a notable example of a form of magic which seeks to purify the natural world by bringing physical things into more perfect conformity with their governing Ideas. This redemption of nature can be performed only by an adept who has previously been spiritually purified by Christ.[8]

Ficino sometimes describes the perfection of the human psyche itself as a form of alchemical sublimation. The ascent toward God involves both "internal action" (i.e., reflection) and "external action" (art). In contemplation we strive to unite with each object in the cosmic hierarchy by contemplating the Ideal Forms within the Mind. "Hence," Ficino says, "in trying to become all things the intellect tries to become God, in whom all things exist."[9] Becoming aware of the soul's divinity is like seeing "the pure gold freed from the defilements of earth" (*Opera*, 1:659, trans. in Robb, 87). The human will, however, is not satisfied with contemplation alone, and art therefore becomes a necessary continuation of human striving toward complete spiritual and intellectual fulfillment. God Himself, when He made the world, first created a perfect universe of Ideas; since all perfect essences possess the power to produce likenesses of themselves, the Ideas acted in turn as the causes of various aspects of the lower world (Kristeller, *PMF*, 125–39, esp. 137–38). Similarly, when human artists imitate God, they must first clarify within themselves the Ideas within the Mind; only after the contemplative withdrawal from physical things can we return to the lower world in order to perfect it (*PMF*, 304–6).

Magic, the noblest of the arts, springs from the final completion of the contemplative ascent. The soul which performs miracles is "that which commands the fantasy to lie silent, and burning with desire for the supernal divinity, relies not on the common discourse of natural reason, but lives in the Mind alone, becomes an angel, and receives God entirely within its breast. This is what Zoroaster means when he says . . . 'The soul of humankind contracts God, in a sense, within itself, when, retaining nothing mortal, it is intoxicated with a divine liquor. . . .' In such a manner, the theology of the divine John says, the soul is born again of God."[10] Temperate and pure living facilitates the process of ascent by freeing the reason from troublesome humors and keeping it from becoming oppressed by physical concerns. An "honest and religious education," Ficino emphasizes, can ennoble the soul by bringing it to desire good for all humankind. It thus comes to resemble God and is chosen by Him as His instrument.[11] "If a soul, in its own nature, rises above the frame of the world and through inferior powers works wonders on other bodies," Ficino adds, "what shall we believe it shall do when it ascends to its source and becomes angelic? . . . Then, indeed, filled with a greater power, it shall not only fascinate a weaker person or heal an ailing man, it shall hold sway over the elements of the spheres."[12]

The reader of book 13 of the *Theologia* continually asks why the soul, once it has united with God, should care to concern itself with the governance of worldly affairs at all. Ficino answers the question by reminding us that the human soul, like God Himself, always desires to care providentially for the entire created world (*Theologia,* 2:241). Our soul is in love with both the intelligible and the physical, and it always seeks to unite them. The Reason turns to the Mind and receives from it the universal Forms, then turns to lower things and seeks to re-create them in the likeness of their governing Ideas. The soul thus forms its own body as a reflection of itself, and it also forms external matter, using its body as a tool, through art. When the soul of the magician unites with God, it receives supernatural powers, and it may either transfigure its own body, as happened in the case of Saint Paul, or project the power which flows through it onto a body other than its own (*Theologia,* 2:231–40; Kristeller, *PMF,* 315). The soul can even transcend its own body in a spiritual ecstasy, and it then exerts a magical, transforming power upon any part of the cosmos to which its affection (*affectus*) leads it:

> As long as it is devoted to this body it controls the elements of this little world, that is, the four humors, and it induces heat, cold, moisture, dryness, and all complexions and feelings.... Therefore when, released from this body, it emerges into greatness [*in amplum*], it moves the humors of this larger animal, that is, the elements of the greater world, as if they were its own, since it has become, as it were, the soul of the world, or of that part of the world toward which it is most inclined.... Because it surpasses the entire mass of body in the hierarchy of nature and in dignity, the soul can fill and move the entire structure of the world itself no less than any part of it. (*Theologia,* 2:238)

With this rather impressive assertion Ficino climaxes his treatment of the soul's immortality as manifested in its creative power. He has praised, in due order, each of the activities celebrated by Renaissance humanists and artists, then dwelled at great length on the highest art and the final proof of the soul's divinity: the power of humanity to perform redemptive magic. The structure of Ficino's argument makes clear that his doctrine of the soul's divinity and its ability to perform miracles is a logical extension of the humanists' emphasis on human dignity, and his understanding of magic as a means of governing and purifying the created world is an expansion of the humanists' belief that one serves God best not solely through contemplation, but also through active and charitable involvement in the affairs of this world.

Ficino does not say that he himself has experienced the final union with God or acquired the power to perform miracles. He did, however, practice a more humble form of magic, using it primarily as an aid to contemplation. He briefly alludes to the specific techniques of magic in the *Theologia* (e.g., 2:238), but in order to attain full comprehension of actual magical procedures we must turn to *De vita coelitus comparanda.*

In the introductory and the concluding chapters of *De vita* Ficino summarizes several relevant aspects of his cosmology. Ideas in the Divine Mind are reflected in the "seminal reasons" (*rationes*) of the World Soul, which in turn impress their images upon the corporeal world. He emphasizes that the influences of the *rationes* reach the lower world through the mediation of the heavens: each *intellectus* in the Angelic Mind governs and is reflected in a group of stellar souls, which in turn govern the *species* of things in the physical realm. He describes the influence of higher powers as light, which is form as well as power (*actus*); the influence is transmitted by means of *spiritus,* the intermediary between soul and body. "In the spirit dwells soul," Ficino tells us in *De vita,* "and in the soul intelligence shines forth." [13] Natural objects thus participate in the power (*virtus*) of the stellar and planetary souls on whom they depend. The entire universe is saturated with spiritual forces, and visible things are reflections of the forms of the invisible. Lower creatures depend upon and, in a sense, are united with their superiors. Ultimately, all creation is one with God (*Opera,* 1:531–35 and 570–72; Kristeller, *PMF,* 35–47, 60–170).

Neoplatonic magic depends upon the operator's knowledge of this complicated system of occult virtues and sympathies. Magicians gather and manipulate natural objects so as to concentrate their virtues, and they may construct symbolic forms and/or perform ceremonies which attract spiritual powers. These methods produce effects either upon the natural world or upon the soul of the operator. Forms of magic which influence the soul may be purely subjective, aiming only at effects within the magician, or they may become transitive, in which case a power introduced into the soul of the operator is projected upon the outside world. [14]

The media of nondaemonic [15] forms of magic are the human *spiritus* and the *spiritus mundi,* both of which are intermediaries between body and soul. The human spirit is similar to the spirit of the world but not, at least in Ficino, quite identical to it. In ordinary perception the human fantasy forms *spiritus* into images which are neither purely physical nor purely mental, and when it conveys these images from the soul to the body it causes physical movements. Conversely, *spiritus* also receives the images of physical objects from the senses and conveys them to the higher powers.[16]

Subjective magic seeks to draw the *spiritus mundi* into the magician, mingle it with the operator's own *spiritus,* and thus enhance the individual's mental and physical well-being. In the most advanced forms of subjective magic, only hinted at in *De vita* but clearly implied in the *Theologia* and developed in detail by Agrippa and others, the magician's knowledge of God and the cosmos can be perfected. Once the divine Ideas within the Mind have been awakened, we see more clearly the spiritual realities which lie behind the appearances of external nature. Many occult philosophers sought only to attain this visionary state, and performed no transitive operations at all. Others, however, believed that the perfection of one's own knowledge brought with it the power, as well as the responsibility, to transform the outside world. The operator's fantasy could imprint his or her *spiritus* with the *species* of a particular power and project it—through the eyes, for example—into a laboratory vessel as part of an alchemical process, or use it to produce psychological effects upon other persons, perhaps bringing them under the operator's control.[17] Many Renaissance magicians asserted that any very sophisticated form of transitive magic could be performed only by an adept who had previously performed subjective magic and rituals of purification, for no one could execute a complicated operation without complete knowledge of occult virtues and sympathies. A rudimentary knowledge of the properties of various materials and forms might be gained from simple observation, but genuinely miraculous works were possible only for those who had completed the contemplative process.

Ficino opens *De vita coelitus comparanda* by asserting that we can literally re-form natural objects which have deteriorated by directing the influence of higher powers into them.[18] *De vita libri tres* is primarily a medical treatise, however, and in most of the third book Ficino concentrates upon the reformation of the human body and soul. In the lowest forms of astrological medicine, he tells us, the operator simply utilizes the occult virtues of natural objects themselves, without attempting to reach the higher powers on which lower things depend. Zinzibar, for example, which receives a great influx of *spiritus* from the sun, can prevent fainting. Gentian has the power to cure rabies and, he adds, to frighten away serpents (*Opera*, 1:547). To increase the power of natural objects one can gather together and arrange properly a number of materials belonging to the same heavenly body.[19] Thomas Aquinas and other authorities, as Ficino points out, had approved the use of the occult virtues of natural objects for medical purposes; but Ficino begins to tread dangerous ground when he discusses higher forms of magic, those involving not only natural objects, but also talismans, magical words, and astrological music. The basic theory behind these more powerful types of magic is that anything which imitates the form of a stellar soul will attract its influence. Talismans, for example, impose upon natural substances a form (*figura*) which corresponds to the higher forms more perfectly than do natural objects, and therefore the talismans attract a more forceful influx of *spiritus* than do natural substances unaltered by human art. Ficino suggests that talismans, powders, and unguents are much more potent in medicine than natural objects alone because they gather together and concentrate the virtues which in nature are dispersed throughout an entire genus of objects.[20]

Ficino is particularly enticed by the possibility of constructing a "figure of the world," a model of the universe which would imitate both the structure and the systematic movements of the cosmos (cf. figs. 3 and 5). Built so as to shield out the rays of Saturn and draw in the life-giving influence of the sun, such a *mundi figura* could serve as an object of contemplation which would promote both physical and psychic health. Ficino tells us that Archimedes and, more recently, a Florentine named Laurentinus have built such figures and endowed them with motion. Contemplating an artistic microcosm such as this, Ficino suggests, can enable us to perceive the unity and order which lies behind the apparent flux and multiplicity of nature. If we construct our figure of the world in our bedchamber or a place of contemplation, and if we do not merely look at it, but truly ponder it in our souls, when we leave our house we shall perceive "not so much the spectacle of individual things as the figure of the universe" (*Opera*, 1:559). By far the best imitation of the heavens, however, is the one we construct within ourselves. We should strive to order our own souls so that they are as orderly as the heavens, to think thoughts as temperate as those of Jupiter. Then indeed can we hope for divine gifts from above (1:559–60).

Even more effective than the *mundi figura* as a means of harmonizing the human personality is the Orphic singing which Ficino himself practiced and which D. P. Walker has treated at length in *Spiritual and Demonic Magic*. Like talismans and other artificial forms, music can be designed so as to attract an influx of *spiritus* from specific planets in order to produce profound psychological effects. In passages which provide a detailed philosophical rationale for the magical power of music in works such as *The Tempest,* Ficino explains that music is more potent than images, vapors, or other medical preparations because the disembodied mathematical proportions of which the sounds are composed are more pure than forms which are compounded with matter. In addition, music imprints itself on the air, and consequently it can mingle freely with the *spiritus* which lies within the human ear. The harmoniously ordered forms are in motion, as are actual celestial influences, and they communicate that patterned movement, through the *spiritus,* to the soul. Finally, music can be accompanied by a text which carries an intellectual content and thus reaches the higher faculties (*Opera,* 1:525–26, 561–66, et passim; Walker, 6–24). Harmonious sounds, accompanied with appropriate lyrics, are ideally suited to bring our entire being, body and soul, into perfect harmony.

The Orphic songs which Ficino describes were originally used by non-Christian cults of the late Classical and early Christian eras, and it seems difficult to believe that Ficino did not realize that the songs were addressed to various pagan demigods. Apparently he regarded these subdeities as stellar and planetary souls and as aspects of the one God of Christianity; although his discussions of the subject are often equivocal, he may have thought it permissible to use such spirits in magical operations or as mediators between God and human beings. Perhaps Ficino thought that one could reverence the daemons so long as they were not worshipped with the same devotion one shows to God Himself. Genuinely orthodox Christian authorities, however, including Augustine and Aquinas, had always explicitly condemned the use of talismans or of invocations to these minor deities as evil sorcery (*goetia*), maintaining that the demigods of pagan religions were devils and that the sorcerer who invoked them had made either an explicit or an implicit pact with Satan. Even those who attempted to practice only good magic and to invoke the benevolent angels as God's messengers were deluded if they believed that magical ceremonies could compel a benevolent spirit to do a human's bidding; such attempts at magic, the orthodox tradition insisted, sprang from excessive pride and a foolish conceit of power, and the evil demons who serve Lucifer would play upon the conjurers' egotism, delude them into thinking they had genuine powers, and eventually lead them to perdition.[21]

Ficino attempts in several ways to defend the orthodoxy of good magic (*magia*) and distinguish it from evil sorcery (*goetia*). Aware that he is in dangerous territory, he occasionally says that he does not recommend the use of talismans, but only describes them. At other times he writes as if he advocates operating not with celestial *daemones* themselves, but only with their influences. The line between invoking the daemons per se and attracting their influences, however, is perilously thin: "It is not, strictly speaking, divinities entirely separated from matter which are received through these materials," Ficino says in *De vita*, "but only mundane ones. . . . Mundane, I say, that is, a certain life or something possessing vital power from the soul of the world and the souls of the spheres and the stars, or perhaps a certain vital motion, as if it were a presence from the daemons, or rather as if the daemons themselves were near the materials for a time."[22] At times Ficino speaks of the *numina mundana* as if they were impersonal forces, rather than intelligences. He is quite inconsistent about this, and eventually he gives himself away on the subject of daemons in his commentary on Saint Paul's condemnation of pagan idolatry. In Romans 1:22–23 Paul says that the pagans, "professing themselves to be wise . . . became fools, and changed the glory of the incorruptible God into an image made like corruptible man, and birds, and four-footed beasts, and creeping things," but Ficino offers a somewhat guarded defense of at least the more philosophical pagans. He argues that the learned non-Christian priests regarded images purely as symbols of the daemons; their error was permitting the common people to worship the physical images per se, rather than the spiritual realities which lay behind them. When he alludes to the animation of idols, Ficino is clearly aware that the powers invoked in magical ceremonies were benevolent daemons, not merely aspects of an impersonal *anima mundi*.

"Orpheus," he writes, "the great founder of that religion, devoted many of his hymns not only to celestial [gods], but also to daemons and daemonic men, and added particular fumigations for each." [23] Ficino was much more broad-minded and tolerant than many of his contemporaries, and he believed that the pagans' reverence for the *numina* of nature, though confounded at times with some superstition, was based on at least partially valid religious insights. Apparently he thought that certain aspects of the pagan magical religion—his own Orphic singing, for example—need not be inconsistent with Christianity.

Ficino's efforts to reconcile pagan magical practice with orthodox Christianity were doomed to fail. Daemonic magic, in particular, seeks to invoke spiritual agencies through ceremonies not sanctioned by the church; it is therefore a rival religion and cannot be tolerated (Walker, *Magic*, 83). Moreover, the Neoplatonic and Gnostic religions from which Ficino adopted his magical procedures were not only different from Christianity; they were in some respects fundamentally opposed to it. Despite the important differences between the Hermetic philosophers and the ancient Neoplatonists, both groups attributed to the individual soul a degree of self-sufficiency and power which cannot be reconciled with the orthodox Christian conception of Original Sin. They acknowledge that the soul is limited by its fall into the material world, but they assert that by turning inward to itself through philosophy and/or through non-Christian ritual (including, in some instances, theurgy), it can return to its unfallen condition. R. T. Wallis has observed that Plotinus, for example, differs from Christian mystics in that he "lacks any sense of sin or of the need for redemption. . . . Our true self is eternally saved and all that is required is to wake up to this fact, a process requiring self-discipline, but perfectly within the soul's own power." [24] Participation in a specific ritual, authorized by a particular religious institution, is unnecessary. Plotinus's successors began to emphasize theurgy rather than purely philosophical contemplation, but the contrast between ancient Neoplatonism and Christianity remained largely the same. The Neoplatonists found salvation through contemplation of the soul and of the cosmos; the early Christian church opposed the Neoplatonists by emphasizing the individual's need for divine grace as channeled through specifically Christian institutions. The contrast is underscored by the claims of some of the Neoplatonists that no special intervention of divine grace stood behind Christ's miracles; they claimed that any philosopher who adequately understood cosmology could repeat them. In other words, they denied the uniqueness of Christ's divinity.[25]

The Hermetic books similarly maintain that salvation is found through the awakening of the divine Mind within the human soul, but the relation between the individual and God does not depend upon a savior such as Christ or upon the rituals of a specific institution.[26] The portion of the *Hermetica* which Ficino translated describes humanity as created in the image of God, "the Divine and Sovereign Mind," and God grants to humankind creative powers which are similar to those of "Mind the Maker," the first offspring of God who created the lower world. Once humanity has fallen into the material world, human beings are dual in nature: we possess an immortal soul and, consequently, potential power over all of creation, yet by virtue of our physical nature we suffer the lot of mere mortals, and are subject to Destiny. The knowledge of our divine nature may be awakened in us through mystical experience, in which a novice is introduced to the mysteries of the universe by a spiritual guide. Anyone who has obtained gnosis may eventually act as spiritual advisor to other individuals. Subjective *magia* can free humankind from the limiting control of astrological influences, and transitive magic is the exercise of our awakened powers upon the external world.[27]

Ficino attempted to reconcile certain aspects of the Gnostic and Neoplatonic ideals of self-purification and subjective enlightenment with traditional Christianity by asserting that God chose to confer special knowledge and powers upon individuals who had practiced moral self-discipline, cultivated the reason, and developed a godlike concern for the welfare of humanity. We make ourselves similar to God, and *therefore* we are chosen as His instruments. The regenerative experience described in the *Hermetica* does in fact involve something similar to Christian salvation through divine grace, but there is still no need for a specific religious institution or for Christ as a unique savior.

In general Ficino dealt more cautiously with heretical ideas than did many of his successors in the occult tradition. When challenged, he submitted to authority on such matters as the use of talismans and the invocation of daemons, and he probably would never have dreamed of connecting magic or subjective illumination with radical social, political, or religious reforms. Nonetheless, through his own works and his translations of Hermetic and Neoplatonic texts, Ficino founded a magical tradition whose influence eventually went far beyond anything he could have anticipated.

As we have seen in this chapter, Ficino helped to provide a philosophical rationale for the growing conviction that the human mind could comprehend the inner workings of nature and for the renewed affirmation of human creative power. Recent studies are confirming that Ficino's works have exerted a significant and a positive influence upon our civilization.[28] At the same time, we should place an appropriate emphasis upon those elements of the magical world view which had to be rejected before genuine science could evolve: certainly it should be obvious enough that scientific method is incompatible with the appeal to divine revelation for specific knowledge of nature, with the claim that natural philosophy is esoteric, and with the belief that a single individual can master complete knowledge of the cosmos. In conclusion, however, I would stress those aspects of Ficino's thought which were not always retained by his successors and of which we need to be reminded in our scientific world. I personally am impressed by the beauty of certain elements of Ficino's conception of humanity: we are in love with both God and the world, and it is the very essence of human nature to wish to care providentially for all of life. At certain points in Ficino's work the Renaissance vision of human power appears to be purged, at least momentarily, of the grandiose self-centeredness which so often corrupted it. For Ficino, power ultimately cannot exist apart from goodness. It is a sad fact that certain facets of the history of science and technology, among many other things, may lead us to see Ficino's faith in humanity as sublimely naive. And yet one may feel, simultaneously, that there are aspects of Ficino's idealized vision of humankind which it may be well for us to contemplate, even if we are quite aware that such ideals may never be fully attained.

Chapter Three

Pico della Mirandola:
Christian Cabala, Theurgy,
and Universal Reformation

Those who see the Renaissance as a time of liberation have almost universally praised Giovanni Pico della Mirandola for his affirmation of human dignity and freedom. The *Oratio* which prefaces his nine hundred *Conclusiones,* or theses, has been entitled *Oration on the Dignity of Man* by modern editors, and it is widely cited as a central document in the literature of the movement which eventually freed Western civilization from the limitations of rigid hierarchy and traditional orthodoxy. Referring to Pico's willingness to explore with an open mind "the truth and science of all ages," Burckhardt proclaimed that when we look at this precocious philosopher, regarded as a prodigy by many of his contemporaries as well as by modern scholars, "we can guess at the lofty flight which Italian philosophy would have taken had not the Counter-Reformation annihilated the higher spiritual life of the people" (*Civilization,* 1:210). Although scholars who have dissented from Burckhardt's view of the Renaissance, such as Lynn Thorndike and William G. Craven, have also tended to reinterpret or to reevaluate Pico, thinkers in the mainstream of thought about the period have tended to share Burckhardt's enthusiasm.[1]

Praise of Pico as one of the founders of modern conceptions of humanity took a relatively new turn when Frances Yates emphasized the occult sources of much of Pico's thought, rather than the patristic or scholastic ones, and saw Pico and Ficino as among the first Renaissance thinkers to introduce significant unauthorized sources of religious revelation. Furthermore, Yates asserted that Pico believed the dignity of humanity to be derived not only from our similarity to God and our ability to purify our souls through contemplation, but also from our potential for sharing in God's creative power: the *Oratio* and *Conclusiones,* Yates believed, celebrate humankind's magical powers, and through these works Pico contributed to the new conception of humanity as essentially operative, controlling both its own destiny and the natural world (*Giordano Bruno,* 84–116). Pico della Mirandola and Renaissance occult philosophy thus assumed a more significant role in preparing the way for modern science than most researchers prior to *Giordano Bruno and the Hermetic Tradition* had been willing to concede.

Yates's conclusions concerning Pico, magic, and science have been subjected to careful scrutiny and criticism, and although her work is undoubtedly of fundamental importance, some of her generalizations must be qualified. The magic advocated by Pico and Ficino did contribute to new attitudes which helped to stimulate genuine science, but we should emphasize that it was only one of several important influences. Those who contributed to science and technology in the sixteenth century were often eclectic thinkers, willing to experiment with virtually anything to see if it worked: Hermetic/Cabalist magic, alchemy and Paracelsianism, the technology developed by mechanical artisans in response to economic needs, ancient scientific texts rediscovered by the humanists, Aristotelianism, and other currents of thought interrelate with one another in such a complex fashion that it is often quite difficult to isolate the strands of influence upon any given individual, much less upon the age as a whole. Moreover, progress occurred only as subsequent generations reinterpreted and reevaluated their predecessors: they were stimulated by the occultists' affirmation of human control over nature, but they rejected those aspects of occult philosophy which are incompatible with more advanced forms of rational inquiry. Occult philosophy differs from genuine science in its conception of mathematics as mystical rather than strictly mensurative; in its belief that profound knowledge of nature is esoteric and available only to those who have experienced a special revelation; in the failure of many of its practitioners to criticize their methodological assumptions; and in other important respects. Having acknowledged all of this, we should recognize that the occult tradition was nonetheless a powerful force in undermining received opinion in natural philosophy and in stimulating the widespread hope for an instauration of knowledge. The works of Pico, in particular, helped to promote the concept that human art can help to perfect nature: artists, including magicians, are chosen by God as His agents. As Paolo Rossi has emphasized, the belief that humankind possessed sufficient power to transform its environment had traditionally been regarded as impious, and the challenge to orthodox attitudes concerning human art was essential to the scientific revolution.[2]

Pico's philosophy was widely disseminated, and his work was both directly and indirectly influential in England. Pico's *Conclusiones* were incorporated into Johann Reuchlin's *De verbo mirifico* (*On the Wonder-Working Word,* 1494) and *De arte cabalistica* (*On the Cabalistic Art,* 1517), as well as into Cornelius Agrippa's immensely influential *De occulta philosophia libri tres* (*Three Books on Occult Philosophy,* 1533). In 1570 John Dee reported in his "Mathematical Preface" to Euclid's *Elements of Geometry* that Pico's *Conclusiones* were readily available in England (although he wished they were studied more diligently), and he cites Pico's eleventh mathematical conclusion to the effect that numbers are the key to all knowledge. Although Pico was apparently best known in England for his purely devotional literature, his works on magic were widely read by those who were intrigued by the prospect of expanding human knowledge and human control over nature.[3] Since the claims of magicians in the Hermetic/Cabalist tradition were much more extreme than those of the mechanical artisans or the Aristotelians, and since, as we shall see in Chapter 5, virtually all forms of mathematics or technology were often interpreted as evil sorcery, it is natural that magic would become one of the dominant symbols in English Renaissance literature for all human attempts to control our own destiny.

Pico transformed the entire basis of Renaissance occult philosophy through his addition of the Jewish Cabala to the sources of occult lore which Ficino had used. Pico did not, however, emphasize transitive magic throughout his career as consistently as did Agrippa, Dee, Paracelsus, or some of his other successors. Pico himself seems to have valued the Cabala first and foremost as a means of explicating the Bible and of gaining esoteric knowledge of divine mysteries. He nonetheless emphasized, like Ficino, that once we have completed the contemplative ascent, we should "descend to the duties of action, well instructed and prepared."[4] The Cabala, in fact, intensified Pico's conviction that humanity was responsible for the providential care of the natural world. Moreover, Pico perceived the

Cabala as a means of invoking the influence of the angels as a stage in our ascent toward complete knowledge of and unity with God, and in Reuchlin, Agrippa, and Dee there was increasing emphasis upon the Cabala as a source of techniques for a form of Christian theurgy.

The aim of Pico's Cabalist magic is the redemption of both humankind and the natural world. Like Ficino, Pico conceives of Christ as both the Logos, the pattern of all the created world, and *Humanitas,* the universal from Whom all individual human beings receive their perfection. "Just as humanity is the absolute consummation of all lower things," he writes in *Heptaplus,* "so Christ is the absolute consummation of all human beings. If, as the philosophers say, all perfection in each class is derived by the other members from the most perfect one as from a fountain, no one may doubt that the perfection of all goodness in humankind derives from Christ as a human being. To Him alone the Spirit was given without measure, so that we might all receive it from His fullness" (220). As in Ficino, the Incarnation of Christ makes possible not only the restoration of humanity to its prelapsarian state, but also the renewal of nature. The influence of Gnostic, Neoplatonic, and especially Cabalist doctrine is evident in Pico's conception of Christ as "the image of the invisible God, the first-born of all creation, on Whom all things were founded" (*Heptaplus,* 308) and in his emphasis upon humanity as the mediator between intelligible and physical worlds. In the Cabala the fall of humanity entailed the corruption of all of nature, and it is the mission of the human race to restore the world to perfection.[5] This concept had a profound influence upon Pico, and eventually, through his works and those of other Cabalists, it is one of the factors which intensified the hopes for universal reform during the later Renaissance.

In *Heptaplus,* written after a number of his *Conclusiones* had been declared heretical, Pico says no more than Ficino did when he explained how the created world is purified by human perception and contemplation. In fact, Pico attempts to reinterpret statements which he had made in the *Oratio* and *Conclusiones* so as to disconnect from his philosophy the practical magic and the commerce with angels which he had defended a few years previously. The philosophy of *Heptaplus* is still quite helpful as a source of ideas which can help us to interpret the earlier works, especially since Pico treats the relation between Christ and individual human beings in some detail, and he is still enthusiastic in *Heptaplus* about our ability to transcend mortal limits through contemplation. He emphasizes that we can purify ourselves only with the aid of divine grace, however, and he often speaks of humanity's deification as taking place only within a fairly orthodox eschatological framework.[6]

In the *Conclusiones* and *Oratio* Pico shows much less concern for orthodoxy than he does in his later works. Several of his earlier theses imply that complete perfection of the soul may be possible in this life, and that an individual who fully unites with Christ can receive the power to perfect the external world through transitive magic. *Cabala speculativa,* a contemplative Cabala, could help to perfect the form of the human soul and restore our lost knowledge of God and the cosmos. *Cabala practica* was the application of that knowledge in transitive magical works.[7] In the *Oratio,* the first text which Pico cites as testimony for the soul's divinity and grandeur is *Asclepius,* in which Hermes Trismegistus proclaims that humanity is "a great wonder" because we possess potentially godlike knowledge and powers. Pico summarizes the reasons which are often given as the basis for assertions of human greatness, but he dismisses them as not entirely sufficient. While it is often said that humanity is "the mediator between creatures, familiar with the higher and king of the lower; by the acuteness of the senses, by the searching power of reason, and by the light of intelligence, the interpreter of nature; the part in between the steadfastness of eternity and the flow of time; and, as the Persians say, the bond tying the world together, nay the nuptial bond; and, according to David, only slightly lower than the angels" (*Oratio,* 102), the true basis for the unparalleled dignity and honor of humanity is that the human being is the only creature to whom God has granted unlimited powers of self-determination. Our greatness derives not from our occupying a privileged position *within* the universal hierarchy, but rather from our ability to live on whatever level of that hierarchy we choose. Pico refers to humanity as "a work of indeterminate form" and says that at the moment of creation God spoke to Adam as follows:

No fixed seat, no form of your very own, no gifts exclusively yours have We given to you, Adam, so that whatever seat, whatever form, whatever gifts you choose, those, according to your wish and according to your judgment, shall you have and possess. A limited nature in other creatures has been confined by Us within fixed laws. In conformity with your free will, in whose hands I have placed you, you are enclosed by no boundaries; and you will fix limits of nature for yourself. I have placed you at the center of the world, so that from there you may more conveniently look around and view whatsoever is in the world. Neither heavenly nor earthly, neither mortal nor immortal, have We made you. You, like a judge appointed for being honorable, are the molder and maker of yourself; you may sculpt yourself into whatever shape you prefer. You can degenerate into the lower natures, which are brutes. You can be regenerated, in accordance with your soul's determination, into the higher natures, which are divine.[8]

As microcosm, Pico continues, humanity contains the seeds of all created things, and by cultivating whichever of these we choose, we can become whatever we will to be. If we choose to cultivate the lower faculties, we become brutes; if we choose to cultivate the intellect, we become angels. If we are not content with the limitations of any creature, we can become fully united with God, "who is above all things," and we, too, "will stand ahead of all things. Who does not wonder at this chameleon which we are? Or who at all feels more wonder at anything else whatsoever? Not unjustly did Asclepius the Athenian say that humanity was symbolized by Proteus in the secret rites, by reason of our nature sloughing its skin and transforming itself; hence metamorphoses were popular among the Jews and the Pythagoreans" (*Oratio,* 106–8).

Pico's conception of humanity is a unique compound of humanism, Neoplatonism, Gnosticism, Cabala, and Pico's own esoteric interpretation of Christianity. He frequently cites the Bible, as well as orthodox Christians such as Augustine or Aquinas, and occasionally he refers to authors such as Horace or Seneca, who were revered by the humanists. In the *Oratio* and *Conclusiones,* however, he relies most frequently upon occult sources such as the *Hermetica,* Cabala, or the Orphic hymns, and on Plato, Plotinus, Iamblichus, Porphyry, Proclus, and those Christian thinkers, such as Origen and Dionysius, who were heavily influenced by the same pagan philosophies and religions which fascinated Pico himself. Pico's own thought is not identical to that of any one school or sect; he uses freely whatever appeals to him in various Christian, Jewish, and pagan writings, and in general he ignores their conflicts. I do not mean to suggest, however, that Pico's syncretism is merely an inability to make distinctions; rather, it springs from a conviction that all religions and philosophies may have at least partial validity, and consequently, all should be studied and evaluated by those who search for truth. Pico believed that the Christian revelation is more complete than any other, but since the Bible contains hidden meanings, pagan or Jewish texts may help us to interpret the Scriptures. Moreover, Pico thought that the study of pagan and Jewish texts could help to confirm the central truths of Christianity.[9] But even though Pico is a Christian, his conception of humanity is in some ways closer to the attitudes of Plotinus or the Gnostic heretics than to the orthodox Catholicism of his own day. When he exhorts us in the *Oratio* to discipline our personalities, cultivate the intellect, and eventually unite fully with God, he speaks not primarily of repentance for sin or submission to divine grace, but of self-assertion:

> Let a certain holy ambition take possession of the soul, so that we may not be content with mean things, but may aspire to the highest things and strive with all our forces to attain them: for if we will to, we can. Let us disdain earthly things; let us struggle toward the heavenly. Let us put in last place whatever is of the world; and let us fly beyond the chambers of the world to the chamber nearest the most lofty divinity. There, as the sacred mysteries reveal, the seraphim, cherubim, and thrones occupy the first places. Ignorant of how to yield to them and unable to endure the second places, let us compete with the angels in dignity and glory. When we have willed it, we shall be inferior to them in nothing. (*Oratio,* 110)

Ernst Cassirer pointed out that Pico's doctrine of the soul restores to humanity the absolute freedom which orthodox theologians believed was lost or severely impaired through the Fall ("Giovanni Pico della Mirandola," 319–31). For most Christian thinkers prior to the Renaissance, the will of fallen humanity was so corrupted that we cannot choose the good without the continuous assistance of divine grace. For Pico, however, the Fall is not irrevocable; original sin means not that each soul is born into the world with absolute limitations imposed upon it, but merely that it has the *capacity* to sin. Its propensity toward evil is no stronger than its propensity toward good. We are free to choose the higher or the lower portion of our dual nature, and each time we face that decision we have the opportunity either to repeat the Fall or to overcome it. "Having been born in this state," Pico says "we may be what we will to be" (*Oratio*, 108–10). To be sure, God had extended His grace at the moment of Creation by endowing humankind with the potential to become Godlike; once created, however, we ourselves possess the power to fulfill that potential or not to fulfill it, as we choose.

When Pico describes the actual stages in the process of "purgation, illumination, and perfection," he incorporates the educational philosophies of the Scholastic philosophers and the humanists into his own program, and then he goes a step beyond them. The Schoolmen are generally moderate in their conception of original sin, in that they grant the human mind and soul the power to do some good, with the aid of divine grace, but still maintain that our powers are limited. The humanists, although often somewhat more optimistic about humankind than their Scholastic predecessors and rivals, still retain some sense of human limitations. Pico goes a significant step beyond both the humanists and the Schoolmen by emphasizing the extent to which human beings may gain knowledge and power through the *Mens,* the intuitive faculty which he believed was superior to the *Ratio.* He therefore speaks of the traditional academic disciplines as preparing us for the final stage in the soul's ascent toward union with God. Moral philosophy quells the disturbances of the passions, and then dialectic and natural philosophy can further clarify the reason, banish error, and make the soul fit for its final enlightenment. The final stage of the soul's ascent is the study of theology, culminating in the direct illumination of the *Mens* through the descent of the Holy Spirit.[10]

In many of the Gnostic and Neoplatonic writings which Pico defends in his *Conclusiones,* a faith in the ability of the human soul to perfect itself cannot be fully separated from a belief in magic. Not only does humankind's spiritual and intellectual ascent culminate in the infusion of knowledge which may be applied in transitive magical operations; the process of gaining knowledge itself often involves the invocation of benevolent spirits. The "secret rites" which Pico mentions with obvious approval in the *Oratio* sometimes involve traffic with daemons, and the ancient theologians point to human-kind's power to invoke these spirits as a sign of human greatness. In the *Asclepius,* to which Pico alludes at the opening of the *Oratio,* Hermes Trismegistus' highest praise of humanity occurs in the passage on the animation of idols:

> Marvellous is all that I have told you of [humankind]; but one thing there is, more marvellous than all the rest; for all marvels are surpassed by this, that [humankind] has been able to find out how gods can be brought into being, and to make them. Our ancestors were at first far astray from the truth about the gods; they had no belief in them, and gave no heed to worship and religion. But afterwards, they invented the art of making gods out of some material substance suited for the purpose. And to this invention they added a supernatural force whereby the images might have power to work good or hurt, and combined it with the material substance; that is to say, being unable to make souls, they invoked the souls of daemons, and implanted them in the statues by means of certain holy and sacred rites.[11]

Pico believed that *Asclepius* and other sacred texts of the ancient mystery religions and gnostic cults contained valuable truths and should be studied by Christian philosophers; he was certainly attracted to the Gnostic vision of the human soul and its magical powers. At the same time, he knew that orthodox Christians from the patristic period onward had virtually always declared the daemons worshipped in pagan cults to be the servants of Satan. He therefore introduces magic into Christian philosophy cautiously, at times attempting, like Ficino, to speak of the daemons as if they were impersonal forces. His most important strategy for defending himself against possible charges of heresy, however, is to distinguish between the good magic (*magia*) which he was advocating and the evil magic (*goetia*) which involved the worship of devils. Magical Conclusion number 1 (Kieszkowski ed., 78) states that the infamous magic condemned by the church is indeed *goetia* and can be nothing but an illusion. It is the work of evil demons who serve the Father of Lies. "Natural magic," however, "is the practical part of natural science," and is lawful (Magical Conclusions 2 and 3, p. 78). The Orphic hymns—which Pico admits utilize *nomina deorum*—are not addressed to evil spirits, but to "natural powers" which are distributed throughout the world by God and which may properly be invoked by the wise.[12] Therefore whatever marvelous work is performed by *magia* or Cabala must be attributed principally to God, who grants miraculous powers to contemplative souls who will use them for good purposes (Magical Conclusion 6, quoted below, p. 50).

W. G. Craven has recently argued that magic is much less important in Pico's thought than Yates had believed, and he denies altogether that Pico developed a form of theurgy. He correctly points out that Pico discusses *natural* magic in the *Oratio* as an aspect of natural philosophy, but not in connection with the higher pursuits of theology (Craven, 84–85). At other points in the *Oratio*, however, Pico suggests that we can gain further knowledge of nature by exploring ourselves, and he emphasizes that the final contemplative ascent, culminating in union with God, must be followed by a descent to action (112, 124). The major evidence concerning Pico's interest in theurgy, however, is in the *Conclusiones*. Craven challenges Yates's discussion of these magical and Cabalist theses on the grounds that the *Conclusiones* are "obscure" (128), and it is true that Pico develops his most heretical arguments in an allusive and metaphorical fashion. We can clarify the theses, nonetheless, by interpreting them in the context of the more complete version of Pico's cosmology which we find in *Heptaplus* and by keeping in mind some of the basic concepts of the Cabala and of other philosophies which Pico explicitly draws upon. Such an examination will demonstrate that Yates's original analysis was substantially correct, and that Reuchlin, Agrippa, and Dee also interpreted Pico correctly when they built their conceptions of Christian theurgy and redemptive magic upon Pico's works.

In *Heptaplus* Pico tells us that there are four worlds. One of these is humanity, the microcosm, and the other three are the major subdivisions of the hierarchical universe. Heaven, the intelligible or supercelestial world, is the realm of the angels. Pico, like Ficino, tends to associate this Angelic Mind with the Platonic Ideas which derive directly from God and which are reflected as light or *actus* into the second level of existence, the celestial world. He also tends to equate the Angelic Mind with the Logos, the Logos with Christ. Through the celestial world the reflections of Ideas reach the lowest of the three levels of existence, the terrestrial (*Heptaplus,* 184–98, 246–66, 308–24). The system of harmonious correspondences between the three worlds might thus be described as a consequence of the incarnation of aspects of God Himself in His creation. Pico emphasizes that the same divine Ideas are present, albeit in successively more adulterated forms, in each of the three levels of existence: "Truly, whatever things exist in the lower world are also in the higher ones, but of better stamp; likewise, whatever things exist in the higher ones are also seen in the lowest, but in a degenerate condition and with a nature one might call adulterated. In our world there is the elemental quality of heat, in the heavens there is a heating power, and in angelic minds there is the idea of heat" (*Heptaplus,* 188). "Heaven" is thus literally present in the lower worlds as well as in the supercelestial realm, but in a different mode. In the celestial world it is present as light, or power, and in the terrestrial it is the efficient cause which brings the potential of matter into actuality and perfects it (*Heptaplus,* 204–12, 314).

If we look at the *Conclusiones* and *Oratio* in the context of this cosmology, we realize that the magus who has completed the contemplative ascent intuits within the *Mens,* now fully awakened and aware of its union with the divine Mind, the Ideal Forms from which earthly things are derived. The purpose of transitive magic is to intensify the influence of stellar and supercelestial powers upon terrestrial creatures and thus perfect them. Pico's magic, in other words, is a form of Cabalist alchemy (cf. Blau, 27). The magician unites lower things with the Ideas which govern them and, by doing so, actualizes their full potential:

> There exists no power seminally and separated in heaven or on earth which the magus cannot actuate and unite.

> The miracles of the magical art are performed only through the union and actuation of those things which exist seminally and separated in nature.[13]

The thirteenth Magical Conclusion tells us that "to perform magic is nothing other than to marry the world."[14] In the *Oratio* Pico explains in further detail, making clear that the marriage is between a higher level of reality and a lower one. While evil magic makes us the slaves of the powers of wickedness, good magic grants us the power to rule them. Benevolent magic enables us to contemplate nature and gain intimate knowledge of divine virtues and the system of cosmic correspondences: "Applying to each thing its innate charms . . . as if it were itself the maker, [magic] discloses in public the wonders lying hidden in the recesses of the world, in the bosom of nature, in the storerooms and secrets of God. And just as the farmer marries the elms to the vines, so the magician marries earth to heaven, that is, lower things to the properties and virtues of higher things" (*Oratio,* 152). The magician, as the supreme artist, is in love with the reflections of God which he sees in earthly creatures, and his love impels him to redeem those creatures by freeing them through his magic from all impurity. As we shall see in a subsequent chapter, this conception of cosmic marriage lies behind Prospero's symbolic masque in *The Tempest,* and it may also have influenced Edmund Spenser, who often alludes in a very intriguing fashion to symbolic marriages in *The Faerie Queene.*

Ficino had also sought to purify lower things by bringing the influence of stellar and planetary souls to bear upon them, but Pico, through Cabala, envisioned operating not merely with the mundane or stellar *numina,* but with the angelic powers themselves. As Yates has demonstrated in *Giordano Bruno* (121–23), Pico identified the ten Sephiroth, the Cabalistic "Powers of God," with the the ten angelic hierarchies set forth by Pseudo-Dionysius. Although the Sephiroth themselves exist in the intelligible world, each of them is also the *primum,* or the leader, of a class of spirits who in turn govern various aspects of the lower spheres of the cosmos. Through Cabala one can learn the names and numerological symbols of the Sephiroth, and by manipulation of these names one can bypass the celestial intermediaries and tap directly these highest of all creative forces. Pico's twenty-sixth Magical Conclusion states that pure Cabala can work miracles which no lower form of magic can accomplish because Cabala utilizes "prime agents" rather than intermediaries.[15] Magical Conclusion 15 even says that no magical operation can be of any efficacy unless a work of Cabala is annexed to it.[16]

Under the influence of Neoplatonic and Gnostic conceptions of the Logos, medieval Cabalists developed the conception of Adam Kadmon, the archetype of Humanity who is the first offspring of God and the underlying unity of the ten Sephiroth. Because of the anthropomorphism of this symbolic concept, Adam Kadmon strongly resembles Christ as understood by Pico and Ficino. The Jewish Cabalists believed that the earthly Adam was made in the image of Adam Kadmon and that as long as humanity dwelled in Eden the powers of the human soul participated in those of the Sephiroth. The sixty-sixth Cabalist Conclusion strongly suggests that Pico adopted this view:

> I thus adapt our soul to the ten Sephiroth, so that through its unity it becomes one with the first, through intellect with the second, through reason with the third, through the higher con-cupiscible power with the fourth, through the higher irascible power with the fifth, through free will with the sixth, and through all of this, as it turns itself to higher things, with the seventh, as it turns toward lower things with the eighth, and through the mixture arising from both directions, through its shunning neither or clinging alternately to each, rather than simultaneously containing them, with the ninth, and through the power [it possesses] insofar as it inhabits the highest dwelling place, with the tenth.[17]

In *Major Trends in Jewish Mysticism* (245–86) and *Sabbatai Sevi,* Gershom Scholem has described the apocalypticism and the Messianic ideals which became an increasingly important part of the Jewish Cabalist tradition in the fifteenth and sixteenth centuries. Many Cabalists of the period believed that humankind had originally been created in order to complete the creation of a harmoniously ordered cosmos, but the task was never completed because Adam sinned. The human soul became fragmented and was embodied in fallen individuals who now dwell in an imperfect universe. Through adherence to divine law and through mysticism, however, each individual has the power to purify the soul, unite it to its divine source, and restore its lost powers. Each soul which thus perfects itself hastens the onset of the Messianic Age, when the world will be re-created according to the flawless pattern it was originally intended to follow. Magic, for some Cabalists, was a means of contributing to this process of purifying the fallen world and completing God's creation.

Pico was profoundly impressed by the similarity between the regenerative experience sought by Cabalists and that which is described in the Hermetic books (Yates, *Giordano Bruno,* 106–10). The

Hermetica states that certain "vices" or "punishers" inhabit the soul of unregenerate, earth-bound humanity, and Pico equated these *ultores* with the similar evil forces of the Cabala. In the *Hermetica* these forces are the influences of the evil demons of the zodiac or the planets, and the regenerative experience is described as an ascent through the spheres in which the good forces of each level of existence drive out the corresponding evil ones. "The Powers are One in the Word," Hermes Trismegistus tells an initiate in one Hermetic treatise, "and the soul thus regenerated becomes itself the Word and a Son of God." [18]

For the Jewish Cabalists the Word is Adam Kadmon. For Pico, the Word is Christ, who is born in the soul of the pious and contemplative:

> When we hear "the sun" and "the stars," let us understand not the stars, but the angels presiding over the stars, who, since they are invisible themselves, illuminate an earth which is also invisible, namely, the substance of our souls. . . . For since, as Dionysius says, there are three angelic activities—purgation, illumination, and perfection—they are so distributed that the lowest order purifies, the highest order perfects, and the intermediate one . . . illuminates. Therefore the lower waters purify our earth, whence it becomes bright in appearance; the celestial ones illuminate it when purified; the supercelestial ones perfect it with a fiery and vivifying dew, and often fertilize it for such great felicity that there germinate not healthful herbs but the Savior himself, and not one virtue, but Christ, the fullness of all virtues, is formed in us. (*Heptaplus*, 262)

In the *Conclusiones*, Pico discusses the union of the individual and the archetype in the context of both the Cabala and the Orphic mysteries. The twenty-sixth Orphic Conclusion states that "he who returns entirely to the soul shall make his own form equal to the first form"; the twenty-seventh asserts that "he who attempts the work of the preceding conclusion shall approach the third Jove as living, not as vivifying." [19] Although I cannot be absolutely certain what Pico means by "*Iovem . . . tercium*," it seems reasonable to interpret this last thesis as meaning that the initiate is attempting to approach the Creator as He is in Himself, instead of merely as He is reflected in His creatures. It also seems probable that the experience is similar to that which Pico describes in the eleventh Cabalist Conclusion: "The manner in which rational souls are sacrificed to God by the archangels, which is not explained openly by Cabalists, occurs only through the separation of the soul from the body, not of the body from the soul, unless by chance, as happens in the death of the kiss, of which it is written, *precious in the sight of the Lord is the death of His saints.*"[20]

Several additional *Conclusiones* imply that this regeneration of the soul confers upon the individual the ability to perform miraculous works. Magical Conclusion 12 states that all magical power is dependent upon "the soul of humankind standing, and not falling,"[21] suggesting that the soul of one who does not repeat Adam's sin will still participate in the creative powers of the archetype. Even more explicit is Magical Conclusion 6:

> Every miraculous work which may occur, whether of magic, or of Cabala, or of any other kind, must be attributed principally to glorious and blessed God, *whose grace bountifully rains down supercelestial waters of miraculous powers daily upon contemplative human beings of good will.*[22]

The term "supercelestial" is especially noteworthy, since it implies that the powers referred to in the conclusion come from the highest of the three levels of the cosmos. This conclusion therefore alludes not to the form of magic which relies merely on the operator's knowledge of the virtues of earthly things or on the influences of the stars, but to a higher form of magic which draws upon the powers of the angelic hierarchies which Pico associated with the Sephiroth.

Pico's magical doctrine is an attempt to reconcile an emphasis upon the freedom and the magnificent creative powers of humankind with the traditional belief that the individual is dependent upon God. When the soul restores the image of God within itself and realizes its union with the Creator, it receives the power to participate in God's creative work. The desire to assert the individual personality and the opposed desire to become lost in mystical union with God become paradoxically fused.

The belief that one can become a vehicle of God's power has sometimes led to an identification of the individual with the Messiah. This equation was made by ancient Gnostics such as the infamous

Simon Magus,[23] and we find similar tendencies among occult philosophers and the radical sects of the Renaissance. Pico himself, however, avoided these extremes, although his metaphors and the force of his rhetoric sometimes seem to point in this direction. When Pico says that Christ is born in us, I do not think he means to imply that we become equal to the Creator, but only that the human soul conforms to the image of God and derives certain powers from Him. Our actions as artists or magicians are analogous to God's in that we must build a world of perfect Ideas within the soul before engaging in external creation; but we do not create *ex nihilo* the world of Ideas within the self. Rather, we awaken the seeds which God has graciously planted within us.

In *The Individual and the Cosmos in Renaissance Philosophy* Ernst Cassirer identified the movement toward a paradoxical fusion of subject and object, individual and universal, humanity and God, as central to Renaissance thought. He pointed out that for ancient Neoplatonists, such as Plotinus, Eros was the force which drove creatures in the physical world to strive through ceaseless activity to realize themselves through union with the world of Ideas, but there was no countermovement from the One toward the Many. For Pico and Ficino, however, the love between higher and lower is reciprocal, and it is the love of the deity for His creatures which makes their redemption possible. Quite frequently in the Renaissance, the idea that God Himself is in love with the lower world served to justify humankind's own love for it. Moreover, the new emphasis upon the immanence of aspects of divinity in the natural world was a corollary of the belief that humanity must engage in the reformation of the material world in order for us to realize our own divine potential:

> For matter is no longer conceived of as the mere opposite of form and, therefore, as "evil" pure and simple; instead, matter is that with which all activity of the form must begin and through which the form must realize itself. . . . The enigmatic double nature of the artist, his dedication to the world of sensible appearance and his constant reaching and striving beyond it, now seemed to be comprehended, and through this comprehension really justified for the first time. The theodicy of the world given by Ficino in his doctrine of Eros had, at the same time, become the true theodicy of art. For the task of the

artist, precisely like that of Eros, is always to join things that are separate and opposed. He seeks the "invisible" in the "visible," the "intelligible" in the "sensible." Although his intuition and his art are determined by his vision of the pure form, he only truly *possesses* this pure form if he succeeds in realizing it in matter. The artist feels this tension, this polar opposition of the elements of being more deeply than anyone else. But at the same time, he knows and feels himself to be the mediator. (*Individual and the Cosmos,* 133, 135)

From the tension between the love of this world and the quest for transcendence springs an impulse to embody the universal fully in the particular. What Cassirer has told us about Renaissance art applies equally to Renaissance magic, except that the latter takes the impulse to idealize the actual a step further: whereas the painter, sculptor, or poet creates only images of perfection, the magus controls life itself.

Chapter Four

Cornelius Agrippa and the
Dissemination of
Renaissance Magic

The Hermetic/Cabalist magic which Pico and Ficino formulated was popularized in northern Europe, including England, largely through Cornelius Agrippa's *De occulta philosophia libri tres.* Agrippa's exposition of magical theory and procedures was widely circulated in the Renaissance among those who sought knowledge of occult philosophy, and it was a central influence upon John Dee and Giordano Bruno, both of whom had significant impact upon English society in the late sixteenth century. Agrippa himself was famous as a scholar, physician, jurist, and astrologer, but throughout his life he was continually persecuted as a heretic. His problems stemmed not only from his reputation as a conjurer, but also from his vehement criticism of the vices of the ruling classes and of the most respected intellectual and religious authorities. To a few, Agrippa was a source of inspiration; to many others, he was the most infamous of evil sorcerers, and the legends which grew up about him eventually were combined with those involving Johann Faust. Agrippa's works and his reputation have exerted a considerable influence upon major European authors, including Marlowe, Montaigne, and Goethe.[1]

The transitive side of magic is expanded in Agrippa's *De occulta philosophia,* and at times it is vulgarized. In Pico and Ficino we never lose sight of magic's solemn religious purposes: the magician explores the secrets of nature so as to arouse wonder at the works of God and inspire a more ardent worship and love of the Creator. The magus undertakes transitive operations with reverence, assuming a sacred mission as an instrument of God's will. In certain portions of *De occulta philosophia,* however, the sense of divine mission becomes confounded with self-centered ambition, and Agrippa ironically juxtaposes his exhortations to piety with references to how magic may be used to gain power to achieve one's personal desires. Moreover, passages counseling fervent prayer and ceremonial purification may well be followed by descriptions of cheap and distasteful conjurer's tricks. In book 3, for example, Agrippa warns the prospective initiate to "implore God the Father ... that you may be worthy of His mercy, be clean, within and without, and in a clean place, because it is written in *Leviticus*, 'Anyone who shall approach these things which are consecrated, in whom there is uncleanness, shall perish before the Lord.'"[2] Yet within a few pages he has descended to a catalogue of quaint spectacles: by the "art of images" it comes to pass that at Byzantium snakes are rendered harmless, and jackdaws are prohibited from flying over the walls of the city; in Crete night owls are banished, and in Naples one is never disturbed by the chirping of grasshoppers; at Venice magical images keep the flies out of the barber shops (3.64, p. 344). The consecrated magus can also perform "great works," Agrippa continues, by "the powers of speeches and words": "So Cato testifies that weary Oxen are refreshed by words, and also that by prayers and words, you may command the Earth to produce unusual trees; by this means trees may also be entreated to pass over to another place, and to grow in another ground. Grapes grow larger if they are entreated when they are sown to be beneficial to the farmers, and to their family and neighbors; the Peacock, also, being praised, presently extends his feathers" (3.64, p. 344). At the conclusion of this chapter Agrippa exhorts the reader once again to "take heed in your prayers, lest you desire some vain thing, or that which is against the will of God; for God would have all things good: neither shall you use the name of your God in vain, for one who uses His name for a vain purpose shall not go unpunished" (3.64, p. 345).

Considerable space is devoted to examples of evil sorcery in *De occulta philosophia*, and one might easily come away from the treatise with the impression that Agrippa found witchcraft as intriguing as benevolent magic. He seems fascinated by the grotesque and the obscene as well as the divine. His interest in the more lurid aspects of the occult is evident, for example, in the story he tells of a sorceress named Pamphilia who was "out of her wits" with love of a young man named Baeotius. A maid who was supposed to bring the sorceress hair from Baeotius's head brought instead the hairs of goats. The witch had previously equipped her house with such "suitable equipment" as pieces of iron with images carved upon them, sections of the sterns of wrecked ships, and various portions of corpses she had apparently stolen from their graves: "here noses and fingers, there the fleshy nails of those who had been hanged, and in another place the blood of those who had been murdered, and their skulls mangled with the teeth of wild beasts." She performs various ceremonies, sprinkling the "enchanted entrails" with different liquors, until "through the irrestible power of the magical science, and obscure force of the gods, the bodies of those [goats] whose hairs did smoke ... assumed a human spirit, and felt, and heard, and walked, and came to where the odor of their hair led them, and, instead of the young man Baeotius, came skipping, and leaping with vehement desire into the house" (1.41, p. 47).

Though Agrippa labels this particular ceremony as *goetia,* many of the practices of which he apparently approves are equally ludicrous. Not only are the techniques which he describes sometimes physically revolting, but they often are used not for altruistic purposes, but simply to serve the operator's lusts. In spite of the frequent warnings that whoever works magic only for worldly ends shall "work himself to judgment and damnation," section after section of *De occulta philosophia* explains how magic can bring the operator wealth, love, political power, or revenge on his or her enemies. In book 2 Agrippa tells us quite bluntly that we can construct astrological images "for the success of petitions, and in order to obtain something which has been denied, or taken, or possessed by another" (2.50, pp. 192–93). In other sections the desire for personal power penetrates quite subtly into what otherwise seems to be a sincerely religious context:

There are three guides which bring us to the paths of truth and which rule all our religion, in which it wholly consists, namely love, hope, and faith: love indeed is the chariot of the soul, the most excellent of all things, descending from the intelligences above to the lower world. It congregates and turns our Mind [*Mens*] toward the Divine Beauty, *preserves us also in all our works, gives us events according to our wishes, administers power to our supplications. . . . But hope, when it is certain and not wavering, immovably clinging to those things which it desires, nourishes the Mind*

and perfects it. . . . To conclude, by faith humankind is made some-
what the same with the superior powers and enjoys the same power
with them. (3.5, p. 217; my emphasis)

It is possible to interpret the preceding quotation as referring to magical powers which might be used for unselfish ends, but at the very least the passage reveals the genuine danger that the aspiring magician's desire to enhance his or her own personality might become stronger than the desire to serve as the agent of Providence. Other passages of *De occulta philosophia* go much further: the reader often encounters strikingly paradoxical and sometimes confusing mixtures of the sacred with both the profane and the ridiculous. Lists of magical operations which an adept can perform often include both the beneficent and the destructive, with little or no explicit distinction between *magia* and *goetia*. A good example is Agrippa's list of "bindings" in book 1, chapter 40, in which he tells us that magic can bind individuals into love or hate, sickness or health; armies and navies can be immobilized; mills can be bound so as to prevent their turning, wells to prevent their providing water; the ground can be bound so that it will not produce crops; and we can bind specific locations so that nothing can be built upon them. Fire can be stopped from burning those objects placed into the flames, tempests prevented from inflicting harm, and dogs stopped from barking. Among the more chilling instances of the strange intermingling of *magia* with *goetia* in Agrippa's treatise is his description of how images may be made "not after the likeness of any celestial figure, but after the likeness of that which the Mind of the operator desires":

So that to procure love we make images [of persons] embracing each other: to procure discord, striking each other; to bring misfortune, or destruction or hindrance to a person, or house, or city, or anything else, we make images distorted, broken in members, and parts, after the likeness and figure of that thing which we would destroy or ensnare; and magicians instruct us that in casting or engraving images we should write upon the object the name of the effect: and we should do this on the back when the effect is evil (as destruction), and on the front when good (as love). . . . Moreover, in making the image they advise that prayer for the effect for which it is made must not be omitted. (2.49, p. 191)

At times Agrippa's accounts of how talismans, potions, or the power of imagination may be used to procure love or to control natural forces read like demonic parodies of Ficino's doctrine of Eros. In book 3 Agrippa asserts that the highest forms of magical power are derived from "our mind being pure and divine, inflamed with a religious love," but he then proceeds to describe examples of magic which the reader may find difficult to interpret as consonant with Providence and the natural order: "Hence it comes to pass that though we are stationed within the natural world, yet we sometimes predominate over nature, and cause such wonderful, sudden, and difficult operations, that the spirits of the dead obey us, the stars are disordered, the heavenly powers compelled, the elements made obedient" (3.6, p. 218). There are times in the works of Pico or Ficino when some readers may legitimately wonder whether the fascination with human knowledge and power has become, at least temporarily, of greater interest than submission to Providence, but what we find in the earlier writers seems quite mild when compared to what we encounter in Agrippa. Pico and Ficino were convinced that the highest levels of magical power could be attained only by one who had been sanctified and whose motives were, consequently, entirely pure. As we read through Agrippa and witness how easily the magical ideal can be perverted, we begin to realize how Erasmus or Ben Jonson could condemn as a dangerous madness the belief that the individual can obtain magical power by perfecting the soul.

A potential for the moral ambivalence we encounter in Agrippa is inherent in certain aspects of magical theory itself, particularly in the case of the "force of imagination." As we saw in the section on Ficino, the imagination conveys *species* which participate in the power of the celestial and supercelestial Ideas, and since the passions are closely allied to imagination, a strong desire gives the imaginative power greater force. Sheer intensity of desire and assertion of will can thus enhance the magician's power to project *species* onto the outside world in order to accomplish his or her purposes. Theoretically, the greatest increases in the power of imagination occur only when the *Ratio* and *Mens* are purified and thus "conformed" to the corresponding powers of the universe, and for Pico or Ficino this fact guaranteed that great powers could be attained only by those who sincerely desire to serve God. Agrippa, quite frequently contradicting himself, sometimes seems to say that virtually any strong feeling, pure or impure, can become a source of power:

> The human Mind, when it is intent upon any work, through its passions [*passiones*] ... is joined with the Minds of the stars and the intelligences, and this union causes a marvellous virtue to be infused into our operations. This occurs because there is in [the Mind] the apprehension and power of all things, so that all things have a natural obedience to it, and by necessity are more influenced by that which desires them with a strong desire. ... By this means whatever is affected by the Mind of someone who is vehemently in love has the ability to cause love, and whatever is influenced by the Mind of someone who strongly hates has the power to hurt and to destroy. (1.67, p. 88)

In the next chapter Agrippa actually says that all things obey the mind of a person "who is carried into a great excess of any passion."[3] In book 3, chapters 46–49, he explains that the "passion" which brings power into the soul is not an ordinary emotion, but rather a "heroic frenzy" (*furor*) which enables us to transcend mortal limits, but in other passages he seems to say merely that if magicians desire something strongly enough there is nothing in heaven or earth which can deny it to them. Precisely at this point will the opponents of magic, including Ben Jonson, attack: seizing upon the ambivalence of the terms *passio* and *furor* in magical theory, Jonson will identify the belief that one can transcend mortal limits as a delusion fostered by irrational passion and a diseased imagination. The fantasy of the deluded characters in Jonson's *Alchemist* is stimulated not by a genuinely "heroic" aspiration, but by egocentric ambition and by lust.

Agrippa's *De occulta philosophia* is important for our study not only because it illustrates the manner in which the magical ideal could be perverted, but also because it boldly makes explicit the most heterodox aspects of Renaissance magical theory. To begin with, Agrippa frankly acknowledges the daemonic character of much of the magic which he describes. He sometimes speaks of natural powers simply as "occult virtues," but he subsequently explains that the powers from which these virtues derive are what the Platonists call "gods," "lives," or "souls," and that all of them are aspects of the one God.[4] At one point he repeats almost verbatim Pico's third Orphic Conclusion, but he prefaces it with a remark identifying the "natural and divine virtues" distributed throughout the world with "celestial deities" and "souls."[5] In book 3 he treats daemonology in great detail, citing numerous Christian, Jewish, and pagan sources. He begins his account with a discussion of the highest order of intelligences, the angels or Sephiroth, and he follows Dionysius and Pico in dividing the angels into three hierarchical groups, each of which has specific duties.[6] The supercelestial hierarchies preside over the celestial orders of spirits, reflecting into them the light which they receive directly from God. According to Agrippa these celestial orders are much more numerous than some Christian philosophers have realized. The Peripatetics held that only one intelligence ruled each sphere of the heavens, but since we see that every individual star and each portion of the heavens has its own type of influence, we must conclude that each individual heavenly body has its own ruling spirit. The magicians, therefore, believe in the twelve princes which rule the signs of the zodiac, thirty-six spirits which rule the Decans, and seventy-two which rule the Quinaries of heaven and the languages of human nations, as well the seven governors of the world who are associated with the seven planets. Agrippa does not stop here; he goes on to describe literally dozens of varieties of spirits of the terrestrial orders, the invisible powers who directly govern earthly affairs. He divides them into fiery, aerial, aquatic, and earthy orders, whose powers, respectively, are intuitive, rational, imaginative, and sensitive or vegetative. Among the specific types of *numina mundi* are the spirits whom we call "woodmen, mountaineers ... Gods of the Forest, Satyrs, rural Deities, Nymphs, Naiades, Neriades, Dryads, the Muses, Hamadryades ... the Graces, Genii, Ghosts," and others (3.16, p. 241). Agrippa combines the daemonology of classical, Christian, Neoplatonic, Hermetic, and Cabalist sources with popular myth and legend, never achieving a genuinely coherent synthesis. Apparently he perceives the universe as saturated with spiritual powers: literally every place in the cosmos has its own *numen,* and every natural or supernatural occurrence is the *operatio* of a personified aspect of God.

Each of the three books of *De occulta philosophia* contains instructions for operating with the powers of a different level of the cosmos. Book 1 explains how to utilize the occult virtues of natural objects and how to call upon terrestrial daemons through images, fumigations, or other means. Book 2 describes the invocation of celestial deities through mathematics, geometrical forms, or images of the zodiac and the planets, and book 3 concentrates upon operating with the Sephiroth through Cabalistic names and numerological symbols. Finally, since all of these powers are aspects of the Logos, or Christ, Agrippa tells us, all of the creative power of the universe is concentrated in the magical name "Jesu" (3.12, pp. 233–34). The third book also explains—much more explicitly than Pico did—that since humankind is created in the image of Christ our souls participate in all of these creative powers. Agrippa draws heavily upon the Cabalistic doctrine that unfallen humanity bore the divine image "in all integrity and fullness," and he explains that each of us has the power to restore the soul to its prelapsarian condition (3.40, p. 293). In one passage he incorporates Pico's statement that "magical power derives from the soul of humankind standing and not falling" into his own text, explaining that "there is no work in this whole world so wonderful, so excellent, so miraculous, that the human soul, embracing in love its own image of divinity . . . cannot accomplish by its own power without any external help," and he adds that this perfect union with God's image is what "the magicians call a soul standing, and not falling."[7] He furthermore describes the life-sustaining powers of different areas of the world as emanations, or conduits of divine power, and also as "the members of God," and he asserts that if we conform ourselves to these spirits and are translated into the divine image, we gain the power to carry out God's works (3.13, p. 234).

Much of book 3 explains the specific steps through which our innate powers of command over all of creation may be restored. Agrippa says that moral self-discipline, education, and cultivation of our rational faculties may partially amend the defects of our fallen nature, but religious ceremonies and expiations must complete the process. One must cleanse the body of all disease, the mind of all guilt, for we are prohibited from enjoying our innate knowledge and power by inappropriate passions, deceptive fantasies, and immoderate appetites. Once these are expelled, "divine knowledge and power is suddenly present" within us.[8] In chapters 46–49 of book 3 Agrippa describes this spiritual ascent in terms of the four *furores,* or stages of divine madness. In the final stage, that which Agrippa associates with Venus, the purified soul "is so formed by God, that above any other intelligence, through contact with the divine essence, it knows all things" (3.49, p. 316). In addition to receiving the power of prophecy, such a soul has the ability to perform marvellous works which cannot be performed by nature itself. Such works are properly called miracles:

> For just as heaven performs by its image (both light and heat) things which the power of fire cannot do by its natural quality (which in Alchemy, assuredly, is very well known through experience) thus does God also perform through His image and light things which the world itself cannot perform through its own innate virtue: but the image of God is humankind, or at least one who is made similar to God by a frenzy from Venus, lives solely in the Mind, and receives Jove entirely within the breast. Yet the soul of humankind is defined by the Hebrew doctors and Cabalists to be the light of God, and created in the image of the Word, the cause of causes, the prime exemplar, the substance of God, and figured by a seal whose character is the Eternal Word. Hermes Trismegistus, contemplating this, says that such a person is superior to those who govern the heavens, or at least equal to them. (3.49, p. 316)

Students of Agrippa's *De occulta philosophia* have been hard pressed to explain adequately his motives for writing his famous and influential polemic, *De incertitudine et vanitate scientiarum atque artium (On the Uncertainty and Vanity of the Arts and Sciences),* in which he denies the value of all fields of learning, especially occult philosophy. The treatise was written in 1526, at a time when Agrippa had lost favor at the French court and was suffering financial difficulties, but it was not printed until 1531, the same year in which he published the first book of *De occulta philosophia.* The complete version of the *De occulta philosophia* was published in 1533, two years after Agrippa had declared in print that anyone who attempted magic or practiced Cabala was likely to be damned.[9]

Many readers of *De vanitate* have interpreted the work as sustained irony. Eugene Korkowski has argued that Agrippa is utilizing the popular Renaissance literary devices of mock praise and mock blame in order to parody those orthodox monks and theologians who were themselves prideful and corrupt, yet who were quick to denounce others—including Agrippa himself—as heretics. The anticlerical sections of Agrippa's polemic (chaps. 56–65 et passim) are sincere, Korkowski argues, and the sections which describe the supposed benefits of various fields of learning, including the occult sciences, express Agrippa's genuine convictions. After Agrippa explains the benefits of learning and of magic, he sarcastically reverses himself, but these attacks upon learning, Korkowski believes, are satirical parodies of the extreme positions taken by the conservative theologians and inquisitors who are Agrippa's habitual enemies. Sir Philip Sidney also tells us in his *Defense of Poetry* that Agrippa was "merry" in his railing against learning, and when *De vanitate* created an uproar because of Agrippa's bitter invective against monks, inquisitors, and orthodox theologians, Agrippa himself wrote an *Apologia* in which he professed to be surprised by the number of people who had taken his jokes so seriously. Even James Sanford, whose popular translation of Agrippa's *De vanitate* was published in London in 1569, asserts in his dedicatory epistle and his preface that Agrippa is criticizing not all of learning, but merely its abuses.[10] Another approach to the puzzle of Agrippa's treatise has been suggested by Frances Yates, who proposed in *Giordano Bruno* (131) that Agrippa's rejection of the arts and sciences is disingenuous: *De vanitate* may be a "safety device," an insincere retraction of learning and of occult philosophy which Agrippa published prior to the 1533 edition of *De occulta philosophia* so that when he was attacked as a heretic he could claim that he had already recanted. The treatise might sincerely criticize certain abuses of learning or of occult philosophy, Yates added, but it cannot be taken entirely at face value.

The problem of determining Agrippa's true beliefs is further complicated by the rather vague retraction which appears on signature aa2r–v of the 1533 edition of *De occulta philosophia:* Agrippa defends some magical practices, but he also says that he no longer believes everything which the book contains, and he is publishing it merely because others have circulated erroneous versions of it. Although the 1533 retraction might support the hypothesis that Agrippa's rejection of learning and of occult philosophy in *De vanitate* is sincere, we must account for the fact that Agrippa continued to perform alchemical experiments and study pagan sources of occult wisdom long after he had written *De vanitate*.[11]

Richard Popkin, in his introduction to Agrippa's *Opera* (1:v–xxi) suggests that after the composition of *De vanitate* Agrippa may still have been driven to find a grain of truth in occult philosophy, even though he felt that any discoveries would have to be subjected to the test of consistency with the Bible. Nauert, on the other hand, has proposed that *De occulta philosophia* and *De vanitate* are not, in fact, entirely antithetical to each other: in both works, Professor Nauert argues, Agrippa denigrates human reason and exalts revelation. He sees Agrippa as typical of those Renaissance thinkers for whom skepticism concerning the powers of the human mind was a prelude to reliance upon immediate experience, on the one hand, and divine revelation, often through occult sources, on the other. In some cases empiricism became divorced from religion, Nauert points out, and eventually it led to modern scientific method, but in the sixteenth century the appeal to experience could be combined with faith in the Bible, pagan occult sources, or purely the Holy Spirit itself. In many cases the reliance upon experience and/or immediate revelation entailed the kind of rejection of traditional intellectual and scientific authorities which we find in *De vanitate*.[12]

In spite of all of the obvious irony and exaggeration, the retractions and self-contradictions in Agrippa's works, there is evidence both in the treatise itself and in the biographical circumstances of its composition that *On the Uncertainty and Vanity of the Arts and Sciences* expresses Agrippa's sincere personal confession of intellectual pride and selfish ambition, and that his retraction of many of his earlier opinions is genuine. Agrippa consistently tells us in the treatise that this world is ruled by pride and iniquity, and he expresses bitter remorse for his own personal guilt. Although he alternates between straightforward argument and satire, his attack on the world's vanity and corruption is too intense and at times too carefully reasoned to be dismissed as mere jest. In the opening chapters of *De vanitate* Agrippa proceeds mercilessly through each field of knowledge, demonstrating that all learning which proceeds from human reason is uncertain. He does not, however, consistently argue that all of our claims to knowledge are totally false; his usual procedure is to demonstrate that the various authorities in each field conflict with each other, that their arguments typically derive from premises which cannot be proved, and that consequently each art or science rests upon an insecure foundation. Most importantly, he argues that the reigning intellectual establishment persecutes anyone who dissents from orthodox doctrine, even on questions which can never have definitive answers, and many innocent people of good conscience are forced either to recant their beliefs or be tortured and burned at the stake. Agrippa thus establishes an attitude which is crucial for an interpretation of *De vanitate:* to a considerable extent, his attack on learning is a corollary of his assertion that educational institutions, traditional academic disciplines and authorities, and the established church itself are instruments of oppression, wielded by a corrupt political, religious, and intellectual establishment in order to stifle various forms of dissent which may be based upon genuine divine inspiration. Agrippa may have utilized the genre of the mock encomium so that he could subsequently claim that his criticisms had not been serious, but the disclaimer did not convince most of Agrippa's contemporaries (Nauert, *Agrippa,* 107–11), nor should it convince a modern reader. Despite his relatively transparent cover and some passages actually intended as exaggerations, the central purpose of *De vanitate* is to express Agrippa's sincere and concerted attack upon the social, political, and religious hierarchy, as well as to confess that he himself has attempted to use his reputation as a man of learning and a magician in order to obtain social and financial advantages from a society which he always knew in his heart to be corrupt.

At the very beginning of his treatise Agrippa concedes that some people think that arts and sciences can lead us to divinity, but he insists that only a reformed will and a commitment to living according to the word of God have genuine value for humankind. True felicity is derived not from knowledge, but from living well, "for not a good understanding, but a good will unites humankind with God." [13] Throughout the treatise he maintains that learning springs from excessive pride, and in his chapters on grammar, logic, scholastic philosophy, and scriptural exegesis he argues that the vanity, excessive cleverness, and presumptuous curiosity of scholars can lead them to stray from the literal truth of the Scriptures. In the dedicatory epistle to John Trithemius and in book 3, chapter 3, of *De occulta philosophia,* Agrippa had followed Pico della Mirandola in granting traditional education a role in preparing the soul to receive divine revelation; throughout *De vanitate,* however, Agrippa consistently maintains that the only firm basis of knowledge and of virtue is neither human reason, nor scholastic learning, nor the occult philosophy which bases itself on pagan sources, but rather a humble acceptance of biblical truths, as interpreted by the gift of the Holy Spirit.

As he proceeds through his critique of the various fields of knowledge, Agrippa spends considerable time summarizing and then refuting the claims of the occult tradition. Although exaggeration and sarcasm are fairly common in the treatise, at times the attack upon the foundations of the occult sciences is earnestly and carefully reasoned. In chapter 30, on astronomy (including astrology), Agrippa does not deny entirely the reality of astrological influences, as he might if his criticism were mere satirical raillery. Instead he argues that the precise sources and the interactions of the influences of the heavens are too obscure and too complicated for human beings to comprehend. Astronomers claim that knowledge of the structure and the influence of the heavens is the foundation on which "all things stand, and may be known or done" (2:67–68), but their assertions are undermined by the fact that the same astrological situation will be interpreted in different ways by different individuals. In reality the practice of astrology, which Agrippa admits he himself has engaged in, is founded upon a wicked, prideful curiosity concerning human destiny, or simply upon the astrologer's desire for wealth and fame. When Agrippa discusses alchemy, Cabala, theurgy, and other occult sciences, he repeatedly confesses that he has explored them, but learned through experience that they were vain, and a serious threat to salvation. In chapters 41–43 Agrippa summarizes the theory of magic which he treats in greater detail in the *De occulta philosophia,* alluding to such feats as the animation of statues, and he then concludes by telling the reader that the magicians have gone so far as to imitate Satan, "the promiser of sciences," in their endeavor "to rival God and nature." [14]

Agrippa does not claim, however, that all magicians have consciously made a pact with the devil. On the contrary, in chapters 45–46 he tells us that evil spirits will imitate holy angels, even requiring ritual cleanliness and ceremonies, in order to deceive those who seek occult knowledge and magical powers. He singles out intellectual curiosity as the "damnable" quality of mind which leaves us vulnerable to the snares of the Serpent, who promises knowledge in order to lead us to destruction. We must remember, Agrippa tells us, that ultimately no one approaches God through learning, magic, or theurgy. Indeed, the occult arts are dangerous precisely because they may deceptively appear to be benevolent, especially to those who are fervently seeking divine wisdom. Agrippa focuses consistently in *De vanitate* upon two essential distinctions between genuine sources of revelation and deceptive ones: first, genuine revelation comes to those who seek to comprehend the Christian Scriptures, not to those who study pagan religion and philosophy. Secondly, and most importantly, genuine illumination is granted to those who are humble at heart, not to those who take pride in their own learning, their own power, or their own social status. Agrippa's central argument concerning the vanity of learning is thus a corollary of the sympathy for the poor, the ignorant, and the meek of the earth that permeates the entire treatise.

Consider, for example, Agrippa's passionate criticism of the foundations of "nobility": he begins, in chapters 69 and 70, by criticizing the dissolute behavior, pride, and flattery of courtiers in terms which may sound familiar to readers of Renaissance satire, but he proceeds to an unusually bold and far-reaching critique of the entire system of inherited social privilege. Warfare, Agrippa tells us in chapters 79–80, is frequently praised by the powerful of this world, and prowess in battle is regarded as a prime source of personal honor. In reality, Agrippa asserts, warfare is simply murder, usually pursued merely to extend political empires, and it is rationalized with a false and deceptive rhetoric of military glory. The social institutions of monarchy and aristocracy are based upon brutality and bloodshed, since the most remorseless, and consequently the most successful, soldiers of the past are the ancestors of present-day noblemen and kings. Those who control the governments are simply the most efficient in killing their personal enemies. The laws of human society are typically evil, oppressive, and contrary to the judgments of God. If anyone wishes to advance in such a society and become a nobleman, Agrippa advises, "let him become a mercenary soldier, and hire himself out for a price to commit murder, for this is the true virtue of nobility." There is no greater glory among noblemen than to show oneself through such exploits to be "a powerful and courageous brigand" (2:226). If an ambitious man is unfit to be a soldier, he may purchase a title with money, or rise through flattery, or by pandering to the lusts of the great and powerful, or through some other deceit. These are the ladders and the steps on which the ambitious of this world rise to prominence and to the highest perfection of "nobility." In previous and subsequent chapters (74–75, 99 through the "Operis peroratio," et passim) Agrippa frequently contrasts corrupt noblemen with humble farmers and shepherds, who earn their bread by the honest sweat of their brow, as God commanded. The earnest and straightforward tone of the passages in which Agrippa expresses admiration for the honesty and humility of the working classes is in striking contrast with the bitter invective of the numerous sections in which he attacks the vanity of those who are educated and socially prominent. Moreover, Agrippa's social attitudes are logically consistent with his expressions of faith in the literal truth of the Scriptures and with his affirmation of Saint Paul's admonition that those whom the world deems wise are fools if judged by the wisdom of the Lord. Only humility, Agrippa repeatedly emphasizes, can enable us to find our proper relationship with God.

Agrippa's attack upon the nobility is paralleled by his criticism of the ecclesiastical hierarchy and the oppressive authorities of the church. Throughout the chapters on religion he affirms his faith in the Scriptures as the sole source of ethical and religious wisdom, and at times he suggests that the modern church reform itself in the light of the practices of the apostles and the early church fathers. Whether Agrippa actually remained loyal in any sense to the Roman Catholic community is uncertain, but his extreme criticism of the use of images and relics, of excessive reliance on external ceremonies rather than inner spirituality, of the intolerance of ecclesiastical authorities, and of the vices and worldliness of priests, monks, bishops, and popes certainly places him in the ranks of the radical reformers.[15] In his section on the Inquisition (chap. 96, 2:278–82), Agrippa defends the right of the individual to interpret the Bible according to his or her own conscience. Inquisitors, he says, base their persecution of presumed heretics on canon law and papal decrees, not solely on the literal interpretation of the Scriptures, and Agrippa implies that both the Inquisition itself and the Scholastic philosophy which supports it are allied to the corrupt, worldly political establishment. In this section Agrippa recounts, in dead earnest, the true story of how he personally saved an innocent, humble woman from the hands of a

Dominican inquisitor who claimed that the woman's mother, previously convicted and executed as a witch, had dedicated her child to Satan. Her accuser had claimed that the woman was the offspring of an evil spirit, and he was determined to torture her until she confessed. The inquisitor attempted to support his case against the woman with citations from *Malleus maleficarum* and from "peripatetic theology" (2:281). Agrippa protested to the inquisitor, and subsequently to a new magistrate in Metz, that all of us are born in sin, but that baptism redeems us, unless we lapse into evil of our own free will. He also argued that it was heresy to believe that devils can impregnate human women. At considerable risk to himself, Agrippa accused the inquisitor and his accomplices of engaging in a plot to seize the woman's property and of proceeding in an irregular and illegal fashion. Eventually, he was instrumental in securing the woman's release.[16] This incident, as well as others in which he sought to promote charitable enterprises such as medical care for the indigent (Nauert, *Agrippa,* 72–73), confirms that Agrippa's sympathy with the common people was genuine, and it suggests that his opposition to the Inquisition and to academic traditions which were supported by religious and political authorities was sincere.

In chapters 99, 100, and 101 of *De vanitate* Agrippa elaborates in further detail his assertion that the sole reliable sources of truth are Scripture and divine inspiration. He expresses his anxiety concerning the factual errors and self-contradictions which, he acknowledges, exist in the Bible, but he maintains that the central tenets of the faith are clear, even if the apostles and other authors of Scripture erred in some details. Although only Christ was infallible and possessed the Holy Spirit perfectly, true prophets have always agreed on the most important truths of the Christian religion. The Word of God belongs to all of humankind, not just the learned, and it is not so obscure that we cannot perceive its essential message. As for the more difficult and somewhat less essential points of theology, each individual should strive to comprehend the Bible as fully as possible, according to his or her capacity, and we should practice tolerance of those whose opinions on such matters differ from our own. Citing once again the apostle Paul's statement that God's wisdom transcends reason or the senses, and seems folly to those whom the world deems wise, Agrippa points out that prophetic gifts are granted most frequently not to the "masters of arts" and the powerful of this world, but to the rude, simple commoners, like most of the apostles, those whom the philosophers of this world condemn as "asses."

This last idea provides a transition from Agrippa's discussion of prophecy and Scripture to his satirical "praise of the ass" in chapter 102. In this section Agrippa utilizes an encomium in praise of the "mysteries of the ass" to develop the ideas he propounded in a straightforward manner in the previous section. The ass, he tells us, possesses "fortitude and strength ... patience and clemency" (2:307). The humble ass bears his burdens and accepts his fodder in peace and contentment; Apuleius, we are told, would never have been admitted to the mysteries of Isis had he not been changed into an ass; prophecy came from God to Balaam through an ass. The simple asses of this world possess more genuine knowledge and wisdom than the proud bishops and learned doctors. In his peroration Agrippa reverts once again to a serious tone, but he continues to assert that the humble of the earth are granted revelations which are denied to those who rely upon human traditions and institutions. Most strikingly, Agrippa reaffirms his hope for the restoration of all knowledge and the complete reformation of the human soul, while at the same time rejecting all pagan sources of wisdom and denigrating the human learning which Renaissance humanists often believed could play a role in reforming the world—and which Agrippa himself had apparently accepted as being as of some value in book 3, chapter 3, of the *De occulta philosophia:*

> Wherefore, you Asses who are now ... the messengers and interpreters ... of the true wisdom of Christ's holy Gospel, ... renouncing all human sciences and every quest and discourse of the flesh and blood whatsoever it may be, ... enter not into the schools of philosophers and sophists, but into yourselves, and you will know all things: for the knowledge of all things was created within you, which (as the Academicians confess) the holy Scriptures do witness, because God created all things most good: ... even as He has created trees full of fruits, so also has He created souls as rational trees full of forms and ideas, but through the sin of the first parent all was concealed by a veil, and oblivion, the mother of ignorance, entered [the Mind]. Remove, those of you who may, the veil from your understanding; you who are covered by the shades of igno-

rance, cast out the drink of Lethe with which you have made yourselves drunk with forgetfulness, and await the true light ... for (as John says) ... you need not be taught by anyone, because His anointing [of you] teaches you all things: that alone grants sight and wisdom. David, Isaiah, Ezekiel, Jeremiah, Daniel, John the Baptist, and many other prophets and Apostles were not taught by formal education, but having been shepherds, rustics, and ignorant commoners, were made most highly instructed [by God] in all things.[17]

Remarkably, Agrippa asserts that the Holy Spirit teaches us to understand all of creation, including the secrets of nature, the dispositions of the stars, the true nature of all creatures, and the powers of roots and herbs (2:313–14). In *De vanitate* Agrippa still seeks the perfection of the soul and the perfect knowledge which he attempted to find in his occult studies, but he rejects the worldly and pagan philosophies which had proved, in his judgment, to be unstable. The very revival of learning in the modern age, Agrippa says, has resulted in new heresies, for we have set up our own intellect as the judge of truth, rather than humbly awaiting the Holy Spirit (chap. 101, 2:306). The revival of ancient learning has introduced controversies over such matters as the number of worlds which may exist, or how long the universe shall endure (chap. 51, 2:107–8), and in his desperation to escape doubt and uncertainty Agrippa rejects, at least in *De vanitate,* the movement which we now call the Renaissance, including the occult philosophy which was one of the most radical expressions of the desire to vindicate a degree of human self-assertion and to authorize pagan sources of knowledge. Agrippa's life and works provide a poignant reminder of the fact that those who long most intensely for certain knowledge are often those who ultimately despair of the possibility of attaining truth through systematic inquiry. In the sixteenth century, the reaction against the new learning and against occult philosophy came not solely from those who were consistently conservatives or reactionaries, but from scholars who previously had taken pride in their command of the arts and sciences.

When Agrippa discusses his own career as an ambitious scholar and occult philosopher, he makes several very striking personal confessions. In chapter 13, while retracting his treatise on geomancy, for example, he describes his own work as "superstitious, false, or, if you wish that I say it, even deceptive" (2:42). In chapter 30 he tells us that he learned astrology as a boy from his parents, but subsequently became aware, after much labor in this false discipline, that astrology was based upon trifles, deceptive fables of the poets, mere figments of imagination. Although he renounced astrology long ago, he further confesses, he was led to practice it again by those in positions of power who entreated him to do so. "And my own expediency persuaded me sometimes to make use of their folly, and to humor those who were so desirous of trifles" (2:72). Charles Nauert clearly documents the fact that Agrippa had indeed used his reputation as an astrologer and an alchemist to secure preferment, and Professor Nauert confronts with an admirable frankness the evidence which has suggested to Auguste Prost, Giuseppe Rossi, and others that Agrippa was a charlatan. Nauert cites a letter, for example, in which a friend had urged Agrippa to exploit the curiosity of a certain nobleman of Chalons for profit (*Agrippa,* 25). Although Professor Nauert is reluctant to see Agrippa as totally skeptical about the occult arts or as essentially dishonest, he concedes that Agrippa "doubtless counted on his alchemical work to attract interest and perhaps was not above intimating that his work was more successful than it really was" (*Agrippa,* 25; cf. 198–99). By his own admission, Agrippa himself had participated in the world of ambition and corruption which he denounces so bitterly in *De vanitate,* and he wrote the treatise at a moment when his personal misfortunes apparently had stimulated a period of intense critical self-examination. Paolo Zambelli has provided evidence in "Magic and Radical Reformation in Agrippa" that Agrippa actually held, but often concealed, a sincere belief that Christendom was in need of radical reform, and if this is the case, as seems likely, he must have lived in constant spiritual turmoil as a result of the conflict between his deepest religious beliefs and his social and financial aspirations. Many passages of *De vanitate* are the products of sincere—if perhaps transitory—feelings of remorse; at times one can sense Agrippa's spiritual and emotional release as he confesses his past dissimulations.

Agrippa's life and works are characterized by inconsistency and vacillation. He experienced desperate hopes and profound disillusionments, ambition and otherworldliness, pride and humble repentance. The conflicts of Agrippa's life are in many ways those of the

Renaissance itself, and in our efforts to interpret either the works of individuals or the intellectual history of an entire period, we must beware of seeking to impose a degree of consistency or coherence upon materials which are diverse and self-contradictory. Agrippa's career suggests to us that works such as Marlowe's *Dr. Faustus,* with all of its variations in tone and its paradoxical conflicts, are no more incoherent than the very lives of those individuals whose intellectual and spiritual turmoil such works of art are designed to reflect.

Chapter Five

Magic, Science,
and Witchcraft in
Renaissance England

The immediate context of Elizabethan and Jacobean plays on magic was an intense and wide-ranging controversy concerning the uses of knowledge, the status of traditional authorities, and the limits of the human personality. In addition to those who were influenced directly by the works of Ficino, Pico, and Agrippa, there were technologists, mathematicians, Paracelsian physicians, and many others who argued throughout the sixteenth century that received opinion should be tested by the light of experience, in order that a more firm foundation be established for progress in both theoretical and practical knowledge. Social and economic conditions favorable to the development of science intensified in the 1580s, after the reurn of Francis Drake's treasure-laden ship from its remarkable voyage around the globe encouraged Englishmen to envision the possibility of a British Empire which would rival that of the Spaniards in wealth and power. Militant Protestants such as the earl of Leicester, Christopher Hatton, and Walter Ralegh offered patronage to those whose knowledge of navigation, munitions, and geography promised to give England an advantage over its Catholic rival. After the Armada, the possibilities seemed boundless.[1]

The study of the debates over magic and science in the Renaissance reveals the vigor and the diversity of the forces which were pressing for intellectual and technological change, as well as the power and variety of the conservative and reactionary forces. There were, on the one hand, members of dissenting sects who embraced occult philosophy because they readily perceived its subversive potential; on the other, there were monarchists like John Dee who wished to buttress the political and social status quo and who failed to comprehend their opponents' fears that the overthrow of authorities in natural philosophy could result in the undermining of social, political, and religious authorities as well. Mathematics in general was sometimes suspected of being associated with evil conjurers and antisocial forces, and it was fairly common in the sixteenth century for unfamiliar and impressive mechanical devices, such as the flying *Scarabeus* which Dee constructed for a Cambridge production of Aristophanes' *Pax,* to be regarded as products of demonic aid.[2] At the same time, there were individuals who comprehended the possibilities of applied science and who could distinguish between advanced mathematics or technology and the apparent illusions of magic. In short, although we can be certain that magic was an important and volatile issue, we can posit no one attitude which would be typical of an Elizabethan audience. By exploring the various opinions which existed concerning magic and science in the sixteenth and early seventeenth centuries, we can, however, illuminate the historical and philosophical issues to which Marlowe, Jonson, Shakespeare, and other authors were responding, and we can identify, in some cases, specific influences upon individual dramatists.

MAGIC AND SCIENCE, UTOPIANISM, AND THE UNDERMINING OF AUTHORITY

Assertions that experience is an important teacher exist throughout the Middle Ages. "Experience though noon auctoritee / Were in this world is right ynogh for me," Chaucer's Wife of Bath tells us,[3] and questions concerning the relative value of experience, as opposed to book learning, occur frequently in *The Canterbury Tales,* as in other medieval literary works and philosophical treatises. Explicit confrontations between experience and authority, however—including assertions that inherited opinions must be questioned so that human knowledge can be entirely reformed—begin to multiply quite notably in the mid-sixteenth century in England and intensify until the movement reaches its climax in Francis Bacon. Although the general notion of a reformation of knowledge and the rejection of the absolute authority of Aristotle has roots in humanism, the most outspoken criticism of received authority in sixteenth-century England seems to have developed among practical technologists and physicians, many of whom were influenced by the Hermetic and Neoplatonic traditions.

In 1551, for example, Thomas Rainold argued in a medical treatise that in his own lifetime God had aroused "excellent uertuous witts" who have examined all doctrine of the ancients so rigorously that in a few years, "science wil be so renuid, refreshid, and purgid, that thei which hitherto haue boren al the bruit, & haue obtained al autorite, wil leese a great portion of there creadit."[4] Interestingly, Rainold is a student of alchemy who is critical of the grandiose claims of some practitioners of the art. Although he gives directions for the preparation of an alchemical medicine which will concentrate the "spirites, life, and . . . vertue" of natural substances, he is skeptical of the idea that anyone could concoct an "elixir of life" which would cure all diseases (sigs. D4r, E3v–E4r). Even though Rainold's assumptions concerning natural philosophy are in many ways those of an occult philosopher, he is aware of the relatively new tendency to examine critically the received opinion which has been handed down through books, and he is highly enthusiastic about the renovation of learning: the current revolution in knowledge, Rainold asserts, promises to renew virtually all of the arts and sciences, and in a relatively short period of time many of the ancients will be regarded as having good intentions, but thoroughly outdated. Rainold is aware that some "excellent wits" are afraid to publish their findings, since they fear being criticized by reactionaries, but he admonishes us to remember that contributing to human knowledge, especially in medicine, is an act of Christian charity (sigs. A3r–B4r).

One of the most influential mathematicians of the sixteenth century was Robert Recorde, who was employed by the Muscovy Company to study applied mathematics and navigational technology, and who gave lectures to the company's seamen. Although Recorde died in 1558, his textbooks on mathematics and astronomy were widely used throughout the century, and in these works he promoted the idea that through diligence in the pursuit and application of knowledge Englishmen could affirm human dignity, procure wealth, and improve the quality of human life. The illustration for the title page of the 1556 edition of *The Castle of Knowledge* (fig. 1) illustrates Recorde's belief that knowledge could give humankind a degree of control over its own destiny. On the right is a blindfolded figure, standing on an insecure sphere and apparently turning Fortune's wheel, with the motto, "The wheele of Fortune, whose ruler is Ignoraunce." On the left, in contrast, is a figure holding a pair of compasses and standing on a secure cube, holding "The Sphere of Destinye, whose governour is Knowledge." The textbook itself provides more than one commentary on the emblem. Recorde suggests, first of all, that we can, to some extent, control the course of our own lives through various applications of mathematics and astronomy, including navigation, medicine, and other arts. In order to accomplish this goal, however, we must subject traditional authorities such as Ptolemy to the tests of experience and logical analysis: "Be not abused by their autoritye, but evermore attend to their reasons, and examine them well, ever regarding more what is saide, and how it is proued, then who saieth it: for autoritie often times deceaueth many menne."[5] These progressive and enlightened attitudes exist side by side with a prominent interest in astrology, and Recorde also argues that knowledge of the stars enables us to control our destinies by allowing us to plan the conduct of our affairs in auspicious astrological circumstances. He who understands the heavens

> shall be able not only to avoide many inconveniences, but also to atchive many unlikely attemptes: and in conclusion be a governoure and rulare of the stars accordynge to that vulgare [i.e., commonly known] sentence gathered of Ptolemye:
>
> *Sapiens dominabitur astris*
> The wise by prudence, and good skyll,
> Maye rule the starres to serve his will.
>   (sig. a5v)

Recorde is well aware that mathematics, astrology, and technology are often suspected of being diabolical, especially when striking feats are performed by mechanical or other scientific means. He acknowledges that Roger Bacon, the pride of English scientists, was accused of being a necromancer who conjured with evil spirits, but Recorde insists that the accusation cannot be supported by evidence.[6] Repeatedly he defends the study of astronomy as consistent with piety, pointing out that contemplation of the incorruptible and constant heavens uplifts the mind and inspires us with respect for

God's creative power. As an epigraph for the preface of *The Castle of Knowledge* Recorde provides the following verse:

> If reasons reache transcende the Skye,
>   Why shoulde it then to earthe be bounde?
> The witte is wronged and leadde awrye,
>   If mynde be mar[r]ied to the grounde.

In the 1580s and 1590s intensified aspirations for wealth, military success, and empire generated an increased demand for research and instruction in what we would now call the applied sciences. Francis Drake himself, as well as Richard Hakluyt, William Gilbert, John Dee, Walter Ralegh, and others, insisted on the need for training programs in navigation, geography, cartography, and gunnery. Gilbert's proposal for a new academy in London recommends that "there shalbe placed two Mathematicians, And the one of them shall one day reade Arithmetick, and the other day Geometry, which shalbe onely employed to Imbattelinges, fortificacions, and matters of warre, with the practize of Artillery, and vse of all manner of Instruments belonging to the same.... The other Mathematician shall reade one day Cosmographie and Astronomy, and the other day tend the practizes thereof, onely to arte of Nauigacion, with the knowledge of necessary starres, making vse of Instrumentes apertaining to the same."[7] Richard Hakluyt praised Sir Walter Ralegh for perceiving the importance of such instruction and for employing Thomas Harriot, "a man pre-eminent in those studies," to instruct him and his sea captains. "This one thing I know," Hakluyt told Ralegh, "and that is that you are entering upon the one and only method by which first the Portuguese and then the Spaniards at last carried out to their own satisfaction what they had previously attempted.... There yet remain for you new lands, ample realms, unknown peoples; they wait, yet, I say, to be discovered and subdued, quickly and easily, under the happy auspices of your arms and enterprise, and the sceptre of our most serene Elizabeth, Empress—as even the Spaniard himself admits—of the Ocean."[8]

Eventually Gresham College was established to provide the research and instruction for which Hakluyt, Gilbert, Drake, and others had called, with instructors such as Henry Briggs, an acquaintance of Ralegh and Harriot, and Matthew Gwinne, who had come to know Giordano Bruno. The Muscovy Company continued for decades to instruct its own seamen, with John Dee serving the company in much the same capacity as Robert Recorde had in previous years. Contacts among those who taught at Gresham and those who worked for private companies or for Ralegh were frequent, and the scientific community in London was much more receptive to new ideas than were other segments of Elizabethan society. Copernicanism, atomism, and the concepts of the infinity and homogeneity of the universe, first interrelated by Giordano Bruno, found a favorable reception in these circles; and Jean Jacquot has argued convincingly that the transition from Bruno's magical philosophy to genuine science was effected in part by Thomas Harriot, Nicholas Hill, Walter Warner, and other researchers who were patronized by Sir Walter Ralegh and the earl of Northumberland. Jacquot points out that some of the new philosophical concepts which were conducive to the development of genuine science tended to stimulate the theological heresies of which Harriot, as well as his acquaintance Christopher Marlowe, was frequently accused:

> According to one Mr. Haggar, who was a mathematician and well acquainted with Harriot, [Harriot] could not believe in the story of Genesis, and would say *ex nihilo nihil fit*. Torporley considered that the dogma of Creation was at stake in the controversy of atoms, and sought to prove the contrary maxim: *ex nihilo omnia*. Ancient atomism offered the model of a universe indefinitely extended in space and time, where everything was subject to generation and decay but was made up of indestructible particles of matter. This view could fit neither with Christian eschatology nor Aristotelian cosmology. But such a universe could be conceived as homogeneous, all its parts being subject to the same physical laws. And this suited the purpose of the new astronomy which tended to dispense with qualitative distinctions between different regions of the cosmos.[9]

Denial of the existence of heaven and hell, questions about the Creation, and the rejection of traditional scientific and religious beliefs in the interest of gaining control over nature and obtaining wealth and military power are the heart of Marlowe's *Dr. Faustus*. The remark attributed to Marlowe by Richard Baines, that "Moyses was but a Jugler & that one Heriots being Sir W Raleighs man Can do more then he," suggests that the playwright was familiar with the theory that Moses performed his feats of magic through practical Cabala (or, perhaps, that Moses' feats were merely illusions) and that Marlowe knew that Harriot's scientific knowledge was more genuine—and consequently more potent—than that of his predecessors in the quest for control of nature. Thomas Kyd listed "Harriot, Warner, Royden, and some stationers in Paules churchyard" as those with whom Marlowe had discussed his heretical religious beliefs, and "Warner" is almost certainly the scientist Walter Warner, the close associate and colleague of Harriot's whose philosophy Jacquot has shown to have been extensively influenced by Giordano Bruno and whose research on biology, psychology, and other aspects of natural philosophy in turn influenced Thomas Hobbes. Although Harriot avoided making explicitly heretical statements in print, he was accused throughout his life of asserting that heaven and hell were merely fictions designed to enforce obedience to the state, of denying the immortality of the individual soul, of questioning the biblical account of the Creation, and of conjuring. In a list which he compiled of printed references to himself, Harriot confirms that he feels himself to be the so-called "conjurer" whom Robert Parsons said was the "Master" of Sir Walter Ralegh's "School of Atheism," and at Ralegh's trial for treason in 1603 Chief Justice Richard Popham is recorded to have admonished Ralegh by saying, "And lett not Heriott nor any such Doctor persuade you there is no Eternity."[10] At the inquiry into Ralegh's alleged atheism in 1594, Nicholas Jefferys testified that Harriot had been questioned by the Privy Council concerning his denial of the resurrection of the body, and it is possible that this questioning occurred as a part of the Privy Council's investigation of Marlowe in 1593 (Shirley, *Thomas Harriot: A Biography,* 185, 192–93).

There is, in fact, a remark in Harriot's *A briefe and true report of the new found land of Virginia* which suggests that he regarded the doctrines of salvation and damnation as an effective means of regulating behavior. In discussing the Indians' religion he describes in considerable detail their conceptions of heaven and hell, and he then remarks that "what subtilty soeuer be in the . . . Priestes, this opinion worketh so much in manie of the common and simple sort of people that it maketh them have great respect to their Gouernours."[11] Although it cannot be proved that any of these men were atheists in the modern sense of the term, it is clear that Harriot, Walter Warner, Nicholas Hill, Ralegh, and Marlowe engaged in serious criticism of many traditional beliefs and institutions; what they shared was not a single set of beliefs, but rather a willingness to subject all opinions to rigorous logical analysis. Ralegh was loyal to Christianity, but he struggled with the question of whether religious doctrine could be supported through rational argument, and the evidence brought forward at the Cerne Abbas hearing demonstrates that he frequently engaged in much more open-minded discussion of religion than most of his contemporaries could tolerate.[12] Ralegh, Harriot, and Marlowe differed in many important respects, but they shared a resentment of the attempts of rulers to impose uniformity of belief upon the populace. The use of established churches as a means of enforcing obedience to the government was, of course, an obvious fact of life in the Renaissance; what is remarkable is not that Marlowe or Harriot perceived the situation accurately, but that they had the courage even to hint at it in print or on the stage. Of central importance for the present study is the fact that Marlowe was in contact with several of the most advanced and open-minded scientists and philosophers in Europe, and he was intensely and no doubt uncomfortably aware that among the tools used to suppress freedom of inquiry were accusations of atheism and witchcraft. As I shall argue in detail in the next chapter, the ambivalence of *Dr. Faustus* is in part the product of Marlowe's strategy for questioning his society's condemnation of independence of mind as sinful, while at the same time concealing the playwright's own heterodoxy within the framework of an ostensibly orthodox morality drama.

Ralegh studied occult philosophy extensively, and in the philosophical sections of his *History of the World* he consistently defends the opinions of "the Platonists," including Pico, Ficino, and Plotinus, and the "ancient theologians," such as Hermes Trismegistus and Zoroaster. In book 1, chapter 1, entitled "Of the creation and preservation of the world," Ralegh draws directly upon the Hermetic books and on the Bible, as well as on the works of Ficino, Pico, and other theologians, to support his belief that the nature and powers of God are revealed in the created world.[13] In his preface he quotes Ficino's description in the *Theologia Platonica* of a realm of eternal Ideas, created by God as the archetype of the physical universe, and in his discussion of human nature Ralegh emphasizes that we are endowed by our Creator with an intuitive faculty, the *Mens,* or pure understanding (*Works,* 2:lii, 48–54, 59). His section entitled "Of the free power which man had in his first creation to dispose of himself" is based primarily upon Pico's *Oration:*

> God gave unto man all kind of seeds and grafts of life, to wit, the vegetative life of plants, the sensual of beasts, the rational of man, and the intellectual of angels; whereof whichsoever he took pleasure to plant and cultiv[at]e, the same should futurely grow in him, and bring forth fruit, agreeable to his own choice and plantation. This freedom of the first man Adam, and our first father, was enigmatically described by Asclepius Atheniensis, saith Mirandula, in the person and fable of Proteus, who was said, as often as he pleased, to change his shape. (*Works* 2:62)

Chapter 11 of the first book of Ralegh's *History* is devoted to a defense of magic. Magic is an "art, saith Mirandula," which "few understand, and many reprehend: ... As dogs bark at those they know not; so they condemn and hate the things they understand not" (2:381). Although the name "magic" has sometimes been applied to the practices of witchcraft, the true magician is a servant of God. Magic "containeth the whole philosophy of nature; not the brabblings of the Aristotelians, but that which bringeth to light the inmost virtues, and draweth them out of nature's hidden bosom to human use" (2:384–85). Ralegh accepts astrology and alchemy, but he regards theurgy as an illusion, denying that any magical ceremony can compel either devils or angels. In chapter 6, section 7 (2:181), he quotes Pico's third Orphic Conclusion, explaining that the names within the Orphic Hymns refer to "natural and divine virtues," not demons. Here, as elsewhere, he struggles to reconcile his defense of the occult tradition with his understanding of the Bible. He respects the Cabala, for example, as a tradition based on secrets given by God to Moses and handed down in an oral tradition, but he denies that Cabalist explication of the Scriptures in any way cancels their literal truth (2:72–75, 152–54). Furthermore, he admits that the devil may take advantage of the ambitions of those who pursue even the lawful kinds of magic; Satan has the power to disguise himself as an angel of light and attempt to lead the magus into idolatrous practices such as worshipping the stars, "teaching men to esteem them as gods, and not as instruments" (2:391). Similarly, it is permissible and even pious to utilize the occult virtues of natural objects, but the devil seeks to corrupt legitimate magic by teaching people to believe superstitiously in "the strength of words and letters; (which without faith in God are but ink or common breath)" (2:392). Although many have rejected natural philosophy and mathematics because of these dangers, Ralegh continues, we should not abandon our quest for truth because of the difficulty of separating science from idolatrous superstition; if we permit ourselves to be hindered from practicing benign arts merely because they could be corrupted, "we shall in a short time bury in forgetfulness all excellent knowledge and all learning, or obscure and cover it over with a most scornful and beggarly ignorance" (2:395).

In chapter 3 of book 1 of the *History* (2:84), Ralegh remarks that ancient philosophers, reflecting upon the power of the censors, often feared to express their religious beliefs explicitly. One might be tempted to infer from this remark that Ralegh himself at times expresses his own unorthodox ideas in an indirect fashion. It should be emphasized, however, that regardless of what Ralegh may have believed concerning religious and political institutions or concerning magic, he devotes hundreds of pages in the *History* to reconciling his opinions on occult philosophy, the Creation, and other subjects with his obviously firm belief in the literal truth of the Scriptures. Although he is fascinated by magic and heavily influenced by Renaissance Neoplatonism and the Hermetic/Cabalist tradition, he does not hesitate to criticize those Cabalists who imply that the Bible is purely allegorical. Indeed, one of the most fascinating aspects of the *History* is the conflict between Ralegh's fervent desire to affirm learning— including magic—and his anxiety concerning the manner in which the quest for truth can be corrupted by excessive pride and selfishness. Despite his inquiring mind and his admiration of the descriptions of human dignity, freedom, and power which he has found in the occult tradition, Ralegh never extends his criticism of traditional authorities to the Bible, nor does he entirely abandon the biblical conception of the frailties of fallen human nature. The devil creeps into the minds and hearts of human beings, he tells us, and "sets before them the high and shining idol of glory, the all-commanding image of bright gold. He tells them that truth is the goddess of dangers and oppressions; that chastity is the enemy of nature; and lastly, that as all virtue, in general, is without taste, so pleasure satisfieth and delighteth every sense: for true wisdom, saith he, is exercised in nothing else than in the obtaining of power to oppress, and of riches to maintain plentifully our worldly delights" (2:186).

Ralegh's assertion that the devil tells us that truth is "the goddess of dangers and oppressions" is challenging and enigmatic. Does the remark express Ralegh's commitment to truth despite the "dangers and oppressions" which he himself faced while in prison composing his *History?* Could it refer to the belief, attributed to Harriot and Marlowe, that religion was merely a tool of oppressive governments? If so, is Ralegh expressing his disapproval of opinions which he has heard expressed by his associates? Regardless of how one might answer these questions, Ralegh's *History* reveals the profound self-examination of a man who had sought truth, both through his own studies and through his patronage of scientists and intellectuals, and who came to know that he himself was subject to the passions which make us vulnerable, as he suggests in the passage just quoted, to the wiles of the devil.

Ralegh was a major participant in the cult of Elizabeth which described the Virgin Queen as a reincarnation of the mythical virgin Astraea, the goddess of justice who had returned to earth in order to revive the Golden Age. The rhetoric of universal reform that was developed by Ralegh, Dee, Spenser, and others as an idealistic rationale for the British Empire was influenced in part by the emphasis on the purification of humanity and of the fallen world which lies at the heart of the occult tradition. Much of the Cabala and several of the ancient Hermetic and pseudo-Hermetic treatises contain Messianic elements which eventually became a significant force behind many of the most important utopian and millenarian movements of the period, including those which contributed to the English Revolution.[14] As I mentioned in my previous discussion of Pico della Mirandola, many of the Jewish Cabalists believed that God originally had intended for the earthly Adam to complete the process of creation which had been interrupted by the catastrophic "breaking of the vessels" in which the divine light emanating from Adam Kadmon had become scattered and confounded with matter. The terrestrial Adam had failed to complete the harmonious order of creation only because of his own sin, and in the fifteenth and sixteenth centuries both Jewish and Christian Cabalists placed increasing emphasis on the idea that any individual who refused to repeat Adam's fall could still contribute to the process of *Tikkun,* or restoration. Many of them believed that magic performed by individuals could actually hasten the onset of the Messianic age.[15] The Cabalists' doctrine was one of many variations upon the Gnostic version of the myth of loss and restoration: the *archetypus mundi* had been fragmented, but enlightened and virtuous individuals who have become aware of their divine origins can help to reassemble it. The myth was transformed in numerous intriguing ways in the various branches of the occult tradition, but one central belief always remained intact: the world would become perfect when humanity regained the knowledge and power it had lost through original sin.

One of the most prominent of the sixteenth-century reformers whose vision was inspired by the Cabala was Guillaume Postel. In 1552 Postel felt himself to be reborn through the descent of the Holy Spirit, and thereafter he considered himself to be the prophet and herald of a new age in which religious harmony would be restored and all traces of sin and imperfection would be eradicated from human nature. He planned a missionary effort to convert the entire world to Christianity, and he believed that once all of humankind was truly enlightened, the Messianic Age would begin. He ingenuously described his program to the Holy Roman Emperor, Ferdinand I, in 1560: "Led by the *mater mundi,* who is right reason, I have proposed a method by which the Christian Republic may be preserved uninjured and undisturbed. This is to be accomplished by a universal empire, which will enable the teachings of the Christian religion, confirmed by right reason, to be set forth. In this way, Christ will be seen to restore as much as Satan has destroyed, and it will be as though Adam had never sinned."[16]

Postel centered his hopes primarily on the French monarchy, and the research of R.J.W. Evans, Frances Yates, Peter French, and others has demonstrated that ideas derived from Cabalist and Hermetic sources were also influential in stimulating the cult of mystical imperialism which surrounded Queen Elizabeth. John Dee (fig. 2), one of the most influential spokesmen for Elizabethan imperialism, met Postel in 1550 in Paris, where the young English scholar was lecturing on mathematics; and upon his return to England Dee embarked on a lifelong career of occult studies and promotion of his belief that the English had been chosen by God to renew human knowledge, purify religion, and unite the world in a new Golden Age.[17] As early as 1564, Dee proclaimed in his *Monas Hieroglyphica* (fig. 3) that a successful adept who mastered occult philosophy could help restore to humankind the knowledge and power which had been lost since "the first age of Man" ("vsque ab ipsa prima Hominum aetate").[18] Although it is uncertain whether Dee's phrase "prima Hominum aetate" refers to the ancient world or to the Garden of Eden, he clearly implies that those few magi who have been granted "great wisdom, power over other creatures, and large dominion" (217) have undergone a process of transformation and self-purification similar to that described by Pico della Mirandola in his *Oratio* and *Conclusiones.*[19] Subsequently, in his *Mathematicall Preface* to Sir Henry Billingsley's translation of Euclid's *Elements of Geometrie,* Dee asserts that the human soul is a microcosm which "participateth with Spirites and Angels: and is made to the Image and similitude of God."[20] By the 1580s Dee had begun to use the techniques of Agrippa's *Occult Philosophy* in order to summon the angels and learn from them the secrets of the universe; actual transcripts of the seances make clear that Dee believed himself to have been chosen to purify the church and put an end to religious strife in Christendom.[21] His medium in the seances was Edward Kelley, through whom the angels presumably spoke, and who probably deceived him. Dee approached these experiments in the pious spirit of a man who hoped to be granted a closer relationship with God, but he also planned to use the knowledge he gained from his occult studies and his communion with the angels for practical purposes. The ascent to knowledge of divinity and the subsequent descent to practical technology were, for Dee, two sides of one coin: "The Mathematicall minde, [can] deale Speculatiuely in his own Arte: and by good meanes, Mount aboue the cloudes and sterres [i.e., to the intelligible world]: And thirdly, he can, by order, Descend, to frame Naturall thinges, to wonderfull vses: and when he list, retire home into his own Centre: and there, prepare more Meanes, to Ascend or Descend by: and, all, *to the glory of God, and our honest delectation in earth.*" (*Mathematical Preface,* sig. C3v; my emphasis). Dee believed it was his sacred duty to harness the occult forces of the universe (which he thought of in mathematical terms) in order to ameliorate our earthly condition. This amelioration involved extending to all humankind the benefits of the just rule of Queen Elizabeth and the true religion of English

Protestantism (tempered with Dee's Hermeticism), and he therefore placed his knowledge of applied mathematics, navigation, and geography at the service of Elizabeth's armed forces.

The modern student may find it paradoxical that Dee's vision of world peace under a united and reformed Christendom served to justify what many of us would now regard as the ruthless conquest of "heathen peoples," an activity which Dee felt to be the duty of every Christian ruler (French, 180–207, esp. 197). We also may question Dee's belief that imperialist ventures ought to make England wealthy while at the same time spreading the light of true religion. These contradictions apparently never bothered Dee, who firmly believed that one could procure wealth and political advancement for oneself and one's country while simultaneously pursuing an idealistic mission. Whether Elizabeth herself fully shared Dee's grandiose vision we cannot say, but we do know that she allowed him to play an important role is building up the "Tudor myth" which she used so skillfully in strengthening her ancestral claim to the British throne. In fact, Dee's significance in Renaissance history may derive more from his success as a propagandist than from his contributions to science and technology. The theory that the Tudor monarchs were descendents of the legendary Arthur and ultimately of the Trojan Brutus received considerable support from Dee's antiquarian studies, and he also argued that British title to newly discovered lands was justified by King Arthur's ancient conquests. Both at court and in his own home he discussed his theories of history and his knowledge of geography with the earl of Leicester, Francis Walsingham, Christopher Hatton, Walter Ralegh, Edward Dyer (who was godfather to Dee's son Arthur), and the queen herself. Dee served Elizabeth as an astrologer and, on at least one occasion, as a physician, and his theories about imminent reform in Christendom helped to shape the vision of militant Protestantism which influenced Elizabeth's foreign policy.[22]

In 1583 the Polish prince Albrecht Laski (or Alasco) visited England and was received by Sir Philip Sidney and the earl of Leicester. Sidney and Laski were present at the famous confrontation between Giordano Bruno and the dons of Oxford, and after the debate Sidney took the Polish prince to visit Dee. When Laski returned to the continent later in the year, both Dee and Edward Kelley accompanied him. From Laski's home in Poland Dee and Kelley travelled to the court of Rudolf II, where they came into contact with other occultists who shared Dee's reformist impulses. In Bohemia Dee and Kelley conducted seances which confirmed Dee's belief that he had been chosen to lead a universal religious reform; Dee never fully gained Rudolf II's confidence, however, and eventually the Catholic authorities, convinced that Dee was a conjurer who had been deceived by evil spirits, had him expelled from Bohemia. On his way back to England in 1589 Dee travelled through Germany, and Frances Yates has suggested that important ties were at that time established between the English monarchy and the German Protestant princes. Yates also mentions that in 1586 an alliance was formed between Elizabeth, Henry of Navarre, and the king of Denmark, and she believes that Navarre may well have been influenced by Bruno, who had returned to France from England the year before the alliance was formed. Yates's suggestion that Dee may have been authorized by the queen to conduct affairs on the continent is speculative, but the research of C. H. Josten has verified that in Dee's own mind the journey was connected with the English magician's hopes for universal reform.[23] Ben Jonson alludes prominently to Dee and Kelley's trip to Bohemia in *The Alchemist,* and the context of the allusions suggests that Jonson is aware of the connection between the occultists' prophecies of reform and the political ambitions of various monarchs—including Elizabeth.[24] The fact that the occultists' prophecies concerning the renewal of human society were used by political leaders as propaganda for their own nationalistic ambitions casts the magicians' optimism about human nature in a peculiarly ironic light, and Ben Jonson was not the only playwright to notice that irony. Despite the important differences among the plays by Marlowe, Jonson, and Shakespeare, the feeling that the magicians' idealism about human nature has been undercut by the ruthless actions of those who seek political power is a major thread which ties together *Dr. Faustus, The Alchemist,* and, to some extent, *The Tempest.*

While Dee was on the continent, Giordano Bruno remained in London at the home of the French ambassador, Michel de Castelnau de Mauvissière, and in 1583–85 he published several of his most important works, two of which were dedicated to Philip Sidney. Some of the writings which Bruno published in London—particularly *Spaccio della bestia trionfante (The Expulsion of the Triumphant Beast), De gli eroici furori (The Heroic Frenzies),* and *Cena de le ceneri (The*

Ash Wednesday Supper)—describe an essentially Gnostic religious experience in which the individual purifies his or her personality by expelling vice and corruption and becoming fully aware of the human soul's innate divinity. Although Bruno's works are often allegorical and at times obscure, apparently he entertained a desperate hope that by promulgating a purified Hermetic religion which transcended the dogmatic sectarianism of both Protestantism and traditional Catholicism, he could contribute to the reformation of human society and the elimination of religious warfare. Yates has argued that Bruno's magical philosophy contributed to the utopian dreams of some Elizabethans, and she sees evidence in *The Heroic Frenzies* that Bruno hoped that Elizabeth would play a role in effecting universal reform. Professor Weiner's research has shown that if Bruno did want to promote a conciliatory atmosphere and religious toleration, he was somewhat less successful with such militant Protestants as Philip Sidney, Francis Walsingham, and the earl of Leicester than he wished.[25] As I have suggested above, however, he exerted considerable influence upon important scientists and philosophers, as well as poets, and his notoriety in England undoubtedly intensified the controversies in which magic was the central, symbolic issue. As a result of his publications and his debate at Oxford, Bruno gained a reputation as a conjurer, a bold defender of Copernicus, and a heretical religious thinker who trusted in his own intellect rather than traditional authorities. He had publicized openly his conviction that through heroic exertions of intellect and will the individual could release the divine, magical powers of the soul and thus gain the power to contribute to a reformed world order. In the following passage from *The Ash Wednesday Supper,* Bruno boldly describes himself as the prophet of the new era:

> The Nolan [i.e., Bruno himself] ... has released the human spirit, and set knowledge at liberty. Man's mind was suffocating in the close air of a narrow prison house whence only dimly, and, as it were, through chinks could he behold the far distant stars. His wings were clipped, so that he might not soar upwards through the cloudy veil to see what really lies beyond it and liberate himself from the foolish imaginations of those who ... have with many kinds of deceit imposed brutal follies and vices upon the world in the guise of virtues, of divinity

and discipline, quenching the light which rendered the souls of our fathers in antique times divine and heroic. . . . Behold now, standing before you, the man who has pierced the air and penetrated the sky, wended his way amongst the stars and overpassed the margins of the world, who has broken down those imaginary divisions between spheres—the first, the eighth, the ninth, the tenth, or what you will—which are described in the false mathematics of blind and popular philosophy.[26]

As Yates has demonstrated in her analysis of *The Ash Wednesday Supper,* the new light which Bruno claims to have brought to humankind is the ancient magical philosophy, and the "fools and sophists" who have "imposed brutal follies and vices upon the world in the guise of virtues, of divinity and discipline" are the conservative theologians and philosophers who reject magic and pagan philosophy as Satanic (*Giordano Bruno,* 235–56). Moreover, in a very striking section of the first dialogue of the *Cena de le ceneri,* one of the speakers points out that most people are so thoroughly indoctrinated with the traditional beliefs of their own nation that they believe it to be an act of piety to oppress, conquer, or assassinate those who believe differently. To the question of whether anyone who has been misled by custom and tradition can ever be receptive to an unorthodox truth, Theophil, who speaks for Bruno, replies simply that the capacity to accept revolutionary insights in science or religion is a gift of the gods.[27] In view of passages such as this one, it seems likely that Bruno—who was executed as an unrepentant heretic in Rome in 1600—would have appealed to thinkers such as Harriot or Marlowe not only because of the specific ideas which he asserted, but also because of his courageous, and tragically self-destructive, independence from traditional authorities.

Although Bruno was an important influence upon individual philosophers, scientists, and poets, a much more pervasive revolutionary force was exerted in England by Philippus Aureolus Theophrastus Bombastus von Hohenheim—who apparently called himself "Paracelsus" in order to suggest his superiority to Celsus, the legendary Roman physician. Ralegh, Harriot, and Dee were monarchists who identified their own interests with the establishment of the British empire, and although their critique of traditional authorities in science ultimately contributed to the overthrow of authoritarian casts of mind, they tended to express their unorthodox religious and political ideas either in private or, when they committed themselves to print, equivocally. In Cornelius Agrippa's *De vanitate* we see clearly an assault upon the social, political, and intellectual establishment, but when challenged by the authorities whom he had criticized Agrippa was willing to protect himself by claiming to be a satirical railer whose strident criticism of society was not meant to be taken seriously. When we encounter Paracelsus we are confronted with a degree of boldness and self-assertiveness in challenging the existing order which is unsurpassed in all of Renaissance history. He not only condemned vehemently the standard medical and scientific authorities of his day, such as Galen, Aristotle, and Avicenna, but he also presented himself to the world as a prophet chosen by God to initiate a new age of social revolution and universal enlightenment. Whereas Bruno still regarded *gnosis* as available only to a spiritual elite, Paracelsus predicted that genuine enlightenment would spread throughout the working classes, whose practical experience, he asserted, brought them a more intimate knowledge of reality than could ever be attained through conventional, formal education. Conservatives and reactionaries who were threatened by the revolutionary currents of Renaissance thought found in the life and works of Paracelsus a more than ample justification for their fear that a challenge to the reigning authorities in natural philosophy would lead inevitably to the overthrow of existing social, political, and religious institutions. Consider, for example, Paracelsus' preface to "The Book Concerning the Tincture of the Philosophers":

> From the middle of this age the Monarchy of all the Arts has been at length derived and conferred on me, Theophrastus Paracelsus, Prince of Philosophy and of Medicine. For this purpose I have been chosen by God to extinguish and blot out all the phantasies of elaborate and false works, of delusive and presumptuous words, be they the words of Aristotle, Galen, Avicenna, Mesva, or the dogmas of any among their followers. My theory, proceeding as it does from the light of Nature, can never, through its consistency, pass away or be changed: but in the fifty-eighth year after its millennium and a half it will then begin to flourish. The practice at the same time following upon the theory will be proved by wonderful and incredible signs,

so as to be open to mechanics and common people, and they will thoroughly understand how firm and immovable is that Paracelsic Art against the triflings of the Sophists: though meanwhile that sophistical science has to have its ineptitude propped up and fortified by papal and imperial privileges.[28]

Paracelsus goes on to say that he has a treasure—apparently the philosopher's stone—which neither Pope Leo X nor the Holy Roman Emperor Charles V could purchase, despite their wealth and power. In the present treatise he will explain how to prepare the "Tincture of the Philosophers," so that those who love truth may enjoy its benefits. "By this arcanum," he concludes, "the last age shall be illuminated clearly and compensated for all its losses by the gift of grace and the reward of the spirit of truth, so that since the beginning of the world no similar germination of the intelligence and of wisdom shall ever have been heard of" (1:20).

Paracelsus insisted that the search for occult virtues—the *arcana*, as he termed them—must proceed primarily through practical experience, guided and illuminated by divine grace. Ficino, Pico, and Agrippa (in *De occulta philosophia*) all had retained a deep respect for books, especially the revered classics of the Neoplatonic and Hermetic traditions; the authorities they invoked were often different from the conventional ones, but never did they go so far as Paracelsus in affirming that actual laboratory experiment is of primary importance. One must actually labor at the furnace, prepare one's own medicines, and learn through first-hand observation the properties of various chemicals, Paracelsus insists, if one is to be an effective alchemical physician. Furthermore, one must explore the natural world in order to discover the virtues of plants and herbs, be willing to learn from the practitioners of folk medicine, and, in addition, deal more directly with one's patients than was popular at the time among most university-trained physicians, who generally assessed the symptoms of a disease and left orders for actual treatment with their subordinates. As for traditional medical authorities, Paracelsus' attitude was dramatized during his understandably brief tenure as a professor of medicine at the University of Basel in 1527 when he threw the revered *Canon* of Avicenna into the St. John's Day bonfire.

Paracelsus continually reminds us that alchemy is essentially redemptive: transforming base metals into gold is simply one of many processes which seek to remove the impurities and corruptions of fallen nature. Alchemy is an art which God granted to humanity so that we may ameliorate our fallen condition. We may learn to extract elixirs, tinctures, or quintessences from plants or metals, for example, and utilize them to eliminate diseases and impurities from our bodies and to lengthen our lives. The fact that knowledge of these arts was increasing in the sixteenth century, Paracelsus believed, was a sign of the approaching Millennium: God intended for the Elect to advance steadily in knowledge and power until they eventually overthrew the ignorant who oppose them and who now occupy the seats of power. Human nature itself was to be purified, as our divine potential freed itself from corruption. Alchemical adepts shall become God's agents in reforming not only the physical world, but also society and religion. Although Paracelsus apparently never associated himself formally with a specific Protestant denomination and his relation to the Roman Catholic church remains ambiguous, he did compare his own renovation of medicine and science with Luther's attempts to reform Christianity, and throughout the sixteenth and seventeenth centuries Paracelsus' followers compared their innovations in science—which they described as the recovery of the knowledge which had been lost at the Fall of humankind—with the reform of religion. This Protestant strategy for justifying the renovation of natural philosophy and the overthrow of received opinion was especially common in England, where it was used by Anglicans such as Francis Bacon as well as by adherents of the radical sects.[29]

Some of the English Paracelsians were interested purely in the practical advantages of Paracelsus' chemical medicines and were either indifferent or hostile to the radical social, political, and religious implications of his philosophy. To varying degrees, however, many of them regarded it as their duty to insist that received opinion should be tested through practical experience. John Hester, an apothecary, published translations of a number of Paracelsian treatises in London in the 1580s and 1590s, and Hester's prefaces, as well as the treatises themselves, emphasize that relying upon experiment and questioning received traditions could enable us to contribute to the renovation of knowledge which Paracelsus and others had initiated. In an epistle to Sir Walter Ralegh which prefaces *A Hundred and fourtene experiments and cures of the famous Phisition Philippus Aureolis Theophrastus Paracelsus* (c. 1583), Hester proclaims that the pursuit of knowledge has no limit because the mind of humankind is insatiable.[30] In another dedicatory epistle in 1590 he decries the practice of blindly revering ancient authorities, accepting their conclusions without examining their proofs; we naively assume that a mere *ipse dixit* has the weight of genuine evidence. We should not "peevishly distrust our owne wittes, furnished with so many helpers, and apishly admire other mens, onelie for theyr antiquitie: this were to tie God to times and seasons, & to play bopeepe in a secure shroude of idlenesse, utterly dis-franchising our selves of the free legacie, *Dü laboribus dona dant sua* [the Gods grant their gifts to those who labor]."[31]

Following Hester's death in 1593, his edition of *The Pearle of Practise* was completed by James Forester, an enthusiastic Paracelsian and friend of Hester's, and the book was published in 1594 by Richard Field, a native of Stratford who printed Shakespeare's *The Rape of Lucrece* in the same year and who had published *Venus and Adonis* in 1593. Charles Nicholl has noted this connection and speculated that Shakespeare may have known Forester; Nicholl also notes the interesting fact that Forester's *Pearl of Practise* was dedicated to George Cary, son of Henry Cary, lord chamberlain and patron of Shakespeare's theatrical company. Although Nicholl may very well be correct, we need not rely solely upon evidence of personal relationships with Paracelsians to establish the fact that Shakespeare—or any other dramatist—had access to Hermetic and alchemical treatises. As Nicholl's very thorough research has shown, the resurgence of interest in alchemy and related subjects in late-sixteenth-century England was of such magnitude that one may fairly say that no literate Londoner could be unaware of it. Many of the city's apothecaries, in addition to some of England's most advanced scientists, were heavily influenced by the movement. In addition to books and pamphlets by Paracelsians and Hermetic philosophers such as John Dee, Thomas Tymme, and Samuel Norton, there were new editions of works by medieval alchemists, including several works attributed to Roger Bacon. The growing scientific community in London stimulated renewed interest in investigating alchemical theories and procedures, and the language of alchemy, with its emphasis on the purification of nature and the human personality, struck a responsive chord in the minds and hearts of those who saw the era as one which was about to witness the final purification of religion, the triumph of the arts and sciences, and the full control of humankind over its environment.[32]

In 1585 R. Bostock published a detailed defense of the entire Renaissance occult tradition. He argues that Paracelsus and his followers were restoring to humankind the knowledge which God had granted to Adam but which had become lost or corrupted in the course of human history; this restoration correlated with the purification of religion, and it would occur only when the reigning authorities in natural philosophy were no longer protected by the authority of governments.[33] According to Bostock, the truths of natural philosophy, medicine, and religion were passed down through Adam's children to Abraham, who conveyed them to certain Egyptian priests. Although some of the Egyptians confounded these truths with idolatry, others retained a purer understanding, and Bostock thinks it likely that among these superior priests were the teachers of Moses. Not long after the time of Moses was born Hermes Trismegistus, author of *Asclepius, Pimander,* and other works containing genuine religion and philosophy. The Greeks, in general, had no independent revelation; but Plato, Pythagoras, Aesculapius, and others travelled to Egypt, Judea, or other nations where the ancient wisdom was remembered. Hippocrates wrote down a somewhat corrupted version of the ancient physic; a more serious departure from the truth occurred when Galen, in his commentary on Hippocrates, departed from his master's doctrine by erroneously attributing the causes of diseases and their cures to "bare dead qualities of heat[,] could, &c., which be caused and not causes. And so our later Phisitions, following their Prince and Captaine Gallen, that heathen and professed enemy of Christ, in steade of Phisitions and healers or curers of sicknesses and griefes, are become warmers, or coolers and bathers, whereas Hypocrates teacheth plainly and expressely that diseases are not caused nor cured by the bare dead qualities of heate and cold, &c., but by such things that have power to worke" (sig. H5r). Similarly, Aristotle, motivated by envy and vainglory, dissented from Plato's teaching and attempted to attribute all effects to purely natural causes, rather than to the occult virtues through which God's spiritual power is infused into all living creatures (sigs. ****5r–A7r, H1v). Just as the Roman Catholic religion is a mixture of the pure and the impure, relying on outward ceremonies and traditions which are a hindrance to genuine spirituality, Bostock argues, so are the medicines of the Galenist gross and impure, when compared to those whose spiritual power has been purified by fire (sig. C8v).

Bostock's detailed history of the occult tradition is designed to show that Paracelsus is a reformer who is restoring medicine to its ancient purity, just as Wycliffe, Luther, and Calvin have restored the purity of the church and Copernicus has restored the ancient knowledge of the movements of the heavens (sigs. H7v–H8r). Although Bostock is incorrect in his assertion that Copernicus's contribution to astronomy consists purely of the recovery of Ptolemy's original teachings, which had suffered centuries of corruption, it is true that Copernicus developed *De revolutionibus* as, in many respects, a revision of Ptolemy's *Almagest* in the light of ancient Pythagorean philosophy, as well as his own mathematical calculations; both Bostock and Copernicus himself are prime examples of the fact that in the sixteenth century, the most radical ideas were often defended by the assertion that centuries of corruption had obscured an ancient truth.[34]

Although Bostock believes that the present age has seen magnificent progress toward the renovation of knowledge, he is nonetheless concerned that progress is hindered because "in the scholes nothing may be received nor allowed that savoreth not of Aristotle, Gallen, Avicen, and other Ethnickes, whereby the yong beginners are either not acquainted with this [Paracelsian] doctrine, or els it is brought into hatred with them. And abrode likewise the Galenists be so armed and defended by the protection, priviledges and authoritie of Princes, that nothing can be allowed that they disalowe, and nothing may bee received that agreeth not with their pleasures and doctrine."[35] One may wonder whether Bostock is using the term "abrode" to mean "at large in the world" or "in foreign countries"; although England was not as consistently reactionary as some other nations, English universities and the Royal College of Physicians tended to regard Paracelsianism, like other forms of magic, as subversive of authority. Although some English physicians were able to incorporate aspects of Paracelsian medicine into their practice while remaining socially and politically conservative, Paracelsus' proclamation that practical experience and divine favor often conferred advanced knowledge on the working classes eventually contributed to the growth of revolutionary attitudes. In the seventeenth century, members of the dissenting sects whose doctrines had the most radical political and social consequences, such as the Anabaptists and the Family of Love, quite often found in Paracelsianism an ideology which supported their cause; and during the Puritan revolution many of the radicals claimed that Paracelsus had been a true prophet whose predictions were coming true in seventeenth-century England. When the sects felt increasingly free to express their ideas during the Interregnum, an unprecedented flood of Hermetic and alchemical works was published, and many of the treatises have a strong utopian or millenarian emphasis. Some of them propose such measures as community of goods and complete political egalitarianism, and at times even Oliver Cromwell found it difficult to maintain control of the more radical elements within his own army.[36] Although progress in science and technology initially served the ends of the established monarchy, and the rhetoric of the return of the Golden Age was at the heart of the propaganda of the British Empire, one of the long-range effects of the assault upon authorities in natural philosophy was an awareness that authorities in other spheres of life could also be challenged. The movement ultimately contributed to the forces of intellectual, social, and political change in ways which Marsilio Ficino, Giovanni Pico della Mirandola, or John Dee could not have anticipated.

WITCHCRAFT DOCTRINE, THE REACTION AGAINST LEARNING, AND COUNTER-REFORM MOVEMENTS

Studies of the witchcraft persecutions of the sixteenth and seventeenth centuries have often suggested that the witch-hunts were a means of suppressing virtually all forms of heresy and social deviation, including those generated by attempts at radical religious and social reform. Hugh Trevor-Roper, Norman Cohn, and others have documented the connection between the witchcraft trials and the efforts to destroy heretical sects such as the Waldensians, and Trevor-Roper further pointed out that witchcraft persecutions intensified after the Reformation, as various parties in the religious conflicts of the era felt the need to cast their enemies in the role of servants of Satan. In addition, Trevor-Roper argues that Renaissance Neoplatonists and Paracelsians were, in many respects, progressives who often opposed the witch-hunts and who consequently were identified by the authorities as allies of Satan. In *The Occult Philosophy in the Elizabethan Age,* Frances Yates has gone much further: she argues that the Hermetic/Cabalist philosophy was the dominant school of thought among advanced thinkers in the English Renaissance; the witch-hunts of the sixteenth and seventeenth centuries were, in her view, primarily a reaction against the progressive and revolutionary forces which were associated with the occult tradition. In order to support these generalizations, Yates departs from her earlier conception of the relationships among occult philosophy, humanism, and the Reformation. In *Giordano Bruno and the Hermetic Tradition* she had seen humanism as generally conservative in its conception of human nature and its attitude toward social and religious reform, and she regarded the Hermetic/Cabalist tradition as progressive. In *The Occult Philosophy in the Elizabethan Age,* she asserts that the Cabala itself was at the heart of the new learning promoted by the humanists. Because Cabalist exegesis sought to find new depths of meaning in the Scriptures, she argues, Cabalist studies, as well as humanist scholarship, contributed to the reform movements in both Roman Catholic and, subsequently, Protestant circles. She cites the reaction of conservatives against Johannes Reuchlin's Judaic studies and his interest in the Cabala as evidence that occult philosophy and humanism were allies, both of them opposed to the Aristotelian scholasticism which the existing authorities had chosen as the only sanctioned philosophy. She sees Reuchlin as a precursor of Martin Luther. Both the occult movement and the counter-reaction intensified in the late sixteenth and early seventeenth centuries, Yates points out, and she emphasizes that the efforts of John Dee, Walter Ralegh, and others to promote technology—which they regarded as "natural magic"—are precisely contemporaneous with the most intense period of the European witch-hunts. She credits Jean Bodin, who visited England during the 1580s and whose works were influential there, with intensifying the witch hunts through his *De la démonomanie des sorciers,* in which he condemns Pico and Agrippa for attempting to use Cabala for transitive magic. She also cites Martin Del Rio's *Disqvisitionum magicarum libri sex* (Louvain, 1600), a work utilized by Ben Jonson in *The Alchemist,* as evidence that reactionary activity intensified around the turn of the century and that conservative thinkers perceived occult philosophy as one of the most significant threats to the intellectual and political establishment.[37]

Certainly it is true that the efflorescence of occult philosophy, the increase in challenges to traditional authorities, and the intensification of the witch persecutions occurred simultaneously. The studies of Trevor-Roper, Cohn, Alan Macfarlane, Keith Thomas, and Christina Larner, however, have demonstrated that the witch-hunts served a variety of sociological and psychological functions, and to assert that the intensification of the witch-hunts in the Renaissance was primarily a response to humanism, occult philosophy, or the new science is much too broad a generalization. At the same time, an examination of the treatises on witchcraft which were influential in late-sixteenth- and early-seventeenth-century England reveals that Ficino, Pico, Agrippa, Paracelsus, and others who dissented from authorized versions of natural philosophy were often among the major targets of those who promoted the witch trials. The papal bull which prefaces the inquisitors' manual, *Malleus maleficarum,* reminds us that witches were, first and foremost, arch-heretics, and once the official beliefs about witchcraft were firmly established, they could readily be invoked whenever any form of dissent became a threat. Professor Larner has argued effectively that the persecution of witches was a form of social control; the witch-hunts attempted to eliminate any form of social deviation and to demonstrate the presumed efficacy of the authorities in morally cleansing society. Such persecutions became prominent during the Reformation and the Counter-Reformation because there was an intensified effort to impose ideological unity: the witch became "a personification of all forms of deviance and revolt," and a high percentage of the accused were women who failed to conform to traditional stereotypes of feminine behavior.[38] Although Professor Larner is concerned primarily with the connection between witchcraft and antifeminism, there is considerable evidence that accusations of witchcraft were also used to suppress innovations in natural philosophy, especially when those innovations were perceived as being allied with subversive religious or political beliefs. To Jean Bodin, Martin Del Rio, and King James I, the religious, intellectual, and scientific ferment of the Renaissance was a sign of an increase in monstrous alliances with Satan. Numerous authorities agreed that while some witches were motivated to ally themselves with the devil out of greed, lust, or a desire for revenge upon their enemies, others were prompted by a damnable intellectual curiosity.

We must remember that what was orthodox in one community

was heresy in another, and different authors' conceptions of what must be defended and what forces were subversive sometimes varied considerably. Peter Burke, for example, in his analysis of *Strix*, by Gian Francesco Pico (the nephew of Giovanni Pico, the famous Cabalist), has provided interesting support for the idea that witch persecution was in some cases a reaction against the revival of classical literature and philosophy. Burke points out that the witchcraft ceremonies described and condemned in the younger Pico's treatise strongly resemble pagan religion, and he argues that Gian Francesco Pico feared that humanism and occult philosophy would revive the worship of those Greek and Roman gods whom the orthodox often believed to be devils. Gian Francesco also wrote a widely read biography of his uncle, translated into English by Thomas More, which emphasized the elder Pico's repentance of his excessive pride in learning and his subsequent asceticism; in both the biography and in *Strix* G. F. Pico is critical of the revival of ancient learning, and he strongly reasserts otherworldly values and traditional Roman Catholic orthodoxy.[39]

Jean Bodin, in contrast to Gian Francesco Pico, was a Judaizer who accepted contemplative Cabala, as well as some of the beliefs of the pagan mystery religions, and he therefore would have been regarded by the younger Pico as a dangerous heretic. Bodin condemns the transitive Cabala, which attempts to utilize spirits to perform magical operations, and he explicitly accuses Giovanni Pico and Cornelius Agrippa of witchcraft. The Orphic hymns commended by Pico, Bodin asserts, are in reality addressed to the devil.[40] Bodin seems motivated primarily by genuine fear of the dangerous threat which he feels witchcraft poses to the commonwealth, and he asserts that diabolical practices have at times become so widespread that they have resulted in wholesale rebellion (Preface, fol. c1r). Interestingly, he also emphasizes that the devil has loyal subjects in all estates, and popes, emperors, and princes have at times fallen under Satan's dominion (fol. a4v), an opinion which we shall also encounter in Marlowe's *Dr. Faustus*. Bodin seems fearful of any attempt to control nature, and he associates genuine piety quite closely with the confession of the extreme limitations of the human mind: "All human science," he tells us, "is filled with ignorance" (fol. c2r). This reaction against learning and intellectual presumption is a common thread which runs through many of the witchcraft treatises, even though they sometimes differ in some of their religious and political assumptions. While some of the works on witchcraft react against all learning and all science, others affirm traditional natural philosophy and direct accusations of witchcraft solely against those who are guilty of innovation.

Although the influence of *De la démonomanie* in England was significant, Bodin had many predecessors and contemporaries who similarly argued that the quest for occult wisdom was the epitome of intellectual pride and inevitably led to a pact with Satan. In 1561 Francis Coxe published what he claimed to be his personal confession as a convicted conjurer who had received clemency from the Privy Council and who now felt it his duty "to declare and open the wickednes[s] of those artes and sciences, which hath of late time to [the] provocation of God[']s wrath and almightie displeasure, ben had in suche estimation."[41] Astrology, geomancy, and all forms of prophecy or magic are unlawful and impious inquiries into realms of knowledge which God has reserved to Himself. Included in Coxe's list of conjurers who have been seduced by evil spirits to seek forbidden powers is Roger Bacon, who Coxe says was starved to death as punishment for his crimes, and he also condemns Cornelius Agrippa, whose works, Coxe asserts, are widely circulated and debated (sig. B3v–B4r). Eight years after the publication of Coxe's pamphlet, Agrippa's own confession in *De incertitudine et vanitate scientiarum atque artium* was translated into English by James Sanford. Agrippa's *De vanitate* was undoubtedly one of the most influential documents in the English Renaissance in promoting the idea that magic is a natural consequence of excessive intellectual pride and that it leads the practitioner to fall into the clutches of the devil. Here was the confession of one of Europe's most infamous conjurers, and as my discussion of *De vanitate* in Chapter 4 emphasized, Agrippa describes his own misguided and sinful involvement in occult sciences as the product of his vanity, greed, and social ambition. Elizabethan readers found *De vanitate* an important, unsettling treatise, and it is interesting to notice the ways in which various readers misinterpret the work by accepting only those aspects of Agrippa's critique of pride and worldliness which do not touch them personally. English Protestants, for example, readily accepted Agrippa's criticism of monasticism and the papacy, but they sometimes argued that his condemnation of all of the arts and sciences was merely satirical railing and not to be taken seriously.[42] Although Agrippa acknowledges that witchcraft is a reality, his true account of his defense of an innocent woman who was accused of the crime underscores the fact that his major criticism is directed against the moral corruption of those who seek, or who already possess, worldly power. Despite the complexity of Agrippa's treatise and the varying responses of some Elizabethan readers, it must have been uncomfortably clear to many of them that Agrippa felt it much more likely that the devil would possess the heart of a king than the soul of a humble peasant.

Much more defensive of existing political institutions and fearful of antiauthoritarian forces was Thomas Erastus, whose *Dispvtationvm de medicina nova Philippi Paracelsi (Disputations on the New Medicine of Philippus Paracelsus)* was the only detailed discussion of Paracelsus' philosophy which circulated in England prior to the 1580s.[43] Erastus was a professor of philosophy, theology, and medicine at the University of Heidelberg, and he is best known for his defense of the principle that secular rulers have the authority to oversee the purity of the church and the moral and spiritual life of the populace. In his dedicatory epistle to the elector of Saxony, Erastus says that his motive in the *Disputations* is to stem the rising tide of Paracelsianism and to prevent the further spread of Paracelsus' errors and blasphemies. He is particularly incensed by Paracelsus' claim to unique revelations and his assertion that the common people possess more wisdom than the educated classes. Erastus' intense loyalty to certain features of Renaissance humanism is underscored by his complaint that Paracelsus' works are not only filled with ignorance, self-contradiction, and false doctrine but are also written in an utterly barbaric prose style (sig. a2r–a4v; Pagel, *Paracelsus,* 311-15). He often charges Paracelsus with ignorance of the classics, and it is obvious that Erastus is personally affronted by this commoner who dares to question the wisdom of established university professors.

Erastus' conception of the canon of true authorities is determined largely by his strict Lutheranism. Although he deeply respects Aristotle and Galen, he is sometimes critical of the Scholastic interpreters of Aristotle, and he prefers above all else the evidence of the Scriptures and, secondarily, the early church fathers. In several instances he is even willing to subject Aristotle himself to the test of experience, and occasionally he finds him wanting (e.g., *Dispvtationvm, pars prima,* 25–28, 74, 123). At first it might seem that Erastus and Paracelsus would agree on the primacy of the Bible and of experience, but Erastus perceives quite correctly that Paracelsus' interpretations of Scripture and his natural philosophy are strongly influenced by ideas ultimately derived from Gnosticism, whereas Erastus himself relies primarily upon those traditional academic authorities whose works are still acceptable to the Lutheran church.

Erastus begins his disputations by explaining that Paracelsus' philosophy is similar to the accursed doctrine of the monstrous Gnostic heretics. He points out that Paracelsus' view of the creation of the world resembles the Gnostic idea that the material world and humankind were both created by subordinate deities, or demiurges. If we are tempted to believe the false tales of Paracelsus' marvellous cures and, consequently, to question traditional medical authorities, we should remember that Galen had never been so irrational as to develop so base a conception of the origins of humanity as we find in Paracelsus' works; certainly Galen, whose thought is consistent with Christianity, is to be trusted more than a palpable heretic such as Paracelsus.[44] Furthermore, Paracelsus, like most of the Platonists, erroneously believes that earthly forms, whether natural or artificial, can participate directly in the powers of spiritual forces whose influence is mediated by the heavenly bodies and by the *anima mundi*. Erastus seeks to destroy this claim, which is fundamental to the theory of natural magic, by asserting that both Aristotle and our own experience should convince us that the heavens exert an influence on the lower world only through light and heat; all objects are thus affected uniformly, and nothing on this earth receives a unique, occult virtue from the stars (22–23, 27–28, 107–8, 139–94, et passim). Words, Erastus also asserts, are merely the natural creations of the human mind, and they are not connected with the exemplars of creation, as the Platonists claim. The human mind, which creates language, cannot be directly influenced by the heavens, and Ficino merely revived the ancient heresy of Plotinus when he imagined that earthly events were caused by occult forces (177). Having adduced evidence at great length from Aristotelian physics, Galenic and Hippocratic medicine, and the test of experience (interpreted in the light of orthodox religious doctrine) to the effect that all charms, spells, images, songs, characters, or other devices of magicians are utterly without effect, Erastus concludes that any observed result of a magical procedure must come from one of two sources: either evil spirits have deceived the senses of the observers and produced an illusion, or else God has permitted the sorcerers such powers as may suit His purposes. The Lord may sometimes permit magicians to perform such things as will result in punishment for their idolatry, or He may permit the devil to create trials for the spiritual benefit of the virtuous, as He did in the case of Job. In response to the question of whether some magicians may not simply learn their magical procedures through books, without entering a pact with Satan, or whether indeed it might be possible to control evil spirits, Erastus asserts that, as he has already shown, no magical effect can be wrought without the aid of devils, and any such use of demons, even if we pridefully deceive ourselves into thinking we can control them, constitutes an alliance with the infernal powers (194). Given the major premise that the traditional science of Aristotle and Galen can be supported through references to the Scriptures and orthodox theologians and is therefore God's truth, and the minor premise—established easily enough—that the Paracelsians and the Renaissance Neoplatonists dissent from this doctrine, Erastus draws what he sees as the only valid conclusion: all such dissenters are the servants of Satan.

Controversies over magic, science, and witchcraft were especially intense from the 1570s through the early years of the seventeenth century, and in many treatises one can see various authors struggling to defend their religious beliefs while also endeavoring to respond in some systematic way to the innovations in natural philosophy which have threatened the coherence of their world views. Lambert Daneau, whose book on the relation between religion and science was translated as *The wonderfull woorkmanship of the world* by Thomas Twyne in 1578, argues that the study of nature can enhance our reverence for the Creator, and yet Daneau decries the diversity of opinions which have arisen concerning the creation *ex nihilo* and other aspects of natural philosophy. This distressing variety of theories has evolved, Daneau says, because scholars have too curiously inquired into heathen philosophy and have failed to regard the Bible as the ultimate test of truth. At times Daneau quotes classical authors to support his own opinions, but he insists that the Scriptures alone are infallible. In a passage which seems designed as an ironic allusion to Hermes Trismegistus' exhortation to explore with our minds all levels of the cosmos, Daneau admonishes the reader that we cannot understand all the secrets of the universe, "either bicause they bee higher in heauen than our vnderstanding is able to attain unto them, or perhaps are in vnhabitable regions of the earth: or lie hidden very low in the bottom of the deapths."[45] In *A Dialogue of Witches,* published in London in 1575 in a translation sometimes attributed to Thomas Twyne, Daneau makes clear that the increase in learning has undermined religious dogma and consequently contributed to the spread of witchcraft. Although many of the lower classes are won over to Satan because they hope to escape poverty or gain sufficient power to exert some control over their lives, there are many scholars who become Satan's vassals because they are proud of their presumed intellectual gifts and cannot accept the limitations imposed by the Almighty on the human understanding. Such scholars imagine that the devil can grant forms of knowledge which are, in fact, denied to mortals, or that Satan can grant them power to perform feats which are normally beyond human skill.[46] Explaining why he will not inquire into the details of magic or engage in subtle proofs of his assertions, Theophilus, one of the two major speakers in the dialogue, expresses his fear of becoming subject to that vanity which leads to scholarly debate and dissension: rather than fall prey to such intellectual curiosity, one should "imitate the auncient Christians, who utterly banished all kynde of curious knowledge out of their scooles and assembl[i]es, and threwe their unprofitable bookes into the fire" (sig. B5r). Those who wander beyond the bounds of doctrine are always seeking but never learning, always doubting and never determining the truth. Daneau explicitly condemns both the "Schoolmen" and the Platonists, and he asserts that magic, although common among idolaters of all ages, has increased in the present age because the intensified study of pagan authors has begotten increasing diversity of opinion. God permits Satan to seduce heretics into witchcraft in order to punish them for their apostasy, and in recent years the study of unorthodox philosophy has, lamentably, caused an increasing number of scholars and natural philosophers to abandon ancient truths and to imperil their souls by seeking in vain for new knowledge (sigs. B2r–B7r, D5r–v, K3r–v, et passim).

Accusations of witchcraft were powerful political weapons. An assault upon the social and political hierarchy, such as Agrippa's, was likely to contend that Satan's influence was strongest in the seats of power; on the other hand, those who wished to defend the status quo associated witchcraft with rebelliousness and discontent among the lower classes and/or among those who dissented from government-sanctioned religion and natural philosophy. Until the early years of the Interregnum, when censorship was temporarily relaxed and fear of reprisal diminished, conservative ideas are, of course, dominant in printed books and pamphlets.[47] Treatises which emphasize the social and political implications of witchcraft doctrine often assert that the world is divided into two kingdoms, the servants of God and the slaves of Satan, and the Kingdom of Darkness is described as a demonic parody of the Kingdom of Light. In 1590 Henry Holland characterized Satan as a "tyrannical usurper," and the language of Holland's treatise is heavily laden with images of rebellion and conquest, reinforcing the idea that salvation lay in subjection to proper authorities. In reminding his readers of "the divine maiestie and powerfull might" of the Gospel, Holland emphasizes that "a man must be, as it were conquered [by true religion] before he doe yeelde sincere and sound obedience unto Christ. And certen it is, that before men be brought downe to that subjection, they fall often into daungerous errours in minde."[48] William Perkins, who began his career as a popular and influential preacher and professor of theology at Cambridge while Christopher Marlowe was a student there, asserted that Satan's kingdom is upheld by witches who fall prey to two major categories of temptation: first, there are those who are unwilling to accept their subordinate social status and who wish to use magical powers in order to attain wealth and political power; the second major category includes those who are dissatisfied with the limitations of the human mind and who feel an inordinate thirst for knowledge.[49] Perkins includes in this category all occult philosophers, and he conducts a detailed refutation of the theory used by Pico, Agrippa, Paracelsus, and others as a rationale for what they claimed to be a benevolent form of magic. Perkins bases his argument on the premise that the heavens act upon all areas of the earth uniformly, so that no earthly substance possesses a specific occult virtue. Consequently, all astrology is vain, and charms, spells, amulets, and exorcisms all have no inherent efficacy. Magicians derive whatever actual powers they may possess from the superior scientific knowledge of the devil, who may indeed enable his followers to perform certain feats, either by natural means or through illusions, in order to win himself a following among foolish worldlings. Perkins combines his critique of Neoplatonic and Hermetic philosophy with an assault on the village "cunning men" or "wise women" to whom the ignorant populace frequently turn instead of relying upon genuinely learned and properly licensed physicians. Perkins approves of the use of drugs and other cures when they are provided by university-trained doctors of physic who are loyal to the established medical authorities, but he regards the practitioners of folk medicine, whom Paracelsus had defended, as not merely superstitious or misguided, but as servants of the devil. All who consult them stand in peril of their souls. Perkins' treatise is one of the most detailed and systematic discussions of witchcraft to appear in Renaissance England, and it is clear that, in his opinion, there were three classes of persons who are most likely to become witches: Catholics, whose idolatrous worship, exorcisms, and spurious miracles are all effected by Satan; learned magicians, whose intellectual pride has led them to adopt a fallacious pagan philosophy and to fall prey to Satan's temptations of fame, wealth, and power; and members of the uneducated classes who are presumptuous enough to attempt to compete with trained physicians or who simply wish to escape the humble lot to which God has assigned them.

King James I assumed a leading role in witchcraft persecution largely because of his vision of himself as a philosopher-king and religious teacher. Witches were the ultimate traitors to both God and the state, and their ranks constituted a counter-kingdom of perversion and disorder. James believed that witches' powers diminished in proportion to the hierarchical status of the official who prosecuted them, and his personal involvement in the witch trials, as well as his publication of *Daemonologie,* enabled the king to perform the role of a divinely ordained spiritual and temporal leader.[50] In the published account of the North Berwick case, in which a sorcerer named Dr. Fian and his followers were accused of attempting to shipwreck the king as he sailed from Denmark to Scotland, one of the witches is reported to have testified that the devil had a special enmity to James because "the King is the greatest enemy he hath in the worlde" (*Newes,* 15). The pamphlet describes the interrogation of the accused by the king himself, the means by which they were tortured, their confessions, and their final sentencing to be burned at the stake. It concludes with a paragraph affirming James's heroic courage and his steadfast faith; in the future, as in the past, the reader is assured, the Lord will protect his anointed against the enchantments of Satan's followers.

James's *Daemonologie* is of special interest because of the manner in which the king apparently projects onto learned magicians his own feelings of guilt with regard to intellectual pride. Early in the treatise he explains that the devil appeals to witches through greed, desire for revenge, or an excessive desire for knowledge, and he devotes most of book 1 to the problem of insatiable intellectual curiosity. He sets out to refute the claims of the Renaissance occult tradition and to expose the dangers of those arts and sciences which he terms "the devil's school." James does not condemn all astronomy or mathematics as sinful, as many of the popular demonologists had done; the dangerous branch of the art, he says, is judicial astrology, through which those who have already mastered legitimate knowledge seek to transcend human limitations by learning to predict the future. At first this study seems lawful to them, but "they are so allured thereby, that finding their practize to prooue true in sundry things, they studie to know the cause thereof: and so mounting from degree to degree, upon the slipperie and vncertaine scale of curiositie; they are at last entised, that where lawfull artes or sciences failes, to satisfie their restles mindes, even to seeke to that black and vnlawfull science of *Magie*" (*Daemonologie*, 10). That James feared his own intellectual aspirations is strongly suggested by a close reading of *Daemonologie* in conjunction with Sir John Harrington's account of his personal interview with the king, reprinted by Professor Harrison in his edition of James's treatise. Evidently much of the conversation centered upon James's opinion that "a Kynge should . . . be the best clerke in his owne countrie," and he took great pains to assure himself that his subjects adequately respected his intellect (*Daemonologie*, vii-viii). The most important revelation is that James himself had sought the power of prophecy:

His Highnesse tolde me [the queen's] death was visible in Scotlande before it did really happen, being, as he said, 'spoken of in secrete by those whose power of sighte presentede to them a bloodie heade dancinge in the aire.' He then did remarke much on this gifte, and saide he had soughte out of certaine bookes a sure waie to attaine knowledge of future chances. Hereat, he namede many bookes, which I did not knowe, nor by whom written; but advisede me not to consult some authors which woulde leade me to evile consultations. (*Daemonologie,* viii)

In the *Daemonologie* itself James dwells at length upon the fact that scholars who indulge their "curiosity" with regard to foreseeing the future have taken the first step toward crossing the boundary between lawful and unlawful arts. Perhaps he felt that as God's anointed he was privileged to explore with impunity those subjects which would endanger the souls of lesser mortals. It seems likely, however, that just as the typical demonologist projected his own lust onto the presumably insatiable women whose carnality made them easy prey for the devil, so James's attack on the dangerous presumption of scholars grows from his fear of his own desire to gain forbidden knowledge. Having warned his listener that the devil seduces us by appealing to "passiones that are within our selues" (8), Epistemon, who speaks for King James in the dialogue, expresses profound anxiety over the dangers of learning about prophecy, charms, and conjurations, the rudiments of the devil's school. When asked for further information about these matters, he prefaces his discussion with the comment, "I thinke ye take me to be a Witch my selfe" (16; cf. 8–18). On the one hand, James believed that the king should assume the role of teacher and spiritual guide to his people; on the other, he felt the danger of seeking to be godlike in knowledge and in power. Perhaps an awareness of this mixture of pride and fear in King James may help us to understand how the royal demonologist who had so vehemently denounced intellectual magic could subsequently identify with Prospero, the benevolent royal magician of *The Tempest,* which was performed before the king on November 1, 1611, and again during the winter of 1612/13. It is possible that James had grown somewhat more tolerant as he was influenced by the growing skepticism of the period with regard to witchcraft, but it seems likely that the most significant factor was political: one could write a play about a magician so long as the proper authorities were reaffirmed, rather than challenged.

SKEPTICISM AND COMPROMISE:
REGINALD SCOT AND FRANCIS BACON

During the years when plays on magic and witchcraft flourished on the Elizabethan and Jacobean stage, actual practitioners of the occult arts, of chemistry, and of technology continued to test the theories of alchemists and Hermetic philosophers, and increasingly they dismissed the more grandiose claims of the Hermetic/Cabalist tradition and began to find genuinely reliable methods of investigating nature. As Hugh Plat complained in 1594, the progress of genuine knowledge was hindered both by credulity and by unreflective, dogmatic reaction against all "natural magic," and what was needed was a willingness to test the speculations of the Paracelsians and other natural philosophers with a rigorous method of experimentation.[51] As credulity gradually began to wane, alchemists and Hermetic magi increasingly became the objects of ridicule rather than fear, and satirists such as Gabriel Harvey, Thomas Lodge, and Ben Jonson mocked the occultists as hypocritical charlatans or deluded fools (cf. fig. 6).[52] But the boldest voice in England prior to Francis Bacon was that of Reginald Scot, a justice of the peace who was sufficiently horrified by the torture and execution of alleged witches to publish a detailed refutation of the belief that any mortal could command either benevolent or evil spirits or in any way obtain supernatural powers. In *A Discoverie of Witchcraft* (1584) Scot asserts that the age of miracles has passed, and consequently all accounts of supernatural feats performed by witches or benevolent magi are based on false confessions and fallacious hearsay, or, in some cases, are records of tricks performed by legerdemain—mere "juggling." Anticipating some of the modern explanations of the witchcraft phenomenon, Scot asserts that people need tangible villains to blame for their misfortunes, and by projecting their guilt onto presumed witches they can avoid admitting that adversity may be a punishment for their own sins. Occasionally an old woman who cursed a neighbor who had done her a disservice might be deluded enough to think that she indeed caused whatever ailment or other affliction subsequently befell the family, but more frequently the accused simply break down under severe torture and are willing to confess anything.[53]

Scot demonstrates a thorough knowledge of Renaissance occult philosophy, and he refutes the claim that the magus, emulating God, can purify or renew the fallen world. For "we ought not to take upon us to conterfet, or resemble him, which with his word created all things. For we, neither all the conjurors, Cabalists, papists, sooth-saiers, inchanters, witches, nor charmers in the world, neither anie other humane or yet diabolicall cunning can adde anie such strength to Gods workmanship, as to make anie thing anew, or else to ex-change one thing into another" (12.2, p. 124). Drawing upon Agrip-pa's *De vanitate*, he denies that our knowledge of the influence of the heavens is sufficient to provide a foundation for judicial astrology or other, related occult arts which claim to foretell the future (11.21–22, pp. 120–22; cf. 11.10–11, pp. 113–14 and 14.1–8, pp. 204–16). Scot believes, however, that there is a form of "natural magic" which investigates the virtues and qualities of natural substances, and such science, being totally free of supernatural forces, is lawful; the most obvious example of benevolent use of our knowledge of natural properties is medicine, but Scot also believes that there may be other instances of "natural magic" which experience may prove to be le-gitimate and beneficial to humankind (13.1–4, pp. 163–65). Scot also describes in great detail the manner in which some persons who possess genuine knowledge of nature can—sometimes with the aid of legerdemain—produce feats which the ignorant will attribute to witchcraft. Lamentably, "we are so fond, mistrustfull & credulous, that we feare more the fables of Robin good fellow; astrologers, & witches, & beleeve more the things that are not, than the things that are. And the more unpossible a thing is, the more we stand in feare thereof; and the lesse likelie to be true, the more we beleeve it. And if we were not such, I thinke with *Cornelius Agrippa,* that these divi-nors, astrologers, conjurors, and cousenors would die for hunger" (11.22, p. 121; cf. 13.1–34, pp. 163–203). Although Scot concedes that God chose to work through miracles in the Apostolic era, he denies virtually all supernatural influence in subsequent periods of history, believing firmly that the Creator chooses to work through natural law.

In the preface to *Daemonologie,* King James says that his book is written principally against two damnably misguided authors: Johann Wier, whose defense of witches as mentally ill plainly reveals that he himself was of their profession, and "one called SCOT an Englishman, [who] is not ashamed in publike print to deny, that ther can be such a thing as Witch-craft: and so mainteines the old error of the Saddu-

Figure 1: Title page of Robert Recorde's *The Castle of Knowledge*. (By permission of the Houghton Library, Harvard University.)

Figure 2: Anonymous portrait of John Dee. (By permission of the Ashmolean Museum, Oxford.)

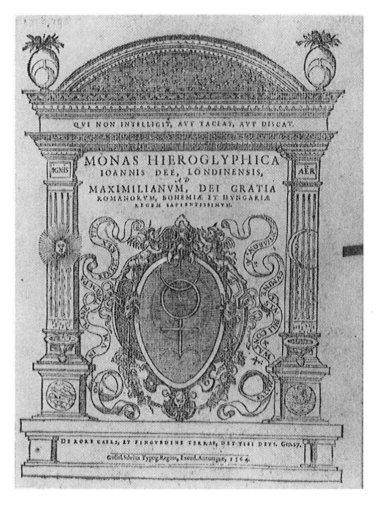

Figure 3: Title page of John Dee's *Monas Hieroglyphica*. (Bodleian Library, 4to Sigma 76. (By permission of the Bodleian Library, Oxford.)

The Tragicall Hiſtorie of the Life and Death of Doctor Fauſtus.

With new Additions.

Written by Cʜ. Mᴀʀ.

Printed at London for *Iohn Wright*, and are to be ſold at his
ſhop without Newgate. 1631.

Figure 4: Title page of *The Tragical History of Doctor Faustus,* 1631. (By permission of the Folger Shakespeare Library.)

Figure 5: Rembrandt, *Dr. Faustus,* sometimes called *The Inspired Scholar.* (By permission of the Trustees of the British Museum.)

Figure 6: Peter Bruegel the Elder, *The Alchemists*. (By permission of Kupfer-stichkabinet, Staatliche Museen Preussicher Kulturbesitz, Berlin [West]. Photograph: Jorg P. Anders.)

Figure 7: William Hamilton, illustration to *The Winter's Tale*, act 5, scene 3: "If this be magic, let it be an art / Lawful as eating." (By permission of the Trustees of the British Museum.)

Figure 8: Frontispiece to Nicholas Rowe's edition of *The Tempest*, 1709. (By permission of the Folger Shakespeare Library.)

Figure 9: John Gilbert, illustration to *The Tempest*, act 1, scene 2: Prospero, Miranda, and Caliban. (From *The Complete Illustrated Shakespeare*, ed. Howard Staunton [New York: Park Lane, 1979], by permission of Crown Publishers, Inc.)

cees, in denying of spirits" (*Daemonologie,* xi-xii). One wonders how many Elizabethans may have shared Scot's skepticism with regard to witches and spirits, as well as his faith in the order of nature, but refrained from expressing themselves out of fear of persecution. Only when Francis Bacon convinced a significant percentage of his countrymen that innovation in natural philosophy need not undermine the traditional authorities in politics and religion could the nation commit its resources to scientific and technological endeavors. Bacon adopted from the occult and alchemical traditions the belief that civilization was on the eve of a renewal of knowledge which would restore to humankind the powers with which God had originally endowed us: "For man by the fall fell at the same time from his state of innocency and from his dominion over creation. Both of these losses can even in this life be in some part repaired; the former by religion and faith, the latter by arts and sciences."[54] The humanist conviction that knowledge must issue in virtuous action had been carried to its logical extreme in occult philosophy and ultimately contributed to Bacon's vision of a society in which science would improve the lot of all social and economic classes. Among the many aspects of occultism which Bacon rejected, however, was the idea that knowledge could be perfected through the vision of an inspired, self-reliant individual. For Bacon and his followers in the Royal Society, science progressed through controlled experimentation and the combined labors of a large community of researchers who replicated each other's findings, and to a considerable extent it was this emphasis upon the limitations of the individual which made it possible for scientists to form an alliance with traditional political and religious authorities. Although the theoretical basis of this alliance has proven acceptable to many of Western civilization's most influential thinkers, there have always remained compelling reasons for some religious and ethical thinkers to question any form of magic or science which sought to compel nature to serve human purposes. As Sir James Frazer pointed out in *The Golden Bough,* miracles wrought by prayer in an orthodox religious context result from an attitude of submission; works accomplished either through magical ceremonies or as a result of genuine science and technology are typically an assertion of human power, of our daring to assert control over our own destiny.[55]

Although we are no longer engaged in debate over the technical details of magical procedure or the existence of witchcraft, many of the fundamental intellectual, social, psychological, and spiritual problems which gave rise to the controversies and the officially sanctioned violence of the sixteenth and seventeenth centuries are still very much with us. We continue to be threatened by the confusion of religious sincerity with dogmatism and self-vindication, and it would be naive indeed to flatter ourselves that rationality and open-mindedness have entirely triumphed in the twentieth century over the need to defend those personal biases which are, in large part, the result of one's economic and social status. Moreover, as the research of Professors Cohn, Larner, and others has reminded us, the desire to destroy entire classes of human beings who are imagined to constitute a subversive counter-society, and onto whom the guilt and the sense of failure of others can be projected, is not merely a characteristic of sixteenth- and seventeenth-century Europe, or of other cultures distant from us in space or time. The psychological roots of such intolerance lie deep within the human personality, and the social dynamics which bring such forces to the surface threaten to appear in virtually all human societies.[56] Science and technology, while capable of bringing incalculable improvement of the quality of human life, have also made it possible for us to witness the destructive consequences of human fear and hatred on a scale which makes the European witch-hunts, as appalling as they are, appear relatively limited by comparison. The history of the twentieth century has intensified, rather than diminished, the perennial questions concerning the limitations of human nature and its potential for benevolence and for destruction. That fact is one of the most compelling reasons for the enduring power of the plays by Marlowe, Jonson, and Shakespeare which we shall examine in the following chapters.

Chapter Six

Vision and Illusion
in Marlowe's *Dr. Faustus*

Magic in *Dr. Faustus* is a unifying symbol which draws together the three aspects of Renaissance thought with which Christopher Marlowe was typically concerned: the indulgence of the senses and the enjoyment of worldly beauty, the quest for wealth and political power, and the pursuit of infinite knowledge. The play itself, as well as the relevant historical and biographical evidence, suggests that Marlowe was aware that each of these pursuits had at times been justified by Renaissance occult philosophers. As we have seen in the preceding chapters, the Florentine Neoplatonists who founded the tradition of Hermetic/Cabalist magic had argued that humankind's love of earthly beauty sprang from our visionary powers and our love of an immanent divinity, and Ficino had asserted that even human political ambitions resulted from the individual's awareness of the immortality and divinity of the human soul. The values and attitudes which Marlowe was contemplating when he composed *Tamburlaine* and *Dr. Faustus,* and which proved so captivating to Elizabethan audiences, are epitomized in Ficino's assertion that "the immeasurable magnificence of our soul may be seen from this, that humankind will not be satisfied with the power of command over this entire world if we learn, having conquered this one, that another world remains which we have not yet conquered. . . . Thus human beings wish no superior and no equal, and we will not suffer anything to remain excluded from our command. . . . This status belongs to God alone; therefore humanity seeks a divine condition." [1]

Through his contact with Thomas Harriot, Walter Ralegh, and others, Marlowe had become intensely aware of the importance of the occult tradition—as well as the genuine science and technology often associated with it—in the controversies over the status of traditional authorities and over the wisdom of attempting to alter or control the natural world. At the same time, his familiarity with orthodox treatises on magic, the public controversies over witchcraft, and popular literary and dramatic traditions made him aware of the many different ways in which various segments of his audience might respond to a stage conjurer. Although he himself was likely to have been capable of distinguishing between *magia* and *goetia* and of seeing through the common confusions among mathematics, technology, magic, and witchcraft, it suited Marlowe's purposes, in a work which responds with a calculated ambivalence to the most radical currents of Renaissance thought, to play upon the widespread fear that a revolution in science would result in revolutions in religion, politics, and other spheres. *Dr. Faustus* focuses, through the multifaceted symbol of magic, upon the central, underlying question of the limits of human nature, but its response to this question is equivocal: *Dr. Faustus* simultaneously reveals and conceals the searching reflections of its author.

In his opening soliloquy, Faustus not only surveys the traditional academic disciplines and spurns them because of their limitations; he systematically rejects all conventional authorities: Aristotle in logic and, by implication, in natural philosophy; Galen in medicine; Justinian in law. He progresses immediately to the rejection of the Bible, the ultimate authority in religion. He willfully misinterprets the Scriptures because to read them accurately would lead him to confess his human limitations, and his pride will not permit him to submit to anything outside himself. Although Faustus wavers in his resolution throughout the play, one of his deepest longings is to free himself from the constraints of orthodoxy, so that he can exalt his own intellect (or, as he tells Valdes and Cornelius, his own "fantasie," A-text, 136) over traditional sources of knowledge.[2] Like the Christopher Marlowe, who, according to Richard Baines, advised men that religion had been invented as a tool of political oppression and that they should "not . . . be afeard of bugbeares and hobgoblins,"[3] Faustus endeavors to reject as superstition all doctrine which threatens to impose limitations upon him. When he says that "Hel's a fable," Mephostophilis' reply—"I, thinke so still, till experience change thy mind" (519–20)—suggests that Faustus has decided, like an increasing number of sixteenth-century "empirics," to adopt a skeptical attitude toward all assertions which his own experience has not proven true. It is not sufficient that Mephostophilis lecture Faustus on astronomy; the conjurer must mount the heights of Olympus and "proue *Cosmography*" (796) for himself. The most obvious effect of Mephostophilis' response to Faustus' skepticism, of course, is to imply that the conjurer eventually will experience hell, and that his attempt to establish complete intellectual freedom is damnably misguided. The play repeatedly alludes to the most notorious varieties of heretical philosophy and iconoclastic freethinking which were abroad at the time *Dr. Faustus* was written, and in many ways it places those unorthodox ideas in an ironic context, apparently affirming the line of reasoning which Erastus, Holland, Perkins, King James, and others had developed in their attacks on the occult tradition and on freethinkers in general: a man so bold as to reject the officially sanctioned authorities in natural philosophy and medicine would not stop short of challenging the authority of God Himself.

Previous interpretations of Marlowe's attitude toward the subversive currents of thought which are evoked in the play generally fall into one of three categories: those who believe that Faustus and Mephostophilis express the dramatist's own rebellious criticism of traditional ideas and institutions; those who interpret *Dr. Faustus* as entirely orthodox; and those who see the play as ambivalent. One of the most influential studies in the first category is Harry Levin's *The Overreacher,* which combines very sound biographical evidence for Marlowe's heretical opinions with a stylistic analysis which emphasizes Marlowe's use of hyperbole, a figure of speech which expresses a desire to transcend normal limitations. In Marlowe's case, Levin argues, "the style is the man himself," and the dramatist's identification with Faustus is suggested by the quality of the verse in those speeches which express radically humanistic aspirations.[4] Professor Levin draws in part on the seminal research of Paul Kocher, who provides detailed evidence of Marlowe's heretical opinions, but who, like many subsequent readers, interprets *Dr. Faustus* as embodying significant self-contradictions. Kocher provides convincing evidence of Marlowe's extensive use of traditional, orthodox treatises which condemn all magic as witchcraft, but he also perceives correctly that Marlowe seizes the opportunity for expressing heretical ideas through the speeches of Faustus and the devils. He observes that the speeches of Faustus or Mephostophilis which express a sense of loss and despair are as powerful as those which embody daring aspirations for knowledge and power. He underestimates, however, the extent to which Marlowe utilizes material from the Renaissance occult tradition, and he tends to attribute the ambivalence of the drama in part to Marlowe's subconscious anxieties. In more recent studies the tendency to see the play as essentially incoherent has often become increasingly pronounced.[5] In this chapter, however, I shall explore the possibility that the play's conflicts and self-contradictions are not the consequence of Marlowe's presumed intellectual or spiritual confusion, nor, despite the obviously genuine textual problems, do they result primarily from collaborative authorship or textual corruption. Our appreciation of *Dr. Faustus* is enhanced if we regard the play's complexities as the product of consciously controlled artistry.

Critics who believe that Marlowe sympathizes with Faustus' rejection of established beliefs and authorities have often had difficulty in dealing with the comic scenes. Some readers have regarded them as extraneous, while others have argued that they provide a satirical commentary on the main action and serve to underscore the incredible folly of Faustus' bargain with the devil. Aware that some of these scenes, though not all of them, were probably written by Marlowe, Levin argues (*The Overreacher,* 120–21) that actions which appear ludicrous to a modern audience may have seemed more impressive to the Elizabethans. Those who see Marlowe's plays as thoroughly orthodox, however, have often pointed out that the comic elements of *Dr. Faustus,* as well as other aspects of the play's structure and imagery, emphasize the degeneration of a person who has imagined himself as self-sufficient and consequently cut himself off from God. The clown in scene 4, whose imagination seems thoroughly captivated by the prospect of being able to transform himself through magic into "a Dog, or a Cat, or a Mouse, or a Rat, or any thing" (381), initiates a continuing strand of animal imagery which suggests that the magician who wishes to ascend the Chain of Being toward godhead ironically transforms himself into a beast. Faustus never attains the grandiose vision of his opening soliloquy; instead, he descends rather quickly to trivial "juggler's" tricks and to crude sensuality. There are also numerous allusions in the play to mythological figures such as Icarus, whose fall was traditionally regarded as a warning against overweening pride, and to Actaeon, whose dismemberment by his own hounds was often interpreted as a lesson in the self-destructive character of excessive sensuality. Those who interpret *Dr. Faustus* as upholding traditional doctrine have also argued that the play's extensive use of the conventions of the morality play implies that Marlowe is affirming theological assumptions which are associated with the genre.[6] In brief, if the character of Faustus embodies the most radical and antiauthoritarian elements of Renaissance thought, then one might reasonably conclude that identifying the magus as a servant of Satan, leading him to display an absurd degree of folly and triviality, and finally carrying him literally off to hell before the eyes of the audience all imply a rather definite rejection of Faustus' radical vision.

As David Bevington has pointed out in what is still the most detailed study of the play in relation to the morality tradition, there is, in spite of all of the apparently orthodox features of *Dr. Faustus,* an ambivalence which results in part from Marlowe's decision to use a semihistorical and in many respects admirable individual as his protagonist; Faustus is a man, not merely a moral abstraction, and he is, moreover, a man whose aspirations and whose daring may well have appealed to the Christopher Marlowe with whom the biographers have acquainted us.[7] The introduction of Faustus' Promethean aspirations into the morality pattern produces a mixed genre and consequently enables the play to evoke complex emotional and intellectual responses. Although neither biographical evidence nor Professor Levin's stylistic argument is entirely convincing when considered in isolation, the weight of these two types of evidence is considerable when they are combined, and an interpretation which somehow comes to terms with the biographical record is more convincing than one which ignores it. Although there may be exaggerations in Richard Baines's testimony to the Privy Council concerning Marlowe's blasphemy and atheism, the combined accusations of Baines, Kyd, Cholmely, and Greene, when considered in the light of the poetry of *Dr. Faustus,* tend to intensify one's feeling that orthodox theology, although undeniably present in the play, is only one of its facets. For many of those who experience the play, the most captivating lines of *Dr. Faustus* are those which express the glorification of humankind and its powers:

But think'st thou heauen is such a glorious thing?
I tell thee *Faustus* it is not halfe so faire

As thou, or any man that breathe[s] on earth.
                    (574–76)

Go forward *Faustus* in that famous Art
Wherein all natures treasure is contain'd:
Be thou on earth as *Ioue* is in the skye,
Lord and Commander of these elements.
                    (101–4)

The appeal of the Faustian vision of human potential and of this world's pleasures must be felt by anyone who is sensitive to the poetry of the apostrophe to Helen or of the description of the powers of magic in Faustus' opening soliloquy. At the same time, the passages which affirm human power and glory are counterpoised by those which evoke fear of damnation:

Why this is hell: nor am I out of it.
Think'st thou that I who saw the face of God,
And tasted the eternall Ioyes of heauen,
Am not tormented with ten thousand hels,
In being depriu'd of euerlasting blisse?
O *Faustus* leaue these friuolous demandes,
Which strike a terror to my fainting soule.
                    (301–7; emendations in 302 and 307 from A)

Dr. Faustus is neither a morality play nor an unambivalent celebration of radical humanism; it is a tragedy which dramatizes a conflict between two irreconcilable systems of value, each of which, we may feel, has at least partial validity and a genuine claim to our allegiance. While Marlowe may have sympathized with Faustus' rejection of traditional authorities and the strict limits which they impose upon human aspirations, he was nonetheless aware that Promethean self-assertion could degenerate into debasing forms of self-aggrandizement. The play thus establishes a dramatic rhythm which initially leads us to experience the appeal of the Faustian ethic which demands that humankind free itself from the bondage of traditional restraints, and subsequently brings us to acknowledge human weakness and limitations. Marlowe's verse paints beguiling portraits of sensual delight and of infinite knowledge and power, and at the same time it brings us to feel pity and terror as we realize the extent of

Faustus' self-delusion. If we respond fully to all aspects of the text, we participate in the protagonist's spiritual conflict.

Many critics have assumed that the protagonist's conflict is, in fact, the conflict of the historical Christopher Marlowe, and it is possible that this is the case. There is considerable danger, however, that this assumption will lead us to perceive in the play a total lack of artistic coherence. Wilbur Sanders, in an important and influential study, attributed the play's apparent inconsistencies to an alleged moral and spiritual chaos in Marlowe himself. To a lesser extent, Paul Kocher, Barbara Traister, and others have also regarded the play's conflicts as beyond authorial control. The problem is compounded by the presence of serious textual corruption and the question of collaborative authorship, both of which have at times been found to introduce such chaos into the texts that they have been seen as providing no more than fragmentary glimpses of the masterpiece which Marlowe originally conceived. In spite of all of these difficulties, there is in the texts as we have them considerable evidence that Marlowe purposely adopted artistic strategies for developing ambivalence in the drama and thereby unsettling his audience. As Annabel Patterson, Stephen Greenblatt, and others have emphasized, subversive ideas were much more common in the Renaissance than is sometimes supposed, and authors of independent mind adopted techniques for expressing their ideas indirectly, in the context of works whose ostensibly orthodox framework would enable them to pass the censor.[8] The hypothesis that *Dr. Faustus* employs such strategies accounts for the discrepancy between the documents which attest to Marlowe's heretical opinions, on the one hand, and the apparent orthodoxy of many aspects of *Dr. Faustus,* on the other; it has the further advantage of encouraging us to perceive the conflicts of the play as the consequences of controlled artistry, rather than Marlowe's presumed moral and spiritual confusion. Even the scenes which may have been written by Rowley and Birde or an earlier collaborator often develop themes which are initiated in lines always attributed to Marlowe, and the presence of the comic material by no means utterly destroys the unity of the work as Marlowe originally designed it. The comic scenes not only emphasize the theme of Faustus' degeneration; they often reinforce the identification, originally established in the opening soliloquy, of the world of political ambition and self-aggrandizement as—metaphorically, perhaps—demonic; they render grotesquely absurd the desire for conquest which was, in fact, sanctioned by the very authorities which portions of *Dr. Faustus* endeavor to subvert. It seems probable that Marlowe, retaining a thoughtful concern for both morality and liberty while rejecting political and religious dogma, has protected himself by placing his own radical ideas in the mouth of the devil—or of a damned conjurer—while skillfully designing a play which implicitly questions the very orthodoxy which it seems to invoke.

This interpretation of Marlowe's purposes becomes even more attractive if we recall that 1592 is the most probable date of the composition of *Dr. Faustus* (especially since we have no firm evidence of the existence of an English *Faustbook* prior to that time), and it was during that year that Robert Parsons initiated a widely read series of pamphlets accusing Sir Walter Ralegh and his associates of maintaining a "schoole of Atheisme" led by a "Coniurer."[9] The magician to whom Parsons alludes as the "master" of the school is almost certainly Thomas Harriot, the accomplished scientist and acquaintance of Christopher Marlowe's. Although we cannot know with certainty that Marlowe intended *Dr. Faustus* to be a response to such accusations, the history of the scandals which attached themselves to Ralegh, Harriot, and Marlowe, as well as the inquiries of the Privy Council and of other authorities into their religious views, is a chilling reminder of the oppressive atmosphere in which these men lived. It is tempting indeed to see Marlowe as protecting himself by writing a play which is in many ways more explicitly orthodox than his earlier works, yet smiling wryly to himself as he contemplates the lines of the bad angel in the following exchange:

> EUILL ANGEL. Go forward *Faustus* in that famous Art.
> GOOD ANGEL. Sweete *Faustus* leaue that execrable Art.
> FAUSTUS. Contrition, Prayer, Repentance? what of these?
> GOOD ANGEL. O they are meanes to bring thee vnto heauen.
> BAD ANGEL. Rather illusions, fruits of lunacy,
> That make them foolish that do vse them most.
>
> (403–8)

The subversive idea which appears most frequently in the biographical documents relating to Harriot and to Marlowe is what Robert Greene apparently alluded to as the "pestilent" Machiavellian doctrine that "the first beginning of Religioun," to use the terms of the Baines document, "was only to keep men in awe."[10] One of the central conflicts of *Dr. Faustus* is whether magic—and the liberating vision of human potential which it symbolizes—are in fact illusions, or whether the illusion is traditional orthodoxy itself.

One aspect of *Dr. Faustus* which appears thoroughly traditional is its apparent denial of the possibility of benevolent magic. Numerous allusions to the alchemical and Hermetic/Cabalist traditions appear in a context which seems to imply that all occult philosophy, despite the disclaimers of magicians who assert that their art is benign, leads inevitably to the worship of demons. Valdes and Cornelius, who instruct Faustus in magic, claim to base their art on authors such as Roger Bacon, who distinguished between legitimate magic and the damnable invocation of demons, and they also profess that the magician relies upon genuine knowledge of astrology, the occult properties of minerals, and the magical power of words. And yet, surprisingly, Faustus does not utilize knowledge of occult virtues, as did Bacon or Paracelsus, or the services of good angels, as described by Dee or Agrippa. Instead, his initial conjuration is a ceremony which seeks to gain power over devils through a combination of propitiation and intimidation, relying in part on the invocation of the power of the name of God in a manner which traditional theologians regarded as blasphemous. As Robert West has correctly shown in his careful examination of the conjuring scene, Faustus' actions are not, at the very outset, fully abandoned acts of devil worship; in fact the line *"valeat numen triplex Iehouae"* (242–43), often translated as "Farewell to the Trinity," should instead be rendered "Let the triple power of Jehovah be strong," a reading which is consistent with Faustus' commanding the spirits to appear by invoking the name of Jehovah, sprinkling holy water, and making the sign of the cross. As Mephostophilis explains to Faustus, and as Erastus, Bodin, James I, and even Roger Bacon himself had argued, such attempts to coerce spirits prove ineffectual, and as soon as Faustus realizes that fact he takes the further, desperate step of agreeing to abjure God and enter the diabolical pact. The assertion that verbal magic possesses no genuine power is an important step in the play's apparent adoption of an orthodox framework ostensibly condemning the Renaissance occult tradition; although Professor Traister is technically correct that the play leaves open the possibility that a more patient magician could succeed at benevolent magic, this possibility is never made explicit in *Dr. Faustus.* The major emphasis falls instead on the suggestion that the devil complies with the requests of a conjurer only insofar as such compliance enables Satan to ensnare the soul of one so foolish as to imagine that he or she can attain superhuman power, and throughout the remainder of the play Faustus' magic is always limited precisely to the kind of feats which could be accomplished, as Perkins, Holland, Erastus, and others tell us, by demonic agency (insofar as God permits the devils to confirm hardened sinners in their damnation) or simply through illusions.[11]

Although Professor West has clearly shown that in many respects *Dr. Faustus* is founded upon orthodox, traditional beliefs concerning witchcraft and demonology, he goes somewhat too far when he states that the tradition of intellectual magic, with its assertion of human nobility and power, "goes unnoticed in Marlowe's play" ("Impatient Magic," 229) and that Faustus, totally lacking in spiritual and intellectual aspiration or any form of altruism, desires purely and simply to serve his physical appetites. West argues that Faustus' professed plans to "wall all *Germany* with Brasse," to levy soldiers with the wealth he shall obtain, and to invent "stranger engines for the brunt of warre, / Then was the fiery keele at *An[t]werpe* bridge" (115–23) are "vain and frivolous" ("Impatient Magic," 230), but it seems likely that a significant portion of Marlowe's audience would regard the military applications of Faustus' magical technology, as well as his desire to learn "the secrets of all forraine Kings" (114) and to gather wealth from the New World, as intensely appealing. Although we might agree that arraying the students in the public schools with silk is a relatively trivial project, surely the scholar's desire to be resolved of all ambiguities is not so petty, and Faustus' insistent questioning of inherited cosmological and theological beliefs recurs throughout the action.[12] Faustus possesses exactly the same mixture of egotism and genuine desire for knowledge, of intoxication with an expansive vision of human potential and desire for the power to serve one's own selfish ends, which Marlowe had observed in such historical figures as Dee, Bruno, Agrippa, and Paracelsus, and in Sir Walter Ralegh and other members of the militant Protestant and imperialist party at Elizabeth's court. Moreover, whereas West argues that we must assume the existence of a Christian God and of the Adversary as "given" in the play, I rather see the entire Christian conception of reality as insidiously questioned in *Dr.*

Faustus by the protagonist's skepticism with regard to traditional doctrine and by systematic allusion to the heretical philosophies of scientists and occult philosophers such as Bruno and Harriot.

The magnificent conclusion of the opening soliloquy, for example, is based clearly upon the occult doctrine that the individual can literally unite with God through knowledge. In the Hermetic books and in works by Renaissance occultists such as Ficino, Agrippa, and Bruno, the magus attains a godlike status through the reflection of the entire cosmos within the magician's own soul: the mind becomes all things, and in doing so, it becomes one with God. In *Corpus Hermeticum*, treatise 12, the Divine Mind addresses Hermes Trismegistus as follows:

> Therefore unless you make yourself equal to God, you cannot understand God; for the like is not intelligible save to the like. Make yourself grow to a greatness beyond measure, by a bound free yourself from the body; raise yourself above all time, become Eternity; then you will understand God. Believe that nothing is impossible for you, think yourself immortal and capable of understanding all, all arts, all sciences, the nature of every living being. Mount higher than the highest height; descend lower than the lowest depth. Draw into yourself all sensations of everything created, fire and water, dry and moist, imagining that you are everywhere, on earth, in the sea, in the sky, that you are not yet born, in the maternal womb, adolescent, old, dead, beyond death. If you embrace in your thought all things at once, times, places, substances, qualities, quantities, you may understand God.[13]

Ficino explicitly embraces this Hermetic doctrine in book 14, chapter 3, of the *Theologia Platonica,* affirming the nobility of the human quest to develop the soul's divine potential through heroic exertions of intellect and will. Through exercise of all the faculties which participate in the various levels of the universal hierarchy, human beings strive for universal knowledge and power: "This is what Hermes Trismegistus was admiring when he said: 'A human being is a great miracle, a living creature to be revered and adored, one who knows the genus of daemons as if one were by nature related to them, or who transforms oneself into God as if one were a god oneself.'"[14] Giordano Bruno, the occult philosopher whose works Marlowe was perhaps most likely to have read, apparently reverted entirely to the ancient Gnostic heresy, abandoning the Christian framework which Pico and Ficino endeavored to retain, and emphasized the power of the individual to attain a genuinely godlike status by attaining universal knowledge.[15] This Gnostic doctrine is the basis of the powerful suggestion in the following lines that the human mind can embrace infinity and thus become godlike:

> O what a world of profite and delight,
> Of power, of honor, of omnipotence
> Is promised to the Studious Artizan?
> All things that moue betweene the quiet Poles
> Shall be at my command: Emperors and Kings,
> Are but obey'd in their seuerall Prouinces:
> Nor can they raise the winde, or rend the cloudes:
> But his dominion that exceeds in this,
> Stretcheth as farre as doth the mind of man.
> A sound Magitian is a Demi-god:
> Here tire my braines to get a Deity.
>   (80–89; emendations in 81 and 86 from A)

One might well argue that placing such references to Hermetic/Cabalist doctrine in the mouth of a magician who is shortly to sell his soul to the devil serves simply to identify the occult tradition as a damnable illusion; but the poetry of these lines communicates the exciting appeal of the magician's vision. The ultimate effect of the opening scene is not to confirm the members of the audience in their comfortable assumptions, but to unsettle them, to raise questions concerning the limits of human nature, to make them wonder whether the individual does, after all, have the right to make his or her own decisions concerning philosophical, scientific, or religious truth.

Repeated images and key terms, including many of the allusions to classical mythology, are similarly designed to elicit an ambivalent response. From the outset of the play Faustus describes his longing for a godlike status in terms of an intense eroticism: "'Tis magick, magick that hath rauisht me" (132), Faustus tells us in the opening scene, and throughout the play the repeated references to "ravishment," "sweetness," and "delight" communicate the intensity of his desires. Along with the allusions to Icarus, Actaeon, and the

Judgment of Paris, as well as traditional reminders of the destructive consequences of pride, intellectual presumption, and excessive sensuality, the eroticism of Faustus' speeches continually reminds us that he is a mortal, physical creature, and his language thus underscores the irony of his utilizing magic, which he initially describes as the ultimate spiritual and intellectual attainment, to serve his physical lusts. Yet all of these aspects of the play's language are double-edged, for the aspiration of Icarus and the love of Actaeon had been regarded in a much more positive light by Renaissance occult philosophers, and the use of erotic imagery to describe the desire to unite with God was a commonplace of the Neoplatonic and Hermetic traditions. Marlowe would certainly have known of the tradition of Platonic love as embodied in Castiglione's *The Courtier,* and he may well have been familiar with Giordano Bruno's characteristically extreme development of the tradition in the *Heroic Frenzies,* the sonnet sequence published in London in 1585. In his preface Bruno explained that the poems referred not to an ordinary passion, but to the love of a human soul for an immanent divinity which "takes possession of the soul, raises it, and converts it into God";[16] he often speaks of the soul as being "ravished" or "consumed" in a mystical ecstasy. The following lines from the *Heroic Frenzies* are relatively unsophisticated as verse when compared to the poetry of Marlowe, but they will serve to illustrate the conventions upon which the dramatist is playing in *Dr. Faustus:*

> Winged by desire and thee, O dear delight!
> As still the vast and and succouring air I tread,
> So, mounting still, on swifter pinions sped,
> I scorn the world, and Heaven receives my flight.
> And if the end of Ikaros be nigh,
> I will submit, for I shall know no pain;
> And falling dead to earth, shall rise again;
> What lowly life with such high death can vie?[17]

> So high a torch, love lighted in the skies,
> Consumes my soul, and with this bow divine
> Of piercing sweetness what terrestrial vies?
> This net of dear delight doth prison mine;
> And I to life's last day have this desire—
> Be mine thine arrows, Love, and mine thy fire.[18]

The erotic imagery in *Dr. Faustus* can refer to the relationship between the magician's soul and an immanent divinity, or to Faustus' losing himself in mere bestial lust. In the prologue Marlowe establishes a pattern in which such references to "sweetness" and "delight" are juxtaposed to terms such as "gluttony" and "surfeit," which remind us of physical excess and of the sickness engendered by it:

> Excelling all, whose sweete delight's dispute
> In th' heauenly matters of *Theologie,*
> Till swolne with cunning of a selfe conceit,
> His waxen wings did mount aboue his reach,
> And melting, heauens conspir'd his over-throw:
> For falling to a diuelish exercise,
> And glutted now with learnings golden gifts,
> He surffets vpon cursed Negromancy,
> Nothing so sweete as magicke is to him,
> Which he preferres before his chiefest blisse.[19]

Faustus vacillates between the ambition to "get a Deity" (89) and his worship of his "owne appetite / Wherein is fixt the loue of *Belzebub*" (398–99). Wagner's accidental substitution of "letcherie" for "loue" in the initial comic scene (207) reminds us of the confusion in Faustus' own mind between his desire to become a god and the desire to obtain the power to serve one's lusts. One might infer that Marlowe regarded the Neoplatonists' attempts to spiritualize the love of woman and of physical beauty as simply a rationalization of human pleasure in the sensual world itself. While Faustus' opening speeches contain a mixture of spiritual and intellectual aspiration and desire for sensual pleasure, sensuality continually overpowers Faustus, and his initial noble ambitions are almost forgotten; at other times the imagery of sweetness and surfeit refer metaphorically to all forms of pride and excess and their terrible consequences. Even the comic scene in which we are told of Faustus' "monstrous" consumption of an entire load of hay (1608) serves to underscore the theme of gluttony, the unnatural overindulgence of the appetites, "a surfet of deadly sin" (1933). Some of the most moving speeches of the play are those in which Faustus attributes divinity to the things of this world, as did many of the occult philosophers, but these passages are inevitably followed by lines which suggest that Faustus' fantasy is deceiving him. The "delight" he experiences in his worldly pleasures has the bewitching power to delude him into seeing the things of this world as more valuable, more genuinely real, than those of the next. Perhaps the most impressive instance of this transvaluation is the apostrophe to Helen of Troy: Helen is the personification of the beauty and the sensual pleasure Faustus has sought, and yet he describes her as a goddess who can make him immortal:

Was this the face that Launcht a thousand ships,
And burnt the toplesse Towers of *Ilium?*
Sweet *Hellen* make me immortall with a kisse:
Her lips sucke forth my soule, see where it flies.
Come *Hellen,* come, giue me my soule againe,
Here will I dwell, for heauen is in these lippes,
And all is drosse that is not *Helena.*
                    (1874–80)

The idea that the human soul can be ravished by God in a mystical union referred to by Cabalists as "the death of the kiss" was a commonplace of the occult tradition, and its presence in the line "make me immortal with a kiss" seems unmistakable: yet at the moment we recognize this allusion to occult doctrine, we must recall that Faustus is losing his soul through the worship of demons and through excessive indulgence in the physical delight which Helen symbolizes.[20] The remainder of this strange and powerful speech refers repeatedly to the ravishment of a mortal by a deity, and on another level, it suggests that whatever Helen represents, Faustus has chosen her instead of God:

O thou art fairer then the euenings aire,
Clad in the beauty of a thousand starres:
Brighter art thou then flaming *Iupiter,*
When he appear'd to haplesse *Semele:*
More louely then the Monarch of the sky,
In wanton *Arethusa's* azure arms,
And none but thou shalt be my Paramour.
                    (1887–93)

Throughout *Dr. Faustus* the imagery of faces presents alternating positive and negative aspects, and it thus contributes to the play's pattern of calculated ambivalence: it begins in the opening scene, when Valdes describes the beauty shadowed in the "Airie browes" of the spirit-maidens who will appear to Faustus (150); it continues through Mephostophilis' bitter memory of being thrown from "the face of heauen" with Satan and exiled forever from the presence of "the face of God" (294, 302); it attains its climax in the apostrophe to Helen; and it reaches its tragic conclusion in the final scene, when Faustus perceives with terrifying anguish the "irefull browes" of God (A-text, 1469). The apostrophe to Helen brings us temporarily to exult with Faustus in his imaginary triumphs, and we feel with him the allurement of Helen's beauty; and yet, as Lucifer and Mephostophilis arise from Hell to oversee the scene immediately following these lines, we are reminded that the image Faustus worships is not even the actual ghost of Helen of Troy, but merely a devil in a fair disguise. The play continually suggests that Faustus' visions of power and pleasure are "idle fantasies" (1909); the poetry of *Dr. Faustus* creates in the minds of the audience the same visions that have ravished the protagonist, yet we never forget for more than a brief moment the tragic context that suggests that these grandiose dreams are damnable.

Even the final scene of the play contains an undercurrent of allusions and images which imply a comparison between Faustus' death and the apotheosis of humankind described by Renaissance magicians. The references to the myth of Actaeon culminate in Faustus' final dismemberment, and for some of the occultists—notably Bruno—Actaeon's death, caused by his gazing at a naked goddess, was an allegory of the death of the body in a mystical vision of divinity. Neoplatonists also sometimes referred to the Divine Mind as "the ocean," and Faustus' wish that his soul "be changde into little water drops, / And fal into the *Ocean,* nere be found" (A-text, 1502–3) may well be another ironic reference to the absorption of the soul into the Platonic Absolute.[21] I do not mean to suggest that all of these references would be immediately understood by everyone in Marlowe's audience, or that they entirely overwhelm our sense of Faustus' damnation. Nevertheless, esoteric symbolism is appropriate for a play whose subject is occult philosophy, and I think that Marlowe is playing systematically upon these symbols, aware that there is more than one possible interpretation of them. If we know that, according to one traditional interpretation of the myth, Actaeon was destroyed by his own lusts, our initial impulse may be to judge Faustus in that light; one might emphasize that the final scene shows the heretical occult philosopher appealing desperately and in vain to his neopagan pantheism and to the doctrine of metempsychosis (2074) as he is literally carried off to hell before our eyes for his presumption. Nonetheless, the concluding scene can still evoke intense sympathy for Faustus and his aspirations: the final chorus, for instance, contains an element of enticement as well as one of admonition:

> *Faustus* is gone, regard his hellish fall,
> Whose fiendfull fortune may exhort the wise
> Onely to wonder at vnlawfull things:
> Whose deepnesse doth intice such forward wits,
> To practise more then heauenly power permits.
> (2117–21)

For members of the audience who have experienced powerful intellectual curiosity or felt a sense of wonder concerning the unknown or the forbidden, the closing lines will seem designed not to destroy the ambivalence about Faustus and his magic, but rather to preserve or even intensify it at the play's conclusion.

Dr. Faustus evokes conflicting responses concerning the desire for conquest and military glory, as well as with regard to Faustus' intellectual and spiritual ambitions. Marlowe makes this theme relevant to an Elizabethan audience through a series of allusions to the political and military contexts of sixteenth-century developments in technology and natural philosophy. The struggle for control of the Netherlands (119–24), the competition with Spain for control of the New World and its legendary wealth (152–54), and the effort to gain control of foreign centers of trade (411) were all issues to which Dee, Ralegh, Harriot, and others had given considerable attention. The "Prince of Parma" was the Spanish governor-general in the Netherlands from 1579 to 1592, and he was commander of the forces with whom the English were in conflict when the play was written. The anti-Catholic gibes are part of a sequence of references associating Faustus with the anti-Spanish and antipapal cause. The historical allusions in several of the comic sections of the play, especially those involving Pope Adrian, the emperor Charles V, and the Saxon Bruno, are occasionally confused, but the pattern of allusions to events of the 1580s and 1590s is especially pronounced in the opening scene, in lines which are virtually always attributed to Marlowe. The anti-

Catholic references would make at least a portion of an Elizabethan audience sympathize momentarily with Faustus, but the play questions the idealistic propaganda which sought to justify England's political and military objectives by associating the interests of the militant Protestants with a character who has professed the love of Beelzebub and whom many would regard as an evil conjurer. We may wonder whether Marlowe felt an imaginative sympathy with Faustus' military and political ambitions, as he did with his spiritual and intellectual aspirations, or whether his anti-authoritarian stance extended to a criticism of the attempts of virtually all governments to expand their power through conquest. The play's exploration of these specific issues is one of several ways in which it continually raises the central question of whether human self-assertiveness and ambition are indeed the manifestations of a godlike spirit which (as Ficino had said) cannot bear to be surpassed, or of a Satanic drive toward self-aggrandizement.

In the apostrophe to Helen, Faustus presents us with a classic image of the glories of warfare, bringing together the themes of love and honor in a manner reminiscent of *Tamburlaine:*

> I will be *Paris,* and for loue of thee,
> In stead of *Troy* shall *Wittenberg* be sack't,
> And I will combat with weake *Menelaus,*
> And weare thy colours on my plumed crest.
> Yea, I will wound *Achilles* in the heele,
> And then returne to *Hellen* for a kisse.
> (1881–86)

The dramatic context of the speech implies that Faustus is as deluded in his poetic idealization of warfare as he is in his dream of sensuality. In addition, the comic scenes provide a satirical commentary upon the struggles of men and devils in the main plot to dominate one another. Regardless of whether Marlowe wrote all of these scenes, and in spite of their occasional historical confusion, they develop themes which are initiated in undoubtedly Marlovian sections: Wagner's bullying of the clown in act 1, scene 4, parodies the power struggle between Faustus and Mephostophilis, and the conflict between Faustus and the knight, Benvolio, whom the magician had "transformed" for mocking him, brings the theme of domination and personal vindication down to the level of the grotesque. In addition to continuing the play's allusions to Actaeon, Benvolio's speeches in act 4, scene 3, present an emblem of the brutality with which men retaliate for an injury to their pride:

> BENVOLIO. First, on his head, in quittance of my wrongs,
> Il'e naile huge forked hornes, and let them hang
> Within the window where he yoak'd me first,
> That all the world may see my iust reuenge.
>
> $\cdot$ $\quad$ $\cdot$ $\quad$ $\cdot$ $\quad$ $\cdot$ $\quad$ $\cdot$ $\quad$ $\cdot$ $\quad$ $\cdot$ $\quad$ $\cdot$ $\quad$ $\cdot$
>
> Wee'l put out his eyes, and they shall serue for buttons to his
> lips, to keepe his tongue from catching cold.
> MARTINO. An excellent policie.
>
> (1431–34, 1438–41)

The struggle between Pope Adrian and the Saxon Bruno similarly reveals the meanness of the quest for worldly power. Despite our questions concerning the authorship of some of these scenes, it is interesting to note the similarity between many of the comic sections of *Dr. Faustus,* especially those which satirize the use of religious doctrine to rationalize the lust for power, and the "savage farce" of *The Jew of Malta.*[22] As the Pope exults vaingloriously in his authority ("Is not all power on earth bestowed on vs? / And therefore tho we would we cannot erre," 960–61), he reveals that he is no less prideful than any other earthly monarch.

Bruno's reference to the Pope as "Proud *Lucifer*" (899) connects with a series of references to the devil himself as a monarch who captures souls because he wishes to "Enlarge his Kingdome," as Mephostophilis tells Faustus (428). Mephostophilis subsequently calls upon Lucifer as "Monarch of hel[l], vnder whose blacke suruey / Great Potentates do kneele with awful feare" (A-text, 1023–24), and when Lucifer himself appears in act 5 he says he has come "To view the subiects of our Monarchy, / Those soules which sinne, seales the blacke sonnes of hell" (1896–97). Satan is thus linked explicitly with ambitious earthly monarchs, and we are brought to realize that the self-aggrandizement manifested by the desire for conquest is the essence of evil. Marlowe has drawn extensively in the play upon the belief affirmed by Renaissance demonologists that the devil's servants indeed occupy positions of power in this world. William Perkins, who began his career as a popular and influential preacher and professor of theology at Cambridge while Marlowe was a student there, proclaimed that "the Devill hath a kingdome, called in Scripture the kingdome of darknes, whereof himselfe is the head and governour, for which cause he is tearmed *the Prince of darknes, the God of this world,* ruling ... in the hearts of the children of disobedience"; the most faithful of Satan's followers are granted powers of witchcraft, Perkins continues, including the ability to create striking illusions which will win them a following among foolish worldlings.[23] In *Dr. Faustus* Marlowe actually goes beyond Perkins, Holland, and others in the extent to which he represents human society as under Satanic influence: he suggests that a world in which the lust for power and sensual delight are dominant is Hell itself.

Mephostophilis endeavors to explain to Faustus that "Hell hath no limits" but is, rather, a mental and spiritual condition which exists wherever demonic influence is present, but the magician responds with the opinion so often attributed to Marlowe himself: "I thinke Hel's a fable" (513, 519). One can imagine Mephostophilis' consternation as he protests, "I tell thee I am damn'd, and now in hell" (529); and the actor who plays Faustus might well gesture toward the stage as *theatrum mundi* when he replies:

> Nay, and this be hell, I'le willingly be damn'd.
> What, sleeping, eating, walking and disputing?
> But leauing this, let me haue a wife, the fairest Maid in
> *Germany,* for I am wanton and lasciuious.
>
> (530–33)

When the Old Man tells Faustus he must check his body to amend his soul, and when Mephostophilis says that because the Old Man's faith is strong, "I cannot touch his soule; / But what I may afflict his body with, / I will attempt" (1860–62), one might well infer that the flesh, as well as the world, is under the devil's control.

The fact that Faustus imagines sensual pleasure and worldly ambition to be "heavenly" rather than hellish is related to the play's extended comparison between magic and poetry. The parallel was a natural one, partly because occult philosophers and poets both laid claim to divine inspiration, which could be conveyed by spirits, and also because both arts were of dubious moral status: poets, like magicians, were at times accused of irrationality and excessive passion, of creating and/or being deceived by illusions. Moreover, both poets and magicians use language as the medium through which the artist's vision, whether genuine or deceptive, is created.[24] The comparison between the two arts is signalled by the parallel between Faustus' references to "heauenly" necromancy (e.g., 77) and the chorus's reference to the poet's "heauenly verse" (7), and it soon becomes apparent that the two arts are similar because both are based upon fantasy and consequently have the power to create intoxicating delusions. Although Faustus initially believes that his "heauenly words" (255) possess genuine power to command spirits and control the forces of nature, the play constantly suggests that his language merely embodies various forms of self-deception. Consider, for example, Faustus' response to Mephostophilis' chilling revelation that the magician has no real control over the devil and that Faustus must worship Lucifer in order to obtain magical powers:

> So *Faustus* hath already done, and holds this principle,
> There is no chiefe but onely *Beelzebub:*
> To whom *Faustus* doth dedicate himselfe.
> This word Damnation, terrifies not me,
> For I confound hell in *Elizium:*
> My Ghost be with the old Phylosophers.
>   (281–86)

To "confound hell in *Elizium*" is to persuade oneself that one can change the nature of things-in-themselves merely by manipulating their names; the alteration takes place in the mind of the magician, not in reality.[25] Moreover, the play often reminds us that "heavenly words" may produce alterations in the perceptions of the audience as well as in the fantasy of the protagonist, and we become critically aware of our tendency to feel empathy, however momentary, with Faustus' vision of warfare as noble rather than brutal, of the delights of the flesh as heavenly rather than base.

Faustus' magical art is eminently theatrical as well as poetic, and *Dr. Faustus* frequently utilizes plays-within-the-play to enhance our sense of the insubstantiality of the worldly goals Faustus has chosen to pursue. Sensual delight, worldly ambition, and magic are repeatedly labelled as shadowy theatrical spectacles. When Faustus wavers in his resolution after signing the infernal contract, Mephostophilis decides to "fetch him somewhat to delight his minde," and stage directions for a miniature play-within-the-play follow:

Enter Deuils, giuing Crownes and rich apparell to
Faustus: they dance, and then depart.
Enter Mephostophilis.
FAUSTUS. What meanes this shew? speake *Mephostophilis.*
MEPHOSTOPHILIS. Nothing *Faustus* but to delight thy mind,
And let thee see what Magicke can performe.

(470–77)

The judgment that earthly crowns, delight, and wealth mean "nothing" is subsequently reinforced by the presentation of Pope Adrian's proud triumph over Bruno as another theatrical "show." The formal, artistic nature of the Pope's worldly power is emphasized in the stage direction which introduces the scene:

Enter the Cardinals and Bishops, some bearing Crosiers, some
the Pillars, Monkes and Friers, singing their Procession:
Then the Pope, and Raymond King of Hungary,
with Bruno led in chaines.

(891–94)

A few lines before the procession begins, Faustus refers to the affairs of the kingdoms of the world as a "show" in which he himself has chosen to be an "actor." In act 4 political power is once again associated with theatrical illusion when Faustus apparently raises the shades of Alexander and his paramour:

Senit. Enter at one [door] the Emperour Alexander, at the other Dar-
ius; they meete, Darius is throwne downe, Alexander kils him; takes
off his Crowne, and offering to goe out, his Paramour meetes him, he
embraceth her, and sets Darius Crowne upon her head; and commi[n]g
backe, both salute the Emperour, who leaving his State, offers to em-
brace them, which Faustus seeing, suddenly staies him. Then trumpets
cease, and Musicke sounds.

My gracious Lord, you doe forget your selfe,
These are but shadowes, not substantiall.
EMPEROUR. O Pardon me, my thoughts are so rauished
With sight of this renowned Emperour,
That in mine armes I would haue compast him.

(1292–1307)

The identification of worldly power and pleasure with theatrical spectacle and hence with illusion is perhaps epitomized in the Masque of the Seven Deadly Sins which Lucifer presents to Faustus in act 2. The stage—which represents the world and which is, at the same time, a place where deceptive imagination reigns—is identified with the realm of privation that is Satan's domain. To find purely sensual fulfillment and to triumph in this world's struggle for conquest is a hollow victory indeed: it is to proceed downward toward a bestial level of existence and ultimately to unite with Lucifer as "Chiefe Lord and Regent of perpetuall night" (443).

All of Faustus' apparent self-delusions ultimately derive from his belief that he is a demigod who can fully realize his divine potential by releasing the powers of the self. Instead of seeking salvation by accepting a subordinate position within the universal hierarchy, he seeks Godhead within the powers of his own mind, and in doing so he enters the realm of his own fantasy. The magicians had believed that magical power was derived from the magus's ability to purify the soul, to return it to its prelapsarian condition: "For there is within our own selves the apprehension and power of all things; but we are prohibited, so ... that we little enjoy these things, by passions opposing us even from the time of our birth, and vain imaginations and immoderate affections, which being expelled, the divine knowledge and power immediately appear within us."[26]

Dr. Faustus suggests that because human beings are creatures in whom good and evil are tragically intermingled, the process of purification which the magicians described is impossible. The human aspiration to attain a godlike status and to exert benevolent control over history is almost inevitably corrupted by selfish desires for wealth, sensual indulgence, and political power. The refusal to admit this is Faustus' fatal error, as is perfectly clear when he reads from Jerome's Bible: "If we say that we haue no sinne, / We deceiue our selues" (69–70).

And yet the play will not permit a sensitive audience to rest comfortably in traditional assumptions concerning the wisdom of confessing one's limits. At the same time that we acknowledge Faustus' tragic self-deceptions, we must concede that the enduring appeal of the play is surely based in part upon the power of Marlowe's verse to encourage us to share Faustus' aspirations. *Dr. Faustus* leads us to appreciate the values of those philosophers and scientists whose vision of human nature and assault upon dogmatic authoritarianism have contributed to modern science as well as to the forces of intellectual, social, and political liberation. Simultaneously, it cautions us to remember the dangers of casting aside too hastily our culture's inherited awareness of the human capacity for idealistic rationalization of our own self-centered desires. *Dr. Faustus* develops a panoply of poetic and theatrical strategies for dramatizing the perennial, unanswerable questions concerning the essence of human nature, and as it explores those questions with emotional intensity, with humor, and with subtlety, it attains the stature of great tragedy.

Chapter Seven

The Renaissance Magus as Mock-Hero: Utopianism and Religious Enthusiasm in Ben Jonson's *The Alchemist*

In Ben Jonson's major plays the radical individualism, utopian dreams, and anti-authoritarian forces of the Renaissance are the objects of skillful and concentrated satiric attack. Jonson's artistic support of Tudor and Stuart monarchs and of the English aristocracy is consistent with his sincere conviction that the good of the community could be maintained only through traditional political and religious institutions, and one of the major threads unifying his diverse canon is an intense fear of subversive forces, especially those which sought to rationalize the overthrow of traditional authorities with spurious claims to private religious revelation, or "enthusiasm." One of Jonson's major aims is to remind us that we are fallen creatures and to convince us that the first step toward making the best of life in this imperfect world is to admit our limitations. In his most successful plays, as well as in his literary criticism and his own practice in the nondramatic poems, Jonson reacts against unquestioned faith in the individual and advocates restraint, discipline, and objectivity. In *The Alchemist* he sets out to ridicule the claim of occult philosophers that human beings are demigods who can literally perfect their own personalities, control time and change, or perfect the fallen world through magical arts. The center of the play is the deflation—or perhaps explosion—of the illusion that the individual can realize a godlike potential through a series of self-transformations and that this perfection of the soul can lead directly to the radical reformation of nature and society. Unlike the royal personages to whom Jonson attributes the power to transform society in his court masques, the reformers ridiculed in *The Alchemist* are, in Jonson's view, hypocrites: they profess noble motives, but in reality they possess partially concealed, self-centered motives. The transformations which they undergo are illusory, and their utopian dreams are merely indulgences of their own lust and ambition.[1]

Like Marlowe, Jonson establishes the context in which he wishes his play to be interpreted through a series of systematic allusions. He mentions John Dee at II.vi.20, and at IV.i.89–91 he refers to Edward Kelley's association with Rudolf II of Bohemia.[2] The play is filled with references to the Paracelsians and to other alchemists and magicians whose philosophies, as we saw in Chapter 5, had profound political implications. The influence of millenary occultism had waned somewhat in the first decade of the seventeenth century, especially because of King James's opposition to the occult tradition, but it was by no means extinct; having lost some of the respectability it had possessed when Dr. Dee was favored by Queen Elizabeth, Renaissance magic in Jacobean England was beginning to go underground into secret societies such as the Rosicrucians, the esoteric brotherhood which Jonson satirizes in *The Fortunate Isles* and elsewhere. The militant Protestants who had previously allied themselves with Dee or even with the more radical Paracelsians hoped that they could influence King James to continue to strengthen the alliances which Elizabeth had formed with Protestant forces on the Continent, but James chose instead to pursue a course of moderation and to avoid confrontation with Catholic nations. Around 1610, however, James began to arrange a betrothal between his daughter, Elizabeth, and Frederick V, Elector Palatine, and the occasion raised illusory hopes among militant Protestants that the marriage would be a step toward the long-awaited political and religious reformation of Europe. Frederick himself may have shared these hopes, for in later years when Ferdinand of Styria assumed the throne in Prague, reversed Rudolf II's policies of religious toleration, and began to persecute the Bohemian Protestants, Frederick accepted the crown which the rebellious Bohemian nobility offered him. In their attempt to expel the Hapsburgs from Prague, however, Frederick and Elizabeth depended upon James's military support, and he failed to send it to them; within a few months they were defeated. It is interesting to note that some of the Hapsburg propaganda against Frederick and Elizabeth accuses them of having an interest in heretical occult philosophy.[3]

The millenarianism of the Rosicrucians originally centered on the widespread hope that Frederick and Elizabeth would initiate a new age of universal reform. One of the sources of the "Rose Cross" symbolism is the Red Cross of Saint George, which appears on the banner of the Order of the Garter, into which Frederick was initiated, and which Spenser's hero in his nationalistic and militantly Protestant epic, *The Faerie Queene*, wears upon his shield. We have no documents attesting the prominence of the Rosicrucian movement until three or four years after *The Alchemist* was written, but the emergence of the Rosicrucian manifestoes at that time underscores the continuation of the close ties between magic and utopianism. Even poets who were not as seriously absorbed in occultism as Spenser was often found in the terminology of Hermetic alchemy the perfect metaphor for the transformation of the present Age of Iron into an era of peace and justice. A striking example is the following poem of Sir John Davies, in which we find the symbol of alchemy combined with the conventional equation of Elizabeth I with the mythical virgin Astraea, the goddess of justice who had fled to the heavens at the close of the reign of Saturn, but who promised to return to earth when the lost Golden Era was restored:

> E arly before the day doth spring
> L et us awake my Muse, and sing;
> I t is no time to slumber,
> S o many ioyes this time doth bring,
> A s Time will faile to number.

> B ut whereto shall we bend our layes?
> E uen vp to Heauen, againe to raise
> T he Mayd, which thence descended;
> H ath brought againe the golden dayes,
> A nd all the world amended.

> R udenesse it selfe she doth refine,
> E uen like an Alchymist diuine;
> G rosse times of yron turning
> I nto the purest forme of gold;
> N ot to corrupt, till heauen waxe old,
> A nd be refined with burning.[4]

This poem epitomizes the ethos which Jonson is satirizing in his portrait of Epicure Mammon. At the time *The Alchemist* was written, there had been attempts to revive the millenary enthusiasm of the late 1500s, and Jonson is intent upon exposing the foolishness and the dangers of the belief that all of the problems of mortal life will magically disappear. In fact Jonson quite pointedly links the magicians with the one other major revolutionary group which had passionately asserted the possibility of radical reform in the Renaissance—the extreme Puritans. The Puritans and the occultists obviously have their differences, but in *The Alchemist* Jonson emphasizes their very real similarities. Most importantly, he links them together because both are "enthusiasts" who regard their own subjective inspiration as superior to any institutional authorities. It is this enthusiasm—or "possession," to use Jonson's own term—which gives rise to the spirited but unintelligible languages of the play, such as the enigmatic jargon of alchemy and the apocalyptic prophecies from Broughton which Dol spews forth in act 4.[5] It is also what deludes some of Jonson's gulls into thinking they can establish a new political, social, and religious order.

Jonson mentions several groups of Puritan enthusiasts in *The Alchemist*, but one of the most important sects is the one to which Tribulation and Ananias belong, the Anabaptists. It is natural that he would focus upon this group in his attack upon extreme Protestants, for the Anabaptists were among the most radical of all dissenting denominations. Their absolute faith in the direct revelations they felt they received from God led them to set themselves above the established laws of church and state. The great majority of the Anabaptists were pacifists, but in several well-known instances the leaders of various splinter movements became violent revolutionary millenarians. They endeavored to initiate an earthly Kingdom of God characterized by egalitarianism and community of goods. By far the most infamous of the revolutionary Anabaptists were the two with whom Jonson has Subtle explicitly link Ananias and Tribulation: Jan Bockelson, better known as John of Leyden, and Bernt Knipperdollinck.[6]

Jonson could not have chosen better examples to illustrate his belief that the rhetoric of individualism and reform can become the tool of a vicious megalomania. After establishing themselves as messianic lords of Münster in the 1530s, Leyden and Knipperdollinck instituted a reign of terror which lasted for nearly a year. Claiming that God had ordered him to transform Münster into the New Jerusalem, Leyden had himself crowned King of the World. He then appropriated for himself and his close followers practically all of the worldly goods of Münster's citizens. He also instituted polygamy and collected for himself a harem of fifteen wives. Emissaries from Münster were sent out to Anabaptist communities in neighboring provinces, and a wave of sympathetic rebellions shook northwestern Germany and the Netherlands. After a six-month blockade Münster was recaptured, but not before the population had been decimated by starvation and by Leyden's fanatical executions. The notorious uprising in Münster was often discussed in Jonson's day (in Nashe's *Unfortunate Traveller,* for example), and there was good reason for the authorities to fear a similar outbreak in England. In 1591, for instance, a self-proclaimed messiah named William Hacket was executed for asserting in public that Elizabeth's rule was at an end and that the English government must be totally reformed. The Anabaptist prophet Edward Wightman was burned as a heretic in 1612, the year of *The Alchemist*'s publication, for calling himself "Elias," or Elijah, the prophet whose return would presage the Second Coming. There is a long tradition of underground radical activity of this sort which surfaced only intermittently until the Puritan Revolution, when a series of utopian schemes and millenarian prophecies broke forth with such fury that even Oliver Cromwell at times found it difficult to control his own supporters. Frequently the radical reformers among the various sects, especially the Family of Love and the Anabaptists, were deeply absorbed in Hermetic philosophy and alchemy. The occultists' theories of illumination and spiritual perfection coincided with those of the sectarians, and the radicals frequently claimed Paracelsus as a true prophet whose predictions of reform were coming true in seventeenth-century England. When the sects felt increasingly free to express their ideas during the Interregnum, an unprecedented flood of Hermetic and alchemical works was published. Often these treatises have a strong utopian or millenarian emphasis.[7]

Jonson uses the allusions to Leyden, Knipperdollinck, Henric Nicholas (an immigrant preacher of Anabaptist background who founded the Family of Love), Dee, Kelley, Paracelsus, Broughton, and others to make clear one of the contexts in which he wishes *The Alchemist* to be understood. At one level, to be sure, the play ridicules ordinary charlatans who may have had little intellectual background and no political or truly religious motivation. But the grandiose utopian dreams of Mammon, Ananias, or Tribulation were not the usual stock-in-trade of the uneducated village wizard or London con artist. They are characteristic of a far more sophisticated and historically significant occult tradition. One of Jonson's major strategies in *The Alchemist* is to reduce that tradition to the level of ordinary fraud. At the heart of the play is a pointed satirical attack upon those who claimed to base a program of radical reform upon the new forms of individualism which Jonson saw penetrating into much of Renaissance political, economic, and religious life. Many of the characters' enthusiasms and pretensions are variations upon what Jonson perceives as a new self-centeredness that threatens to overthrow all stable social order. He was quite aware that this new concept of the individual had received metaphysical justification in the occult tradition, and that is one of the reasons why he chose alchemy as the central, unifying symbol of the play. The quest for gold, which can symbolize either the soul's prelapsarian purity or fallen humanity's cupidity, was uniquely appropriate.

As we enter the opening scene of the play, we should keep in mind the distinction between Jonson's concept of self-knowledge and that of the magicians. For the occultists, self-knowledge is awareness of one's own divine origins, the consciousness of humankind's inherent divinity which may drive human beings, according to Ficino, to seek immediate union with God and to resist all external authorities. This awareness of the "immeasurable magnificence of our soul" can even lead to the desire for universal conquest: "Human beings wish no superior and no equal, and we will not suffer anything to remain excluded from our command."[8] For Jonson, however, this drive for ascendency is simply the consequence of prideful refusal to accept one's limits, a more traditional view and one diametrically opposed to that of the occultists. Self-awareness leads not to assertiveness, but to acceptance of one's position within a static hierarchy. It enables the individual to assume his or her place in the human community and to enjoy the benefits of an ordered society. And the retreat from genuine self-knowledge into a realm of self-flattering illusion lay, for Jonson, precisely in the direction which the occultists, like the Puritans, believed led to truth: the withdrawal into subjectivity.

The interrelated themes of self-knowledge, individual self-transformation, and radical reform are all introduced in the opening lines. We enter in the midst of a heated altercation in which Face and Subtle attack each other's false conceptions of self. When Face demands, "Who / Am I, my mungrill? Who am I?" Subtle retorts, "I'll tell you, / Since you know not your selfe" (I.i.12–14) and proceeds unmercifully to unmask him:

> SVBTLE. Yes. You were once (time's not long past) the good,
> Honest, plaine, liuery-three-pound-thrum; that kept
> Your masters worships house, here, in the *friers,*
> For the vacations— FACE. Will you be so lowd?
> SVBTLE. Since, by my meanes, translated suburb-Captayne.
>
> (I.i.15–19)

This is clearly not the description of himself which Face was asking for, and he seems momentarily crestfallen. Soon he retaliates, though, by reminding Subtle that he first found him a mere beggar, yet took him in, exchanged his ragged clothes for a grand conjurer's costume, and gave him a house in which to practice his con-game artistry. On the last point Face leaves himself vulnerable again, for Subtle reminds him that the house in which they are practicing is not Face's, but his master's. Face is not the great man he has disguised himself to be; he is merely a servant who has managed temporarily to turn his master's home into a haven for a fraudulent alchemist and a prostitute. Throughout the scene we are reminded that we are watching base characters—a dishonest servant, a cheap con man, and a whore—who have tried to rise above themselves through language and through mere clothing.[9] By assuming theatrical costumes and adopting an inflated jargon they have undergone illusory transformations to higher states of being.

The themes of acting and disguise as forms of false metamorphosis are connected with the central metaphor of "translation," or alchemical purification, each of the two con men claiming to have "made" or "sublimed" the other, to have raised him above his normal station in life. The cozeners do not take their role-playing literally, but it is nonetheless a means of acting out imaginatively a seemingly infinite potential. It is also, for them, a delightful means of deception, of turning the base passions of others into gold, of "cockering up their genius," as Volpone, another consummate role player, might put it. Subtle makes the connection between disguise, language, and alchemical transformation clear when he explains how he has taken Face "out of dung" and raised him above the status of mere butler:

> Thou vermine, haue I tane thee, out of dung,
> So poore, so wretched, when no liuing thing
> Would keepe thee companie, but a spider, or worse?
> Rais'd thee from broomes, and dust, and watring pots?
> *Sublim'd* thee, and *exalted* thee, and *fix'd* thee
> I' the *third region,* call'd our *state of grace?*
> Wrought thee to *spirit,* to *quintessence,* with paines
> Would twise haue won me the *philosophers worke?*
> Put thee in words, and fashion? made thee fit
> For more then ordinarie fellowships?
> Giu'n thee thy othes, thy quarrelling dimensions?
> Thy rules, to cheat at horse-race, cock-pit, cardes,
> Dice, or what euer gallant tincture, else?
>
> (I.i.64–76)

The speech moves to a climax in the sublime, symbolic language of the magus, then descends rapidly to bathos in the phrase "Put thee in words, and fashion," which reveals that Face's transformation of Subtle is no more magical than any other ordinary affectation. This movement from the sublime to the ridiculous is typical of many of the speeches of the play, and it characterizes the plot as well. Through disguises and inflated rhetoric the characters attempt to ascend in the social hierarchy, but because their transformations are superficial they are inevitably deflated again. The central action of the play is built upon the model of alchemical ascent and descent, the descending action consisting in part of a stripping away of disguise and a deflation of the dreams of transformation which the grandiose alchemical terms express. Much of the humor of *The Alchemist* derives from Jonson's skillful revelation of the comically ironic gap between the noble roles which the characters endeavor to create for themselves and the base realities to which they are inevitably forced to return.

Jonson's mockery of London con artists is thus a vehicle for another level of satire, one which deflates the illusion that human beings can transcend their limitations. Jonson was widely read in Neoplatonism and occult philosophy, from the *Hermetica* and the ancient Neoplatonists through Ficino, Cornelius Agrippa, and Paracelsus; his attitude toward the occult was informed in part by Martin Del Rio's careful and thoroughly orthodox assessment of Renaissance magic in his *Disqvisitionum magicarum libri sex*.[10] He is clearly aware that Renaissance occult philosophy had promoted the widespread use of metamorphosis and alchemical transformation as metaphors for the ability of human beings to act out their infinite potential, and in *The Alchemist* he skillfully manipulates these symbols so as to reduce to an absurdity the belief that humankind possesses potentially unlimited power. The play is filled with echoes of the occultists' optimistic praise of humanity, but by connecting the celebration of the human race as "a great miracle" with charlatans and gulls he renders it mock-heroic. The suggestion that the ridiculous Dapper is the nephew of the Queeen of Faeries is an absurd parody of Hermes Trismegistus' teaching that humankind is "akin to the race of daemons," and it may also serve as a mockery of Spenser's *Faerie Queene*. The central point of the play is the identification of *magia*, supposedly the highest of all arts and a symbol of human creative potential, with simple fraud. The characters transcend their places in the universal hierarchy only through superficial disguises and their own imagination; the entire operation is a cheat.

The theme of deceptive metamorphosis is closely related to Jonson's satire on Renaissance utopianism and millenarianism. As soon as the opening lines establish the emphasis upon false transformation and role-playing, Dol Common, as she endeavors to put an end to "ciuill warre" and "faction," begins to describe the relationship among the three con artists as a republic or a commonwealth. Their "venter *tripartite*" is a political arrangement in which Face plays the role of "Captain" or "Generall," Subtle that of "Soueraigne" (I.i.82, 135, 172). Although the use of terms such as "Sovereign" and "Royall Dol" (I.i.174) betrays the desire of the trio to see themselves as of exalted social status, Dol insistently reminds Face and Subtle that their "Republique" was initially founded in accordance with the egalitarian ideals that Renaissance thinkers often associated with the lost Golden Age.[11] As she scolds Face and Subtle for the self-centered bickering which threatens to tear their commonwealth apart, she asks what right either of them has to "claime a primacie, in the diuisions" and insist upon being "chiefe" when their "republique" was from the outset a "worke . . . begun out of equalitie? / . . . All things in common? / Without prioritie?" Resolve your differences, she says, "and cossen kindly / And heartily, and louingly, as you should" or she herself will become "factious" (I.i.131–40). Her appeals to their reason and their professed egalitarian principles fail, however, and she finally imposes order only by seizing Face's sword and threatening her partners with physical violence. The problem with the cozener's commonwealth, the play suggests, is that each presumably "equal" partner is always attempting to gain ascendancy over the others. The General attempts to take over the republic, and the Sovereign tries to keep him in awe. Throughout the play they call each other "rebels" and "traitors." Eventually Face and Subtle contribute to their own undoing not only by overreaching themselves, but also by competing with each other for Dol and for Dame Pliant. By describing the trio's relationship as a political venture and then offering us a comic display of their violent dissensions, Jonson endeavors to have his audience laugh themselves into the awareness that fallen creatures simply cannot do without traditional restraints. A society built upon radical individualism and free from law and social hierarchy becomes a chaos in which each person strives to bind all others to his or her own will. We cannot regain our prelapsarian innocence, as some of the reformers had erroneously claimed, and consequently there must be restraints—restraints which Jonson associates with traditional political and religious institutions—upon human pride, greed, and lust.

Once Jonson's satiric themes are established in the opening dialogue, they develop rapidly. The alchemical symbol comes to embrace all of the areas of Renaissance life into which Jonson saw the new individualism (or, in his view, self-centeredness) penetrating—capitalism, religious dissent, republicanism, Epicureanism. The gulls appear in quick succession, all hoping to be "sublimed" or "raised" by Subtle's art. Each of them expects magic to enable him to escape his limitations or to expand his powers. Dapper wishes to become a great gamester and a gallant, Drugger to be transformed from a modest shopkeeper into a great merchant prince, Kastrill to become a fashionable quarreler and rise above his class by marrying his sister to a knight. The Puritans want to become not merely dissenters, but a "faction, / And party in the realme" and perhaps even "temporall lords" themselves (III.ii. 25–26, 52). But all of these fall short of Epicure Mammon, who imagines that he will be lord of a new world, "the enuy of Princes, and the feare of States" (IV.i.114). His fancy carries him far beyond the boundaries of reality, convincing him that with the stone he will control time and change altogether. He echoes an actual claim of Paracelsus' when he tells Surly that he will "make an old man, of fourescore, a childe. / . . . Restore his yeeres, renew him, like an eagle, / To the fifth age; make him get sonnes, and daughters, / Yong giants" (II.i.53–57); and in act 4 he compares Subtle's art to that of Aesculapius, the mythical physician who restored Hippolytus to life and whom Zeus slew lest humankind become immortal. Mammon's lusts are not merely of heroic proportions (he says he will make himself "a back / With the *elixir,* that shall be as tough / As Hercules, to encounter fiftie a night," II.ii.37–39); they are infinite. When he woos Dol in act 4, his description of his boundless appetites culminates in the imagery of disguise and metamorphosis:

> Wee'll therefore goe with all, my girle, and liue
> In a free state; where we will eate our mullets,
> Sous'd in high-countrey wines, sup phesants egges,
> And haue our cockles, boild in siluer shells,
> Our shrimps to swim againe, as when they liu'd,
> In a rare butter, made of dolphins milke,
> Whose creame do's looke like opalls: and, with these
> Delicate meats, set our selues high for pleasure,
> And take vs downe againe, and then renew
> Our youth, and strength, with drinking the *elixir,*
> And so enioy a perpetuitie
> Of life, and lust. And, thou shalt ha' thy wardrobe,
> Richer then *Natures,* still, to change thy selfe,
> And vary oftener, for thy pride, then shee.
>   (IV.i.155–68)

Mammon is one of many characters in *The Alchemist* whose language carries them beyond the limitations of the actual world, and, as an expression of their own peculiar "humor," isolates them from the rest of humanity. He locks himself into a private world in which he imagines himself as a god. We often think of a Jonsonian "humor" as a mere affectation or idiosyncrasy, but in its broadest meaning it is a willingness to abandon the guidance of reason and give way to one's own selfish inclinations. It is allied with instinct, self-love, and inordinate passion.[12] In Jonson's more formidable characters it can become a dangerous monomania. In *The Alchemist* the idea of a "humor" as an all-consuming passion is linked to the theme of enthusiasm, or excessive religious zeal, to the concept of heroic or poetic *"furor,"* to the idea of being possessed by a spirit, and to the madness caused by inhaling the fumes of an alchemical laboratory. Since madness may be caused by syphilis, it is also associated with lustfulness, disease, and perhaps even with the plague which threatens London.

Tribulation makes some of these associations clear when he tells Ananias that even though Subtle's inhalation of fumes may stimulate excessive passion, "This heate of his may turne into a zeale" (III.i.31) and more firmly ally the alchemist with the Anabaptists. Subtle himself describes Mammon as "possessed" (I.iv.16), and the testimony of Mammon's own speeches bears out the accusation. In Mammon's case the peculiar excessive passion, or "humor," is luxuriousness, and the language which expresses it is highly imaginative poetry. Like the jargon of alchemy, Kastrill's quarreling tongue, or the Puritans' religious cant, Mammon's poetic raving serves to block communication rather than to promote it. Instead of employing language to reach out to others, Mammon uses it to project the self-enclosed world of his own fantasy, an unreal world in which he can escape mortality and indulge his seemingly boundless lusts.

Jonson's exposure of Mammon's delusions is an important aspect of his general attack upon the claims of occultists, prophetic poets, or any other enthusiasts to have special insights into the nature of reality. He reduces such claims to absurdity in part by destroying the idealistic theories of imagination on which they often rested. The occult philosophers, in particular, had claimed that the magus's imagination could become linked to the *Mens* and that therefore the individual could attain visionary powers. Since images supplied by the fantasy were connected with archetypal Ideas within the *Mens,* the magus could thus apprehend the meaning of the forms of created things. The aim of the alchemist—and, in a sense, of the poet-as-magician—is to bring physical things into greater conformity with the Ideas that govern them. To be able to do this one must have passed through various stages of enlightenment and have attained at least momentary union with God. The desire to thus purify oneself was described as a "divine" or "heroic" passion, and stages of the soul's ascent were referred to as the four *"furores."* [13]

It is largely on the ambivalence of these terms in Neoplatonic philosophy and magical theory that Jonson bases his attack on occultism and, by association, other forms of enthusiasm. He rejects the claim that the imagination can become linked with the mind's intuitive faculties and asserts the traditional view that it is allied with the senses and with physical desire. He agrees with those conservative Renaissance moral psychologists who believed that excessive emotion could distort the fantasy and cause it to form images which did not correspond to physical reality. If strict rational restraint were not exercised, objects of desire might deceptively appear more attractive than they really were. This could in turn stimulate even greater passions, so that the soul became trapped in a vicious cycle in which passion and imagination continually heightened each other. This cycle could continue until it produced actual madness, a complete divorce from reality.

Almost all of Jonson's characters in *The Alchemist* suffer to some extent from this kind of malady. Their idealized view of themselves and of the objects of their desire is not a true vision of a higher reality or of genuine human potential, but simply an illusion prompted by pride, lust, and a diseased imagination. The gulls come to Lovewit's house predisposed to certain delusions, and it remains for Face and Subtle only to intensify their ambitions somewhat and allow them to gull themselves. Obviously the con artists themselves never take occultism at face value; in Face and Subtle Jonson has drawn portraits of the enthusiast-as-charlatan, while in the Puritans and in Mammon he shows us the enthusiast-as-deluded-fool. But there is, nonetheless, a sense in which Face and Subtle do have an absurdly exaggerated faith in their own powers. As we saw in the opening dialogue, they use their disguises and trickery to inflate their self-esteem, and in the course of the action they become so elated by their own display of wit (see, e.g., the image of ascent at IV.v.96–100) that they imagine they can fool an infinite number of gulls simultaneously.[14] At the height of their success their plots explode, and they, much like the gulls, are forced to reassume their normal social identities. The effect of all of this is to render absurd the notion that one can rise above one's place through a "heroic frenzy" or "divine ambition"; the "frenzy" that grips Jonson's characters is not a "heroic passion," but an ordinary madness.

Jonson dramatizes the self-delusions of his characters by showing us that their imagination leads them to "see" things which do not in reality exist. Mammon and Surly make this theme explicit in the first scene of act 2:

> MAMMON. But when you see th' effects of the great med'cine!
> Of which one part proiected on a hundred
> Of *Mercurie,* or *Venus,* or the *Moone,*
> Shall turne it, to as many of the *Sunne;*
> Nay, to a thousand, so *ad infinitum:*
> You will beleeue me.   SVRLY. Yes, when I see't, I will.
> But, if my eyes doe cossen me so (and I
> Giuing 'hem no occasion) sure, I'll haue
> A whore, shall pisse 'hem out, next day.
>   (II.i.37–45)

Many of the characters in *The Alchemist* are unlike Surly in that they are quite willing to "see" things which are not there, or to see themselves and the fallen world as more exalted or divine than they really are. Among the most entertaining examples are Mammon and Dapper, who see Dol Common as a kind of goddess. When Face tells Dapper, "You are made, beleeue it, / If you can see her" (I.ii.154–55), what he really means is that if Dapper can delude himself into seeing Dol Common as the Faery Queene, he can be made a victim of Subtle's fraud. In act 5 when Dapper actually believes the woman whom the audience recognizes as the ridiculously disguised prostitute to be the mysterious Queen of Faeries, the absurdity of his delusion becomes physically visible. When Mammon courts Dol in act 4, he similarly deceives himself about her appearance. To begin with, he manages to see in her face the features of all the noble houses of Europe, while at the same time Face points out that "Her father was an Irish costar-monger" (IV.i.57). As Mammon continues, he begins to wax poetic and to worship Dol. We may grant, of course, that Dol might well possess a kind of earthy attractiveness; but the earthiness should be apparent enough to give the lie to Mammon's perception of "a certaine touch, or aire" in her face "That sparkles a diuinitie, beyond / An earthly beautie" (IV.i.64–66). What Mammon, like Dapper, sees in Dol is more a projection of his own desires and an indulgence of his own extravagant fantasy than it is a true perception of the mortal woman that stands before him. Jonson implies, I think, that something similar is true of all enthusiasts—

lovers, poets, or magicians—who seriously claim to see in the physical world or in mortal women a reflection of a suprasensual reality. His criticism of the tendency to idealize the world (as was often done in the romances to which he mockingly alludes throughout the play) or to project into poetry a subjective spiritual vision is what makes him, in large part, the father of English neoclassicism. Jonson's canon is diverse, and he displays a command of a variety of poetic styles; in *The Alchemist*, however, as in other major plays for the public theater, visionary dreams and highly idealized poetry appear in a context which reminds us of the need to accept the realities and limitations of the physical, mortal world.[15]

The retreat into subjectivity, as I have previously suggested, not only encloses the individual in a realm of illusion, but also gives him or her a false sense of self-sufficiency which leads to the resistance of discipline and social or legal constraints. The satire on enthusiasm in *The Alchemist* is thus quite intimately related to its exposure of millenary schemes as merely sophisticated forms of outlawry. Jonson saw the traditional hierarchical order as a system in which love and law work together as the motivating force and the structure of society, and he alludes to love or charity and to law throughout the play. In the new "Golden Age" of which the "venture tripartite" is a caricature, however, individuals dispense with laws and obey only the dictates of their own selfish humor. Subtle sums up the libertarian Golden Rule of the new era in a casual remark to Dapper, "Your humor must be law" (I.ii.70). Jonson also establishes the theme of lawlessness by having Face threaten to bring Subtle "within / The *statute* of *sorcerie, tricesimo tertio,* / Of Harry the eight" (I.i.111–13), and by frequently reminding us that alchemy is illegal. He develops the idea that the new age will be a time of anarchy and self-indulgence most fully, of course, in his characterization of Mammon, his greatest satiric portrait of those who proclaimed the Renaissance as a new era of freedom in which the individual's potential could be fully unleashed. The deluded knight describes the Golden Age he will make with the stone as a time in which all restraints normally placed upon humankind's powers (that is, its lusts) will be done away with. He is a mock savior who preaches as the good news of his new dispensation, "*be rich.* / This day, thou shalt haue ingots; and, to morrow, / Giue lords th' affront" (II.ii.6–8). Epicure Mammon is anarchy personified, yet he masquerades as a prophet of humanitarian reform. Jonson establishes this ambivalence in the speech in which Subtle introduces Mammon to us:

> This the day, I am to perfect for him
> The *magisterium*, our *great worke*, the *stone;*
> And yeeld it, made, into his hands: of which,
> He has, this month, talk'd, as he were possess'd.
> And, now, hee's dealing peeces on't, away.
> Me thinkes, I see him, entring ordinaries,
> Dispensing for the poxe; and plaguy-houses,
> Reaching his dose; walking *more-fields* for lepers;
> And offring citizens-wiues pomander-bracelets,
> As his preseruatiue, made of the *elixir;*
> Searching the spittle, to make old bawdes yong;
> And the high-waies, for beggars, to make rich:
> I see no end of his labours. He will make
> Nature asham'd, of her long sleepe: when art,
> Who's but a step-dame, shall doe more, then shee,
> In her best loue to man-kind, euer could.
> If his dreame last, hee'll turne the age, to gold.
>
> (I.iv.13–29)

The Alchemist as a whole builds up a grandiose, mock-heroic portrait of Mammon as an altruistic reformer whose magical power to reform the ills of our fallen condition surpasses those of Nature herself; at the same time the play continually deflates this illusion by revealing that what Mammon really wants is to destroy the social hierarchy and to serve his own lusts, to "Giue lords th' affront" and make old bawds young again.

Aspects of Mammon's personality are reflected in several of the less important characters, but the most significant parallels are between Mammon and the Anabaptists. The Puritans, too, have a dream of reforming society, of remaking the modern world in accordance with biblical Christianity. Tribulation calls their plan a "holy worke" (III.ii.16), identifying it as a type of alchemical *magnum opus* and thus bringing it within the scope of Jonson's central metaphor. They have hopes of "rooting out . . . th' *Antichristian Hierarchie*" (II.v.82–83) of the established church and destroying all traditions which conflict with their private revelations. The themes of enthusiasm or "possession" and of the contempt for law are naturally very highly developed in their case, particularly in Jonson's characterization of Ananias. In fact, in act 3 when Ananias's excessive zeal apparently threatens to alienate Subtle, Tribulation actually attempts to command the "spirit (of zeale, but trouble)" to silence within him (III.ii.84–85). Ananias is "a man, by reuelation, / That hath a competent knowledge of the truth" (III.ii.113–14), and he depends entirely upon his own conscience, not external authority, in deciding questions of ethics. When Tribulation raises the question of whether "casting of money" is lawful (III.ii.142–58), Ananias vehemently protests that the brethren are not subject to temporal authorities.

Emphasizing that the Anabaptists' appeal to conscience permits them simply to decide that counterfeiting for the benefit of the cause is lawful is one of several ways in which Jonson suggests that the Puritans' brand of radical individualism is, like all others in the play, self-serving. They claim they will use the stone as "medicine" for society's ills, but in reality they plan to use it to corrupt all forms of order. *"Aurum potabile"* is "The onely med'cine, for the ciuill *Magistrate,* / T'incline him to a feeling of the cause" (III.i.41–43), Tribulation tells Ananias, and Subtle explains at length how the stone can obtain political influence for the brethren. He makes it clear that to grant power to the Puritans would be to promote chaos:

> You cannot
> But raise you friends. Withall, to be of power
> To pay an armie, in the field, to buy
> The king of *France,* out of his realmes; or *Spaine,*
> Out of his *Indies:* What can you not doe,
> Against lords spirituall, or temporall,
> That shall oppone you? Tribulation. Verily, 'tis true.
> We may be temporall lords, our selues, I take it.
> Svbtle. You may be any thing.
> (III.ii.45–53)

Jonson deals with serious social and moral issues in his treatment of Tribulation, Ananias, and Mammon, and occasionally we may feel that the comedy of *The Alchemist* verges toward the dark satire of *Volpone.* The play maintains its comic mood, however, by reducing the stature of its characters. For example, while Mammon's language is as powerful as Volpone's, he himself is never really as formidable a threat to society: we can hardly forget that he is essentially a fool. When Lovewit appears at the end of the play, Mammon and practically all of the other characters, gulls and knaves alike, prove quite helpless. This ending, though, is controversial; many readers who quite properly look for social and moral purposes in a Jonsonian comedy are disturbed because Lovewit collaborates with Face in the final act and wins both Dame Pliant and the cozeners' accumulated pelf. The problem is compounded, it seems, by the fact that Face shares the benefits of Lovewit's success, and even Dol and Subtle escape any real punishment.[16]

These problems begin to resolve themselves if *The Alchemist* is seen not only as an attack upon greed and dishonesty, but also as a mockery of the dream that individuals can magically transform themselves or the world in accordance with their private desires. If Jonson's aim, as I have argued, is to mock his characters' pretensions and to expose their Faustian impulses as prideful self-delusions, then Lovewit quite logically appears on the scene as a man whose clear-sightedness, good nature, and common sense contrast sharply with the credulity and wild imagination of Mammon or the Puritans. Lovewit is not perfect, but at least he suffers from no delusions. He has wit enough to take advantage of what chance provides him, but he would hardly attempt to control Fortune herself, as Dapper wished to do. He is secure in his station as proper master of his household, and when Face tries to persuade him that the unusual occurrences at his home are "Illusions" or are caused by "some spirit o' the aire" (V.iii.66), he dismisses the notion rather quickly and demands the plain truth. He does not force Dol, Face, and Subtle, into prison, but he does at least require them to give up their costumes and assumed personalities. Face, in particular, reassumes his proper identity as Jeremy the Butler and is allowed by an indulgent master to remain in service. As Judd Arnold has pointed out, Lovewit is a self-possessed and intellectually superior aristocrat, a member of that class of persons whom Jonson most desired to please.[17] He is indeed not the sort of character one would create if one's purpose were to reform the knaves and gulls of the play, but if we realize that Jonson's aim is simply to deflate his characters' illusions, we can see that Lovewit suits his purposes admirably well.

Deflating illusions, of course, is Jonson's typical comic business. In *The Alchemist* he effectively turns his wit against those who had embarked upon a subjective quest for a vision of perfection and for the power to make that vision an objective reality. The accuracy of his analysis of portions of Renaissance history is startling. Only in recent years have we begun to understand fully some of the implications of Renaissance occult philosophy which Jonson perceived with exceptional clarity. The Renaissance occult tradition had promoted the belief that one could find within oneself a world of perfect form; the most noble of human creative activities was to embody that form in physical reality. The Hermetic alchemist thus believed that humankind could perfect the *species* of all created things, and as alchemy blends into millenarianism, we encounter the belief that the magus can bring back the Golden Age, the lost prelapsarian world. When Neoplatonism and occult philosophy exert an influence upon poetics, we find increasing emphasis upon the idealization of nature in the Golden World of art. In the next chapter we shall explore the intriguing question of why Jonson, who questions all of these things so masterfully in *The Alchemist,* himself drew upon Platonic traditions and the rhetoric of the Golden Age in some of the early plays and in his court masques. At present it may suffice to suggest that Jonson never permits us to take magic at face value, nor does he imagine that the virtuous and benevolent society which he presents in his masques and in some of his nondramatic poems is anything more than a distant ideal toward which mortal creatures must strive, but which we may never attain. At the heart of his mature and most satisfying works is the conviction that our own limitations and those of the world around us are something we must learn to live with.

Chapter Eight

Neoclassicism and the
Scientific Frame of Mind:
Ben Jonson and "Mystick Symboles"

Ben Jonson's neoclassicism is grounded firmly upon the moderate Christian humanism which was cultivated in England by scholars and educators such as Thomas More, Erasmus, Roger Ascham, John Cheke, and William Camden. Jonson's art is typical of this tradition in that he is concerned primarily with social and ethical problems, and his sense of civic duty and propriety is derived in large part from those Roman authors—especially Horace, Virgil, Seneca, and Cicero—whom he deeply revered. There is considerable justification for Frances Yates's use of the phrase "Latin humanism" to refer to this educational and literary movement, which is concerned with human beings as social creatures, not as magnificent demigods or magicians. While the Latin humanists were more concerned with the development of the individual personality than were most medieval thinkers, they avoided the radical assertion of humankind's dignity and freedom which we find in Pico, Ficino, and others whose works were more heavily influenced by Hermetic sources. The term "Latin" suggests this moderate stance and the pragmatic, social orientation of those who adopted a Ciceronian morality and who wrote satire as a significant part of their program of social reform. The term need not imply an ignorance of Greek, but the Plato reverenced by Thomas More and Ben Jonson was the social theorist of *The Republic,* not the poetic or religious metaphysician of *Phaedrus* or *Ion.*[1]

A significant aspect of Jonson's loyalty to the Roman spirit of Latin civic humanism is his conscious rejection of the subjective quest for selfhood or for a personal vision of reality as the primary subjects of art; he insists instead upon the artist's role as advisor to those in positions of political power. Although Jonson is loyal in many important ways to the ideals of the early Renaissance, his reaction against the more radical movements of the period leads him to become much more socially conservative than More or Erasmus had been. From the perspective of the early 1600s it was painfully obvious that the Golden Era predicted by Renaissance humanists from Erasmus through Spenser would never materialize, and Jonson is intensely aware of the limitations imposed upon reformers. From this later position in history Jonson could perceive, as Erasmus and More initially could not, that an insistence on the immediate relation between the individual soul and God would tend to destroy institutional authorities. Having witnessed revolutions led by religious and political radicals such as the Anabaptists of Münster, Jonson feared that if one fails to exercise conscious, rational control over one's personality, one may unleash powers which are bestial or Satanic, rather than those which are godlike. His conception of human nature is thus somewhat more pessimistic than that of many of the earlier humanists, and his insistence upon adherence to the limitations and restraints of rational law is more rigorous.[2] In his self-conscious adherence to authority and his fear of social innovation he is closer to Samuel Johnson or Jonathan Swift than to More or Erasmus. Yet in his court masques, Jonson himself employs the rhetoric of the return of the Golden Age, as well as methods of symbolism which *Discoveries, The Alchemist,* and other plays and poems seem to criticize quite severely. The exploration of this apparent paradox in Jonson's life and work is the subject of this chapter.

Discoveries, which consists largely of Jonson's private reflections and which consequently possesses a special status as a revelation of Jonson's own critical and moral assumptions, consistently emphasizes discipline, rational self-control, and acceptance of one's limitations in both aesthetics and social and political thought. Jonson repeatedly condemns excessive innovation, extravagant rhetoric, and the use of "far-fet" metaphors as a dangerous self-indulgence. "The true Artificer," he writes, "will not run away from nature, as hee were afraid of her; or depart from life, and the likenesse of Truth; but speake to the capacity of his hearers. And though his language differ from the vulgar somewhat; it shall not fly from all humanity, with the *Tamerlanes,* and *Tamer-Chams* of the late Age, which had nothing in them but the *scenicall* strutting, and furious vociferation, to warrant them to the ignorant gapers." [3] Although he affirms the importance of invention, Jonson makes clear that poets or dramatists who strive only for novelty may become so caught up in pride in their own wit that they fail to communicate—to "speake to the capacity of [their] hearers"—and he therefore subordinates the individual's imagination to custom and tradition in the selection of diction and figures of speech. Judging from *Discoveries,* Jonson has no tolerance whatsoever for ambiguity: "Many Writers perplexe their Readers, and Hearers with meere *Non-sense*. Their writings need sunshine. Pure and neat Language I love, yet plaine and customary. A barbarous Phrase hath often made mee out of love with a good sense; and doubtfull writing hath wrackt mee beyond my patience" (1868–73).

In his "Execration upon Vulcan," written after the catastrophic fire which destroyed his house and possessions in 1623, Jonson provides a catalogue of literary vices, and the chains of association in the poem are intriguing:

Had I wrote treason there, or heresie,
    Imposture, witchcraft, charmes, or blasphemie,
I had deserv'd, then, thy consuming lookes,
    Perhaps, to have beene burned with my bookes.
    ·   ·   ·   ·   ·   ·   ·   ·   ·   ·   ·
Had I compil'd from *Amadis de Gaule,*
    Th' *Esplandians, Arthurs, Palmerins,* and all
The learned Librarie of *Don Quixote;*
    And so some goodlier monster had begot:
Or spun out Riddles, and weav'd fiftie tomes
    Of *Logogriphes,* and curious *Palindromes,*
Or pomp'd for those hard trifles, *Anagrams,*
    ·   ·   ·   ·   ·   ·   ·   ·   ·
Thou then hadst had some colour for thy flames,
    On such my serious follies.
        (8:203–4, lines 15–18, 29–35, 40–41)

In a rather brief compass Jonson proceeds from political treason and religious heresy through the unnatural myths and monsters of romance to the obscure and trivial puzzles of literary riddles. Here, as in his critical prose and elsewhere, Jonson makes clear his strong preference for traditional morality and religion, realism, and clarity.

The purpose of figurative language in Jonson's work is typically to adorn and to clarify, and his criteria for evaluating poetry are thus diametrically opposed to those of the dominant schools of twentieth-century criticism. "The chiefe vertue of a style is perspicuitie," he insists in *Discoveries,* "and nothing so vitious in it, as to need an Interpreter" (1930–31).

This demand for clarity springs from Jonson's concern with the social function of poetry, but it is also a corollary of his belief that all human beings operate within the same limits of perception. A writer who uses complex, symbolic language may claim that he has access to a sphere of knowledge higher than that perceived by ordinary mortals; Jonson, however, frequently dismisses such claims as self-delusions or as conscious attempts to deceive one's audience. He assumes that cryptic or highly ambiguous language is pretentious, inept, and often meaningless. The assumption behind most of his critical pronouncements is that truth is that which is clear, universal, and capable of being perceived by human reason, not that which is secret or obscure, clothed in mystic symbols, or perceived by a lone, inspired prophet or seer. While he believes that poetry teaches religion as well as morality, he trusts in the traditions of established churches, rather than personal visions, as the reliable source of religious wisdom, a view which correlates with his insistence that the language of the poet must be that which lies within the public domain.

In *The Alchemist,* as I mentioned briefly in the previous chapter, Jonson links highly imaginative, symbolic forms of poetry with the mystical characters and obscure language used by occult philosophers. Subtle makes this connection explicit by describing both alchemy and poetry as "arts" in which the initiates disguise their secret knowledge in "mystick symboles" and "perplexed allegories" (II.iii.198–207). When Jonson describes Subtle's construction of an absurd magical sign for Drugger's shop, he identifies the use of such esoteric symbols with fraud, as well as with the prideful quest for mere novelty:

> FACE. What say you to his *constellation,* Doctor?
> The *Ballance?* SVBTLE. No, that way is stale, and common.
> A townes-man, borne in *Taurus,* giues the bull;
> Or the bulls-head: In *Aries,* the ram.

A poore deuice. No, I will haue his name
Form'd in some mystick character; whose *radii,*
Striking the senses of the passers by,
Shall, by a vertuall influence, breed affections,
That may result vpon the partie ownes it:
As thus— FACE. NAB!   SVBTLE. He first shall haue a bell,
   that's ABEL;
And, by it, standing one, whose name is DEE,
In a rugg gowne; there's *D.* and *Rug,* that's DRVG:
And right anenst him, a Dog snarling *Er;*
There's DRVGGER, ABEL DRVGGER. That's his signe.
And here's now *mysterie,* and *hieroglyphick!*
FACE. ABEL, thou art made.
              (II.vi.10–25)

Drugger actually believes that Subtle's esoteric knowledge enables him to create a symbol with genuine magical power, and he
is awestruck. In reality, Subtle is cozening poor Nab, and the "hieroglyphick" he constructs is a meaningless absurdity. In the preface to
The Alchemist, Jonson connects this kind of cozening with contemporary poetry: "For thou wert neuer more fair in the way to be
cos'ned (then in this Age) in *Poetry,* especially in Playes" (4–5). The
action of some plays is so fantastic, he continues, as "to runne away
from Nature" (7), and presumably we are to infer that we shall be
cozened if we accept such action as a reflection of reality. Although
the preface focuses primarily upon "the Concupiscence of Daunces,
and Antickes" (6) and other breaches of decorum, *The Alchemist* itself
stresses the similarity between certain kinds of poetry and occultism,
suggesting that obscurely symbolic or visionary poetry can cozen us
just as Subtle has cozened Drugger. A poet who attempts to become
an inspired magus or a visionary leads us not to a higher sphere of
truth, but into a realm of illusion. Truth for Jonson is fidelity to
nature, and nature is the world of observable fact: citing Aristotle as
his authority, Jonson defines a poet as "a Maker, or a fainer: His Art,
an Art of imitation, or faining; expressing the life of man in fit measure, numbers, and harmony" (*Discoveries,* 2348–50). In most of Jonson's works, his symbols are not shadows of a suprasensual reality,
but metaphors or emblems whose meaning can be explicated ration-
ally. As we saw in the discussion of Epicure Mammon as visionary

poet in Chapter 7, Jonson seems to regard the belief that the poet can see beyond physical nature as a mere humor. Like Mammon's perception of "a diuinitie, beyond / An earthly beautie" (IV.i.65–66) in Dol, it is an illusion prompted by pride and created by a diseased imagination.

In his court masques, Jonson displays masterful control over methods of symbolism and uses of mythology and romance which he criticizes quite rigorously in his other works. In *The Golden Age Restored, The Fortunate Isles and their Union,* and elsewhere, Jonson praises the apparent power of King James to transform the present age into an Era of Gold, promoting peace and justice and embodying ideal virtues which are founded upon true religion and humanistic learning. Graham Parry has argued that Jonson took great pleasure in his ability to devise symbols based heavily upon traditional iconography and sufficiently complex to appeal to a monarch who took pride in his own intellect and erudition. Jonson's increasing use of emblematic method was initiated by his design for the triumphal arches through which the king passed during his progress through London in 1604: the elaborate symbolism includes personifications of Theosophia, or Divine Wisdom; Agrypnia, or Vigilance; Agape, or Loving Affection; and many other attributes of the British monarchy and its empire. Jonson's published commentaries on the arches, as well as the speeches he had written for the occasion, reveal the extent to which he had drawn upon his immense learning as he developed an elaborate iconology which he further employed in his subsequent court masques. In *Hymenaei,* for example, Jonson utilizes Juno as a mystical symbol of the power of love and reason to effect union and harmony, and in one of his marginal glosses on the masque he tells us that he has adopted from Macrobius the allegorical interpretation of Zeus's golden chain as the emanation of the world soul from the Divine Mind; Jonson thus draws upon a theory of cosmic harmony quite similar to that of Pico and Ficino. Douglas Brooks-Davies has argued for a level of allegory which goes beyond that which is explained in Jonson's own glosses: he believes that the figure of Mercury in Jonson's court masques is an esoteric symbol of the king as a royal messenger of the gods whose magical power to reform the world is similar to that of Hermes Trismegistus.[4] One might conclude that Jonson possesses the singular distinction of having composed the most effective satire against magic and esoteric symbolism in English literature and, almost simultaneously, having developed an exquisitely sophisticated use of occult philosophy and mystical symbols when they suited his own purposes.

One of the simplest explanations of Jonson's apparent self-contradiction is that his desire to adapt himself to the tastes of the court, especially those of the royal family itself, led him to abandon the principles which he enunciated in *Discoveries* and in many of his other works. One might well argue that Jonson accused his rivals and those whom he wished to regard as his social inferiors as misguided visionaries, while he himself practiced whatever his audience demanded. To see Jonson's life and work as embodying this degree of disingenuousness, however, is a serious distortion. There are events in Jonson's life which suggest that he did not fear to speak his mind to a nobleman, as he reportedly did when he criticized the Lord Salisbury's hospitality (*Ben Jonson*, 1:141), or when he proclaims himself in the dedication of *Cynthia's Revels* to be the "seruant, but not slaue" (4:33) of the court itself. Indeed, the entire dedication of *Cynthia's Revels,* far from being an act of flattery, is an admonition to the court to live up to the ideals which the poet will reveal. As Stephen Orgel has demonstrated in *The Jonsonian Masque,* Jonson strove with increasing success to incorporate material imposed by the expectations of his courtly audience into an art form which was genuinely his own. Among the most interesting facets of his courtly spectacles are those through which Jonson hints that the poetic ideals of the masque are not accomplished facts upon which the king and his court may pride themselves, but distant goals which an imperfect society must continually struggle to attain. We find Jonson struggling to distinguish properly between genuine and false reformers, true and false art, proper and improper symbolism, and his masques often reveal his ambivalent attitude toward the symbolism and conventions of the genre.[5] Evidently he feared that his own symbolic method—dictated in part by genre, occasion, and his royal audience—might be confounded with mere obscurantism.

Jonson introduces satirical references to Rosicrucians, alchemists, or other occult philosophers into his masques at moments when he is particularly anxious to distinguish between his own art and the pretenses of those who take seriously the claims of the Hermetic tradition. While Jonson himself may utilize symbols drawn from Platonic philosophy, he reminds us that he is creating a fiction;

in contrast, the alchemists in *Mercury Vindicated from the Alchemists at Court* and the Rosicrucians of *The Fortunate Isles and their Union* are engaged in deception, endeavoring, in a dangerous departure from nature, to delude rather than to enlighten their audiences. The occultist and the false poet both attempt to obscure their intellectual emptiness with false "hieroglyphicks," which may be distinguished from genuine symbols in that they mean nothing. In *Mercury Vindicated,* Mercury himself ridicules the claims of the alchemists who have promised social advancement through magic:

> A poore *Page* o' the Larder, they haue made obstinately beleeue, he shalbe *Phisician* for the Houshold, next Summer: they will giue him a quantity of the quintessence, shall serue him to cure kibes, or the mormall o' the shinne. . . . A child o' the *Scullery* steales all their coales for 'hem too, and he is bid sleepe secure, hee shall finde a corner o' the *Philosophers* stone for 't, vnder his bolster. . . . And so the Blacke guard are pleased with a toy. (72–87)[6]

Jonson does not, however, confine his satire to deflating the ambitions of the working classes. Mercury continues to mock the even more incredible dreams of the court:

> But these are petty Engagements, and (as I saide) below the staires; Marry aboue here, Perpetuity of beauty, (doe you heare, Ladies) health, Riches, Honours, a matter of Immortality is nothing. They will calcine you a graue matron (as it might bee a mother o' the maides) and spring vp a yong virgin, out of her ashes, as fresh as a *Phoenix:* Lay you an old Courtier o' the coales like a sausedge, or a bloat-herring, and after they ha' broil'd him enough, blow a soule into him with a paire of bellowes, till hee start vp into his galliard, that was made when *Monsieur* was here. They professe familiarly to melt down all the old sinners o' the suburbes once in halfe a yeere, into fresh gamesters againe. Get all the crack'd maiden-heads, and cast 'hem into new Ingots, halfe the wenches o' the towne are *Alchymie.* (90–104)

Professor Brooks-Davies is correct to point out that the alchemists and Rosicrucians of the masques are purveyors of a false, unauthorized revelation, and his discussion of Mercury as the bearer of genuine heavenly knowledge is in many ways illuminating. But I would emphasize that at the moment in the masque when Mercury turns to the king, he is rejecting a belief in literal magic and relying instead upon the knowledge channeled through traditional religious and political institutions. The moment of transformation which Jonson made central to the masque form is a literary symbol for the power of reason, education, and self-discipline, aided by divine grace, to effect moral reform in both the individual and society. As Stephen Orgel has observed, "When magic appears in the masques, it is regularly counteracted not by an alternative sorcery, black magic defeated by white magic, but by the clear voice of reason, constancy, heroism" (*Illusion*, 56). The characters who are associated with the royal family and with virtuous noblemen do not perform magical ceremonies, a genuine alchemy, or exorcism; as Jonson reminds us in *Pleasure Reconciled to Virtue*, their virtue derives from the cultivation of reason, symbolized by the "*hill* of *knowledge*" (204) in which the courtiers of the masque have received their "*roial education*" (223). Daedalus, the true artist who "doth in sacred harmony comprize his precepts" (245–46) is the composer of the final songs and designer of the emblematic dances which "*figure out*" (257), or illustrate, a lesson in moderation, the Aristotelian golden mean. Unlike the unnatural and monstrous antimasque, the final dances are pleasurable, yet orderly, like a well-governed life; one cannot tell "*which lines are Pleasures, and which not*" (256). The dancers' controlled and "numerous" movements are visual symbols of the reasonable life, in which the emotions are not denied but are controlled by reason. Jonson insists, perhaps somewhat anxiously, that an apt member of the audience will be enlightened:

> Then, as all actions of mankind
> are but a Laborinth, or maze,
> so let your Daunces be entwin'd,
> yet not perplex men, unto gaze.
> But measur'd, and so numerous too,
> as men may read each act you doo.
> (261–66)

Using such an emblem to communicate moral and religious truths is quite distinct from the enthusiast's pompous use of esoteric style in order to pretend to possess profound knowledge and to conceal the actual emptiness of one's head—or, to use the metaphor of *The Alchemist* and earlier works, the fact that the light of the soul is obscured by the vapors of one's humor.[7]

Jonson's own annotations for the printed editions of the masques frequently reveal his anxious efforts to assure the reader— and perhaps himself—that he can utilize allegorical symbols without being guilty of obscurity. The clearest example is *Hymenaei,* which Jonson prefaces with the assertion that the soul of a masque is not the ephemeral spectacle, but the meaning, which must be based on sound learning and "should always lay hold on more remou'd *mysteries*" (18–19). The soul of *Hymenaei,* a wedding masque, is the mysterious power of love and reason to effect harmonious union on all levels of creation: in marriage, in the commonwealth, and in the cosmos. Jonson asserts that those who have criticized his use of philosophy in the masque possess "little, or (let me not wrong 'hem) no braine at all" (22), and in the annotation to line 112, explaining the correspondences between the microcosm and the body politic, he excuses himself for expounding what should be obvious: "And, for the *Allegorie,* though here it be very cleare, and such as might well escape a candle, yet because there are some, must complaine of darknesse, that haue but thicke eyes, I am contented to hold them this Light." Despite his use of terms such as "mystery" and "mystical" (gloss to line 40, evidently meaning "allegorical"), Jonson planned from the outset to make sure that the proper interpretation of the masque was communicated, for he provides a character whose name is "Reason" to act as explicator. Reason provides order within the masque and simultaneously explains the significance of symbolic movements and costumes, emphasizing the concepts of universal order and harmony which inform both the masque itself and the marriage ceremony. Apparently the commentary of Reason was deemed by some spectators to be inadequate, and, like an impatient scholar endeavoring to make clear to a dull class the glories of a masterpiece of philosophical literature, Jonson subsequently added the marginal notes, including, in the note to line 320, a long quotation from Macrobius explaining that Zeus's golden chain symbolizes the unity of all levels of creation as they descend from, and are illuminated by, the Divine Mind. For a man who insisted that we must not "draw out our *Allegory* too long, lest either wee make our selves obscure, or fall into affectation, which is childish" (*Discoveries,* 2019–21), and who declared that the chief vice of style was to require an interpreter, the need to provide the glosses apparently provoked some ambivalence—as well as anger. At the same time, Jonson insists that his glosses only emphasize what should have been obvious to an intelligent, rational observer. Such insistence is consistent with Jonson's affirmation of Reason—not the *Mens* or intuition—as the highest of human faculties. Although he draws on some of the same aspects of the Platonic tradition as did Pico, Ficino, Agrippa, Bruno, and Dee, Jonson omits all reference to poetic "frenzy," intuition, or prophetic imagination, insisting repeatedly that Reason and authority are the proper guides. Despite his use of Neoplatonism in *Hymenaei*, Jonson's commentary reveals that his symbolism is intended not as a shadow of a mystery which could not be understood in rational terms, but rather as an analogy which may be interpreted with perfect clarity.

Despite all of these distinctions and explanations, Jonson never feels entirely at ease with mythological symbolism and fantasy, and his quarrels with Inigo Jones, whom he accused of sacrificing meaning to appearances, were no doubt intensified by his discomfort in being required by social and economic circumstances to use a genre whose conventions in some ways violated the standards enunciated in detail in *Discoveries*, in *The Alchemist*, and in many of his nondramatic poems.[8] Jonson's struggle to maintain his personal and artistic integrity was genuine, and with regard to his apparent idealization of the king as well as his use of myth and symbolism, it is misleading to recognize only the element of self-interest in his endeavor to fulfill the role of court poet. Throughout the Renaissance, humanists had professed that one could influence a monarch most effectively not by confronting that ruler with direct criticism, but by creating an image to which one wished the ruler to conform, and Jonson often asserts his allegiance to this tradition.[9] In his dedicatory epistle to his *Epigrams*, entitled "To the Great Example of Honor and Vertue, the Most Noble William, Earle of Pembroke, Lord Chamberlayne," Jonson reveals candidly his awareness that his depiction of the virtue of historical persons was idealized: "If I haue praysed, unfortunately, any one, that doth not deserue; or, if all answere not, in all numbers, the pictures I have made of them: I hope it will be forgiuen me, that they are no ill pieces, though they be not like the persons" (8:26). Jonson's fear of becoming a flatterer is revealed with even greater clarity in the poem "To My Muse," which begins with a rejection of the Muse who had inspired him to commit "most fierce idolatrie" by praising a "worthlesse lord." The Muse had not only betrayed the poet by leading him into praising an unworthy subject, the speaker complains, but had even denied him his material reward, leaving him in the same poverty in which he began. At the very conclusion of the poem, however, after he has expressed his self-condemnation in the most severe terms, Jonson reverses his line of argument, consoling himself with the traditional assertion that the poetry of praise may serve as a scourge as well as a compliment:

> Shee [his new Muse] shall instruct my after-thoughts to write
>   Things manly, and not smelling parasite.
> But I repent me: Stay. Who e're is rais'd,
> For worth he has not, He is tax'd, not prais'd.
>   (8:48, lines 13–16)

In the most successful of his masques, Jonson's apparent idealization of the English monarchy and its court is accompanied by hints that the ideal is a fiction. A prominent example is *Pleasure Reconciled to Virtue,* which concludes with a song underscoring the transitory nature of the masque itself and reminding us that virtue must be continually reestablished through hard labor:

> You must returne unto the Hill,
>   and there aduance
> with labour, and inhabit still
>   that height, and crowne,
> from whence you euer may looke downe
>   upon triumphed Chaunce.
> She, she it is, in darknes shines.
>   'tis she that still hir-self refines,
>   by hir owne light, to euerie eye,
> more seene, more knowne, when Vice stands by.
>   And though a stranger here on earth,
>   in heauen she hath hir right of birth.
>   (333–44)

If the imagery of darkness is insufficient to remind us that the ideal realm of the masque is not fully embodied in the actual world, the final two lines leave no doubt that Jonson perceives virtue to be a "stranger" in the mortal realm. Even at the court of James, perfect virtue is not an accomplished fact, and the purpose of the masque is not merely to congratulate the king and his court, but to inspire them to continued labor.

In *The Fortunate Isles,* Jonson's most sustained satire on occult philosophy in the masques, Merefool, a "Melancholique Student" (18) who resembles the gulls of *The Alchemist,* is mocked for falling prey to two illusions. First, he believes that the Rosicrucians have the power to provide a familiar spirit which can make him "Principall Secretarie to the Starres," permitting him to "Know all their signatures, and combinations" (136–37) and attain the power to command the elements. Secondly, he fails to understand that the masque in which he himself appears as a character is a fiction. The spirit Jophiel—having made excuses for failing to produce the spirits of Hermes Trismegistus, Zoroaster, Iamblichus, Porphyry, Proclus, or Plato—finally presents two sturdy English satirists, Henry Scogan and John Skelton. Having been regaled by the two poets' verses, Merefool expresses profound gratitude and naive admiration:

> MERE-FOOLE
> What! are they vanish'd! where is skipping *Skelton?*
> Or morall *Scogan?* I doe like their shew
> And would haue thankt 'hem, being the first grace
> The Company of the *Rosie-Crosse* hath done me.
> IOPHIEL
> The company o' the *Rosie-crosse!* you wigion,
> The company of *Players.* Go, you are,
> And wilbe stil your selfe, a *Mere-foole;*
>
> .   .   .   .
>
> See, who has guld you.
> (425–33, 435)

These lines have the effect of identifying as fiction not only the preceding segment of the masque but also the subsequent vision of England as a nation in which

> There is no sicknes, nor no old age knowne
> To man, nor any greife that he dares owne.
> There is no hunger there, nor enuy of state.

Nor least ambition in the *Magistrate*.
But all are euen-harted, open, free,
And what one is, another striues to be.
$$(508–13)$$

These lines are delivered by Proteus, the archetypal shape-shifter, who embodies the spirit of acting and theatrical illusion. The audience is "gulled," however, only if it is so naive as to imagine with Merefool that the vision is to be taken literally. In the context of this theatrically self-conscious masque, the final chorus, addressed to King James, is not a recognition of existing perfection, but a fervent entreaty, or perhaps a prayer:

And may thy subiects hearts be all one flame,
Whilst thou dost keepe the earth in firme estate,
And 'mongst the winds, do'st suffer no debate,
But both at Sea, and Land, our powers increase,
With health, and all the golden gifts of Peace.
$$(643–47)$$

Even those works which make us intensely aware of ideals of perfection sustain our interest through devices which call attention to the gap between poetic ideals and social realities. This intriguing compound of idealism and satiric realism, the struggle to conform to the conventions of the poetry of praise while retaining a degree of objectivity, and the use of highly imaginative, symbolic poetry in a context which underscores the symbol's fictional, illusory quality are all characteristic of the artist who provides the transition between the literary art of the Elizabethan Renaissance and the more re-strained, conservative, and socially cautious movement which we now term English neoclassicism. We can understand Jonson's desire for objectivity and his modulation of Renaissance ideals as a corollary of the reaction against subjectivity which eventually destroyed the fervent ideals of the magicians and contributed to Baconian science. Too often we assume that politically conservative thinkers of the early seventeenth century always regarded the new science as prideful meddling into the secrets of God's creation. In an important article on seventeenth- and eighteenth-century intellectual history, however, Donald Greene has pointed out that the new insistence on the need for empirical verification of the individual's observation of nature frequently came to be considered a healthy—and Christian—skepticism with regard to the powers of the human mind.[10] Bacon and his followers believed that the old scientists—both the Scholastics and the magicians—depended too much upon individual genius. The belief that the human mind contained innate Ideas which were keys to ultimate truth about the structure of the cosmos was specifically singled out by the new scientists as a prideful dependence upon the powers of the individual intellect. In Abraham Cowley's ode "To the Royal Society," for example, we find this attitude, anticipated in many ways by Jonson, in highly developed form. Referring to the lingering desire to retain the methods of the old scientists, Cowley writes:

> Yet still, methinks, we fain would be
> Catching at the Forbidden Tree;
> We would be like the Deitie,
> When Truth and Falsehood, Good and Evil, we
> Without the Sences aid within our selves would see;
> For 'tis God only who can find
> All Nature in his Mind.[11]

Many of the old scientists (as well as several of the earlier founders of the new science, such as Kepler) believed that because the Creator had revealed Himself in the symbolic forms of the natural world, the knowledge of nature was inseparable from the knowledge of God. The exploration of nature served to awaken the archetypal Ideas within the human mind, and these in turn made it possible for us to see more clearly the significant forms and structures behind physical reality. Such knowledge was the common province of the scientist (or magician), the poet, the sculptor, the philosopher, or the enlightened statesman—in other words, of all artists. For Bacon, however, this faith in the powers of the individual mind was hubris. In Baconian science there are no innate ideas, and consequently knowledge tends to become fragmented. The symbolic approach to the interpretation of nature is no longer viable, and there is an increasing tendency to separate religion from natural philosophy. Although Bacon still suggests that the scientist may be moved to admire the rational design of the cosmos, he does not feel intensely God's immediate presence in the natural world. He accepts the Christian revelation, but he is suspicious of intensely emotional religious feeling, and like Jonson, he relies upon traditional institutions, rather than subjective illumination, as the proper guide in matters of religious doctrine. He sees in nature no vestiges of the divine presence, no glimpses of an immanent spirit. Rather, he attributes the perception of such things to the individual's deceptive imagination, which may be influenced by fear or desire. "Astrology, Natural Magic, and Alchemy," Bacon writes in *The Advancement of Learning* (1605), "have had better intelligence and confederacy with the imagination of man than with his reason." These arts have noble purposes, but in practice they are "full of error and vanity; which the great professors themselves have sought to veil over and conceal by enigmatical writings, and referring themselves to auricular traditions, and such other devices to save the credit of impostures."[12]

Bacon agrees with Jonson that those who practice such imposture are likely to be credulous and gullible themselves: their pride contributes simultaneously to "delight in deceiving, and aptness to be deceived; imposture and credulity; which, although they appear to be of a diverse nature, the one seeming to proceed of cunning, and the other of simplicity, yet certainly they do for the most part concur." As those who are busily inquisitive also tend to be garrulous, "so upon the like reason a credulous man is a deceiver: as we see it in fame, that he that will easily believe rumours will as easily augment rumours and add somewhat to them of his own" (3:287–88). Obscurity of style, in Jonson's plays and literary theory as in Bacon's account of the errors of traditional learning, is quite frequently the attempt of confused, ignorant, and pretentious authors to conceal their own intellectual poverty from both themselves and their audiences.

Jonson's enthusiasts in *The Alchemist* and in other works are the victims of Bacon's Idols of the Mind, particularly the Idol of the Tribe: they fail to acknowledge the limitations imposed upon their powers of intellect and perception by flaws inherent in human nature itself. Jonson's praise of Bacon's wisdom, virtue, and style in *Discoveries*, culminating with the observation that Bacon was "one of the greatest men, and most worthy of admiration, that had beene in many Ages" (941–43), underscores the two authors' deeply shared values. I would emphasize, however, not that Jonson was influenced by Bacon, but rather that the two men shared the desire to moderate, qualify, or restrain the heroic or poetic enthusiasms of the Elizabethan era. Jonson was in some respects more conservative than Bacon, especially with regard to the possibility of social progress and the amelioration of our fallen condition. But Jonson's conception of human nature is, nonetheless, much closer to Bacon's than to that of the magicians, for in Bacon's view progress would eventually result not from the work of a lone, inspired genius, but through the cooperative efforts of a vast community of scientists, all of whom would continually strive to correct one another's errors of judgment and perception.

Jonson is forever devising ingenious artistic strategies for criticizing or containing those passions, fears, and delights which lay deep within his own nature. What we know of Jonson's life confirms William Drummond's judgment that he was "passionately kynde and angry," as well as "oppressed with fantasie, which hath ever mastered his reason" (1:151). Frequently quoted is Jonson's revelation to Drummond that he had spent an entire night watching his great toe, about which he had seen Tartars and Turks, Romans and Carthaginians, fighting in his imagination (1:141); much more moving is Jonson's account of having been moved to fearful prayer by a prophetic vision which presaged the death of his eldest son by the plague. The boy appeared, Jonson told Drummond, "of a Manlie shape & of that Grouth that he thinks he shall be at the resurrection" (1:140). For a student of *The Alchemist,* the following anecdote, also recorded in Drummond's record of his conversations with Jonson, is even more directly pertinent: "He can set Horoscopes, but trusts not jn them, he with ye consent of a friend Cousened a lady, with whom he had made ane apointment to meet ane old Astrologer jn the suburbs, which she Keeped & it was himself disguysed jn a Longe Gowne & a whyte beard" (1:141). Jonson's delight in Subtle and Face's extravagant wit and theatrical talent is obviously genuine; but so is the rational and moral framework through which Jonson consciously sought to contain—perhaps to exorcise—his own ambition and imagination.

In the changing currents of seventeenth-century thought occult philosophy was a key issue, and Jonson's response to the occult tradition and to language which claims to embody mystical insights points clearly toward the solutions to Renaissance problems which subsequent writers will find sensible. His successors in the neoclassical tradition, seeking to restrain uncontrolled individualism, will reject all forms of Platonism and ally themselves with the new Baconian science, which imposes strict limits upon the individual's powers of cognition even as it promises new knowledge through discipline and cooperative effort. As L. A. Beaurline has suggested, Jonson's tendency to set strict limits to works of art such as *The Alchemist* and to exhaust all possibilities within those self-imposed limitations is parallel to the new scientific frame of mind which delimits its fields of inquiry.[13] I would add, however, that Jonson also endeavored to restrict the very *kinds* of subjects with which he, as an artist, can deal, striving to treat only those subjects which the conscious, rational intellect can fully control. Ben Jonson's affirmation of rationality and discipline, his ridicule of magical, Puritan, or poetic enthusiasm, and his tendency to limit his own art to the treatment of the practical affairs of social and political life are what make him the acknowledged founder of a new literary movement. Like Pope, Swift, or Samuel Johnson in the next century, all of whom satirized occultism at some point in their major works, Jonson struggles to contain his sympathy for the romantic longing for the absolute which leaves us wavering between exultation and despair and which characterizes so much of Renaissance literature. In his major works he suggests that the subjective quest for esoteric knowledge is self-centered escapism, and he dramatizes as mere jest the belief that we can totally reform the world. In fact he does not even regard the disillusionment of the romanticist as tragic—that would bring *The Alchemist* or *The Fortunate Isles* quite close to *Dr. Faustus*—but as merely comical. In the speeches of Epicure Mammon, as well as those of other characters, Jonson demonstrates his command of the "mighty line" which expresses the most intense aspirations of the Renaissance, but he almost always deflates the hyperbolic speech with a jest which leaves but little doubt that Jonson willingly reduces his vision of human stature. His art is not often as captivating as that of Marlowe or Shakespeare, because it is not meant to be. Its value is of another order. Its purpose is to convince us that what is genuinely important is not an imaginary vision of humankind's infinite potential or the secrets of another world, but the concrete possibilities of the here and now.

Chapter Nine

Magic as Love and Faith:
Shakespeare's *The Tempest*

In his Jacobean tragedies Shakespeare calls into question the idealistic conception of humanity which had been developed by Renaissance humanists and carried to its logical extreme in the occult tradition. Hamlet's discovery of lust and treachery begets his profound disillusionment with human nature, and he tells Ophelia that he himself, as a representative of humankind, is "proud, revengeful, ambitious, with more offenses at my beck than I have thoughts to put them in, imagination to give them shape, or time to act them in. What should such fellows as I do crawling between earth and heaven?" he continues, "We are arrant knaves, believe none of us" (III.i.126–29).[1] He tells her to enter a nunnery, to abandon the world and the flesh which Hamlet sees as thoroughly corrupted. In his earlier speech to Rosencrantz and Guildenstern Hamlet juxtaposes the eloquent praise of humanity which we find in earlier Renaissance thinkers such as Pico and Ficino with his own intense awareness of human mortality and corruption: "What [a] piece of work is a man, how noble in reason, how infinite in faculties, in form and moving, how express and admirable in action, how like an angel in apprehension, how like a god! the beauty of the world; the paragon of animals; and yet to me what is this quintessence of dust? Man delights not me—nor women neither, though by your smiling you seem to say so" (II.ii.303–10).

King Lear, Troilus and Cressida, and other plays of the early 1600s dramatize the discrepancy between the noble ideals of Renaissance philosophers and the actual world in which we live. In theory, human beings are rational creatures who can control their own souls and the world around them. They are capable of being motivated by love, faith, and honor. In reality, these plays at times seem to imply, we are subject to bestial lust and selfish ambition, and the world we create in attempting to fulfill our desires is one of anarchy. Although it is difficult to say precisely what answers the tragedies may or may not offer to the questions raised within them, it is readily apparent that many Shakespearean plays of the first decade of the seventeenth century center upon a crisis of faith.

A loss of faith in humanity in Shakespeare is often paralleled by a loss of faith in Providence and by an inability to love. Human nature at times threatens to become merely a part of an amoral realm of nature which is ruled by totally selfish appetites. Perhaps the most powerful, desperate statements and questions occur in *King Lear:*

> As flies to wanton boys are we to th' gods,
> They kill us for their sport.
> (IV.i.36–37)

> If that the Heavens do not their visible spirits
> Send quickly down to tame [these] vild offenses,
> It will come,
> Humanity must perforce prey on itself,
> Like monsters of the deep.
> (IV.ii.46–50)

The catastrophe of *Othello* is caused by the protagonist's loss of faith in Desdemona and, by implication, in the values with which she is associated. One recalls the magnificently suggestive lines,

> Perdition catch my soul
> But I do love thee! and when I love thee not,
> Chaos is come again.
> (III.iii.90–92)

In the romances Shakespeare reaffirms the faith in humanity which he permits us to question in the tragedies.[2] The final plays are a series of experiments in developing a genre which encloses the perspective of the tragedies in a broader frame of reference, permitting us to acknowledge the consequences of human evil while simultaneously emphasizing that such consequences are not ultimate. The romances affirm the possibility of regeneration in a more emphatic manner than most of Shakespeare's previous works: the villains of

Pericles, Cymbeline, and *The Tempest* inflict genuine suffering upon others, but the emphasis—especially in *The Tempest*—falls upon the process of restoration rather than the period of destruction. While we are never permitted to forget the bestial, potentially destructive dimension of human nature, we are reminded forcefully of the human capacity for love, faith, and spirituality, and each of these plays suggests that human beings, as they exert the transforming power of love, can choose to act as agents of a beneficent providential order.

It is quite natural that in *The Tempest,* the most fully realized of the romances, Shakespeare would focus upon the figure of the magus, the most fully developed expression of Renaissance hopes for the development of humankind's moral, intellectual, and spiritual potential. Through years of study, contemplation, and reflection upon his experience, Prospero has brought his own soul into harmony with the cosmic order, and consequently his art is a means through which God's will is accomplished. On one level of the play Prospero's magic orders the vital forces of nature so as to make them fruitful rather than destructive. It strives to bring about the harmonious union between the natural and the supernatural dimensions of reality which is symbolized by the marriage of earth and heaven in Prospero's hymeneal masque. But it is highly significant that the masque is never quite completed: the final, harmonious dance is interrupted by "*a strange, hollow, and confused noise*" (IV.i.138 SD), and at this crucial moment Shakespeare stresses the limitations of Prospero's art. By forcing Prospero to halt his spirits' enchanting performance in order to deal with Caliban's plot against his life, the playwright reminds us that there are some creatures on whose nature nurture will never stick. Because there are dimensions of evil in human nature which can never be entirely eliminated from it, the magicians' vision of universal harmony will never be perfectly realized in this world. In his portrait of Prospero Shakespeare confirms the belief of the magicians—and of many of the civic humanists, as well—that human art can become a vehicle of divine power, and he also affirms the importance of the visionary imagination. Shakespeare's conception of human nature is more conservative than Ficino's or Pico's, however, as he suggests that no one can live entirely the life of the mind and thus escape the limitations associated with our physical nature. In addition, *The Tempest* questions the sometimes excessive emphasis on self-assertiveness which we often find in the occult tradition. Pico's *Oration* and *Conclusions,* we recall, placed greater emphasis upon self-assertion in the process of spiritual purification than upon an attitude of submission or repentance, and even for Ficino the awareness of one's divine potential could rationalize the desire for conquest: the individual's unwillingness to serve and the desire to dominate others were the consequence of "the immeasurable magnificence of our soul."[3] To some degree Shakespeare is similar to Jonson—and to Pico, Agrippa, and perhaps even Marlowe at certain moments in their lives—in that he returns to a more traditional emphasis upon confessing one's mortal passions and excessive ambitions. He is unlike Jonson, however, in the extent to which he believes that once the individual is fully aware that there are elements of human nature which must be disciplined and restrained, one can exert considerable control over one's own personality and one's destiny. We fulfill ourselves not by escaping the physical aspect of our nature, as some of the occultists had believed, but by bringing it into harmony with the spiritual. It is well to remember that Prospero is a mortal who must continually struggle to maintain the degree of self-mastery which he has attained, but we may also recognize that it is Prospero's attainment of an unusual degree of harmony within his own personality which has conferred upon him his magical power. By mastering his passions and cultivating his higher faculties, Prospero has obtained the power to command the forces of nature, and in the course of the play he brings all of the other characters under his control. But the most impressive of his feats—indeed, the one to which all of his other powers serve as means to an end—is his power to bring others toward the same self-knowledge he has found within himself.

The fact that Shakespeare does not adhere in a doctrinaire fashion to the details of magical theory has led some very well-informed and sensitive readers to suggest that the relationship between Prospero's art and the benevolent magic described by Renaissance occult philosophers is ambiguous. Robert West, while conceding that Prospero in many ways resembles the beneficent Renaissance magus, argues that Prospero and his art are, nonetheless, of ambivalent moral status. Shakespeare does not stress the relationship between the magician's art and divine providence, West believes, and, since Prospero commands spirits, he must have attained his power through ceremonies—not depicted on the stage—which orthodox theologians condemned as damnable. "No magician, however 'white,'" West writes, "could be supposed to rule in the hierarchy of being all the way to its top. At some stage he had to supplicate, and *unless he was a 'holy magician' like the Apostles,* this supplication was directed well short of the Christian Godhead. Prospero's impious need to pray to finite spirits the Globe audience could have been well aware of, for it was an item of pulpit theology that all spirit magic was illicit because all required such praying."[4] Ariel himself is of ambiguous nature, West argues, especially because Prospero refers to him at I.ii.257 as "malignant," and in Prospero's description of his "rough magic" at V.i.33–57 he includes magical acts of dubious moral character:

> I have bedimm'd
> The noontide sun, call'd forth the mutinous winds,
> And 'twixt the green sea and the azur'd vault
> Set roaring war; to the dread rattling thunder
> Have I given fire, and rifted Jove's stout oak
> With his own bolt; the strong-bas'd promontory
> Have I made shake, and by the spurs pluck'd up
> The pine and cedar. Graves at my command
> Have wak'd their sleepers, op'd, and let 'em forth
> By my so potent art.
>   (V.i.41–50)

Professor West, always admirably faithful to the evidence of the primary sources, concedes that some Renaissance texts assert that there are means of raising the dead which derive directly from God and which consequently hold the status of miracle rather than of evil magic. Although raising the dead typically was condemned by orthodox demonologists as evil necromancy, he continues, "Prospero's claim, made but in passing, saying nothing of ends and little of means, may be held ambiguous rather than clearly evil. But it is hardly redeemable for an effect of an unmixedly good magic, and certainly Shakespeare makes no effort to redeem it. It must, then, signify the dubiety of Prospero's magic" (92).

Barbara Mowat, in a thoroughly researched and carefully reasoned essay which builds upon West's prior arguments, emphasizes that Shakespeare has drawn not only upon the Hermetic and Cabalist sources which were the foundation of Renaissance occult philosophy, but also on classical myth and legend, the wizards of medieval and Renaissance romances, and popular entertainers, or "jugglers." Professor Mowat believes that this conflation of sources, as well as Prospero's abjuration of his art, underscores the ambiguity of magic in *The Tempest*, a mysteriousness which is appropriate, she suggests, for a work which reveals the ambiguities of life itself. While C. J. Sisson felt that the lines quoted above (V.i.41–50), based on Ovid's portrait of Medea, reveal that Shakespeare has been careless in introducing apparently negative elements of his source material into an otherwise positive characterization of Prospero, Mowat sees the ambivalence as the essence of the play.[5] In view of the work of West, Mowat, and others, it no longer seems tenable to view Prospero and his magic as essentially evil, but the arguments in favor of the ambiguity of Shakespeare's magician and his art are formidable.

I would certainly agree that in *The Tempest* as in other plays Shakespeare drew on a variety of sources in an eclectic fashion, adapting and transforming what was appropriate to his own unique artistic vision and ignoring what did not suit his purposes. Yet, as I shall endeavor to show in greater detail in the following sections of this chapter, our knowledge of specific ideas from the occult tradition can illuminate many important facets of the play. Our awareness of the significance of Hermetic/Cabalist magic in Renaissance intellectual history is of fundamental importance in encouraging us to recognize the extent to which one of Shakespeare's central purposes in *The Tempest* is to reflect upon the vision of humankind initiated by Renaissance humanists and carried to its logical extreme in the occult tradition. In addition, while I shall emphasize that Prospero's art is a multifaceted symbol which must be interpreted on several parallel levels, an awareness of the influence of Renaissance occult philosophy upon *The Tempest* helps to confirm that on all of these levels Prospero's art is benevolent, and Shakespeare is affirming—although with significant qualifications—the belief of Ficino and his successors that human beings obtain genuine power by aligning themselves with the order of Providence. Shakespeare draws upon a panoply of sources, and his response to the occult tradition is complex, but it does not necessarily follow that *The Tempest* is characterized essentially by unresolved conflict; instead, I would suggest, Prospero's magic functions on several harmonious levels simultaneously. On one level Prospero's art is, quite literally, Hermetic magic; on another, as Frank Kermode has recognized, it is "art" in the broadest sense of the term, the civilizing power of education and moral self-discipline. On yet another, Prospero's magic is theatrical art, which Shakespeare sees as analagous to magic not only in that it creates visions, but also in that it strives to effect moral and spiritual reform. One of the most fascinating aspects of *The Tempest* is the manner in which Shakespeare correlates all of these dimensions of the play, so that they complement and enrich one another. He draws upon those aspects of occult philosophy which reinforce the parallels among magic, learning, and drama as forms of art which endeavor to perfect nature.

PROSPERO AS BENEVOLENT ARTIST

Doubts concerning the benevolence of Prospero's art derive in part from many interpreters' emphasis upon the attitudes of the orthodox "pulpit theologians," to use Professor West's term, rather than on the attitudes of Ficino's *Theologia Platonica,* Pico's *Oration* and *Conclusions,* Agrippa's *Occult Philosophy,* or other works in the occult tradition which had captured Shakespeare's imagination at the time he wrote his last plays. Magical acts of the kind Prospero describes in the lines prefacing his promise to abjure his "potent art" (V.i.50) were precisely those which, Ficino tells us, the perfected magus, as agent of God, can perform: a human soul dedicated to God may be granted the power to "command the elements, rouse the winds, gather the clouds together in rain," cure human diseases, and perform other miraculous feats which may suit God's purposes.[6] In prominent references to "Providence divine" (I.ii.159; cf. V.i.189), Shakespeare carefully aligns Prospero and his art with the workings of the cosmic order. In this context, as Agrippa and others tell us, even Prospero's raising of the dead could be sanctioned. As Jackson Cope has recognized, the lines may be read in connection with "a motif of miraculous resurrection" which becomes prominent in *Pericles* and *Cymbeline,* as well as *The Tempest,* as a corollary of Shakespeare's intensified concern with the visionary and potentially redemptive character of art; like Ariel's mysterious song at I.ii.397–405, the image of resurrection may remind us, on one level, of the process of regeneration which Prospero's art endeavors to bring about as it leads Alonso and others to reflect upon their past transgressions.[7]

Prospero's application of the term "malignant" to Ariel is a major consideration, for in Shakespeare's day one of the most common meanings of the word was "disposed to rebel against God or against constituted authority; disaffected, malcontent" (*OED*). In context, however, "malignant" probably refers to Prospero's somewhat exaggerated accusation that Ariel is resistant to the magician's orders, not that he is essentially evil, and the accusation itself evokes speeches from Ariel which develop the contrast between Prospero's art—which the airy spirit does, in fact, obey—and the witchcraft of Sycorax, with which Ariel had refused to comply. Moreover, Prospero's intellectual and spiritual self-purification has given him a degree of control over his spirits which is based not on supplication of these lower spiritual orders, but on the participation of the awakened human soul in the very highest levels of the cosmic hierarchy. As we saw in previous chapters, occult philosophers had asserted that the magus becomes aware of the innate ideas within the *Mens,* the intuitive, suprarational faculty within the soul, and once this occurs, the magician possesses the power to connect, in contemplation and/or transitive magic, the things of this world with the archetypal forms that govern them. Alchemy, in particular, is an attempt to purify the fallen world by bringing earthly creatures into more perfect unity with their governing Ideas, and Shakespeare may well have been aware of the alchemical meaning of the term *tempest:* it is a boiling process which removes impurities from base metal and facilitates its transmutation into gold. Because the human *Mens* is a part of the series of minds which constitutes the order of Providence, the magus gains intimate knowledge of God's providential purposes and consequently becomes an agent of the divine Creator. Through assent to Providence the magus could then liberate himself from the control of Fortune, gaining the true freedom which comes from aligning oneself with the will of God. The magus possesses the power to manipulate stellar influences and to contribute to the course of earthly events, but the power of the benevolent magician consists solely of the ability to help fulfill providence, never to thwart it: Ariel's assertion that he and his fellows are "ministers of Fate" (III.iii.61) is literally true. An evil magician, such as Faustus or Sycorax, might obtain rudimentary powers, but never anything approaching Prospero's. In fact, many Renaissance occultists agreed with orthodox theologians that an evil magician's powers are almost entirely illusory.[8]

Prospero's renunciation of his art suggests a qualification of the ideals of the magicians, but not a fundamental doubt concerning the moral status of the art. Although Renaissance occultists themselves stressed that the magician must use his art in the service of humankind, they nonetheless placed somewhat more emphasis on the virtues of pure contemplation than Shakespeare wishes to do at the end of his play. Prospero's promise to drown his book before he returns to Milan and resumes his political office suggests that contemplation, book learning, and theatrical art are not permanent escapes from life, but preparations for it. Just as Prospero removes his magic robes in scene 2 before his intimate paternal conversation with Miranda, he resolves to make involvement in the human community, not the retreat into his library, his first priority after he dons once again his ducal robes. If one notices the many assurances throughout the play that Prospero's aim is to reform his enemies, not to seek vengeance, his promise to renounce his "rough magic" appears as a part of his initial plan, rather than a change of heart. In order to ensure the success of his project he continues, in fact, to practice his magic until the very end, closing the final scene itself with an order to Ariel that he provide "calm seas, auspicious gales" (V.i.315) for the journey homeward. The adjective "rough" quite probably carries the meanings of "rigorous, severe," or perhaps "stormy, tempestuous" (*OED*), with reference to the literal and the psychological tempests which Prospero creates in order to stimulate reflection upon human limitations. Professors West and Mowat have clearly established that among the members of a Renaissance audience one could expect to find a variety of attitudes toward magic, and I certainly agree that our appreciation of the play is enhanced if we retain a sense of wonder in our response to Prospero's art. In my reading of the play, however, the text as a whole encourages us to see Prospero as benign from the very outset, and Shakespeare is affirming the position enunciated in *The Winter's Tale*'s scene of apparently magical resurrection: "If this be magic," Leontes proclaims after witnessing Hermione's apparently magical restoration to life, "let it be an art / Lawful as eating" (*WT* V.iii.110–11; see fig. 7).

Those who see Prospero's promise to renounce his art as a suggestion of its moral ambivalence often argue that Prospero suffers from excessive pride and vengefulness in the beginning of the play and that he undergoes a transformation in act 5, scene 1, when he tells Ariel that he will feel compassion for all of those—even his enemies—who are now in his power. There is little or no motivation, however, for a major change of heart in Prospero at the outset of act 5, nor do the magician's plots assume a new direction at this point. The dramatic climax of the main action occurs not when Prospero converses with Ariel, but in act 3, scene 3, when Alonso's repentance makes it possible for the magician to free Milan from its subjugation to Naples and to reassume his position as duke. If Prospero had initially planned vengeance, he could easily have annihilated his enemies in the initial storm scene; instead, he endeavors to bring the wrongdoers to repentance. At the outset of the play he takes pains to demonstrate that the magician intends to harm no one:

> Wipe thou thine eyes, have comfort.
> The direful spectacle of the wrack, which touch'd
> The very virtue of compassion in thee,
> I have with such provision in mine art
> So safely ordered that there is no soul—
> No, not so much perdition as an hair
> Betid to any creature in the vessel.
> (I.ii.25–31)[9]

Central to *The Tempest* are symphonic variations upon two major symbols: the first is the storm, which is associated with tragic experience and which can, if we perceive events appropriately, become a blessing in disguise. Prospero's initial shows of severity are mere pretenses, and they provide a specific instance of the general principle that events which appear threatening can, if we respond properly, lead to spiritual rebirth. The second major symbol is the "sea-change" of which Ariel sings in act 1:

> Full fadom five thy father lies,
>   Of his bones are coral made:
> Those are pearls that were his eyes:
>   Nothing of him that doth fade,

> But doth suffer a sea-change
> Into something rich and strange.
>
>   (I.ii.397–402)

As G. Wilson Knight has suggested, the song may intimate a change from a mortal state to an eternal one. Most obviously, however, it foreshadows the change of heart in Alonso which, in turn, makes possible the restoration of proper order in Milan. In the broadest terms, the changes which Prospero's art facilitates are from discord to harmony, tragedy to comedy, and they occur on the psychological, political, and spiritual levels. The agent of change, the sea, is time and experience, as Shakespeare draws upon the traditional analogy between life and a sea voyage, and simultaneously it is the mind, as suggested by the lines which announce the rising consciousness of Alonso and the court party in act 5:

> Their understanding
> Begins to swell, and the approaching tide
> Will shortly fill the reasonable [shores]
> That now lie foul and muddy.
>
>   (V.i.79–82)

Changes must sometimes occur in modes of human perception before the restoration of harmony can occur in human history. Prospero's art seeks to restore love and faith, qualities which lead to creativity and to genuine self-fulfillment within the human community; these powers are contrasted throughout the play with the destructive forces of self-aggrandizement, vengefulness, and cynicism. Shakespeare draws a close parallel between the faith which envisions a benevolent order beneath the apparent meaninglessness and disorder of earthly events, and interpersonal faith, an ability to see the potential for goodness, as well as evil, in human nature. Only those who are willing to develop their capacity for this kind of vision can respond to Prospero's art or participate in the harmonious order which it helps to establish.

Acting in concert with the cosmic order, Prospero's magical art provides experiences through which various characters are granted an opportunity to acknowledge their mortality and, consequently, learn that the human community must be based on mutual forgiveness. Through the storm, which is itself an instance of magical/dramatic art conceived by Prospero and enacted by spirits whom he subsequently terms his "actors," Alonso and the others in his party are confronted with events that impress upon them the limitations of human power. Prospero himself had learned of his mortal limitations years prior to the opening of the play, when he, like King Lear, was deprived of his throne and began his own tempestuous, redemptive voyage. An example of his awareness of the subordinate status of his art within the cosmic order occurs when he informs Miranda that his success

> doth depend upon
> A most auspicious star, whose influence
> If now I court not, but omit, my fortunes
> Will ever after droop.
> (I.ii.181–84)

Although the entire plot of *The Tempest* is in a sense a product of Prospero's magic, there are several brief theatrical performances within the larger play which assist the characters in interpreting the events of their own lives and which consequently exert a potentially redemptive influence. One of these is the broken feast in act 3, which symbolizes the communion from which Alonso, Sebastian, and Antonio have exiled themselves. Obviously this spectacle, along with the admonitions composed by Prospero and spoken by Ariel, is intended not merely to torment Prospero's enemies, but to teach self-knowledge and evoke repentance. In Alonso's case the scene has the desired effect:

> O, it is monstrous! monstrous!
> Methought the billows spoke, and told me of it;
> The winds did sing it to me, and the thunder,
> That deep and dreadful organ-pipe, pronounc'd
> The name of Prosper; it did base my trespass.
> (III.iii.95–99)

At the moment when Alonso feels remorse, his perception of events begins to change. In his imagination the discordant sounds of the tempest are miraculously transformed into music.[10] The storm is a mysterious song that whispers to Alonso the secret of his own soul.

Awareness of our mortality and our capacity for evil is only one component of the self-knowledge which Prospero's art endeavors to convey to us. The other is an awareness of the spark of the divine which Antonio correctly associates with the moral conscience but refuses to acknowledge as his own. When asked by Sebastian how his "conscience" could permit him to supplant Prospero, Antonio reveals his thoroughly materialistic conception of human nature:

> Ay, sir; where lies that? If 'twere a kibe,
> 'Twould put me to my slipper; but I feel not
> This deity in my bosom.
> (II.i.276–78)

Much of *The Tempest* is a dramatic debate over the question of whether humanity is bestial or godlike, Caliban or Ariel; the implied answer is that we are both and that our lower faculties must be guided and disciplined by the mind and spirit. One of the central symbolic scenes of the play is the masque of Juno, Ceres, and Iris, which reveals to us that the power of heaven both stimulates creativity and, at the same time, restrains nature within its proper boundaries. The symbolic union of earth and heaven suggests, among many other things, that the marriage between higher and lower faculties within the human personality can create a harmonious and properly ordered life. In the occult tradition, the metaphor of marriage refers to the magician's ability to reform nature by bringing earthly creatures into more perfect conformity with their governing Ideas.[11] In *The Tempest*, Shakespeare stresses the reformation of the self which may occur as a consequence of the harmonious union of higher and lower faculties within the individual personality. In spite of Prospero's reference to it as a "vanity of mine art" (IV.i.41), the masque reveals to us an essential aspect of the vision of *The Tempest* as a whole.

The disruption of the concluding dance of the masque by Prospero's remembrance of the rebellious plot of Caliban, Stephano, and Trinculo does not entirely invalidate the scene's symbolic vision. Quite recently A. Lynne Magnusson has argued that the interruptions of various scenes and speeches in *The Tempest* suggest that Shakespeare is confessing that art expresses the need of the human mind to create more order and coherence than exists in external reality. Like many modern critics, Magnusson feels that *The Tempest* dramatizes relativism rather than revelation.[12] While the interruption does remind us that Prospero's "majestic vision" (IV.i.118) excludes the destructive forces ever-present in human life, *The Tempest* as a whole, I believe, suggests that the masque embodies an ideal which may be fully realized in the lives of those who choose to align themselves—as Prospero has done—with the order of Providence. The interruption of the masque reminds us that in the fallen world not all mortals will choose to assume their rightful places within the natural order, and consequently the power of Prospero's art to reform life is limited: the artist is genuinely powerful, but he is far from omnipotent. As both Alvin Kernan and Barbara Traister have emphasized, Shakespeare is intensely aware that the artist has no power over the minds and souls of members of the audience who do not respond with a sympathetic imagination.[13] Throughout Shakespeare's canon there are oracles, ghosts, and prophetic visions which are associated both with fantasy and with a genuine spiritual dimension of reality, and faith in Providence in Shakespeare very often entails a willingness to trust these objects of imagination. In *The Tempest,* the plays enacted by Prospero and his spirits serve much the same function that dream visions or other forms of prophecy and magic serve in *Julius Caesar, Pericles, Cymbeline, The Winter's Tale,* and other plays.[14] Ferdinand and Alonso respond positively to Prospero's art and consequently learn profound truths from it; Antonio and Sebastian resist the power of Prospero's magic and remain unaffected by it.

Shakespeare emphasizes the subjective element in our perception of reality itself, as well as art, in the scene in which we first see Alonso, Sebastian, Antonio, Gonzalo, and the others after their shipwreck. As the scene opens, Gonzalo and Adrian are attempting to persuade the other members of Alonso's party to count their blessings. Although they have been stranded on a mysterious island, Gonzalo says, they somehow have been miraculously preserved, and therefore they have cause to rejoice. "The air breathes upon us here most sweetly," Adrian comments, and Gonzalo points out that the isle contains "every thing advantageous to life." To Sebastian and Antonio, however, the air breathes "As if it had lungs, and rotten ones" or "as 'twere perfumed by a fen" (II.i.47–9). Even the physical appearance of the island is subject to dispute:

GONZALO. How lush and lusty the grass looks! How green!
ANTONIO. The ground indeed is tawny.
SEBASTIAN. With an eye of green in't.
ANTONIO. He misses not much.
SEBASTIAN. No; he doth but mistake the truth totally.
GONZALO. But the rariety of it is—which is indeed almost
beyond credit—
SEBASTIAN. As many vouch'd rarieties are.
GONZALO. That our garments, being (as they were) drench'd in
the sea, hold notwithstanding their freshness and glosses, being
rather new dy'd than stain'd with salt water.
ANTONIO. If but one of his pockets could speak, would it not
say he lies?
SEBASTIAN. Ay, or very falsely pocket up his report.
                                        (II.i.53–68)

Shakespeare provides several hints that Gonzalo's view of things is the correct one. In the scene just prior to this one, for instance, Ariel has already assured Prospero that the travelers have been protected, and "On their sustaining garments not a blemish, / But fresher than before" (I.ii.218–19). Another confirmation of Gonzalo's perspective occurs as the conversation turns to the marriage of Alonso's daughter, which has just taken place at Tunis, and Gonzalo remarks that the city has not had a comparable queen "since widow Dido's time." The remainder of the party are surprised by the mention of Dido, since she was queen of Carthage and not, they insist, of Tunis. Gonzalo replies, "This Tunis, sir, was Carthage," but Sebastian and Antonio are incredulous:

ANTONIO. His word is more than the miraculous harp.
SEBASTIAN. He hath rais'd the wall, and houses too.
ANTONIO. What impossible matter will he make easy next?
SEBASTIAN. I think he will carry this island home in his pocket,
and give it his son for an apple.
                                        (II.i.87–92)

The point here is that the site of Tunis actually is contiguous with the site of ancient Carthage, and in the Renaissance the two cities were often referred to as one and the same; many geographers used the term "Tunis" to refer to the entire region in which both cities were located. More importantly, historians such as Leo Africanus, whose account was incorporated into Richard Hakluyt's *Voyages* and Richard Eden and Richard Willes's *The History of Travayle in the West and East Indies* (from which Shakespeare apparently took the name "Setebos") asserted that the survivors of the ruined Carthage founded Tunis, so that the latter city was, in a sense, Carthage reborn.[15] Gonzalo is correct, despite the incredulity and cynicism of Antonio and Sebastian, and the action of *The Tempest* as a whole confirms that he is correct in his optimism concerning the events of the shipwreck as well. *The Tempest* not only suggests that there are subjective elements in our perception of the world; it endeavors, furthermore, to persuade us that some interpretations of life are more valid than others: events which seem "impossible" or "miraculous" to some observers may eventually be proven literally true.

Norman Rabkin is correct when he points out that "Shakespeare reminds us in his last plays of the Renaissance commonplace that the artist is a second God creating a second nature . . . in order to share a more profound perception that God has created our universe as a work of art";[16] Prospero's description of the physical world, "the great globe itself," as an "insubstantial pageant" which shall one day "dissolve, / And . . . Leave not a rack behind" (IV.i.153–56) underscores the analogy between the playwright's art and that of the divine Creator. Moreover, Shakespeare also suggests that the human artist, working in concert with the divine, can help us to interpret life correctly. Just as the drama of the broken feast revealed to Alonso the meaning of the previous events of his life, the art of *The Tempest* as a whole is intended to assist the audience in seeing beyond the literal level of the events of earthly history and apprehending their significance; the purpose of genuine art in *The Tempest* is to reveal which interpretation of reality is genuine. In the epilogue, however, when the analogy between Prospero's art and Shakespeare's becomes most prominent, the playwright makes clear that he has no power without the audience's imaginative participation— our faith, as it were—in the work of art. It is our "gentle breath"— our higher faculties, associated with the airy spirit, Ariel—which will either confer a degree of reality upon the play, and hence send Prospero to Naples, or leave him confined upon the "bare island" of an empty stage. Prospero's closing lines draw attention to the very close similarity between participation in a community of grace and willing participation in a work of theatrical art:

> Now I want
> Spirits to enforce, art to enchant,
> And my ending is despair,
> Unless I be reliev'd by prayer,
> Which pierces so, that it assaults
> Mercy itself, and frees all faults.
> As you from crimes would pardon'd be,
> Let your indulgence set me free.
> (Epilogue, 13–20)

As Prospero responds charitably to those within his power, so he requests from us a charitable response and an exertion of our visionary imagination which will permit us to assist the artist in his miraculous transformation of the brazen world in which we live into the Golden World of art.

SHAKESPEARE, OCCULT PHILOSOPHY, AND RENAISSANCE CONCEPTIONS OF HUMAN NATURE

The Tempest arrives at its final vision of human nature through a dialectical process which initially presents us with two diametrically opposed extremes of the Renaissance debate concerning the limits of the human personality. The first clear statement of the pessimistic view of humankind occurs in Miranda's description of Caliban in act 1, scene 2: he is an "Abhorred slave / Which any print of goodness wilt not take, / Being capable of all ill" (I.ii.351–53).[17] If Miranda's lines on Caliban remind us of Jean Calvin's view of fallen human nature, her response to her first sight of Ferdinand recalls Pico's *Oration:* "What, is't a spirit?" she exclaims, "Lord, how it looks about! Believe me, sir, / It carries a brave form. But 'tis a spirit" (I.ii.410–12). Prospero seeks to qualify her naive enthusiasm about Ferdinand by telling her that although "A goodly person," he is still—at least in part—a mere mortal: "it eats, and sleeps, and hath such senses / As we have" (I.ii.417, 413–14). Unaffected by the moderate words of her father, the young, enraptured lover remains awestruck:

> I might call him
> A thing divine, for nothing natural
> I ever saw so noble.
> (I.ii.418–20)

Miranda retains her innocent faith in humankind throughout the play. When she first sees Alonso and his company in the final scene, she expresses her admiration in what may well be the most famous lines in *The Tempest:*

> O wonder!
> How many goodly creatures are there here!
> How beauteous mankind is! O brave new world
> That has such people in't!
> (V.i.181–84)

Although Shakespeare places these lines in the mouth of a naive adolescent, they nonetheless epitomize the sense of exhiliration felt by those early Renaissance humanists and philosophers who proclaimed that they were entering a new era in which human nature would fulfill its divine potential. Since the audience has become familiar with Antonio, Sebastian, and the others by this point in the play, we hardly need Prospero's line, "'Tis new to thee" (V.i.184), to underscore the irony of the speech; and yet I do not believe that Shakespeare's aim is to discredit Miranda's assessment of humankind entirely. Her faith needs to be qualified, not destroyed, and her innocence and trust are necessary components of the genuine charity which exerts its transforming power throughout the play. Such innocence can be destroyed by experience, but it may subsequently be restored in a more mature form, as it has been in Prospero, whose trial, like that of Pericles and of Leontes in Shakespeare's previous romances, restores to him the somewhat qualified trustfulness and the ability to love which enable him to forgive his enemies in spite of his awareness that some of them may not respond to his clemency. The difference between Miranda's faith and her father's is that Prospero is always aware of the tragic discrepancy between what human beings can become and what most of them actually are; the similarity between Miranda and her father is their shared awareness that humankind possesses a divine spirit which confers upon us a potential for benevolence and creativity. When Miranda tells us that

"nothing ill can dwell in such a temple" as Ferdinand's "brave form"
(I.ii.457, 412), we should recall Saint Paul's well-known words in his
first letter to the Corinthians:

> Know ye not, that your bodie is the temple of the holie
> G[h]ost, *which is* in you, whome ye have of God? and ye are
> not your owne.
> For ye are bo[u]ght for a price: therefore glorifie God in
> your bodie, and in your spirit: for they are God[']s.[18]

An echo of this same passage reverberates in the final line of Gonzalo's summary of the events of *The Tempest:*

> In one voyage
> Did Claribel her husband find at Tunis,
> And Ferdinand, her brother, found a wife
> Where he himself was lost; Prospero, his dukedom
> In a poor isle; and all us, ourselves,
> *When no man was his own.*
> (V.i.208–13, my emphasis)

Shakespeare emphasizes humanity's divine potential in his romances
much more insistently than he had in most of his previous works,
and this change of emphasis correlates with a striking alteration in
Shakespeare's treatment of magic. In the history plays and the tragedies, from the witchcraft of Joan of Arc in *Henry VI, Part One,* and
the sorcery of Owen Glendower in *Henry IV* through the player-
villain's poison produced by "natural magic" in *Hamlet* (III.ii.259)
and the evil witches of *Macbeth,* Shakespeare typically associates
magic and sorcery with subversion of proper order and with deception. In *Love's Labor's Lost* he suggests that the ambition to seek
knowledge of "Things hid and barr'd ... from common sense"
(I.i.57) springs from a proud and foolish attempt to distinguish oneself from ordinary mortals, whom Dumaine terms "the gross world's
baser slaves" (I.i.30), and in this early comedy Shakespeare repeatedly mocks the suggestion that study can make us "godlike"
(I.i.58).[19] While there is some precedent for benevolent magic in *A
Midsummer Night's Dream* and for a positive view of Paracelsian medicine in *All's Well That Ends Well* and elsewhere,[20] only in the romances does Shakespeare affirm boldly the belief that humankind

possesses a divine potential which may be fully realized through knowledge, self-discipline, love, and faith. The most explicit statment occurs in act 3 of *Pericles,* when Cerimon, a magus like Prospero, tells us that "Virtue and cunning" are "endowments greater / Than nobleness and riches," since the latter are things which one's worldly heirs can dissipate, whereas "immortality attends the former, / Making a man a god" (III.ii.27–31). To the sound of mysterious music, Cerimon miraculously resurrects Thaisa; his art, inspiring wonder in those who witness it, is a means through which heaven rewards those whose love and faith are constant. Similarly, Paulina, in the final scene of *The Winter's Tale,* instructs the repentant Leontes to awaken his faith as she calls for music and restores to him his lost queen in a scene obviously modelled on the account of the magical animation of statues in the Hermetic *Asclepius.* Although Paulina's art is not literal magic, as is Prospero's, the scene suggests the extent to which Hermetic sources have stimulated Shakespeare's imagination as he seeks to perfect a genre which will affirm the power of love and faith to dignify humankind and to renew life. Paulina's art achieves its effect through an illusion which becomes reality as Leontes responds to it, and the scene thus suggests the same metaphorical identification between benevolent magic and theatrical art which Shakespeare develops in further detail in *The Tempest.*

Aware of the dangers of asserting individual freedom, dignity, and power to the exclusion of the value of sustaining the human community, Shakespeare distinguishes carefully in the romances between true and false conceptions of human nobility. In act 2 of *The Tempest,* when Antonio endeavors to persuade Sebastian to kill Alonso, he tells him, in speeches which may remind us of *Tamburlaine* or *Dr. Faustus,* that a man who bears a noble mind should assert his power over his fellow human beings. If Sebastian boldly seizes the opportunity which Fortune has offered him, Antonio suggests, he can master his own destiny. As I suggested in the previous section, Antonio's false conception of nobility is a corollary of his materialistic and cynical conception of the human personality, his denial of the "deity" within the human bosom (II.i.278). Genuine awareness of one's spiritual potential in *The Tempest,* tempered by an acknowledgment of human passions and limitations, leads not to the desire to dominate, but to the desire to serve; the attempt to destroy the bonds which unite the individual with all of humankind leads, ironically, to enslavement to one's own passions and ambitions.

False conceptions of human nobility and freedom are associated with *goetia,* such as the evil magic of Sycorax, a travesty of Prospero's benevolent art. Although I am indebted to Frank Kermode's discussion of this contrast between *magia* and *goetia* in his important introduction to *The Tempest,* I would qualify his suggestion that the *goetia* of Sycorax is "natural" magic, whereas Prospero's is "supernatural" (xxiv–xxv, xl–li); the contrast, as I perceive it, is between evil magic, which is unnatural, and benevolent magic, which draws upon both natural and supernatural powers in order to bring nature to fulfillment. Benevolent art such as Prospero's is in a sense "natural" in that it restores harmony within the natural order. In addition, benevolent art is effected through the human mind, itself a product of nature, although disciplined by art and enlightened by grace. A pertinent explanation occurs in *The Winter's Tale,* when Polixenes explains to Perdita that

> Nature is made better by no mean
> But Nature makes that mean; so, over that art
> Which you say adds to Nature, is an art
> That Nature makes. You see, sweet maid, we marry
> A gentler scion to the wildest stock,
> And make conceive a bark of baser kind
> By bud of nobler race. This an art
> Which does mend Nature—change it rather; but
> The art itself is Nature.
> (IV.iv.88–97)

Polixenes' explanation of how art "mends" or "changes" nature is similar to Pico's description of benevolent magic in his *Oration* and to Prospero's art in *The Tempest.* It is an art which improves uncultivated nature—"the wildest stock"—by marrying it to something more noble. The change occurs when art releases the potential of nature and guides the development of that potential purposefully. It is helpful to recall the emphasis in *The Tempest* upon marriage as a means of guiding natural creative powers into constructive channels: the physical dimension of nature becomes fulfilled through institutions which are associated with the controlling power of our higher faculties, and the process is completed through religious ceremonies which invoke the aid of divine grace. Our natural powers are gifts which, if used properly, enable us to participate in the process of creative love which defeats time and change; if we abuse them, they become destructive. Prospero's repeated admonitions to chastity, although they may seem overly zealous or even comical to a modern audience, are in accordance with this principle: if Ferdinand keeps his procreative desires within the bounds of the divinely sanctioned institution of marriage, his union with Miranda will be harmonious and fruitful; if not, it will be barren and filled with discord (IV.i.13–22). The marriage ceremony itself is a form of divinely inspired art, just as Prospero's masque or Ariel's music is. It is a means through which grace effects a miraculous change in nature.

The second scene of *The Tempest* introduces several important terms which help to convey this conception of magic as an art that amends or reforms uncultivated nature. When Prospero describes Antonio's usurpation of Prospero's dukedom, he says that Antonio,

> Being once perfected how to grant suits,
> How to deny them, who t' advance, and who
> To trash for overtopping, new created
> The creatures that were mine, I say, or chang'd 'em,
> Or else new form'd 'em; having both the key
> Of officer and office, set all hearts i' th' state
> To what tune pleas'd his ear, that now he was
> The ivy which had hid my princely trunk,
> And suck'd my verdure out on't.
>   (I.ii.79–87)

Antonio's "art" is of course evil, a form of *goetia* which saps the life of the proper order rather than invigorating it, and it is thus an inverted parody of Prospero's benevolent art, but the words "perfected," "new created," "changed," and "new formed" nonetheless help to establish at an early stage of the play the central emphasis on transformation. The passage also alludes to the magician's marriage of the elm and the vine, and to music, both of which refer in the occult tradition to the influence of heavenly powers upon earthly creation. Music, in particular, was widely believed to possess the power to restore harmony among the faculties of the human personality.[21] The passage thus contributes to our growing awareness that

Prospero's art seeks to effect restorative transformations. To summarize the contrast between *magia* and *goetia* in *The Tempest,* one should say that benevolent magic fulfills and perfects natural processes, whereas evil magic endeavors to destroy or pervert them. Prospero's art brings nature into conformity with the rational and spiritual planes of reality and thus with Providence. It renews the bonds uniting the human community, whereas *goetia* seeks to destroy those bonds in order to confer illegitimate power upon a single individual.

The subplot involving Caliban, Trinculo, and Stephano dramatizes a comic version of the *goetia* which parodies Prospero's benevolent art. Caliban ironically subjugates himself to Stephano in an attempt to escape his true master, Prospero, and his false sense of freedom is contrasted with the genuine liberation found by Ferdinand when he submits to Prospero's discipline. While Ferdinand and Miranda become united through mutual service and devotion, the characters in the subplot are united only by self-interest, and hence their union is unstable and transitory. And just as Ferdinand and Miranda perceive each other as godlike, so Caliban regards Stephano as "a brave god" who "bears celestial liquor" (II.ii.117). He wonders whether Trinculo and Stephano have just dropped from heaven. The irony of his remarks is underscored by Stephano's gross jest (II.ii.105–7) that Trinculo, who has been hiding under Caliban's cloak, appears to be the monster's excrement. The episode reminds us of Prospero's reference to Caliban himself as "filth" (I.ii.346). The effect of the scene may be to render absurd—at least temporarily—the idea that the individual is a kind of deity, but the absurdity is relevant only to those characters who exist on a level of development far below Prospero's. The low humor contributes to the debate concerning human nature by reminding us of the basest elements of the human personality, but the purpose of the comic plot, with its perverted worship and its attempt to commit murder in an effort to further the ambitions and lusts of a trio of misguided fools, is to contrast the genuine magic and genuine fulfillment dramatized in the main action. The use of liquor is prominent in the subplot because drunkenness tends to extinguish the higher faculties and leave the appetites without conscious control.[22] The clowns' drunkenness also produces a false sense of self-expansion which contrasts with the true self-fulfillment found by Ferdinand and Alonso. This false sense of self-realization entails severing one's ties with one's fellow human beings, whereas true self-fulfillment entails a commitment to the good of the human community.

As Arthur Lovejoy and others have pointed out, *The Tempest* is in part a satirical commentary upon the optimism concerning uncultivated human nature which Montaigne seemed to express in his essay "On the Cannibals." [23] This "soft" primitivism, which claims that art corrupts rather than perfects nature, is expressed in somewhat whimsical fashion by Gonzalo when he says that if he had "plantation" of the isle, he would establish an ideal commonwealth that would "excel the golden age" (II.i.144, 169). His scheme, reminiscent of the utopianism mocked by Jonson in *The Alchemist,* would restore humankind to its lost innocence and thus eliminate the need for law or social organization. There would be no hierarchy, no private property, no learning. Although it is possible that Gonzalo is expressing his own naive optimism, it seems more likely that he himself is aware that he is indulging in a fantasy and that Shakespeare is utilizing Gonzalo's speeches to introduce a more extreme optimism concerning the possibility of social reform than any character in the play would seriously profess. Sebastian and Antonio's cynical commentary provides immediate qualification of this naive point of view, not least because we are soon reminded of the human capacity for brutality embodied by Antonio in particular. But perhaps the most devastating critique of the apparent idealization of "natural" humankind is Shakespeare's characterization of Caliban, who serves as a flesh-and-blood example of what uncultivated human nature is really like. Although Caliban develops into a character who eludes complete categorization, he is, in part, representative of human nature in a fallen and perverted condition, a reminder of what human beings may become if our baser elements are uncontrolled. In the tragedies, perhaps most notably *King Lear,* unnatural cruelty and egotism are repeatedly described as "monstrous"; in *The Tempest,* the verbal image is replaced by a visual one, an actual monster whom we find to be "as disproportion'd in his manners / As in his shape" (V.i.291–92). One of the ways in which *The Tempest* contains the potential for tragic destruction epitomized in Caliban is by the creation, in Prospero, of a character who has attained the power to master the destructive potential of such a beast. Moreover, *The Tempest* suggests the process through which such mastery is achieved, as we watch Prospero teaching both Ferdinand and Alonso to remember not only their potential for godlike benevolence but also the guilt which is their mortal inheritance. As Prospero admits his own mortal limits when he points to Caliban and says, "this thing of darkness I / Acknowledge mine" (V.i.275–76), the play closes with an admonition that our better selves can be liberated only if we remember those aspects of our personalities which must be controlled if they are to be fulfilled and, perhaps, transcended.

Each of the works explored in this study is unique in its artistic methods and its philosophical implications, and it is obvious that no final comparison can be exhaustive. Yet I would venture to say that the distinctive character of *The Tempest* derives in large part from its calm—one is tempted to say serene—sense of balance. The play permits us to entertain the possibility that humankind possesses an unknown, perhaps indeterminate, creative potential, and yet the heart of the work is its insistence that we cannot fulfill ourselves until we discover our proper relationship with our fellow human beings. One of Shakespeare's most impressive achievements is his ability to face the truth about the human capacity for destruction, yet leave us with a feeling of hope. As we appreciate the intricacy of the symbolic structure of *The Tempest,* we may also feel that the quality of our aesthetic experience is derived from the play's power to make us feel with renewed intensity the validity of those insights, attitudes, and values which confer upon human life its deepest significance.

Eugenio Garin has described with moving eloquence the essential motivation behind the studies and the teaching of the humanist movement initiated in the Renaissance. To the humanists, Garin writes,

> antiquity was indeed not only a field in which to exercise their scholarly curiosity, but also a living example. In their eyes, classical antiquity had achieved a wonderful fullness of life and of harmony and had both expressed these achievements and handed them down in works of art and thought as perfect as that life itself. To come into contact with these monuments and with the minds behind them was like an ideal conversation with perfect men and allowed one to learn from them the

meaning of existence. If one opens one's heart humbly to those wonderful works and transforms oneself, as it were, through love into them, one can regenerate oneself by absorbing so much human richness and thus reconquer the mastery over all the treasures of the mind.[24]

The critical habits of mind which Professor Garin himself admires make it difficult for us to accept the word "perfect," and modern criticism has raised formidable doubts concerning the possibility of the form of communion which Garin describes. *The Tempest* itself makes us aware of the limitations of art, and it encourages us to affirm the revelatory and redemptive power of Shakespeare's work only with significant qualifications. And yet the play also invites us to an act of faith. It suggests that if we exert our imagination, our vision may, in fact, coincide with that of the artist. If such a miracle does in fact occur, it may contribute to a magical transformation of our perception of ourselves and the world around us.

The vision of human dignity and power which was stimulated by Renaissance Neoplatonism is a primary source of the passionate affirmation of much of Renaissance literature.[1] At the same time, the inevitable questioning of those affirmations provides a counterpoint to the assertion of human grandeur and creative prowess. While their achievements are diverse and the texts are complex and multifaceted, each of the major works which we have studied focuses upon the same essential questions: the issue of the potential and the limitations of the human personality, the possibility of human control over the natural world, the hope for the perfection of human society, and the role which individual human beings, in relation to God and to traditional institutions, might play in a process of universal reformation. *Dr. Faustus* establishes a tragic rhythm which calls into question the status of traditional authorities, beliefs, and institutions. *The Alchemist,* as well as many of Jonson's masques, endeavors to contain such revolutionary energies and to reaffirm traditional authorities, yet it does so in a manner which reflects Western civilization's advancement toward genuine science, the tool through which progress toward a chastened version of the dream of the return of the Golden Age would in some ways actually be accomplished. *The Tempest,* through its marvelously resonant symbolism, suggests a balanced view of the human potential for creation and destruction, encouraging us to affirm the power of human art and science while at the same time reminding us of our limitations.

The connections among Neoplatonism and occult philosophy, an affirmation of human power, and utopianism continue throughout much of the subsequent history of Western civilization. Following the era of Marlowe, Shakespeare, Spenser, and Milton there was a period of reaction in which the major authors of the Neoclassical movement followed in Ben Jonson's footsteps, satirizing the occult philosophy which had contributed to the most radical currents of the Renaissance. During the Romantic period, the renewed assertion of human visionary and creative power correlated with a resurgence, in the works of Goethe, Blake, Coleridge, Shelley, and others, of interest in the Neoplatonists. In the late nineteenth and early twentieth centuries William Butler Yeats, perhaps the greatest of the modern poets to become inspired by the occult tradition, lamented the diminution of spirituality and its replacement by positivism. As Yeats recognized, the most influential utopian movements of our time are founded not upon spiritual longing, but upon materialist philosophies, and we do well, whatever our own philosophical or religious persuasion, to ask ourselves which attitudes and values associated with our religious heritage need to be retained and which may need to be rejected.

Utopian movements of all eras have sometimes been rendered destructive through the capacity of human beings to rationalize the desire for self-aggrandizement. We choose to forget what Marlowe, Jonson, and Shakespeare, despite their differences, all would identify as a bestial or Satanic drive for conquest. The continuing significance of these authors' texts springs from their ability to stimulate our utopian dreams, yet to foster in us that capacity for self-examination without which it is surely impossible to relate wisely the interests of the individual to the good of humankind.

Notes

PREFACE

1. E. D. Hirsch, Jr., *Validity in Interpretation* and *The Aims of Interpretation;* John Wallace, "'Examples Are Best Precepts': Readers and Meanings in Seventeenth-Century Poetry." Wayne Booth responds to Hirsch's work and addresses the problems of reconstructing authorial intention quite sensibly in *Critical Understanding.* Fundamental, for example, is his distinction between "the announced intentions of the author" and "the intentions of the work (that is, the author's choices as finally embodied)" (369).

1. RENAISSANCE MAGIC AND THE RETURN OF THE GOLDEN AGE

1. Excellent surveys of recent scholarship in various areas of Renaissance studies appear in *The Renaissance: Essays in Interpretation,* by André Chastel, Paul Kristeller, and others. Jacob Burckhardt's classic study, *The Civilization of the Renaissance in Italy,* available in several editions, has been published with an introduction on Renaissance historiography—and a qualified defense of Burckhardt—by Benjamin Nelson and Charles Trinkaus. Among those who have reacted against the views of the Renaissance derived from Burckhardt are Douglas Bush, *The Renaissance and English Humanism;* Lynn Thorndike, *A History of Magic and Experimental Science* and "The Renaissance," in *Encyclopaedia Britannica,* 1971 edition; and William G. Craven, *Giovanni Pico della Mirandola, Symbol of His Age: Modern Interpretations of a Renaissance Philosopher,* discussed below in Chapter 3. Additional influential studies include John Herman Randall, *The Making of the Modern Mind;* Wallace K. Ferguson, *The Renaissance in Historical Thought: Five Centuries of Interpretation;* Hiram

Haydn, *The Counter-Renaissance;* Fritz Caspari, *Humanism and the Social Order in Tudor England;* Hans Baron, *The Crisis of the Early Italian Renaissance;* Myron P. Gilmore, *The World of Humanism;* Erwin Panofsky, *Renaissance and Renascences in Western Art* and *Studies in Iconology: Humanistic Themes in the Art of the Renaissance;* Tinsley Helton, ed., *The Renaissance: A Reconsideration of the Theories and Interpretations of the Age;* Ernst Cassirer, *The Individual and the Cosmos in Renaissance Philosophy;* Eugenio Garin, *Italian Humanism: Philosophy and Civic Life in the Renaissance* and *Science and Civic Life in the Italian Renaissance;* Charles Trinkaus, *"In Our Image and Likeness": Humanity and Divinity in Italian Humanist Thought;* Peter Burke, *Culture and Society in Renaissance Italy;* Charles Singleton, ed., *Art, Science, and History in the Renaissance;* Robert Mandrou, *From Humanism to Science, 1480–1700.* Several of Paul Kristeller's most important essays have been published in updated form in *Renaissance Thought and Its Sources.* Among his previous works are *The Philosophy of Marsilio Ficino; Studies in Renaissance Thought and Letters; Renaissance Thought: The Classic, Scholastic, and Humanistic Strains; Renaissance Thought II: Papers on Humanism and the Arts;* and *Renaissance Concepts of Man, and Other Essays.*

2. In addition to *Giordano Bruno* and *The Occult Philosophy in the Elizabethan Age,* see Frances Yates's *The Art of Memory; Theatre of the World; The Rosicrucian Enlightenment; Shakespeare's Last Plays: A New Approach; Astraea: The Imperial Theme in the Sixteenth Century;* and *Lull and Bruno, Collected Essays;* Peter French, *John Dee: The World of an Elizabethan Magus;* R.J.W. Evans, *Rudolf II and His World: A Study in Intellectual History, 1576–1612;* Christopher Hill, *Intellectual Origins of the English Revolution* and *The World Turned Upside Down: Radical Ideas during the English Revolution;* Paolo Rossi, *Francis Bacon: From Magic to Science* and "Hermeticism, Rationality, and the Scientific Revolution"; Allen Debus, *The English Paracelsians; The Chemical Dream of the Renaissance; The Chemical Philosophy: Paracelsian Science and Medicine in the Sixteenth and Seventeenth Centuries;* and *Man and Nature in the Renaissance.* Gordon Worth O'Brien, in *Renaissance Poetics and the Problem of Power,* provides a moving account of the importance of the Platonic tradition in promoting a conception of human dignity and power which inspired the greatest Renaissance poets and which gave much of Renaissance literature its unique character. Professor O'Brien covers several figures whose works I do not treat in detail—

Plotinus, Nicholas of Cusa, and John Milton, as well as a host of lesser figures—and although my discussion of the relationships among humanism, Neoplatonism, and science are different from Professor O'Brien's, his work is in many ways complementary to my own.

While many of the controversies over Renaissance occultism are covered below, I should mention at the outset, in addition to the relevant works already cited in note 1, the contributions of the following: Nesca Robb, *Neoplatonism of the Italian Renaissance;* Walter Pagel, *Paracelsus: An Introduction to Philosophical Medicine in the Era of the Renaissance;* Marie Boas Hall, *The Scientific Renaissance, 1450–1630;* P. M. Rattansi, "Paracelsus and the Puritan Revolution"; Charles Nauert, *Agrippa and the Crisis of Renaissance Thought;* Daniel P. Walker, *Spiritual and Demonic Magic from Ficino to Campanella* and *The Ancient Theology;* Gershom Scholem, *Major Trends in Jewish Mysticism; On the Kabbalah and Its Symbolism;* and *Sabbatai Sevi: The Mystical Messiah;* Keith Thomas, *Religion and the Decline of Magic;* Peter Mathias, ed., *Science and Society, 1600–1900;* Antonia McLean, *Humanism and the Rise of Science in Tudor England;* S. K. Heninger, Jr., *"Touches of Sweet Harmony": Pythagorean Cosmology and Renaissance Poetics;* Robert S. Kinsman, ed., *The Darker Vision of the Renaissance: Beyond the Fields of Reason;* Charles Zika, "Reuchlin and Erasmus: Humanism and the Occult Philosophy"; Jacob Bronowski, *Magic, Science, and Civilization;* J. Peter Zetterburg, "The Mistaking of 'the Mathematicks' for Magic in Tudor and Stuart England"; Brian Easlea, *Witch Hunting, Magic, and the New Philosophy;* and John W. Shirley and F. David Hoeniger, eds., *Science and the Arts in the Renaissance.*

3. Charles Trinkaus, *"In Our Image and Likeness,"* esp. xiv–xxiv, 476–508, and 519–24; Wayne Shumaker, *The Occult Sciences in the Renaissance,* 201–48. Andrew Weiner's "Expelling the Beast: Bruno's Adventures in England" is a carefully researched and balanced evaluation of Yates's assertion that Bruno was widely influential in Elizabethan political life; Weiner confirms much of what Yates has said about Bruno's ideas, but he suggests that Bruno was unsuccessful in his effort to promote peaceful solutions to religious conflicts. Brian Vickers' comment appears in *Occult and Scientific Mentalities,* 6. Professor Vickers' research, as well as that of many of the scholars whose work he reviews in his essay, is discussed below, esp. Chap-

ters 3 and 5. The chapter on Pico also responds in detail to William G. Craven's very challenging study, *Giovanni Pico della Mirandola, Symbol of His Age.*

4. Barbara Mowat, drawing in part upon Robert West's *Shakespeare and the Outer Mystery,* has argued, in her "Prospero, Agrippa, and Hocus Pocus," that because of Prospero's resemblance to the wizards of popular romance, to the stage magicians of the commedia dell'arte tradition, and to ordinary street-corner "jugglers," we cannot identify him unambivalently with the Renaissance magus of the Hermetic/Cabalist tradition. Professor Mowat's scholarship on the various magical traditions is very thorough, and it is true that some playwrights are more directly influenced by purely literary traditions or popular entertainments than by Hermetic/Cabalist magic; as the following chapters will indicate, however, I feel that there is sound historical and textual evidence for us to believe that Marlowe, Jonson, and Shakespeare are responding primarily to the Hermetic/Cabalist tradition and to the birth of science. Barbara Traister, in *Heavenly Necromancers,* does an excellent job of demonstrating that the mixture of influences from the traditions of intellectual occultism, popular romance, and Renaissance epic made possible a wide range of complex audience responses to the stage magician. She disproves, for example, the assertion of Kurt Tetzeli von Rosador, in *Magie im elisabethanischen Drama,* that stage magicians were descended primarily from the Vice figure of morality plays and were "automatically viewed as evil by an Elizabethan audience" (Traister, 33). I place greater emphasis than Professor Traister does, however, upon Neoplatonism as the source of the conception of the magician as artist.

Additional studies of social, literary, and intellectual contexts for the plays on magic include Robert R. Reed, *The Occult on the Tudor and Stuart Stage;* David Woodman, *White Magic and English Renaissance Drama;* and Anthony Harris, *Night's Black Agents.* Robert West's *The Invisible World* accomplishes well its stated aim of clarifying the action and dialogue of various plays by referring to current beliefs about magic and demonology. Although West's purpose is not to connect beliefs about demonology with other historical currents, his analyses of the range of possible responses an Elizabethan audience might experience are carefully reasoned and based on impressively extensive reading in the primary sources. My own study differs from previous ones in part by placing greater emphasis upon the dramatists' awareness of the influence of occult philosophy on the emergence of science and on the reform movements which I discuss in the remainder of this chapter.

5. A. W. Ward's comments appear in his edition of *Dr. Faustus* and *Friar Bacon and Friar Bungay,* 254–55, cited by Yates, *Giordano Bruno,* 210–11. Chronological surveys of Tudor and Stuart plays on magic may be found in Woodman's *White Magic,* Reed's *The Occult on the Tudor and Stuart Stage,* Harris's *Night's Black Agents,* and Traister's *Heavenly Necromancers;* all these studies indicate that plays on magic were most popular from the 1580s through the 1620s, but they differ in their explanations of the phenomenon. Charles Nicholl demonstrates clearly the resurgence of interest in alchemy during this period in *The Chemical Theatre;* the standard history of English Paracelsianism is Debus, *The English Paracelsians.* Renaissance treatises on other aspects of magic and science are surveyed below, in Chapter 5. Among the recent histories of trials for witchcraft in England are Thomas's chapters on the subject in *Religion and the Decline of Magic;* Alan Macfarlane, *Witchcraft in Tudor and Stuart England;* and Hugh Trevor-Roper, *The European Witch-Craze of the Sixteenth and Seventeenth Centuries.*

6. See Garin's *Italian Humanism* and *Science and Civic Life in the Renaissance.* Although John Herman Randall in *The Making of the Modern Mind,* Douglas Bush in *The Renaissance and English Humanism,* and others have argued that humanism did not contribute to scientific inquiry, more recent studies such as Eric Cochrane's "Science and Humanism in the Italian Renaissance" have supported Garin's thesis. See the survey of scholarship in "Problems of the Scientific Renaissance" by Marie Boas Hall in *The Renaissance: Essays in Interpretation,* 273–96.

7. Kristeller, *Renaissance Thought and Its Sources,* 23. In a footnote Kristeller cites Garin's *Italian Humanism* as an instance of this tendency.

8. Charles Zika, for example, in "Reuchlin and Erasmus: Humanism and the Occult Philosophy," has defined humanism purely and simply as equivalent to the interests of Erasmus, and he argues that Johannes Reuchlin, frequently regarded as a humanist, does not merit the title because of his interest in the occult philosophy to which Erasmus objected. John G. Burke, on the other hand, in "Hermetism as a Renaissance World View" (111) has argued that

"of the great humanists, only Erasmus held reservations about magic." Kristeller himself, while retaining his definition of humanism per se, acknowledges that "the influence of humanism went beyond the *studia humanitatis* to touch every level of Renaissance culture" ("The Renaissance in the History of Philosophical Thought," in *The Renaissance: Essays in Interpretation,* 135).

9. Kristeller, *Renaissance Thought and Its Sources,* 30–32, 169–72, et passim.

10. Nesca Robb, *Neoplatonism of the Italian Renaissance,* 27–30. My conception of the relationships among humanism, Neoplatonism, and occult philosophy has also been influenced by Cassirer's *Individual and the Cosmos in Renaissance Philosophy;* Kristeller's *Philosophy of Marsilio Ficino,* esp. 10–29; and Trinkaus's *"In Our Image and Likeness."*

11. Cassirer, *Individual and the Cosmos,* 65–66. Quoting from Ficino's *Opera* (Basel, cited by Cassirer as n.d.), Cassirer cites, among other references, the following:

(1) *De visione Dei,* chap. 7: "Cum sic in silentio contemplationis quiesco, tu Domine intra praecordia mea respondes, dicens: sis tu tuus, et ego ero tuus. O Domine . . . posuisti in libertate mea ut sim, si voluero, mei ipsius. Hinc nisi sim mei ipsius, tu non es meus. . . . Et quia hoc posuisti in libertate mea, non me necessitas, sed expectas, ut ego eligam mei ipsius esse."

(2) *De christiana religione,* chap. 35, fol. 74: "Non cogit ad salutem Deus homines quos ab initio liberos procreavit, sed assiduis inspirationibus singulos allicit, quod si qui ad eum accesserint, hos durat laboribus, exercet adversitatibus, et velut igne aurum, sic animum probat difficultate."

(3) *Epistolae,* bk. 2, fol. 683: "Si quis autem dixerit, mentem ab alienis vel extrinsecis ad intelligentiam non moveri, sed ipsam et propria et mirabili quadam virtute suas sibi species, sua objecta concipere, dicemus ex eo sequi mentem esse incorpoream penitus et aeternam, si nequaquam ab alio, sed a seipsa movetur."

12. See below, Chapter 3.

13. See, for example, Cassirer, *Individual and the Cosmos,* 37–45 and 66 ff.; Robb, 31–56; Trinkaus, *"In Our Image and Likeness,"* xiii–xx

et passim; and Harry Levin, *The Myth of the Golden Age in the Renaissance,* 145 ff.

14. Panofsky, *Studies in Iconology,* 129–230.

15. Levin, *The Myth of the Golden Age,* xv–xx, 32–43, 139–67, et passim. Levin draws upon Arthur Lovejoy and George Boas's influential study, *Primitivism and Related Ideas in Antiquity* and upon George Boas's *Essays on Primitivism and Related Ideas in the Middle Ages.*

16. Ficino, *Opera* (Basel, 1576), 1:944, as translated by Levin, *Golden Age,* 39. References to the 1576 *Opera* are always to the page numbers of the original edition, not to those added at the bottom of the pages of the modern facsimile.

17. See, for example, *Pleasure Reconciled to Virtue,* in *Ben Jonson,* 7:479–91. *The Golden Age Restored* appears in 7:419–29. See also Graham Parry's *The Golden Age Restored: The Culture of the Stuart Court;* Stephen Orgel, *The Jonsonian Masque* and *The Illusion of Power;* and below, Chapter 8.

18. *Opus Epistolarum Des. Erasmi Roterdami,* 2:526–28 (no. 566), trans. in *Collected Works of Erasmus,* 4:309–11. Levin, *Golden Age,* 144–45 and 220, mentions this letter, as well as two others which seem to substantiate Erasmus' sincerity: *Opus Epistolarum,* 2:487–92 (no. 541, quoted below in F. M. Nichols' translation) and 3:587–93 (no. 967). These two letters are translated in *Collected Works,* 4:261–68 and 6:365–72.

19. I have chosen to retain F. M. Nichols' elegant translation from *The Epistles of Erasmus,* 2:506.

20. Baldesar Castiglione, *The Book of the Courtier,* trans. Charles Singleton, 303.

21. "Of Education," in *The Works of John Milton,* 4:277.

22. Occult and alchemical influences upon Renaissance millenarianism are explored by Norman Cohn in *The Pursuit of the Millennium,* esp. 150–54, 170–274, et passim; Rattansi, "Paracelsus and the Puritan Revolution"; and Hill, *The World Turned Upside Down.* Ronald A. Knox traces the roots of the radical sects back to ancient Gnosticism in *Enthusiasm: A Chapter in the History of Religion,* esp. chapters 5, 6, and 7.

23. See J. H. Hexter's introduction to More's *Utopia,* xcii–cv; Gilmore, *The World of Humanism,* 204–28; and Steven Ozment's *Mys-*

ticism and Dissent: Religious Ideology and Social Protest in the Sixteenth Century.

24. This point is central to Trinkaus's argument throughout *"In Our Image and Likeness."* For additional evidence in support of the generalizations in the present paragraph, see also, in addition to Chapters 2–5 below, Cassirer's *Individual and the Cosmos in Renaissance Philosophy;* Robb, *Neoplatonism of the Italian Renaissance;* and Kristeller, *The Philosophy of Marsilio Ficino.*

25. Ficino's *Pimander* and an edition of the Latin *Asclepius* appear in *Opera omnia,* 2:1836–71. The standard modern edition of the *Corpus Hermeticum* is by A. D. Nock, with a French translation by A. J. Festugière. An English translation (parallel texts) is available in Walter Scott's *Hermetica,* but many scholars prefer the Nock and Festugière edition because of the rearrangements which Scott makes in the text. Yates summarizes the most important points of these works, as well as Ficino's commentary on them, in *Giordano Bruno,* 20–42.

26. *Corpus Hermeticum,* 2:326 ff.; Ficino, *Opera,* 2:1858–71; Scott trans., 1:286–377. *Asclepius* is discussed by Yates, *Giordano Bruno,* 35–42. Yates, 40, cites Paul Kristeller, *Supplementum Ficinianum,* 1:cxxx ff., to the effect that the commentaries on *Asclepius* in the 1576 edition of Ficino's *Opera omnia* are in reality written by Lefèvre d'Etaples. The fact is important, since the commentary condemns as heretical the magical practices described in *Asclepius.*

27. Yates, *Giordano Bruno,* 49–57, 68–72. *Picatrix* is one of numerous works dealing with magic or alchemy which were associated with or attributed to Hermes Trismegistus, but which actually were written later than the *Corpus Hermeticum* itself. Modern scholars often apply the term "pseudo-Hermetic" to these later works, but the distinction between the two groups of texts was not usually applied during the Renaissance. See Yates, *Giordano Bruno,* 44–61.

Nicholas Clulee is correct to remind us, in "At the Crossroads of Magic and Science: John Dee's Archemastrie," that the occult tradition has diverse sources; John Dee, for example, draws heavily upon such medieval alchemists as Roger Bacon, as well as upon Renaissance Neoplatonists and Arabic philosophers. In the following chapters, however, I shall provide evidence that Renaissance magic was transformed by the renewed emphasis upon the original Hermetic texts and certain associated works (such as *Picatrix*), especially since the view of the grandeur and power of the human soul in these writings goes far beyond anything asserted by Roger Bacon or most other medieval alchemists. (See, for example, Bacon's *Letter Concerning the Marvelous Power of Art and of Nature and Concerning the Nullity of Magic,* 16). If one studies Dee's canon as a whole, the influence of Hermeticists such as Ficino, Pico, and Agrippa is prominent. In addition, the use of the term "Hermetic magic," rejected by Clulee, is also justified by Renaissance practice, since pseudo-Hermetic works and related texts such as *Picatrix,* the *Emerald Tablet,* and those collected in the *Hermetic Museum,* were included in the term.

28. Trans. in Kristeller, *The Philosophy of Marsilio Ficino,* 56.

29. Ficino, *Theologia Platonica,* ed. Raymond Marcel, 2:260. In translating the *Theologia* I have consulted, wherever possible, the numerous translations from Ficino which appear in Trinkaus's *"In Our Image and Likeness."*

30. See Haydn's *The Counter-Renaissance;* Nauert's *Agrippa and the Crisis of Renaissance Thought;* and Zika's "Reuchlin and Erasmus: Humanism and the Occult Philosophy." Peter French bases much of his interpretation of John Dee (see esp. 20–39) upon Yates's discussion of this problem.

31. Trinkaus establishes a continuity between humanism, Neoplatonism, and occult philosophy in *"In Our Image and Likeness,"* and the line of development he outlines is genuine; I place somewhat more emphasis than Trinkaus does, however, upon the importance of Hermetic/Cabalist magic in extending the humanists' emphasis upon the active life and thereby contributing to the evolution of science. Cf. Garin, *Italian Humanism,* 111–13 and 199–221, and *Science and Civic Life in the Renaissance,* 145–65.

2. ART AND MAGIC IN THE PHILOSOPHY OF MARSILIO FICINO

1. Major studies of Ficino's magic are Daniel P. Walker's *Spiritual and Demonic Magic from Ficino to Campanella;* Yates, *Giordano Bruno,* 62–83; and Brian P. Copenhaver, "Scholastic Philosophy and Renaissance Magic in the *De vita* of Marsilio Ficino." Thomas Moore's *The Planets Within: Marsilio Ficino's Astrological Psychology* rejects a historical approach and interprets *De vita* as a "revelation" of the psyche, understood in Jungian terms.

References to *De vita* are from Paul Kristeller's facsimile edition of the 1576 *Opera omnia*. Page numbers cited are those of the original folio, not those added at the bottom of the pages of the modern facsimile.

2. Kristeller, *Philosophy of Marsilio Ficino* (cited hereafter as *PMF*), 246: "Since Ideas are conceived by God and so are inherent in His mind, they are also identical with His substance and, therefore, through His substance are identical with each other. In other words, each Idea is merely a particular aspect of the divine essence, or to use a figure of speech, a particular color in the fullness of divine light."

3. On the doctrine of the rational soul in Ficino see *Theologia Platonica*, bk. 3, chap. 2, ed. Marcel, 1:137–43. Josephine L. Burroughs has published a translation of this section in *Journal of the History of Ideas*, 5 (1944): 227–32. All subsequent references to the *Theologia* are to the Marcel edition; translations are my own unless I note otherwise.

Ficino summarizes his conception of the universal hierarchy quite succinctly in *Theologia Platonica*, 2:206–7:

> Principio sub Deo mentes illas omnino solutas a corpore ponimus secundum Platonem, quos vocat Dionysius angelos purissimos, scilicet intellectus. Addimus inferiorem mentium gradum, earum scilicet quae iam corporibus uniuntur et quasi quidam angeli videntur esse, obtinentes quodammodo gradum infimum angelorum, quorum in numero sunt animae omnes rationales, sive mundi, seu mundanarum sphaerarum, syderum, daemonum atque hominum. Tertio loco sunt globi caelorum, elementarum, humorum. Proinde angelorum caput Deus est, quia radium suum rerum omnium creandarum rationibus praeditum per angelos omnes demittens, gradatim format omnes, ita ut in singulis universam describat mundi figuram. Neque solum sublimes illos intellectus angelosque purissimos sic exornat, verumetiam per illos tamquam medios in mentes quoque rationalium animarum quasi quosdam infimos angelos radium eumdem traducti, quasi quosdam infimos angelos radium eumdem traducti, iisdem praeditum rationibus. Huiusmodi rerum dispositio lexque divina inscripta mentibus providentia nuncupatur.

For detailed treatment of Ficino's concept of the unity and coherence of the cosmos, see Kristeller, *PMF,* 60–73, 92–120. On the relation between form and matter see 38–39, 126–27.

4. On the concept of humanity as microcosm and on the relation of the powers of the human soul to the universal hierarchy, see *Theologia Platonica,* 2:206–7 ff.; Trinkaus, *"In Our Image and Likeness,"* 476–77; Kristeller, *PMF,* 368 ff. Kristeller points out that Ficino is not precisely clear on the relation of the innate ideas of the human *Mens* to those of the Angelic Mind. Throughout this study I have capitalized the term "Mind" only when it refers to the highest, intuitive faculty within the soul or to the Angelic or Divine Mind; it is not capitalized when it is used in a more general sense.

5. Ficino, *Opera,* 1:373, trans. in Kristeller, *PMF,* 110. For Ficino's concept of the human soul and of *"primum in aliquo genere,"* see also *PMF,* 146–70 and 405–6. For a sensitive discussion of the influence upon Renaissance drama of Neoplatonic theories of humankind's visionary power, see Jackson Cope's *The Theater and the Dream,* esp. 14–28.

6. *Theologia Platonica,* 2:223, my emphasis. The term *spiritus,* discussed below, does not necessarily refer to the same kind of spiritual power as does the word *daemon;* Ficino's use of the term is ambiguous. On the importance for modern science of the departure from the Aristotelian concept of "imitation," see Paolo Rossi, "Hermeticism, Rationality, and the Scientific Revolution," 251–52, and Rossi's *Francis Bacon: From Magic to Science,* 16–27 et passim.

7. *Corpus Hermeticum,* 2:347–49; trans. Ficino, *Opera,* 2:1870; Scott trans., 1:359. On the importance of this passage in the tradition of Renaissance magic, see Yates, *Giordano Bruno,* 40–68.

8. On the hierarchical arrangement of species within each genus see Kristeller, *PMF,* 81–83. Cf. also Mircea Eliade's treatment of alchemy in *The Forge and the Crucible,* esp. 171–72 and 203–4.

9. *Theologia Platonica,* bk. 14, chap. 3, Burroughs trans., 237. The entire section translated by Burroughs is relevant.

10. *Theologia Platonica,* 2:237: "Quisnam animus haec agit? Qui phantasiam iubet silere, ac etiam superni numinis desiderio flagrans, consuetis rationis naturalis discursibus non confidit, sola vivit mente, evadit angelus, et toto capit pectore Deum. Haec significat Zoroaster, ubi sic inquit . . . 'Anima hominum Deum quodammodo contra-

hit in seipsam, quando nihil retinens mortale, tota divinis haustibus ebriatur. . . . ' Huiusmodi animum divi Ioannis theologia nasci iterum dicit ex Deo."

11. E. g., *Theologia Platonica,* 2:236, my emphasis:

Sed redeamus ad illos iam animos, per quos Deus quasi per instrumenta miracula perfecit. Quid confert illis ad hanc excellentiam habitudo corporis temperata, ut ratio illorum sit expeditior, nullo excedentium humorum turbata tumultu? Quid modicus purusque victus, ut non sit anima corporis sui sarcina praegravata? *Quid educatio illa honesta atque pia, ut et optet hominibus bona, et tamquam Deo quodammodo similis adiuvetur a Deo immo tamquam instrumentum a Deo ducatur?* Denique cum ratio eminentior phantasia, quando ipsa dedita Deo tota ad unum hoc opus beneficii conferendi dirigitur, remittitur admodum naturalis ille prior affectus animi quo proprio corpori copulatur, et ab eo soluta agit in alienum.

For a more detailed treatment of the process of purification, see 2:239–41.

12. *Theologia Platonica,* 2:237–38: "Si anima natura sua excedit mundi machinam perque vires inferiores mira operatur in corporibus etiam alienis, quid illam putamus acturam, quando in caput surrexerit suum evaseritque angelica? . . . Tunc igitur non unum quemdam amplius aut tenerum fascinabit, aut sanabit hominem aegrotantem, sed sphaeris imperabit elementorum."

13. *Opera,* 1:570: "In spiritu uiget anima, in anima fulget intelligentia."

14. For more detailed exposition of these types of magic, see Walker, *Spiritual and Demonic Magic,* 75–84, and Copenhaver, "Scholastic Philosophy," 523–54.

15. I have adopted the spelling *daemon* or *daemonic* in order to distinguish the spirits regarded by the Neoplatonists as benevolent from those evil spirits which the spelling *demon* normally brings to mind.

16. On the theory of *spiritus* in Ficino see *De vita coelitus comparanda,* chaps. 3 and 4, *Opera,* 1:534–36; Kristeller, *PMF,* 372 ff.; Walker, *Spiritual and Demonic Magic,* 3–24 and 38–44.

17. In addition to Walker's *Spiritual and Demonic Magic,* see Sherwood Taylor, *The Alchemists,* 226–30. Ficino discusses the "force of

imagination" in *De vita, Opera,* 1:553–54. Cornelius Agrippa, in his *De occulta philosophia libri tres* (1533), discusses both subjective and transitive forms of magic in great detail: on transitive magic and the force of the imagination, see bk. 1, chaps. 40, 50, 58–65; and bk. 3, chaps. 6 and 43. Book and chapter numbers in the 1533 edition and the 1651 English translation are identical.

18. *Opera,* 1:531: "[A]nima mundi totidem saltem rationes rerum seminales diuinitus habet, quot ideae sunt in mente diuina, quibus ipsa rationibus totidem fabricat species in materia. Vnde unaquaeque species per propriam rationem seminalem propriae respondet ideae, facileque potest per hanc saepe aliquid illinc accipere, quandoquidem per hanc illinc est effecta. Ideoque si quando a propria forma degeneret, potest hoc medio sibi proximo formari rursum, perque id medium inde facile reformari, ac si certe cuidam rerum speciei, vel indiuiduo eius rite adhibeas multa, quae sparsa sunt, sed etiam ideae conformia. Mox in materiam hanc ita opportune paratam, singulare munus ab idea trahes, per rationem uidelicet animae seminalem. Non enim intellectus ipse proprie, sed anima ducitur."

19. Ficino probably has such procedures in mind in the passage cited in note 18, above, although he may also be referring to talismans. Such groupings were quite common in magical procedures; see, for example, Agrippa's *De occulta philosophia,* bk. 1, chap. 35.

20. *Opera,* 1:548–49. Ficino discusses talismans at 1:530 and 548–61. See also Walker, *Spiritual and Demonic Magic,* 13–16; Yates, *Giordano Bruno,* 62–83; and Copenhaver, "Scholastic Philosophy," esp. 538.

21. On Ficino, pagan religion, and daemons, see Yates, *Giordano Bruno,* 66–68 and 79–83; Walker, *Spiritual and Demonic Magic,* 36–53; and Copenhaver, "Scholastic Philosophy." Walker cites *Contra Gentiles,* 3.104–6, and *Summa Theologica* 2da, 2dae, q. 96, a.ii, as relevant passages in Thomas Aquinas. For Augustine's attitude see *The City of God,* bks. 8–10. Robert West presents an excellent discussion of Renaissance sources in *The Invisible World,* 1–48.

22. The entire passage (*Opera,* 1:571) is as follows: "His fermē exemplis ipse Plotinus utitur, ubi Mercurium imitatus ait veteres sacerdotes, siue Magos in statuis sacrificiisque in sensibilibus diuinum aliquid & mirandum suscipere solitos. Vult autem unā cum Trismegisto per materialia haec non proprie suscipi numina penitūs ā materia segregata, sed mundana tantum, ut ab initio dixi, & Synesius

approbat. Mundana, inquam, id est, uitam quandam, uel uitale aliquid ex anima mundi, & sphaerum animis, atque stellarum, vel etiam
motum quendam, & uitalem, quasi praesentiam ex daemonibus,
immo interdum ipsos daemones eiusmodi adesse materiis." The disclaimer in Ficino's *Apologia* for *De vita* (1:573) is more precise: "Neque de magia haec prophana, quae cultu daemonum nititur, uerbum
quidem ullum asseuerari, sed de magia naturali, quae rebus natural-
ibus ad prosperam corporum ualetudinem coelestium beneficia cap-
tat, effeci mentionem."

23. *Opera,* 1:440: "Iam ueró Orpheus, magnus religionis illius
author, hymnos quamplurimos non solum coelistibus, sed etiam daemonibus daemonicisque hominibus consecrauit, certasque certis sub
fumigationes adhibuit." Except for the spelling of *daemon,* I have followed the translation in Walker, *Spiritual and Demonic Magic,* 49–50.
The phrase "celestial gods" is, perhaps, a free translation, but the
original passage certainly makes clear that Ficino knew the songs to
be addressed to daemons. See Walker's comments on this passage,
48–53.

24. R. T. Wallis, *Neoplatonism,* 90.

25. Wallis describes the conflicts between Plotinian Neoplatonism and Christianity on pp. 100–110 of *Neoplatonism.* He discusses
the role of theurgy in later Neoplatonism on pp. 3–4, 105–10, and
153–57.

26. See Scott's discussion in his introduction to *Hermetica,* esp.
1:12–13. My summary of Hermetic doctrine is based upon Ficino's
translation in *Opera,* 2:1837–56, as well as Yates's discussion in *Giordano Bruno,* 22–38. Relevant passages are translated by Scott, esp.
1:119–23.

27. In *The Occult Sciences in the Renaissance,* 206–14, Wayne Shumaker attempts, like Scott (1:1), to free the philosophical treatises
which we now regard as the *Corpus Hermeticum* proper from any
association with magic. As Yates points out, however, in *Giordano
Bruno,* 44–49 et passim (drawing upon A. J. Festugière's authoritative
La Révélation d'Hermès Trismégiste), the early philosophical works traditionally were understood as closely related to the magical treatises
which were also attributed to Hermes. The *Corpus Hermeticum* contains much of the astrology and daemonology on which magic depends, and the idol-vivification passage in *Asclepius* occupies an
important position in the philosophical works. The regeneration of

the soul described in the *Corpus Hermeticum* often involves the defeat of evil daemons and an escape from astrological influences. Furthermore, operative magic is the logical extension of the optimistic conception of humanity as creator which we find in the Hermetic books and which is illustrated in the passages I have just discussed. See also Yates's review of *The Occult Sciences in the Renaissance* in the *New York Review of Books*, 25 January 1973, 41–42.

28. See, for example, Alistair C. Crombie's "Science and the Arts in the Renaissance: The Search for Truth and Certainty, Old and New," 15–26.

3. PICO DELLA MIRANDOLA

1. Thorndike, in *A History of Magic and Experimental Science*, 4:485, asserts that "one cannot but feel that the importance of Pico della Mirandola in the history of thought has often been grossly exaggerated. . . . The darling of enthusiasts for the so-called Italian Renaissance, his reputation must decline with its." Professor Craven's more recent and very formidable arguments are considered below.

Pico is central to such classics of scholarship as Ernst Cassirer's *The Individual and the Cosmos in Renaissance Philosophy* (see 2–3, 59–72, 83–89, 115–21, et passim), and Eugenio Garin's *Italian Humanism* (78–135). See also Cassirer's influential two-part article, "Giovanni Pico della Mirandola: A Study in the History of Renaissance Ideas." Paul Kristeller offers judicious assessment of the significance of Pico's thought and of Florentine Neoplatonism in general in *The Renaissance Philosophy of Man*, ed. Ernst Cassirer, Paul Kristeller, and John Herman Randall, Jr., 215–22; *Eight Philosophers of the Italian Renaissance*, 54–71; and *Renaissance Thought and Its Sources*, 167–210.

2. For thorough discussion of the importance of stressing the differences between occult philosophy and genuine science, see Brian Vickers' introduction to *Occult and Scientific Mentalities in the Renaissance*, 1–55, and Paolo Rossi's "Hermeticism, Rationality, and the Scientific Revolution," 247–73. Professor Rossi's article, combined with his book, *Francis Bacon: From Magic to Science*, provides a precisely balanced discussion of the subject.

Robert Westman, in "Magical Reform and Astronomical Reform: The Yates Thesis Reconsidered," in *Hermeticism and the Scientific Revolution*, 1–91, raises formidable questions about Yates's assertion that Hermetic philosophy—especially the idea that the source of life should logically make itself visible at the center of the cosmos—provided theological justification for the adoption of Copernicanism. Westman concedes, however, that Hermeticism may have helped to undermine dogmatic adherence to Aristotelian natural philosophy, and he does not address the question of whether the occultists' exaltation of humanity as essentially creative and in control of nature contributed to the evolution of science. Yates's conclusions concerning these aspects of the influence of occult philosophy have been corroborated by Debus, Hill, and others; see below, Chapter 5.

3. On the dissemination of the Christian Cabalism initiated by Pico, see Joseph Blau, *The Christian Interpretation of the Cabala in the Renaissance;* Yates, *Giordano Bruno* and *The Occult Philosophy in the Elizabethan Age;* and Zika's "Reuchlin and Erasmus: Humanism and the Occult Philosophy." John Dee's remarks on Pico's *Conclusiones* appear on sig. *4r of *The Mathematical Praeface to the Elements of Geometrie of Euclid of Megra, 1570.* George P. Parks provides evidence for the popularity of Pico's purely devotional literature in "Pico della Mirandola in Tudor Translation," 352–69. A rather surprising and intriguing Elizabethan reference to Pico occurs in John Foxe's *Actes and Monuments* (1583), 2:843 (misnumbered, in the copy I have examined, as 2:841), in which Foxe includes Pico in his list of praiseworthy Renaissance scholars who had prepared the way for the Reformation by spreading learning and thereby enabling people to see through the abuses of the church. Sir Walter Ralegh's extensive use of Pico's occult philosophy is discussed below, in Chapter 5.

4. Giovanni Pico della Mirandola, *Oratio (De hominis dignitate)* in *De hominis dignitate, Heptaplus, De ente et uno, e scritti vari,* ed. Eugenio Garin, 114–16. Quotations from the *Oratio* and *Heptaplus* are my translations of the Latin text edited by Garin. I have made close comparisons to the excellent translations of Charles Glenn Wallis and Douglas Carmichael in *On the Dignity of Man, On Being and the One, Heptaplus* and I am indebted to their work.

Charles Trinkaus endeavors to minimize the importance of transitive magic in Pico's philosophy, but his treatment of Pico's thought is based almost entirely upon *Heptaplus,* which was written after Pico's *Conclusiones* had been declared heretical. Trinkaus himself concedes (*"In Our Image and Likeness,"* 524) that a consideration of Pico's other writings might yield results quite different from his own.

5. Invaluable discussions of relevant aspects of the Cabala appear in Gershom Scholem's *Major Trends in Jewish Mysticism,* 144–46, 245–48, and 265–80; and in his *On the Kabbalah,* 115–17. My discussion of Pico's Cabalist magic is intended to corroborate and extend Yates's commentary in *Giordano Bruno,* 84–116.

6. For Pico's eschatology in *Heptaplus,* see pp. 286, 324–38, and 372. An explicit disavowal of talismanic magic appears on p. 244. Louis Valcke provides valuable insight into the significance of Pico's reversal of his former opinions in "Magie et miracle chez Jean Pic de la Mirandole," esp. 164–69.

7. On the two types of Cabala see Pico's second set of Cabalist Conclusions, nos. 1–3, in *Conclusiones,* ed. Bohdan Kieszkowski, p. 83; *Apologia,* in *Opera omnia,* 1:180–81; and Yates's commentary in *Giordano Bruno,* 92–97. Except as noted, references to the *Conclusiones* and *Apologia* are to these editions. Kieszkowski's edition retains *e* for *ae* in many instances, as well as *c* in some places in which classical Latin (and some texts of Pico's *Conclusiones*) would use *t* (e.g., "pocius" for "potius"). As I note below, there are a few instances in which I prefer readings from the 1557 *Opera* which differ from those of the Kieszkowski edition. Professor Kieszkowski has, however, examined the relevant manuscripts and early editions, and he corrects a number of serious and misleading errors which appear in the 1557 text.

8. *Oratio,* 104–6: "Nec certam sedem, nec propriam faciem, nec munus ullum peculiare tibi dedimus, o Adam, ut quam sedem, quam faciem, quae munera tute optaveris, ea, pro voto, pro tua sententia, habeas et possideas. Definita ceteris natura intra praescriptas a nobis leges coercetur. Tu, nullis angustiis coercitus, pro tuo arbitrio, in cuius manu te posui, tibi illam praefinies. Medium te mundi posui, ut circumspiceres inde commodius quicquid est in mundo. Nec te caelestem neque terrenum, neque mortalem neque immortalem fecimus, ut tui ipsius quasi arbitrarius honorariusque plastes et fictor, in quam malueris tute formam effingas. Poteris in inferiora quae sunt bruta degenerare; poteris in superiora quae sunt divina ex tui animi sententia regenerari."

The Creator's speech to Adam is crucially important, and its interpretation has figured prominently in debates concerning Renaissance intellectual history. William G. Craven is correct to emphasize that Pico is not celebrating "promiscuous metamorphosis" (*Gio-*

vanni Pico della Mirandola, 35); he is exhorting us to cultivate the higher levels of the human personality. As I shall emphasize in the remainder of this chapter, however, the extent to which Pico attributes to humankind the ability to surpass even the angels goes far beyond what most orthodox theologians could accept.

9. Pico found what he believed were references to the Trinity in many of the occult writings, and he claimed to have discovered that the Jewish Cabalists' own methods of textual exegesis of the Scriptures proved that Jesus was indeed the Messiah of Old Testament prophecy. See Magical Conclusion no. 9; Orphic Conclusions 8 and 9; Cabalist Conclusions 5–7, 10, and 14–15 (Kieszkowski ed., pp. 79, 81, and 83–85).

10. Pico describes these stages of development in the *Oratio,* 116–24. He mentions the perfection of humanity through the descent of the Holy Spirit in the context of Cabalist mysticism in Cabalist Conclusion no. 15, Kieszkowski ed., p. 85: "Per nomen Iod, he, uahu, he, quod est nomen ineffabile, quod dicunt Cabaliste, futurum esse nomen Messie, euidenter cognoscitur futurum eum Deum dei filium per spiritum sanctum hominem factum, et post eum ad perfectionem humani generis super homines paraclytum descensurum."

11. *Hermetica,* trans. Scott, 1:359; the passage also occurs in Ficino's *Opera,* 2:1870.

12. Orphic Conclusion no. 3, Kieszkowski ed., p. 80: "Nomina deorum, quos Orpheus canit, non decipientibus demonum, a quibus malum et non bonum prouenit, sed naturalium uirtutum, diuinarumque sunt nomina, et uero Deo in utilitatem maxime hominis." The 1557 *Opera,* 1:106, adds the following, omitted in the Kieszkowski edition: " . . . si eis uti sciuerit, mundo distributarum."

13. *Conclusiones,* Kieszkowski ed., p. 79:

5. Nulla est virtus in celo et in terra seminaliter et separata, quam et actuare et unire magus non possit.

11. Mirabilia artis magice non sunt nisi per unionem et actuacionem eorum, que seminaliter et separate sunt in natura.

14. Ibid.: "Magicam operari non est aliud quam maritare mundum."

15. Ibid., p. 80: "Sicut per primi agentis influxum, si sit specialis

et immediatus, fit aliquid quod non attingitur per mediacionem causarum, ita per opus cabale, si sit pura Cabala et immediata, fit aliquid, ad quod nulla Magia attingit." Craven (128) argues that this conclusion need not necessarily refer to transitive Cabalist magic. He proposes the following as a possible translation: "Just as the influence of the first agent, if it is special and immediate, does something which is not affected by the mediation of causes, so what is done by way of Kabbalah, if it is pure and immediate, is not affected by magic." A much more probable reading, in my opinion, would be as follows: "Since something may be done through the influence of a prime agent, if it be special and immediate, which cannot be attained through the mediation of secondary causes, thus through a work of Cabala—if it be pure and immediate Cabala—one can accomplish something which ordinary magic cannot attain." Surely the term "influxum" refers to astrological influence, and Pico is saying that the "prime agents" (i.e., the Sephiroth, the highest angelic powers) possess greater power than intermediary spirits. It is also possible, as Craven acknowledges, that the "prime agent" is God Himself.

See also Pico's references to magical Hebrew names and numerological symbols in Magical Conclusions 19–25 and Cabalist Conclusions 6–8 (Kieszkowski ed., pp. 79–80, 84). John F. D'Amico, in "Paolo Cortesi's Rehabilitation of Giovanni Pico della Mirandola," points out that those who wished to make Pico acceptable to orthodox authorities had to ignore altogether the esoteric and Cabalist aspects of his thought, especially with regard to the *Conclusiones*.

16. *Conclusiones,* ed. Kieszkowski, p. 79: "Nulla potest esse operatio magica alicuius efficacie, nisi annexu habeat opus cabale explicatum, uel implicitum."

17. Ibid., 90: "Ego animam nostram sic decem Sephirot adapto, ut per unitatem suam sit cum prima, per intellectum cum secunda, per racionem cum tercia, per superiorem concupiscibilem cum quarta, per superiorem irascibilem cum quinta, per liberum arbitrium cum sexta, et per hoc totum ut ad superiora se conuertitur cum septima, ut ad inferiora cum octaua, et mixtum ex utroque pocius per indifferenciam uel alternariam adhesionem, quam simultaneam continenciam cum nona, et per potenciam qua inhabitat primum; habitaculum cum decima." My translation assumes that the final semicolon (omitted in the

1557 *Opera*, 1:113) is an error. See also Yates, *Giordano Bruno*, 100–102.

18. This quotation is from Yates's account of *Corpus Hermeticum*, Treatise 13, in Yates, *Giordano Bruno*, 30. For the entire treatise, see Nock and Festugière, 2:200–9; Scott trans., 1:239–55; Ficino, *Opera*, 2:1854–56.

19. *Conclusiones*, ed. Kieszkowski, p. 83:

> 26. Qui perfecte in animam redierit, prime forme suam formam equauerit.
> 27. Qui precedentis conclusionis opus tentauerit, Iouem adibit tercium, ut uiventem, non ut uiuificantem.

20. Ibid., 84: "Modus quo racionabiles anime per archangelum Deo sacrificantur, qui a Cabalistis non exprimitur, non est nisi per separacionem anime a corpore, non corporis ab anima nisi per accidens, ut contigit in morte osculi, de quo scribitur *praeciosa in conspectu domini mors sanctorum eius.*"

21. Ibid., 79: "Forma totius magice uirtutis est ab anima hominis stante et non cadente."

22. Ibid.: "Quodcumque fiat opus mirabile, siue sit magicum, siue cabalisticum, siue cuiuscunque alterius generis, principatissime referendum est in Deum gloriosum et benedictum, *cuius gracia supercelestes mirabilium uirtutum aquas super contemplatiuos homines bone voluntatis quotidie pluit liberaliter*" (my emphasis).

23. See Hans Jonas, *The Gnostic Religion*, 103–11.

4. CORNELIUS AGRIPPA

1. Studies of Agrippa's influence include Nauert's *Agrippa and the Crisis of Renaissance Thought*, esp. 195–97, 298, and 314–34; Yates, *Giordano Bruno*, 130–56 et passim; and Peter French, *John Dee*, 28–30 and 62–125 passim.

2. *De occulta philosophia*, bk. 3, chap. 64, p. 341. All quotations from *De occulta philosophia* are my translations of the 1533 edition. Subsequent references are to book, chapter, and page numbers; book and chapter numbers of the 1533 Latin text and the 1651 English translation are identical. I have found that the 1651 translation by J. F. is generally accurate, but occasionally (though certainly not always) the translator has toned down the heretical aspects of Agrippa's thought.

3. "Omnes res obediunt illi, quando fertur in magnum excessum alicuius passionis" (1.68, p. 89).

4. On the use of occult virtues, see 1.2, pp. 1–3 and 1.9–12, pp. 13–16. Agrippa equates these virtues with "gods" or "souls" in 1.13–14, as in the following passage:

> Democritus autem & Orpheus, & multi Pythagoricorum coe-
> lestium vires inferorumque naturas diligentissime perscrutati,
> omnia plena diis esse dixerunt: nec abs re, siquidem nulla res
> est tam praestantibus viribus, quae uiduata diuino auxilio sui
> natura contenta sit. Deos autem uocabant uirtutes diuinas in
> rebus diffusas: quas Zoroaster diuinas illices, Synesius symbol-
> icas illecebras, alii uitas, alii etiam almas nominabant; & ab his
> uirtutes rerum dependere dicebant: quia solius animae sit, ab
> una materia extendi in res alias, circa quas operatur: sicut
> homo, qui extendit intellectum ad intelligibilia, & imaginati-
> onem ad imaginabilia. (1.14, p. 19)

J. F. (p. 32) cautiously substitutes "God" in the first clause for "diis." The substitution is, in a sense, justifiable, since Agrippa re-gards subordinate deities as aspects of God, as he explains in 3.16, p. 239:

> Dico autem daemones hic non illos quos diabolos uocamus,
> sed spiritus sic uocatos ex uocabuli proprietate, quasi scientes,
> intelligentes & sapientes. Horum vero secundum magorum
> traditionem tria genera sunt, quorum primos supercoelestes
> uocant, atque mentes a corpore penitus se iunctas, & quasi
> intellectuales sphaeras, deum unum tanquam ipsorum fir-
> missimam stabilissimamque unitatem siue centrum colentes:
> quapropter illos iam etiam deos nuncupant, propter diuinitatis
> participationem quandam: quia semper sunt deo pleni, divin-
> oque nectare ebrii.

J. F. translates "daemones" as "angels," which, although a more cautious word, is precisely what Agrippa means. On the lesser dei-ties as aspects of God, see also 3.24, esp. p. 255.

5. "In syderibus quoque zodiaci, duodecim ponebant Pythago-rici particulares deos, siue animas.... Ipseque antiquissimus Or-pheus ad Museum scribens ampliora istis enumerat coelorum nu-mina.... Nemo ergo putet haec malorum & decipientium

daemonum nomina esse: sed naturalium diuinarumque virtutum, a uero deo in ministerium & utilitatem hominis qui eis uti sciuerit, mundo distributarum" (2.58, pp. 203–4).

6. The following discussion of daemonology is based upon bk. 3, chaps. 10 and 14–25, esp. chaps. 14–17, pp. 235–43.

7. "Nullum opus sit in tota mundi serie tam admirabile, tam excellens, tam miraculosum, quod anima humana suam diuinitatis imaginem complexa, quam uocant Magi animam stantem & non cadentem, sua propria uirtute absque omni externo adminiculo non queat efficere" (3.44, p. 310).

8. Bk. 3, chap. 3, p. 214. This entire chapter discusses the importance of education and religious ceremonies. See also the dedicatory epistle to bk. 3, pp. 209–10; 3.45–49, pp. 310–16 (on the four "furores," or stages of inspiration); and 3.53–64, pp. 322–45 (on rapture, prophecy, penitence, and ceremonial purifications). For specific descriptions of the union of the individual with God, see 3.11, pp. 227–32; 3.36, pp. 284–89; and 3.59, pp. 331–34. Agrippa affirms his personal belief in the possibility of the deification of humanity in two letters attached to the *De occulta philosophia*, pp. 346–48.

9. Except as noted, my account of the events of Agrippa's life and of the dates of composition of his works is derived from Nauert's *Agrippa and the Crisis of Renaissance Thought*. The 1531 edition of Agrippa's skeptical treatise was entitled *De incertitudi[n]e et vanitate scientiarum declamatio invecta;* the titles of subsequent editions vary somewhat. The title which I have quoted in the text appears in Agrippa's *Opera*, n.d., facsimile edition by Richard Popkin, and will subsequently be abbreviated as *De vanitate*.

10. Eugene Korkowski, "Agrippa as Ironist," 594–607; Philip Sidney, *Defence of Poetry*, 49; James Sanford, "To the Reader" in *Of the vanitie and vncertaintie of the artes and sciences*, sig. *ii r–*iv r. On Agrippa's *Apologia*, see Nauert, *Agrippa*, 196–97.

11. Wolf Dieter Müller-Jahncke, in "The Attitude of Agrippa von Nettesheim (1486–1535) towards Alchemy," has shown that Agrippa's correspondence during the years 1528–31 reveals that he continued to experiment with alchemy, but that he became progressively disillusioned. The initial draft of *De vanitate* had already been written by 1526, but it was not published until 1531.

12. Nauert, *Agrippa*, 44–50, 104–15, 194–221. Although Professor Nauert is correct to emphasize the quest for certainty through

divine revelation as the most enduring characteristic of Agrippa's thought, the study of occult philosophy is seen in both *De occulta philosophia* (esp. bk. 3, chap. 3) and *De vanitate* as an extension of traditional learning, and Agrippa's rejection of magic quite naturally follows his rejection of other arts and sciences. See also above, Chapter 1, esp. 19–21.

13. Cornelius Agrippa, *De vanitate,* chap. 1, in *Opera,* ed. Popkin, 2:5. All references to *De vanitate* are to volume and page numbers of Popkin's facsimile edition of Agrippa's *Opera.* Quotations in the text are my translations of this edition; chapter numbers in the Latin text are identical to those of the 1569 translation by James Sanford.

14. "Ars data est mortalibus, qua res posteriores quasdam generarent, non quidem veritatis & divinitatis participes, sed simulachra quaedam sibi ipsis cognata deducerent: atque eovsque progressi sunt magi homines audacissimi omnia perpetrare, favente maxime antiquo illo & palido serpente scientiarum pollicitatore, vt similes illi tanquam simiae, Deum & naturam aemulari conarentur" (2:92). This passage is a precise reversal of Ficino's belief that art and magic reveal humankind's godlike potential.

15. For additional evidence of Agrippa's radical views, see *De vanitate,* chaps. 54 and 56–63; Nauert, *Agrippa,* 157–93; and Zambelli's "Magic and Radical Reformation in Agrippa of Nettesheim."

16. Details of the case are documented in Nauert, *Agrippa,* 59–61. A translation of one of Agrippa's letters to a magistrate concerning this case appears in *Renaissance Letters: Revelations of a World Reborn,* ed. Robert J. Clements and Lorna Levant, 143–44.

17. *De vanitate,* 2:311–12. Cf. 1 John 2:20–27.

5. MAGIC IN RENAISSANCE ENGLAND

1. See Marie Boas Hall's survey of major studies in "Problems of the Scientific Renaissance," in *The Renaissance,* by André Chastel and others. Important for the present chapter are the following studies of the social and intellectual contexts of the development of science in England: Christopher Hill, *Intellectual Origins of the English Revolution;* Paolo Rossi, *Francis Bacon: From Magic to Science;* Antonia McLean, *Humanism and the Rise of Science in Tudor England;* John W. Shirley, ed., *Thomas Harriot: Renaissance Scientist;* Shirley, *Thomas Harriot: A Biography* (on the importance of Francis Drake's influence, see esp. 72–74); Allen Debus, *The English Paracelsians, The Chemical*

Dream of the Renaissance, and *The Chemical Philosophy*. Mordechai Feingold has presented considerable evidence in *The Mathematicians' Apprenticeship: Science, Universities, and Society in England, 1560-1640*, that Oxford and Cambridge were somewhat less conservative than previous studies have suggested.

2. See J. Peter Zetterburg, "The Mistaking of 'the Mathematicks' for Magic in Tudor and Stuart England."

3. "The Prologe of the Wyves Tale of Bathe," in *The Complete Poetry and Prose of Geoffrey Chaucer*, ed. John H. Fisher, 107, lines 1–2.

4. Thomas Rainold, *A Compendious Declaration of the Excellent vertues of a certain lateli inventid oile*, sig. B3v–B4r. I should mention at the outset that all primary sources cited in this chapter were either printed in England or influential there through imported editions. On the extent of the import trade, see, for example, William Proctor Williams, "Other Patterns of Stoicism, 1530–1670."

5. Robert Recorde, *The Castle of Knowledge*, 1556 ed., 127 (misnumbered, in the copy I have examined, as 129). Recorde cites examples of the benefits of learning on sig. a6r–a7v et passim; for a discussion of Recorde's influence, see Hill, *Intellectual Origins*, 17, 20–24, 30–31, et passim; McLean, *Humanism and Science*, 71, 131–33; Rossi, *Francis Bacon*, 39–40.

6. Preface to Robert Recorde, *The Pathway to Knowledg[e]*, sig. 3v.

7. British Library, Lansdowne MS 98, art. 1, leaf 2. Published by F. J. Furnivall in the Publications of the Early English Text Society, Extra Series, 8 (London, 1869), 4–5, as quoted by Shirley in *Thomas Harriot: A Biography*, 79.

8. Document 56 in E.G.R. Taylor, *The Original Writings & Correspondence of the Two Richard Hakluyts*, 2:362–69, as quoted by Shirley in *Thomas Harriot: A Biography*, 80.

9. Jean Jacquot, "Harriot, Hill, Warner, and the New Philosophy," 108. Haggar's remarks were recorded by Anthony à Wood in *Athenae Oxonienses* and passed on to John Aubrey, *Brief Lives*, 1:286. Wood's account omitted several words and erroneously read "He [Harriot] could not believe the old position *ex nihilo nihil fit*," but Jacquot, Shirley, and others have corrected the error. See Shirley, *Thomas Harriot: A Biography*, 199, n. 55. Additional evidence of Bruno's influence on Harriot appears in Daniel Massa's "Giordano Bruno's Ideas in Seventeenth-Century England," esp. 240–42.

10. Marlowe's remarks on Moses, including an additional suggestion that Moses' apparent miracles were the "subtleties" of a magician, appear in British Museum, Harleian MS 6848, fols. 185–86, reproduced in C. F. Tucker Brooke, *The Life of Marlowe*, 98–100. Kyd's remarks appear in a letter to John Puckering, Harleian MS 6849, fol. 218, quoted by Brooke, 105. Robert Parsons' remarks are quoted from *An Advertisement Written to a Secretarie of my L. Treasurers of Ingland*, 18. Two versions of Popham's remarks are quoted by Shirley, *Thomas Harriot: A Biography*, 316. On the heretical religious beliefs of Harriot, Hill, and Warner, see Jean Jacquot, "Thomas Harriot's Reputation for Impiety," and "Harriot, Hill, Warner, and the New Philosophy"; David B. Quinn and John W. Shirley, "A Contemporary List of Hariot References"; and the extensive discussion throughout Shirley's *Biography*. The theory developed in Muriel Bradbrook's *The School of Night*, Frances Yates's *A Study of "Love's Labor's Lost,"* and elsewhere that Ralegh, Marlowe, Harriot, and others formed a close circle and shared a common "doctrine" has been effectively criticized, but subsequent research has confirmed that the men knew each other and discussed religion, philosophy, and science. Shirley's *Thomas Harriot: A Biography* is the most recent relevant study, but there is significant additional evidence in Brooke, *The Life of Marlowe*, and John Bakeless, *The Tragicall History of Christopher Marlowe*, esp. 1:134–36. Paul Kocher, in *Christopher Marlowe: A Study of His Thought, Learning, and Character*, 3–68, provides carefully reasoned and still convincing arguments in favor of the significance of the Baines document as providing insight into Marlowe's opinions.

11. Thomas Harriot, *A briefe and true report of the new found land of Virginia*, sig. E3v. Stephen Greenblatt constructs a detailed argument concerning the subversive implications of Harriot's pamphlet in "Invisible Bullets: Renaissance Authority and Its Subversion."

12. Essential documents relating to the Cerne Abbas inquiry are reproduced in an appendix to G. B. Harrison's edition of *Willobie his Avisa*. Detailed examination of Ralegh's religious beliefs and his skepticism with regard to the powers of human reason appear in Ernest A. Strathmann's *Sir Walter Ralegh: A Study in Elizabethan Skepticism*.

13. Sir Walter Ralegh, *History*, in *Works*, ed. Oldys and Birch, 2:1–42, esp. 1–5. All references are to this edition.

14. In addition to the discussion of utopian and apocalyptic as-

pects of the occult tradition in Chapters 1–4 above, see Yates, *Giordano Bruno,* 54–56, 205–90, and 360–97; Yates, *Astraea: The Imperial Theme in the Sixteenth Century;* P. M. Rattansi, "Paracelsus and the Puritan Revolution"; Keith Thomas, *Religion and the Decline of Magic,* 124–46 and 371–78; Norman Cohn, *The Pursuit of the Millennium;* and Christopher Hill, *The World Turned Upside Down: Radical Ideas during the English Revolution.* Andrew Weiner offers judicious qualification of some of Yates's conclusions concerning the influence of Bruno's efforts at reform in his article "Expelling the Beast: Bruno's Adventures in England."

15. See above, Chapter 3, and the sources cited there, esp. in notes 3 and 5.

16. Quoted by William J. Bouwsma in *Concordia Mundi: The Career and Thought of Guillaume Postel,* 215–16. Important new research on Postel and his influence appears in Marion L. Kuntz's *Guillaume Postel, Prophet of the Restitution of All Things: His Life and Thought.*

17. The most thorough account of Dee's career is Peter French, *John Dee;* see pp. 28–32 on Dee's visit to Paris and contact with Postel. In addition to French, I have drawn upon Yates, *Giordano Bruno,* esp. 205-10, and *The Rosicrucian Enlightenment;* Evans, *Rudolf II and His World,* 219–28; and McLean, *Humanism and Science,* 133–45.

18. "A Translation of John Dee's 'Monas Hieroglyphica' (Antwerp, 1564), with an Introduction and Annotations," ed. and trans. C. H. Josten, 167, 166; cf. 120–23. All references to *Monas Hieroglyphica* are to this parallel-text edition.

19. See *Monas Hieroglyphica,* 159–65, and Josten's commentary, 99–111.

20. John Dee, *The Mathematical Praeface to the Elements of Geometrie of Euclid of Megra, 1570,* ed. Allen Debus, sig. c4r–v.

21. See esp. the transcripts provided by C. H. Josten in "An Unknown Chapter in the Life of John Dee," 243–57; and *A True and Faithful Relation of What passed for many Yeers Between Dr. John Dee . . . and Some Spirits.*

22. For discussion of Dee's ideas and evidence of his influence see, in addition to previously cited works by French, Evans, and Yates, *The Private Diary of Dr. John Dee,* ed. James Orchard Halliwell, 2, 4–6, 9, 18–21, 37, 49, 52, et passim; Dee, *Compendious Rehearsal,*

in *Autobiographical Tracts,* ed. James Crossley; and Ralph Sargent, *At the Court of Queen Elizabeth.*

23. Yates, *The Rosicrucian Enlightenment,* 30–40; Yates, *Giordano Bruno,* 203–10, 231, 292–94, 340–44; Evans, *Rudolf II,* 219–28; Josten, "An Unknown Chapter in the Life of John Dee."

24. *The Alchemist,* in *Ben Jonson,* II.vi.20 and IV.i.89–91. The context of the allusions is discussed below, Chapter 7.

25. Yates, *Giordano Bruno,* 229, 287–92, 317; Weiner, "Expelling the Beast: Bruno's Adventures in England."

26. Bruno, *Cena de le ceneri,* in *Dialoghi italiani,* 29–33, as translated by Yates, *Giordano Bruno,* 236–37.

27. *Cena de le ceneri,* 17–22; *The Ash Wednesday Supper,* trans. Stanley L. Jaki, 68–71.

28. Paracelsus, *The Hermetic and Alchemical Writings,* trans. A. E. Waite, 1:19–20. All references to Paracelsus' works are to this translation. My account of Paracelsus and his influence draws upon Walter Pagel, *Paracelsus;* Allen Debus, *The English Paracelsians;* and Charles Webster, *From Paracelsus to Newton: Magic and the Making of Modern Science.*

29. On alchemy as a redemptive art and on the progression in human knowledge as a sign of the approaching Millennium, see Paracelsus' "The Aurora of the Philosophers," 1:48–71; "Alchemy: The Third Column of Medicine," 2:148–64; "Preface" to bk. 10 of *Archidoxes,* 2:81–83; and Pagel, *Paracelsus,* esp. 36, 59–77, and 113–14. The influence of the parallel between the renewal of religion and the renewal of natural philosophy is stressed by Charles Webster throughout *From Paracelsus to Newton.*

30. John Hester, ed. and trans., *A Hundred and fourtene experiments and cures of the famous Phisition Philippus Aureolis Theophrastus Paracelsus* (*STC* 19179.5, formerly 19181), 3. The 1596 edition of the treatise (*STC* 19180) is severely corrupted. Additional translations by John Hester, many with his own prefaces and commentaries, are listed in the bibliography. On the influence of Hester's works, see Debus, *The English Paracelsians,* 65–70.

31. Dedicatory epistle to *An excellent Treatise teaching howe to cure the French Pockes . . . Drawne out of the Bookes of that learned Doctor and Prince of Phisitians, Theophrastus Paracelsus,* trans. John Hester, sigs. ii v–iii r.

32. See, for example, Thomas Tymme's dedicatory epistle to his translation of Joseph Du Chesne's *The Practise of Chymicall and Hermeticall Physicke*. The flourishing of alchemy, its emphasis on redemption, and the reaction against it are thoroughly documented by Charles Nicholl in *The Chemical Theatre*; discussion of Shakespeare's possible acquaintance with Forester appears on pp. 76–77. In addition to the treatises I am discussing in this chapter, see those listed in the bibliography under Roger Bacon, Hugh Plat, Thomas Norton, Thomas Charnock, and George Ripley.

33. The following discussion of R. Bostock's work is based primarily upon "The Authors obtestation to almightie God" (sigs. ****1r–A8r), and chaps. 1–3 (sigs. B1r–C3r) and 10–19 (sigs. F4r–I3r) of *The difference betwene the auncient Phisicke, first taught by the godly forefathers, consisting in vnitie[,] peace and concord: and the latter Phisicke proceeding from Idolaters, Ethnickes, and Heathen: as Gallen, and such other consisting in dualitie, discorde, and contrarietie*. "R.B." has been variously identified as Robert Bostock and Richard Bostock. Chaps. 13 and 14 are misnumbered in Bostock's text.

34. Marie Boas emphasizes this principle in her discussion of the Copernican revolution in *The Scientific Renaissance*, 68–89.

35. Bostock, sig. F2v. The preceding paragraph is also based upon "The Authors obtestation to almightie God," esp. sigs. ****1v–****3v; and chaps. 1–3, sigs. B1r–C3r; cf. also sig. E3r.

36. Debus, *The English Paracelsians* and *The Chemical Dream of the Renaissance*; Rattansi, "Paracelsus and the Puritan Revolution"; Hill, *Intellectual Origins of the English Revolution* and *The World Turned Upside Down*; Thomas, *Religion and the Decline of Magic*, 124–26 and 371–78; Cohn, *The Pursuit of the Millennium*, 150–55, 172–80, et passim.

37. Hugh Trevor-Roper, *The European Witch-Craze of the Sixteenth and Seventeenth Centuries*, 90–192; Cohn, *Europe's Inner Demons: An Enquiry Inspired by the Great Witch Hunt*; Yates, *The Occult Philosophy in the Elizabethan Age*, esp. 61–71; Jean Bodin, *De la démonomanie des sorciers*, bk. 1, chaps. 3 and 5, and bk. 2, chap. 2. Cohn also traces the belief in witchcraft to the practice of ritual magic in the late Middle Ages and early Renaissance.

38. Alan Macfarlane, *Witchcraft in Tudor and Stuart England*; Thomas, *Religion and the Decline of Magic*; Heinrich Kramer and James Springer, *Malleus maleficarum*, trans. Montague Summers, xliii–xlv; Christina Larner, *Enemies of God: The Witch-Hunt in Scotland* and

Witchcraft and Religion. The quotation is from *Enemies of God,* 5. There are major differences among the studies of witchcraft which I have cited, and many issues remain unresolved. Although there is no single explanation which applies to all accusations of witchcraft, the characterization of witches as arch-heretics and rebels against divinely sanctioned authority is obviously of central importance.

39. Peter Burke, "Witchcraft and Magic in Renaissance Italy: Gianfrancesco Pico and His *Strix.*" Thomas More's translation of the biography, entitled *Here is conteyned the Lyfe of Johan Picus . . . with dyvers epistles & other warkis (STC* 19897.7), apparently was published for the first time in 1510 and went through several editions, including the version included in the 1557 edition of More's *Complete Works.*

40. Bodin, *De la démonomanie,* preface, fol. c1r–v; bk. 1, chap. 3, 19v–20r. All references are to the 1580 edition. See also Christopher Baxter, "Jean Bodin's *De la démonomanie des sorciers:* The Logic of Persecution."

41. Francis Coxe, *A short treatise declaring the detestable wickednesse of magical sciences,* sig. A4v. All references are to this edition.

42. See, for example, Sanford's "To the Reader," esp. sigs. *3v–*4r, and the discussion above, Chapter 4.

43. Pagel provides a comprehensive discussion of Thomas Erastus' *Dispvtationvm de medicina nova Paracelsi* in *Paracelsus,* 311–33. On the influence of Erastus in England, see Debus, *The English Paracelsians,* 37. References to Erastus' work in the present chapter are from part 1 of the disputations, 1572 ed.

44. Erastus, *Dispvtationvm, pars prima,* 1–29. Throughout *The difference betwene the auncient . . . and the latter Phisicke,* Bostock explicitly presents his defense of Paracelsus' religious purity and his attack on Galen's heresy as a refutation of Erastus.

45. Lambert Daneau, *The wonderfull woorkmanship of the world,* fol. 14v. See also the dedications by both Daneau and Twyne, sigs. A2r–A3v. Cf. *Corpus Hermeticum,* Treatise XI, summarized by Yates in *Giordano Bruno,* 32, and translated by Ficino, *Opera,* 2:1850–52.

46. Lambert Daneau, *A Dialogue of Witches,* sigs. E2v–E3r.

47. Christopher Hill discusses the evolution of radical ideas and their expression during the Interregnum in *Intellectual Origins of the English Revolution* and *The World Upside Down: Radical Ideas during the English Revolution.*

48. Henry Holland, *A Treatise Against Witchcraft,* sig. A3r; Hol-

land's discussion of the two kingdoms begins on A2r. Cf. also Daneau's *Dialogue*, B2r. Stuart Clark discusses additional sources of the doctrine of the two kingdoms in "King James's *Daemonologie:* Witchcraft and Kingship," esp. 173–81.

49. William Perkins, *A Discourse of the Damned Art of Witchcraft . . . Framed and Delivered by M. William Perkins, in his ordinarie course of Preaching, and now published by Tho. Pickering*, 8–11. The account of Perkins' ideas in the remainder of this paragraph is a summary of arguments which he develops in detail on pp. 55–180.

50. James I, *Daemonologie*, 21, 34–37, et passim. References to *Daemonologie* and to the account of the North Berwick case in *Newes from Scotland* are to G. B. Harrison's combined single-volume facsimile edition of the two works. See also Stuart Clark's "King James's *Daemonologie.*"

51. Hugh Plat, *The Jewel House of Art and Nature*, sigs. A2r–B4v.

52. In addition to Chapters 7 and 8 below, see, for example, Gabriel Harvey's mockery of "Empiriques, Spagiriques, Cabalists, Alchimistes, Magicians, and occult Philosophers" in *Pierces Supererogation; or, A New Prayse of the olde Asse*, 251; Thomas Lodge, *The Anatomie of Alchymie;* and cf. the skeptical attitude of Samuel Harsnet, *A Declaration of egregious Popish Impostures*. Additional satirical works are discussed by Nicholl, *The Chemical Theatre*, 7–14.

53. Reginald Scot, *Discoverie of Witchcraft*, bks. 1 and 2, pp. 1–22; bk. 7, chap. 7, pp. 78–79. See also Sidney Anglo's "Reginald Scot's *Discoverie of Witchcraft:* Scepticism and Sadduceeism"; and Robert West, *Reginald Scot and Renaissance Writings on Witchcraft*. All references to the *Discoverie* are to book, chapter, and page number in Montague Summers' edition.

54. Francis Bacon, *Works*, 4:247–48. My discussion of Bacon and his influence draws upon Hill, *Intellectual Origins*, esp. 85–130; Rossi, *Francis Bacon: From Magic to Science* and his "Hermeticism, Rationality, and the Scientific Revolution"; Joseph Mazzeo, *Renaissance and Revolution*, 161–234; and Donald J. Greene's "Augustinianism and Empiricism: A Note on Eighteenth-Century English Intellectual History." Additional discussion of the connection between the new science and Neoclassicism appears below, Chapter 8. Rupert Hall, in "Science, Technology, and Utopia in the Seventeenth Century," has questioned whether the association between science and utopian ideas was widespread in the period, but, although Hall makes some

instructive comments, he does not refute the evidence of the previous studies I have listed.

55. Sir James George Frazer, *The Golden Bough,* 1:220–25, discussed by West, *Invisible World,* 229–30, n. 47.

56. In addition to Cohn's *Europe's Inner Demons* and Larner's *Enemies of God* and *Witchcraft and Religion,* see Cohn's *The Pursuit of the Millennium,* esp. the appendix on twentieth-century mass movements.

6. VISION AND ILLUSION

1. *Theologia Platonica,* ed. Marcel, 2:260, my translation. For further discussion of Ficino's philosophy, see above, Chapters 1 and 2.

2. Except as noted, line references to *Dr. Faustus* are to the B-text as reproduced in *Marlowe's "Dr. Faustus," 1604–1616: Parallel Texts,* ed. W. W. Greg. I have expanded some abbreviated speech prefixes and occasionally emended punctuation. In my adoption of readings from the A-text, I have been guided in part by the commentaries of Greg, of Fredson Bowers' *The Complete Works of Christopher Marlowe,* and of additional studies cited below, as well as my own comparisons of the texts.

Obviously any discussion of Marlowe's intentions must confront the problem of which scenes may have been added by collaborators, a question which can never be definitively resolved. I can only say that my interpretation does not depend upon scenes or lines which have been regarded in major studies or editions as non-Marlovian, and I shall, furthermore, argue that even if Rowley and Birde added some of the material unique to B, they nonetheless comprehended Marlowe's original purposes and sought to further them. I agree with the arguments of Constance Kuriyama, "Dr. Greg and *Doctor Faustus:* The Supposed Originality of the 1616 Text," in favor of Samuel Rowley as the author of some the B-text's comic scenes, but I do not share her judgment that these scenes transform B into "an aesthetic monstrosity" (177); in particular, I shall stress that the comic scenes of the B-text, often regarded as inferior to the comic material of A and as largely irrelevant to the central plot, in fact continue important themes—such as the conception of the world as Satan's domain and the emphasis on "gluttony"—which are initiated in the opening chorus and the tragic scenes which are common to both A and B. For important discussions of textual and authorship issues, see Greg,

97–139; Bowers, 2:123–59; Kuriyama; Michael J. Warren, *"Doctor Faustus:* The Old Man and the Text"; Michael H. Keefer, "Verbal Magic and the Problems of the A and B texts of *Doctor Faustus*"; and David Ormerod and Christopher Wortham, *Dr. Faustus: The A-Text.* Additional studies are surveyed by Ormerod and Wortham and by Robert Kimbrough in *The Predecessors of Shakespeare,* ed. Logan and Smith, 28–30. While I concede that the B-text has major problems, I do not find it to be as fully incoherent or as opposed in meaning to the A-text as several recent studies suggest, and I accept Fredson Bowers' rationale for choosing B as copy-text and adopting emendations from A.

3. British Museum, Harleian MS 6848, fol. 185v, as reproduced in C. F. Tucker Brooke's *Life of Marlowe,* 99. Another of Baines's comments which is relevant to this chapter is the accusation that Marlowe found Paul to be the only one of the apostles who "had wit[,] but he was a timerous fellow in bidding men to be subiect to magistrates against his Conscience" (Brooke, 99). Corroboration of certain aspects of Baines's remarks may be found in Brooke's *Life,* including the documents collected in Brooke's appendices; in Frederick Boas, *Christopher Marlowe;* and in John Bakeless, *The Tragicall History of Christopher Marlowe.* The discussion of Paul Kocher, in *Christopher Marlowe,* esp. 3–68, remains convincing. Additional evidence for the association between Harriot, Marlowe, Ralegh, and others and discussion of their unorthodox scientific and religious ideas appears above, Chapter 5.

4. Harry Levin, *The Overreacher,* viii–xi, 2–27, 108–35; the quotation appears on p. xi.

5. Kocher, *Christopher Marlowe,* 89–119, 138–72, 300–334. J. B. Steane, who provides fine commentary on Marlowe's verse in *Marlowe: A Critical Study,* also sees the play's ambivalence as an expression of Marlowe's "doubts and fears" (164). Wilbur Sanders, in *The Dramatist and the Received Idea,* 205–42, argues that the incoherence of *Dr. Faustus* reflects Marlowe's inability to exert conscious control over his own psychological conflicts; his negative assessment of the play and of Marlowe himself have recently been carried even farther by Harry Redner in *In the Beginning Was the Deed: Reflections on the Passage of Faust,* 186–95. Barbara Traister comments intelligently on many of the play's problems in *Heavenly Necromancers,* 89–107, but she is led by her consideration of the textual problems to regard

many of the work's ambiguities as largely "accidental" (89). Critics whose explorations of the play's ambivalence have led them to more positive assessments include Richard Sewall, *The Vision of Tragedy,* 57–67; Frank Manley, "The Nature of Faustus"; and Max Bluestone, "*Libido Speculandi:* Doctrine and Dramaturgy in Contemporary Interpretations of Marlowe's *Doctor Faustus.*"

6. The seminal work on the degeneration of Marlowe's protagonists is M. M. Mahood's *Poetry and Humanism,* 54–86. Studies which see traditional morality and/or religion in *Dr. Faustus* and which comment on aspects of the play discussed in this paragraph include Douglas Cole, *Suffering and Evil in the Plays of Christopher Marlowe,* 191–243; Robert Ornstein, "The Comic Synthesis in *Doctor Faustus*"; Charles Masinton, *Christopher Marlowe's Tragic Vision: A Study in Damnation,* 3–13, 113–42; W. L. Godshalk, *The Marlovian World Picture,* 169–202; and Judith Weil, *Christopher Marlowe: Merlin's Prophet,* esp. 10–11, 50–81. Joel Altman, although he is interested throughout *The Tudor Play of Mind* in the ambivalence of much of Renaissance drama, asserts that in *Dr. Faustus,* when "for the first time Marlowe reverts to the moral frame technique of the older drama, . . . his action proper is 'contained' in a way that it has never been before" (372). Important recent discussions of techniques which reveal the distance between Marlowe and his protagonists include Marjorie Garber, "'Infinite Riches in a Little Room': Closure and Enclosure in Marlowe"; Michael Goldman, "Marlowe and the Histrionics of Ravishment"; and Lawrence Danson, "Christopher Marlowe: The Questioner." Professor Danson argues that the rhetorical questions in Marlowe's plays could have been answered by an Elizabethan audience in a manner different from that of the protagonists, and consequently, we may be made aware of the protagonists' limitations; he wisely acknowledges, however, that "the sense of tragic completion is subverted by the sense of disquieting incompleteness attendant on the questioning mode" (28–29).

7. David Bevington, *From "Mankind" to Marlowe,* 245–62, esp. 260. See also Andrew V. Ettin's "Magic into Art: The Magician's Renunciation of Magic in English Renaissance Drama," esp. 273–74.

8. Annabel Patterson, *Censorship and Interpretation: The Conditions of Writing and Reading in Early Modern England;* Stephen Greenblatt, "Invisible Bullets: Renaissance Authority and Its Subversion." Greenblatt's essay focuses initially upon Thomas Harriot and men-

tions Marlowe; Professor Greenblatt's interpretation of Marlowe's plays in *Renaissance Self-Fashioning from More to Shakespeare,* 193–221, is, however, quite different from my own. On the views of Sanders, Traister, and others, see above, note 5.

9. Parsons, *An Advertisement Written to a Secretarie of my L. Treasyrers,* 18. The original Latin version was licensed for publication in late 1591 and published in 1592: see Strathmann, *Sir Walter Ralegh,* 25–40, and John W. Shirley, "Sir Walter Ralegh and Thomas Harriot," in *Thomas Harriot: Renaissance Scientist,* 23.

10. Robert Greene, *Groatsworth of Wit,* 43; Baines's accusation appears in British Museum, Harleian MS 6848, reprinted in Brooke's *Life of Marlowe,* 98.

11. Robert West, "The Impatient Magic of *Doctor Faustus,*" and *The Invisible World,* 110–22 et passim; Traister, *Heavenly Necromancers,* 90–96; cf. also William Blackburn, "'Heavenly Words': Marlowe's Faustus as a Renaissance Magician." For the opinions of Erastus, Bodin, Holland, and James I, see above, Chapter 5. Roger Bacon's opinions are summarized in his *Letter Concerning the Marvelous Power of Art and of Nature and Concerning the Nullity of Magic.*

12. F. R. Johnson, for example, has demonstrated in "Marlowe's Astronomy and Renaissance Skepticism" that, although Marlowe does not mention Copernicanism in *Dr. Faustus,* Mephostophilis' discussion of astronomy at lines 607–35 endorses a critique of traditional opinion: Renaissance scientists who asserted the superiority of experience over received authority had denied the existence of the fiery and crystalline spheres. Greg asserts that "Mephostophilis denies the fiery and crystalline spheres because they were the abode of God and the angels" (338, note to lines 630–31).

13. Translated by Yates, *Giordano Bruno,* 32; Ficino's Latin version of the treatise appears in *Opera,* 2:1850–52.

14. Ficino, *Theologia Platonica,* 2:257: "Quod admiratus Mercurius Trismegistus inquit: 'Magnum miraculum esse hominem, animal venerandum et adorandum, qui genus daemonum noverit quasi natura cognatum, quive in Deum transeat, quasi ipse sit deus.'" The entire chapter is relevant; it has been translated by Josephine L. Burroughs in the *Journal of the History of Ideas* 5 (1944): 235–38.

15. See the discussion of Bruno in Chapter 5, above, and Yates, *Giordano Bruno,* esp. 235–56. James Robinson Howe, in *Marlowe, Tamburlaine, and Magic,* provides a good survey of the evidence for

Marlowe's acquaintance with Bruno's work. Similar ideas could be found, of course, in other texts which were influenced by Hermeticism and were available to Marlowe.

16. Giordano Bruno, *Eroici furori*, in *Dialoghi italiani*, 937, trans. Yates, *Giordano Bruno*, 278.

17. This sonnet is by Luigi Tansillo, but Bruno quotes it in the *Eroici furori* and interprets it in his commentary in accordance with his own philosophy. I have used the translation of I. Frith, quoted in Eleanor Grace Clark's *Ralegh and Marlowe*, 354. The *Heroic Frenzies* has been translated in its entirety by Paul Eugene Memmo, but because Memmo's prose renditions sometimes fail to emphasize significant images I have occasionally preferred the translations provided by Clark or Yates.

Professor Clark sees *Dr. Faustus* as primarily a condemnation of Bruno, and she regards the moments of sympathy with Faustus as symptoms of Marlowe's lack of authorial control. Her research on the relationships among Ralegh, Harriot, Bruno, and Marlowe has been largely superseded by the work of Kocher, Shirley, and Jacquot.

18. Trans. Frith, quoted by Clark, *Ralegh and Marlowe*, 355.

19. A-text, 19–28. I have followed Fredson Bowers' edition in the emendations of lines 19–20, 23, and 25.

20. On the "Death of the Kiss," see above, Chapter 3, and Edgar Wind, *Pagan Mysteries in the Renaissance*, 60, 154 ff. Two of the works which Wind cites are Bruno's *Heroic Frenzies* and Castiglione's *The Courtier*, both of which were widely read in England. Wind also discusses Renaissance allegorizations of pagan myths in which Jove or other deities come to earth to make love to mortals; his entire chapter "Amor as a God of Death" is relevant to the imagery and the patterns of allusion in *Dr. Faustus*.

C. L. Barber, in "The Form of Faustus' Fortunes Good or Bad," has also linked the themes of "sweetness" and "delight" to the concepts of "gluttony" and "surfeit" and to the imagery of "faces" and "breasts" which culminate in the apostrophe to Helen. He interprets these images in Freudian terms, however, suggesting that Faustus mistakenly seeks an incarnation of divinity in "carnal and aesthetic satisfactions" (106). He sees Faustus' gluttony as a perverted manifestation of the primitive impulse to gain power by consuming another—especially a deity—which underlies the Mass. The Reformation, with its attack on religious ceremonies and transubstantiation, has denied the German Protestant Faustus access to the only true magic, and his evil magic and his indulgence of his appetites, Barber contends, are perverted attempts to make contact with the source of life from which he has been exiled.

Although I am indebted to several aspects of Barber's treatment of *Dr. Faustus*, I would emphasize Marlowe's controlled manipulation of concepts and images which come directly from traditional allegorization of pagan myths and from the occult tradition. Magicians actually did explain their love for the sensuous beauty of the physical world by seeing earthly beauty as a reflection of divinity, and a number of them saw human love of earthly creatures as the first step toward apotheosis: *Eros* leads the mind toward union with the *species intelligibilis* of the entire spectrum or "wheel" of created things and reminds us of the divinity within ourselves. Bruno, for instance, asserts in part 1, dialogue 3, of the *Heroic Frenzies* that one can rise from lower forms to higher ones and eventually attain Godhead: "By intellectual contact with that godlike object, he becomes a god" (Memmo trans., 108).

21. See Bruno's use of the myth of Actaeon in *Heroic Frenzies,* trans. Memmo, 123–29; cf. also Don Cameron Allen's references in *Mysteriously Meant,* 173 and 243, to the tradition which compares Actaeon to Christ. On the soul as a "water drop," Eugenio Garin translates the following passage from Bruno's *Lampas triginta statuarum* in *Italian Humanism,* 205: "The spirit that is in me, in you . . . comes from God and returns to God . . . even as any particular drop of water comes from, depends on and returns to water in general." Garin cites *Opera latine,* 3:59 ff., as the source of the ideas which he is discussing in this section; the specific page number for this quotation is not cited.

22. The original, brief commentary on *The Jew of Malta* as farce in T. S. Eliot's "Christopher Marlowe," in *Essays on Elizabethan Drama,* 62–64, has been elaborated by Steane, *Marlowe,* 166–203. Steane and others typically regard the comic scenes of *Faustus* as inferior to those of *The Jew of Malta,* and in some instances I agree; the caricatured villainy of the exchange between Benvolio and Martino, however, impresses me as quite similar to that of the scene between Barabas and Ithamore in act 2, scene 3, of the earlier play.

23. William Perkins, *A Discourse of the Damned Art of Witchcraft,* 5; see also Marcellus Palingenius, *The Zodiake of Life,* 138, and the dis-

cussion of witchcraft and demonology in Chapter 5, above. Clifford Davidson, in "Doctor Faustus of Wittenberg," makes clear that the emphasis in Elizabethan Protestant theology on the widespread influence of Satan and his legions grows directly from Luther, Melanchthon, and other Protestant theologians who taught at the University of Wittenberg, the setting of Marlowe's play.

24. For studies of the influence of Neoplatonic and Hermetic philosophy on English Renaissance theories of imagination and inspiration, see French, *John Dee,* 126–59; Jackson Cope, *The Theater and the Dream;* S. K. Heninger, Jr., *"Touches of Sweet Harmony"*; and Yates, *Giordano Bruno,* 205–56 and 275–90. Important primary sources on poetic inspiration include Bruno's *Heroic Frenzies;* Agrippa's *Occult Philosophy,* bk. 3, chaps. 3 and 43–59; and Gian Francesco Pico della Mirandola, *On the Imagination.* Thorough treatment of the traditional distrust of the imagination may be found in William Rossky's "Imagination in the English Renaissance: Psychology and Poetic." Obviously the magicians had no monopoly on the belief in visions and divine inspiration, but, as I shall emphasize in subsequent chapters, the opponents of the occult tradition, such as Erastus, Perkins, and Ben Jonson, increasingly emphasized the danger of the magicians' "enthusiasm."

Professor Traister, in *Heavenly Necromancers,* emphasizes that magicians appear in drama as literary artists largely because of the influence of medieval romances and Renaissance epics, in which magicians were frequently the presenters of illusory "shows." The connection between magic and poetry has also been explored by D. J. Palmer, in "Magic and Poetry in *Dr. Faustus*"; A. Bartlett Giamatti, "Marlowe: The Arts of Illusion"; and Ettin, "Magic into Art." None of these three studies discusses the manner in which the occultists' theory of imagination makes the connection logical, and each of them stresses the affirmation of a traditional sense of human limitations in the play.

25. C. L. Barber makes a similar point in "The Form of Faustus' Fortunes, Good or Bad," 115–16.

26. Cornelius Agrippa, *De occulta philosophia,* 3.3, p. 214.

7. THE RENAISSANCE MAGUS AS MOCK-HERO

1. On the relationship of Jonson's artistic style to his political convictions, see David Norbrook, *Poetry and Politics in the English*

Renaissance, 175–94. Annabel Patterson, in *Censorship and Interpretation,* 49–58, suggests that Jonson may have progressed from republican sentiments to support of absolutism after he gained royal patronage. There is virtually no doubt, however, concerning Jonson's sincere and confirmed royalist position by the time he wrote *The Alchemist.* Jonson's use of the rhetoric of the Golden Age to support the monarchy, discussed only briefly in the present chapter, is considered in further detail in Chapter 8.

2. All quotations from Jonson's works are from C. H. Herford and Percy Simpson's *Ben Jonson.* References to the plays are to act, scene, and line numbers.

3. Christian of Anhalt, Frederick's chief advisor and one of the leaders of the opposition to the Catholic Hapsburgs, visited James in 1610. Although the formal betrothal ceremony occurred in 1612, negotiations probably began at least as early as Anhalt's visit. See Yates, *The Rosicrucian Enlightenment,* 16 ff., and Claus-Peter Clasen, *The Palatinate in European History.* Anhalt's 1610 visit is recorded by John Nichols in *Progresses . . . of King James I,* 2:369.

4. John Davies, *Complete Poems,* as quoted by Frances Yates in "Queen Elizabeth as Astraea," 63. Yates's *Astraea: The Imperial Theme in the Sixteenth Century,* in which the earlier essay is reprinted, contains a wealth of information on sixteenth-century utopianism and mystical imperialism, especially the cult of Elizabeth.

5. Complementary to my own discussion of Jonson's attitude toward utopianism and religious enthusiasm is Gerard H. Cox's recent article, "Apocalyptic Projection and the Comic Plot of *The Alchemist.*" Cox provides enlightening commentary on the plot structure of the play in terms of protasis, epitasis, and catastrophe. On the historical connection between the magicians and the radical Puritans, see above, Chapter 5, esp. notes 14 and 36, and below, note 7.

6. Allusions in *The Alchemist* to Leyden and Knipperdollinck occur at II.v.13 and III.iii.24. Additional allusions to historical figures discussed below occur at II.iii.230, II.iii.238, V.v.117, et passim. For a detailed account of these and other revolutionary Puritans, see Norman Cohn, *The Pursuit of the Millennium,* and Steven Ozment, *Mysticism and Dissent.* As I am focusing—as did Jonson—upon a splinter movement whose violence was atypical of the Anabaptist movement as a whole, I feel it is appropriate to mention the eloquent and moving testimony of two Anabaptist martyrs whose dissent was thor-

oughly pacifist: see Andreas Ehrenpreis and Claus Felbinger, *Brotherly Community: The Highest Command of Love.*

7. *The Works of Thomas Nashe,* 2:232–41; Keith Thomas, *Religion and the Decline of Magic,* 124–46 and 371–78; P. M. Rattansi, "Paracelsus and the Puritan Revolution"; Christopher Hill, *The World Turned Upside Down.*

8. Ficino, *Theologia Platonica,* 2:260. Further discussion of Ficino and his influence appears above in Chapters 1 and 2.

9. Alvin Kernan has discussed the theme of false metamorphosis in Jonson's work in *The Cankered Muse* and in his introductions to the Yale editions of *Volpone* and *The Alchemist;* cf. also Thomas M. Greene, "Ben Jonson and the Centered Self." Although I differ from Kernan and Greene in several respects, I regard many of their insights as quite basic to our understanding of Jonson. For additional analysis of the language of the play in relation to the alchemical process, see Edward Partridge's *The Broken Compass,* esp. 144 and 156–58.

10. Herford and Simpson list the books in Jonson's library and provide evidence of his use of Del Rio's *Disqvisitionum magicarum libri sex* and other works in *Ben Jonson,* 1:250–71, 2:88–98, 10:46–116 passim, and 11:593–603; see also Jonson's marginal notes to *The Masque of Queenes.* Studies of Jonson's knowledge of Neoplatonism and the occult include Edgar Hill Duncan, "Jonson's *Alchemist* and the Literature of Alchemy"; D. J. Gordon, "The Imagery of Ben Jonson's *The Masque of Blacknesse* and *The Masque of Beautie*"; Gordon, "*Hymenaei:* Ben Jonson's Masque of Union"; and Don Cameron Allen, "Ben Jonson and the Hieroglyphics."

11. I discuss the myth of the Golden Age as a program for social reform above, esp. in Chapters 1 and 5. Chapter 5 includes discussion of the connection between the occult philosophers and the radical Puritans.

12. On the relation between Jonson's theory of humors and his moral purposes, see Hiram Haydn's *The Counter-Renaissance,* 385–87; and James D. Redwine, Jr., "Beyond Psychology: The Moral Basis of Jonson's Theory of Humour Characterization." Valuable discussion of the relationship between affectation in language and the loss of genuine self-knowledge appears throughout Jonas Barish's *Ben Jonson and the Language of Prose Comedy.*

13. See Bruno's *Heroic Frenzies;* Agrippa, *De occulta philosophia,*

bk. 3, chaps. 3 and 44–49; Gian Francesco Pico della Mirandola, *On the Imagination;* and above, Chapters 4 and 6. Studies of the changing attitudes toward imagination in the Renaissance and seventeenth century include French, *John Dee,* 126–59; Jackson Cope, *The Theater and the Dream;* S. K. Heninger, Jr., *"Touches of Sweet Harmony": Pythagorean Cosmology and Renaissance Poetics;* William Rossky, "Imagination in the English Renaissance: Psychology and Poetic"; Yates, *Giordano Bruno,* 205–56 and 275–90; and George Williamson, "The Restoration Revolt against Enthusiasm."

14. Cf. Robert Knoll's discussion of the Promethean aspirations of Subtle, Mammon, and others in *Ben Jonson's Plays: An Introduction,* 132–35.

15. L. A. Beaurline, in *Jonson and Elizabethan Comedy,* explores the differences between the strategies of realistic plays such as *The Alchemist,* on the one hand, and other works, such as the early comedies and the masques, in which ideals are prominent. Jonson's own use of the symbolic and idealized art is discussed in further detail below, in Chapter 8.

16. Among the most significant discussions of this issue are the following: John Enck, *Jonson and the Comic Truth,* 159–68; Alan C. Dessen, *"The Alchemist,* Jonson's 'Estates' Play" and *Jonson's Moral Comedy,* 105–37; Jonas Barish, "Feasting and Judging in Jonsonian Comedy," 25–28; and Alexander Leggatt, *Ben Jonson: His Vision and His Art,* esp. 29–35. I would concede that there is a considerable element of pure festivity in the suspension of rigorous moral judgment at the conclusion of the play, but I would emphasize that the conclusion also banishes enthusiasm and associated subversive forces and reestablishes the social and political status quo. My position is consistent with that of Judd Arnold in "Lovewit's Triumph and the Jonsonian Morality." "Lovewit's Triumph" and Arnold's subsequent *A Grace Peculiar* provide a survey of criticism and a detailed discussion of this problem.

17. Arnold, "Lovewit's Triumph" and *A Grace Peculiar,* esp. 1–7, 55–61.

8. NEOCLASSICISM AND THE SCIENTIFIC FRAME OF MIND

1. For a discussion of the different strands of Platonism in the Renaissance and of the influence of Plato's social theory on civic humanism, see Sears Jayne's "Ficino and the Platonism of the En-

glish Renaissance," and above, Chapter 1. Jonson's loyalty to the ideals of Latin humanism has recently been explored by Katherine Eisaman Maus in *Ben Jonson and the Roman Frame of Mind.*

2. Hiram Haydn discusses the civic humanists' concept of rational law and the Neoplatonists' departure from it in chaps. 5 and 6 of *The Counter-Renaissance.*

3. *Discoveries,* in *Ben Jonson,* 8:587, lines 772–79. All references to Jonson's works are to this edition; subsequent references to *Discoveries* will be to the line numbers in this volume. Herford and Simpson's introduction (11:210–13) suggests that there are signs that Jonson intended to publish at least some portion of the material in *Discoveries,* but the collection as we have it includes many of Jonson's miscellaneous private notes and papers. Certainly the collection is in a category altogether different from the masques or other works which Jonson composed with the interests of a particular audience in mind. The ideas which I am focusing upon here are developed in detail in lines 668–958, 1509–21, and 1755–2820.

4. Graham Parry, *The Golden Age Restored: The Culture of the Stuart Court,* 4–6, 42–43, 70–75, and 165–90; *Ben Jonson His Part of King James his Royall and Magnificent Entertainment* in Herford and Simpson, 7:65–117; *Hymenaei,* in Herford and Simpson, 7:205–41, esp. the gloss on 221; D. J. Gordon, *"Hymenaei:* Ben Jonson's Masque of Union"; Gordon, "The Imagery of Ben Jonson's *The Masque of Blacknesse* and *The Masque of Beautie"*; Douglas Brooks-Davies, *The Mercurian Monarch,* esp. 1–10 and 85–123; and Don Cameron Allen, "Ben Jonson and the Hieroglyphics."

5. L. A. Beaurline, in *Jonson and Elizabethan Comedy,* illuminates what he terms the "Platonic rhetoric" of *Cynthia's Revels* and other early comical satires, in which Jonson reveals the perfect Idea to which we should conform and ridicules our failure to do so. He acknowledges that Jonson's later plays become both more tolerant and more realistic, but the ideals reappear in the masques. Important discussions of the tension between realism and idealism in Jonson's works, as well as the problems of true and false art and of maintaining one's integrity while considering the demands of a courtly audience, are the following: Stephen Orgel, *The Jonsonian Masque* and *The Illusion of Power;* Alexander Leggatt, *Ben Jonson: His Vision and His Art,* esp. 1–44; Annabel Patterson, *Censorship and Interpretation,* esp. 49–58; Jonas Barish, "Jonson and the Loathed Stage." Although my con-

clusions differ in some respects from those of Professor Barish's in *Ben Jonson and the Language of Prose Comedy,* I have often found Barish's discussion of Jonson's style in relation to seventeenth-century intellectual history to be illuminating. I agree entirely with his belief that "Jonson's most successful art is that in which unmasking and casting out have fullest scope. More and more often into the ceremoniousness of the masques intrude outbreaks of the critical spirit that cannot credit the reality of the vision being created" (88).

6. References to the masques are to line numbers; all masques appear in vol. 7 of *Ben Jonson.*

7. In addition to the discussion of *The Alchemist* in this chapter and the previous one, see *Every Man in His Humor,* quarto version, 5.3.261 ff.

8. In addition to the examples I have previously cited, see especially "An Expostulation with Inigo Jones," in Herford and Simpson, 7:402–6, and Jonson's translation of "Horace his Art of Poetry," 7:303–55.

9. A persuasive article relating Jonson's work to this tradition is E. W. Talbert's "The Interpretation of Jonson's Courtly Spectacles."

10. Donald Greene, "Augustinianism and Empiricism: A Note on Eighteenth-Century English Intellectual History." I am also indebted to Joseph Mazzeo's chapter on Francis Bacon in *Renaissance and Revolution* and to Robert B. Hinman's "The Apotheosis of Faust: Poetry and New Philosophy in the Seventeenth Century."

11. *Poems,* vol. 1 of *English Writings of Abraham Cowley,* 449.

12. Bacon, *Works,* 3:289. All references are to the Ellis, Spedding, and Heath edition.

13. L. A. Beaurline, "Ben Jonson and the Illusion of Completeness" and *Jonson and Elizabethan Comedy,* 193–213.

9. MAGIC AS LOVE AND FAITH

1. References to Shakespeare's plays are to *The Riverside Shakespeare,* ed. G. Blakemore Evans and others.

2. Douglas Peterson provides fine commentary on the restoration of faith in the romances in *Time, Tide, and Tempest,* esp. 3–36. I should add, however, that I do not think it necessary to abandon altogether G. Wilson Knight's suggestion that the last plays embody what Knight terms "the triumphant mysticism of the dream of love's

perfected fruition in eternity stilling the tumultuous waves of time" (*The Crown of Life*, 26). Professor Peterson implies (e.g., 45) that he feels obliged to disagree with Knight in this respect, arguing that in Shakespeare's view of time, "the Augustinian dichotomy between the eternal and the temporal no longer separates this world from eternity, but is now manifest in things. Thus man can no longer simply dismiss temporality for the sake of contemplation" (21). While I agree with much of Peterson's commentary, I would stress that Renaissance thinkers often regarded the eternal as both immanent and transcendent; an ambivalent attitude toward the mutable world is therefore characteristic of much of Renaissance literature, including Shakespeare. Moreover, the central, unifying metaphor of the "sea-change" in *The Tempest* points toward the operation of universal principles of order on more than one ontological level: love and faith renew life both on the level of the world of generation on which Professor Peterson focuses and on the transcendent level with which Professor Knight is concerned.

3. Ficino, *Theologia Platonica*, 2:260. For discussion of Ficino's view of human nature and of the historical context of the *Theologia*, see Chapters 1 and 2, above. Additional support for the generalizations about occult philosophy in the present chapter also appears above, Chapters 1–5.

4. West, *Shakespeare and the Outer Mystery*, 86, emphasis altered. My contention, of course, is that Prospero is a "'holy magician' like the Apostles," in accordance with Renaissance Neoplatonic theory.

5. Mowat, "Prospero, Agrippa, and Hocus Pocus"; C. J. Sisson, "The Magic of Prospero." See also Mowat's *The Dramaturgy of Shakespeare's Romances*, esp. 30–31. The comparison of the magus to the benevolent monarch is developed in various ways by Sisson; Stephen Orgel, *The Illusion of Power*, 44–49; Gary Schmidgall, *Shakespeare and the Courtly Aesthetic;* and R.A.D. Grant, "Providence, Authority, and the Moral Life in *The Tempest.*" Additional discussions of Prospero's art as corrupt or ambiguous include Cosmo Corfield, "Why Does Prospero Abjure His 'Rough Magic?'"; Patrick Grant, "The Magic of Charity: A Background to Prospero," esp. 8–9; and David Young, *The Heart's Forest*, 146–91.

Barbara Traister, in *Heavenly Necromancers*, 1–64 and 125–49, recognizes the multiple sources of *The Tempest* while developing a convincing argument concerning the benevolence of Prospero's art.

Walter Clyde Curry's *Shakespeare's Philosophical Patterns*, 141–99, con-tributed much to our understanding of the nature of Prospero's magic, but his book was written long before the important recent research on Renaissance occultism. Relying more heavily on ancient and Hellenistic philosophers than on Ficino, Pico, or Agrippa, for example, Curry asserts that the goal of the magician was to attain the impassive status of the gods (cf. also Traister, 140–43); more characteristic of Renaissance occultists—and of *The Tempest*—is the conviction that the magus imitates God by caring providentially for the lower world.

I am indebted to Derek Traversi's discussion of the pattern of disruption and restoration of harmony in "The Last Plays of Shake-speare" and his *Shakespeare: The Last Phase*, 193–272; and to Frank Kermode's treatment of Prospero's art as a civilizing force in his Introduction to *The Tempest*, xxiv–lxiii. While specific points of in-debtedness and disagreement appear below, I may say in general that whereas Traversi and Kermode tend to stress Prospero's rational control of the passions, my own primary emphasis is on the supra-rational and visionary dimensions of the magician's art.

6. Ficino, *Theologia Platonica*, 2:229: "Hinc admiramur quod animae hominum Deo deditae imperent elementis, citent ventos, nubes cogent in pluvias, nebulas pellant, humanorum corporum cur-ent morbos et reliqua." All of bk. 13, chaps. 4 and 5 (2:229–45), is relevant.

7. Jackson Cope, *The Theater and the Dream*, 236–44. Barbara Mowat, in "Prospero, Agrippa, and Hocus Pocus," points out cor-rectly that Agrippa is, quite typically, inconsistent on the matter of raising the dead, condemning it in his initial disclaimer and subse-quently "claiming that sometimes the magus 'receiveth this miracu-lous power' to 'command the Elements, drive away Fogs, raise the winds . . . raise the dead'"; this quotation from Agrippa (obviously revealing Agrippa's debt to Ficino's *Theologia*, 2:229 et passim) is from the 1651 translation, 357, quoted by Mowat, 288, n. 14.

8. See Ficino, *Theologia Platonica*, 2:206 and 243–45; and cf. Curry, 177 ff. On the "tempest" as an alchemical process, see Wayne Shumaker, *The Occult Sciences in the Renaissance*, 191. On the limita-tions of evil magic, see Pico's *Oratio* (*De hominis dignitate*), ed. Garin, 148–54; Lambert Daneau, *A Dialogue of Witches*, sigs. F1r–G2v et

passim; William Perkins, *A Discourse of the Damned Art of Witchcraft,* 157–59; and James I, *Daemonologie,* 4 et passim.

9. See also I.ii.217. Prospero's concern extends not only to Ferdinand, whom he wishes to marry Miranda, but to every soul on the ship.

10. On this scene, see Reuben Brower's "The Mirror of Analogy: *The Tempest,*" 116–17, and Traversi, *Shakespeare: The Last Phase,* 251–54.

11. See Pico's *Oratio,* ed. Garin, 152: "Et sicut agricola ulmos vitibus, ita Magus terram caelo, idest inferiora superiorum dotibus virtutibusque maritat" ("As the farmer marries elms to vines, so the magus marries earth to heaven, that is, lower things to the gifts and virtues of higher things"). Pico also refers to humankind as the intermediary between the spiritual and material worlds, the "nuptial bond" which unites "the steadfastness of eternity and the flow of time": "Horum dictorum rationem cogitanti mihi non satis illa faciebant, quae multa de humanae naturae praestantia afferuntur a multis: esse hominem creaturarum internuntium, superis familiarem, regem inferiorum; sensuum perspicacia, rationis indagine, intelligentiae lumine, naturae interpretem; stabilis aevi et fluxi temporis interstitium, et (quod Persae dicunt) mundi copulam, immo hymenaeum, ab angelis, teste Davide, paulo deminutum" (Garin ed., 102). Pico goes on to praise the human soul's marvellous powers of self-transformation as the basis of human dignity and freedom: see above, Chapter 3.

12. A. Lynne Magnusson, "Interruption in *The Tempest.*" Among the most important and closely reasoned arguments in favor of the relativism and/or ambivalence of *The Tempest* are those of Barbara Mowat's "Prospero, Agrippa, and Hocus Pocus," David Young's *The Heart's Forest,* 146–91, and David Lindley's "Music, Masque, and Meaning in *The Tempest.*" D. D. Carnicelli has argued, in "The Widow and the Phoenix: Dido, Carthage, and Tunis in *The Tempest,*" that Shakespeare's art "stands closer to Pirandello and to Beckett and Ionesco and the Theatre of the Absurd than to the techniques we have come to expect of Elizabethan and Jacobean drama" (433).

13. See Alvin Kernan, *The Playwright as Magician,* 129–59; and Traister, *Heavenly Necromancers,* 125–49. Robert Egan, in *Drama within Drama,* 90–119, has argued that because Prospero himself can-

not initially accept human imperfections, his art, throughout most of the play, is too highly idealized to withstand the intrusions of reality.

14. Cf. Kenneth J. Semon, "Fantasy and Wonder in Shakespeare's Last Plays"; Cope, *The Theater and the Dream,* 236–44. Joan Hartwig, in *Shakespeare's Tragicomic Vision,* 137–74, comments perceptively on the "transference of ultimate control to a human actor" (137) in the play, as well as upon Prospero's art as an effort to expand the vision of other characters. My own previous study of dream visions in Shakespeare occurs in "Structure, Source, and Meaning in *A Midsummer Night's Dream.*"

15. On the geography of the region, see, for example, Abraham Ortelius, *Epitome of the Theater of the World,* sigs. 106v–107r. I am also indebted to Professor Carnicelli's thorough research in "The Widow and the Phoenix" on the historical and geographical works by Africanus, Hakluyt, and Eden and Willes. (Richard Eden's *Decades of the New Worlde* was enlarged by Eden and his follower Richard Willes and published as *The History of Travayle.*) Professor Carnicelli argues, however, that because there were various traditions concerning Dido's moral character and, to a lesser extent, the question of whether Tunis and Carthage were identical or merely contiguous, the scene suggests a form of relativism rather than a confirmation of Gonzalo's point of view. I find it difficult to see how this conclusion follows from Carnicelli's research on Carthage and Tunis, especially in view of his own important observation that among the texts available in Shakespeare's day there was "an almost eerie unanimous willingness—almost an eagerness—to accept Carthage as a vivid example of the endless process of historical decay and renewal" (432).

16. Norman Rabkin, *Shakespeare and the Problem of Meaning,* 139.

17. Many modern editors (G. B. Harrison, for example, in *Shakespeare: The Complete Works*) have attributed Miranda's speech to Prospero. Except for sentimentality with regard to Miranda, however, there is little justification for thus altering the reading of the folio. In fact, assigning this speech to Prospero tends to diminish the contrast between Miranda's lines on Caliban and her description of Ferdinand.

18. 1 Cor. 6:19–20, quoted from the Geneva Bible. On Shakespeare's use of the Geneva Bible, see Peter Milward, *Shakespeare's Religious Background,* 86.

19. See also Berowne's comic reference to himself as being "like

a demigod" at IV.iii.78. Occult philosophy is only one of several kinds of false learning which *Love's Labor's Lost* satirizes, however; studies such as Frances Yates's *A Study of Love's Labor's Lost* and Muriel Bradbrook's *The School of Night,* although they offer some tantalizing suggestions, ultimately become lost in speculation concerning topical references rather than focusing upon the spirit of the plays as a whole. Similar problems occur in Yates's discussion of the romances in *Shakespeare's Last Plays.*

20. Allusions to the Paracelsian emphasis on spiritual and psychic harmony are explored by J. Scott Bentley in "Helena's Paracelsian Cure of the King: *Magia Naturalis* in *All's Well That Ends Well.*"

21. On the role of music in magical theory, see above, Chapter 2. In addition to the uses of music in Shakespeare's romances, one may recall the prominence of music in the restoration scene in act 4 of *King Lear.*

The relationship between *magia* and *goetia* in *The Tempest* illustrates yet another facet of Shakespeare's use of parody and analogical structure, techniques which have been explored in detail by Joan Hartwig in *Shakespeare's Analogical Scene;* for Hartwig's discussion of these devices in *The Tempest,* see 182–90.

22. See Traversi, "Last Plays," esp. 444–45.

23. Arthur Lovejoy, *Essays in the History of Ideas,* 238, cited by Kermode, xxxiv. Kermode expands Lovejoy's point on xxxiv–xliii.

24. Garin, *Italian Humanism,* 77.

EPILOGUE

1. For discussion of Renaissance authors whom I have not focused upon in the present study, see Gordon O'Brien's *Renaissance Poetics and the Problem of Power.*

The bibliography contains all works cited, plus a selection of additional primary and secondary works which are relevant to the subjects of this study. For the convenience of readers who are using the notes, the entries are arranged in a single alphabetized list. Brief annotations are provided for some items, especially those not discussed in the text or endnotes. A number of the primary sources are available from University Microfilms in the Early English Books series.

Numbers used in the bibliography and notes to distinguish between various editions of an early printed book are from A. W. Pollard et al., *A Short-Title Catalogue of Books Printed in England, Scotland, and Ireland, and of English Books Printed Abroad, 1475–1640 (STC).*

Abelson, Joshua. *Jewish Mysticism: An Introduction to the Kabbalah.* 1913. Reprint. New York: Herman Press, 1969.

Agrippa von Nettesheim, Heinrich Cornelius. *De incertitudi[n]e et vanitate scientiarum declamatio invecta.* Cologne: M[elchior] N[ovesianus], 1531.

———. *De occulta philosophia libri tres.* [Cologne]: n.p., 1533.

———. *Dialogus de homine.* Ed. Paola Zambelli. *Rivisita critica di storia della filosofia* 12 (1958): 47–71.

———. *Of the vanitie and vncertaintie of artes and sciences.* Trans. Ia[mes] San[ford]. London: Henry Wykes, 1569.

———. *Opera.* 2 vols. Lyons: per Beringos fratres, n.d. Reprint, with introduction by Richard Popkin. New York and Hildesheim:

Georg Olms, 1970. The original imprint may be fictitious; see Nauert, *Agrippa*, 336.

———. *Three Books of Occult Philosophy*. Trans. J. F. London: R. W. for G. Moule, 1651.

Allen, Don Cameron. "Ben Jonson and the Hieroglyphics." *Philological Quarterly* 18 (1939): 290–300.

———. *Mysteriously Meant: The Rediscovery of Pagan Symbolism and Allegorical Interpretation in the Renaissance*. Baltimore: Johns Hopkins Univ. Press, 1970.

Allen, Michael J. B. "Marsilio Ficino on Plato, the Neoplatonists, and the Christian Doctrine of the Trinity." *Renaissance Quarterly* 37 (1984): 555–84.

———. "Marsilio Ficino on Plato's Pythagorean Eye." *Modern Language Notes* 97 (1982): 171–82.

———. *The Platonism of Marsilio Ficino: A Study of His Phaedrus Commentary, Its Sources and Genesis*. UCLA Center for Medieval and Renaissance Studies, no. 21. Berkeley and Los Angeles: Univ. of California Press, 1984.

———. "The Sibyl in Ficino's Oaktree." *Modern Language Notes* 95 (1980): 205–10. Reply to Frederick J. Purnell's "Hermes and the Sibyl" (q.v.).

Allen, Paul, ed. *A Christian Rosenkreutz Anthology*. 2nd ed. Blauvelt, N.Y.: Rudolph Steiner Publications, 1974. A 702-page collection of Rosicrucian documents.

Allen, Phyllis. "Scientific Studies in the English Universities of the Seventeenth Century." *Journal of the History of Ideas* 10 (1949): 219–53.

Altman, Joel B. *The Tudor Play of Mind: Rhetorical Inquiry and the Development of Elizabethan Drama*. Berkeley and Los Angeles: Univ. of California Press, 1978.

Alvis, John, and Thomas G. West, eds. *Shakespeare as Political Thinker*. Durham, N.C.: Carolina Academic Press, 1981.

Anglo, Sydney. "Reginald Scot's *Discoverie of Witchcraft*: Scepticism and Sadduceeism." In Anglo, *The Damned Art*, (q.v.), 106–39.

———, ed. *The Damned Art: Essays in the Literature of Witchcraft*. London: Routledge and Kegan Paul, 1977.

Aquinas. See Thomas Aquinas, Saint.

Arnold, Judd. *A Grace Peculiar: Ben Jonson's Cavalier Heroes*. University Park, Pa.: Penn. State Univ. Press, 1972.

———. "Lovewit's Triumph and the Jonsonian Morality: A Reading of *The Alchemist.*" *Criticism* 11 (1969): 151–66.

Ashmole, Elias, ed. *Theatrum Chemicum Britannicum.* London, 1652. Reprint edited by Allen G. Debus. New York: Johnson Reprint, 1967. Includes numerous alchemical treatises (e.g., works by or attributed to Thomas Charnock, George Ripley, Thomas Norton, Edward Kelley, and others), many with utopian elements. Valuable introduction by Debus on the history of English alchemy.

Aubrey, John. *Brief Lives.* Ed. Andrew Clark. 2 vols. Oxford: Clarendon Press, 1898.

Augustine, Saint. *The City of God.* Trans. Marcus Dods. The Modern Library. New York: Random House, 1950.

Bacon, Francis. *Works.* Ed. James Spedding, Robert Leslie Ellis, and Douglas Denon Heath. 15 vols. 1857–74. Reprint. New York: Garrett Press, 1968.

Bacon, Roger. *Libellus Rogerii Baconi . . . de retardandis senectutis.* Oxford: Officina typographica Iosephi Barnesii, 1590.

———. *The Mirror of Alchimy.* London: Richard Olive, 1597. A collection of several alchemical treatises, two of which are attributed to R. Bacon.

———. *Roger Bacon's Letter Concerning the Marvelous Power of Art and of Nature and Concerning the Nullity of Magic.* Trans. Tenney L. Davis. Easton, Pa.: Chemical Publishing, 1923. Reprint. New York: AMS, [1982].

Bakeless, John. *Christopher Marlowe: The Man in His Time.* New York: Morrow, 1937.

———. *The Tragicall History of Christopher Marlowe.* 2 vols. Cambridge: Harvard Univ. Press, 1942. Reprint. Westport, Conn.: Greenwood Press, 1970.

Barber, C. L. "The Form of Faustus' Fortunes Good or Bad." *Tulane Drama Review* 8, no. 4 (Summer 1964): 92–119.

Barfield, Owen. *Saving the Appearances: A Study in Idolatry.* New York: Harcourt, Brace and World, 1965. Contrasts medieval and modern epistemology.

Barish, Jonas. *Ben Jonson and the Language of Prose Comedy.* Cambridge: Harvard Univ. Press, 1960.

———. "Feasting and Judging in Jonsonian Comedy." *Renaissance Drama,* n.s. 5 (1972): 3–35.

————. "Jonson and the Loathed Stage." In Blissett, Patrick, and Van Fossen, *A Celebration of Ben Jonson* (q.v.), 27–53.

————, ed. *Ben Jonson: A Collection of Critical Essays.* Englewood Cliffs, N.J.: Prentice-Hall, 1963.

Barkan, Leonard. *Nature's Work of Art: The Human Body as Image of the World.* New Haven: Yale Univ. Press, 1975.

Baron, Hans. *The Crisis of the Early Italian Renaissance.* 2 vols. Princeton: Princeton Univ. Press, 1955.

Barnes, Celia. "Matthew Parker's Pastoral Training and Marlowe's *Doctor Faustus.*" *Comparative Drama* 15 (1981): 258–67.

Barton, Anne. *Ben Jonson, Dramatist.* Cambridge: Cambridge Univ. Press, 1984.

Bateson, Frederick Wilse. *English Poetry and the English Language.* Oxford: Clarendon Press, 1934. On changes in language as reflections of changes in world view.

Batman, Stephen. *Batman vppon Bartholome, his booke "De Proprietatibus Rerum."* London: T. East, 1582. A Renaissance revision of a medieval encyclopedia; useful for research on traditional beliefs concerning science and philosophy.

Baxter, Christopher. "Jean Bodin's *De la démonomanie des sorciers:* The Logic of Persecution." In Anglo, *The Damned Art* (q.v.), 76–105.

Beaurline, L. A. "Ben Jonson and the Illusion of Completeness." *PMLA* 84 (1969): 51–59. See also Jensen and Beaurline, "L. A. Beaurline and the Illusion of Completeness" (q.v.).

————. *Jonson and Elizabethan Comedy: Essays in Dramatic Rhetoric.* San Marino, Calif.: Huntington Library, 1978.

Bentley, J. Scott. "Helena's Paracelsian Cure of the King: *Magia Naturalis* in *All's Well That Ends Well.*" *Cauda Pavonis: The Hermetic Text Society Newsletter,* n.s. 5, no. 1 (Spring 1986): 1–4.

————. "The Hermetic Tradition in Three Shakespearean Romances: *Pericles, The Winter's Tale,* and *The Tempest.*" Ph.D. diss., Univ. of Oregon, 1986. For abstract, see *Dissertation Abstracts International* 47 (1987): 2591A.

Berger, Harry, Jr. "Miraculous Harp: A Reading of Shakespeare's *Tempest.*" *Shakespeare Studies* 5 (1969): 253–83.

Berger, Karol. "Prospero's Art." *Shakespeare Studies* 10 (1977): 211–39.

Bevington, David. *From "Mankind" to Marlowe: Growth of Structure in* the Popular Drama of Tudor England. Cambridge: Harvard Univ. Press, 1962.

———. *Tudor Drama and Politics: A Critical Approach to Topical Meaning*. Cambridge: Harvard Univ. Press, 1968.

Blackburn, William. "'Heavenly Words': Marlowe's Faustus as a Renaissance Magician." *English Studies in Canada* 4 (1978): 1–14.

Blanpied, John W., ed. *Shakespearean Metadrama*. MLA Convention Special Session 711, December 1977. Rochester, N.Y.: Univ. of Rochester, Department of English, 1977.

———. *Shakespearean Metadrama*. MLA Convention Special Session 206, December 1978. Rochester, N.Y.: Univ. of Rochester Department of English, 1978.

Blau, Joseph Leon. *The Christian Interpretation of the Cabala in the Renaissance*. New York: Columbia Univ. Press, 1944.

Blissett, William; Julian Patrick; and R. W. Van Fossen, eds. *A Celebration of Ben Jonson*. Toronto: Univ. of Toronto Press, 1973.

Bluestone, Max. "*Libido Speculandi:* Doctrine and Dramaturgy in Contemporary Interpretations of *Doctor Faustus.*" In *Reinterpretations of Elizabethan Drama,* ed. Norman Rabkin, 33–88. New York: Columbia Univ. Press, 1969.

Boas, Frederick Samuel. *Christopher Marlowe: A Biographical and Critical Study*. Oxford: Clarendon Press, 1940.

———. *Marlowe and His Circle: A Biographical Survey.* 1929. Reprint. New York: Russell and Russell, 1968.

Boas, George. *Essays on Primitivism and Related Ideas in the Middle Ages*. Baltimore: Johns Hopkins Press, 1948.

Boas, Marie [Marie Boas Hall]. *The Scientific Renaissance, 1450–1630.* Vol. 2 of *The Rise of Modern Science*. New York: Harper and Row, 1962.

Bodin, Jean. *Colloquium of the Seven about Secrets of the Sublime*. Trans. Marion L. D. Kuntz. Princeton: Princeton Univ. Press, 1976.

———. *De la démonomanie des sorciers*. Paris: Chez Iaques du Puys, Libraire Iurè, 1580. References in the present study are to this edition.

———. *De magorum daemonomania*. Strassburg: B. Jobin, 1591.

———. *De magorum demonomania libri IV.* Basel: per T. Guarinum, 1581.

Bond, Donald F. "'Distrust' of Imagination in English Neo-classicism." *Philological Quarterly* 14 (1935): 54–69.

Bonelli, Maria Luisa Righini, and William R. Shea, eds. *Reason, Experiment, and Mysticism in the Scientific Revolution.* New York: Science History Publications, 1975.

Booth, Wayne C. *Critical Understanding: The Powers and Limits of Pluralism.* Chicago and London: Univ. of Chicago Press, 1979.

B[ostock], R. *The difference betwene the auncient Phisicke, first taught by the godly forefathers, consisting in vnitie[,] peace[,] and concord: and the latter Phisicke proceeding from Idolaters, Ethnickes, and Heathen: as Gallen, and such other consisting in dualitie, discorde, and contrarietie.* London: Robert Walley, 1585.

Bouwsma, William J. *Concordia Mundi: The Career and Thought of Guillaume Postel.* Cambridge.: Harvard Univ. Press, 1957.

Bowers, Fredson, ed. See Marlowe, Christopher.

Bradbrook, Muriel C. *The School of Night: A Study in the Literary Relationships of Sir Walter Ralegh.* Cambridge: Cambridge Univ. Press, 1936.

Briggs, K. M. *Pale Hecate's Team: An Examination of the Beliefs on Witchcraft and Magic among Shakespeare's Contemporaries and His Immediate Successors.* London: Routledge and Kegan Paul; New York: Humanities Press, 1962.

Bronowski, Jacob. *Magic, Science, and Civilization.* New York: Columbia Univ. Press, 1978.

Brooke, C. F. Tucker. *The Life of Marlowe* and *The Tragedy of Dido, Queen of Carthage.* Vol. 1 of *The Works and Life of Christopher Marlowe,* ed. R. H. Case. 1930. Reprint. New York: Gordian Press, 1966.

——. "The Reputation of Christopher Marlowe." *Transactions of the Connecticut Academy of Arts and Sciences* 25 (1922): 347–408. Includes documents not reproduced in Brooke's *Life of Marlowe.*

Brooks-Davies, Douglas. *The Mercurian Monarch: Magical Politics from Spenser to Pope.* Manchester, Eng.: Manchester Univ. Press, 1983.

Brower, Reuben. "The Mirror of Analogy: *The Tempest.*" In *The Fields of Light,* 95–122. New York: Oxford Univ. Press, 1951. Reprint. Westport, Conn.: Greenwood Press, 1981.

Brown, Beatrice Daw. "Marlowe, Faustus, and Simon Magus." *PMLA* 54 (1939): 82–121.

Brune, Lester H. "Magic's Relation to the Intellectual History of Western Civilization." *Journal of Thought* 18 (1983): 55–64.

Bruno, Giordano. *The Ash Wednesday Supper.* Trans. Edward A. Gosselin and Lawrence S. Lerner. Hamden, Conn.: Archon Books, 1977. This edition contains valuable commentary; see also the translation by Stanley L. Jaki, listed below.

———. *The Ash Wednesday Supper.* Trans. Stanley L. Jaki. The Hague: Mouton; Atlantic Highlands, N.J.: Humanities Press, 1975. Quotations in the present study are from Jaki's translation.

———. *Cause, Principle, and Unity.* Trans. Jack Lindsey. 1962. Reprint. Westport, Conn.: Greenwood Press, 1976.

———. *La cena de le ceneri.* [London: J. Charlewood], 1584.

———. *Concerning the Cause, Principle, and One.* See Greenburg, Sidney Thomas.

———. *De gl' heroici fvrori.* London: J. Charlewood, 1585.

———. *De l'infinito vniuerso et mondi.* London: J. Charlewood, 1584.

———. *Dialoghi italiani.* Florence: Sansoni, 1958.

———. *The Expulsion of the Triumphant Beast.* Trans. Arthur D. Imerti. New Brunswick, N. J.: Rutgers Univ. Press, 1964.

———. *The Heroic Frenzies.* Trans. Paul Eugene Memmo, Jr. Chapel Hill: Univ. of North Carolina Press, 1966.

———. *On the Infinite Universe and Worlds.* See Singer, Dorothea.

———. *Opere latine.* 1879–91. Reprint. Stuttgart: F. Frommann, 1961–62.

———. *Spaccio della bestia trionfante.* London: J. Charlewood, 1584.

Bryant, Joseph A., Jr. *The Compassionate Satirist: Ben Jonson and His Imperfect World.* Athens: Univ. of Georgia Press, 1972.

Burckhardt, Jacob. *The Civilization of the Renaissance in Italy.* Ed. Benjamin Nelson and Charles Trinkaus. 2 vols. New York: Harper and Row, 1958.

Burckhardt, Titus. *Alchemy: Science of the Cosmos, Science of the Soul.* Trans. William Stoddart. Baltimore: Penguin, 1971.

Burke, John G. "Hermetism as a Renaissance World View." In Kinsman, *The Darker Vision of the Renaissance* (q.v.), 95–117.

Burke, Peter. *Culture and Society in Renaissance Italy.* New York: Charles Scribner's Sons, 1972.

———. "Witchcraft and Magic in Renaissance Italy: Gianfrancesco Pico and His *Strix.*" In Anglo, *The Damned Art* (q.v.), 32–52.

Burnham, Frederic B. "The More-Vaughan Controversy: The Revolt against Philosophical Enthusiasm." *Journal of the History of Ideas* 35 (1974): 33–49.

Burroughs, Josephine L., trans. See Ficino, *Platonic Theology.*

Burton, Robert. *The Anatomy of Melancholy.* Ed. Floyd Dell and Paul Jordan-Smith. New York: Farrar and Rinehart, 1927.

Bush, Douglas. *English Literature in the Earlier Seventeenth Century, 1600–1660.* 1945. Reprint. New York: Oxford Univ. Press, 1952.

———. *The Renaissance and English Humanism.* Toronto: Univ. of Toronto Press, 1939.

Butler, Eliza Marian. *The Fortunes of Faust.* Cambridge: Cambridge Univ. Press, 1952.

———. *The Myth of the Magus.* Cambridge: Cambridge Univ. Press; New York: Macmillan, 1948.

Campanella, Tommaso. *The City of the Sun: A Poetical Dialogue.* Trans. Daniel J. Donno. Berkeley and Los Angeles: Univ. of California Press, 1981.

Cantor, Paul A. "Prospero's Republic: The Politics of Shakespeare's *The Tempest.*" In Alvis and West, *Shakespeare as Political Thinker* (q.v.), 239–55.

Carleton, George. *The Madnesse of Astrologers.* 1624. Reprint. The English Experience Series, no. 53. Amsterdam: Theatrum Orbis Terrarum, 1968.

Carnicelli, D. D. "The Widow and the Phoenix: Dido, Carthage, and Tunis in *The Tempest.*" *Harvard Library Bulletin* 27 (1979): 389–433.

Casaubon, Meric, ed. See Dee, *A True and Faithful Relation.*

Caspari, Fritz. *Humanism and the Social Order in Tudor England.* Chicago: Univ. of Chicago Press, 1954.

Cassirer, Ernst. "Giovanni Pico della Mirandola: A Study in the History of Renaissance Ideas." *Journal of the History of Ideas* 3 (1942): 123–44, 319–46.

———. *The Individual and the Cosmos in Renaissance Philosophy.* Trans. Mario Domandi. New York: Harper and Row, 1964.

Cassirer, Ernst; Paul Oskar Kristeller; and John Herman Randall, Jr., eds. *The Renaissance Philosophy of Man.* Chicago: Univ. of Chicago Press, 1948. Translations of works by Petrarch, Valla, Ficino, Giovanni Pico della Mirandola ("Oration on the Dignity of Man"), Pompanazzi, and Vives. Valuable introductions to each author, as well as a general introduction on Renaissance philosophy and humanism.

Castiglione, Baldesar. *The Book of the Courtier.* Trans. Charles S. Singleton. Garden City, N.Y.: Doubleday, Anchor Books, 1959.

Charlton, K. *Education in Renaissance England.* London: Routledge and Kegan Paul, 1965.

Charnock, Thomas. *The Breviary of Naturall Philosophy.* 1557. Reprinted in Ashmole, *Theatricum Chemicum Britannicum* (q.v.).

Chastel, André; Cecil Grayson; Marie Boas Hall; Denys Hay; Paul Oskar Kristeller; Nicolai Rubinstein; Charles B. Schmitt; Charles Trinkaus; and Walter Ullmann. *The Renaissance: Essays in Interpretation.* London and New York: Methuen, 1982. Surveys of the current state of knowledge on many facets of the Renaissance.

Chaucer, Geoffrey. *The Complete Poetry and Prose of Geoffrey Chaucer.* Ed. John H. Fisher. New York: Holt, Rinehart and Winston, 1977.

Chaudhuri, Sukanta. *Infirm Glory: Shakespeare and the Renaissance Image of Man.* Oxford: Clarendon Press, 1981.

Cheney, Patrick. "Love and Magic in *Doctor Faustus:* Marlowe's Indictment of Spenserian Idealism." *Mosaic: A Journal for the Interdisciplinary Study of Literature* 17, no. 4 (Fall 1984): 93–109.

Christianson, Paul. *Reformers and Babylon: English Apocalyptic Visions from the Reformation to the Eve of the Civil War.* Toronto: Univ. of Toronto Press, 1978.

Clark, Cumberland. *Shakespeare and Science.* Birmingham, Eng.: Cornish Brothers, 1929. Includes astrology and alchemy.

Clark, Eleanor Grace. *Ralegh and Marlowe: A Study in Elizabethan Fustian.* New York: Fordham Univ. Press, 1941.

Clark, G. N., and others, eds. *The New Cambridge Modern History.* 14 vols. Rev. ed. Cambridge: Cambridge Univ. Press, 1957–79.

Clark, Stuart. "King James's *Daemonologie:* Witchcraft and Kingship." In Anglo, *The Damned Art* (q.v.), 156–181.

Clasen, Claus-Peter. *The Palatinate in European History.* Oxford: Basil Blackwell, 1963.

Clements, Robert J., and Lorna Levant, eds. *Renaissance Letters: Revelations of a World Reborn.* New York: New York Univ. Press, 1976. Includes a translation of one of Cornelius Agrippa's letters concerning the woman accused of witchcraft in Metz.

Clulee, Nicholas. "At the Crossroads of Magic and Science: John

Dee's Archemastrie." In Vickers, *Occult and Scientific Mentalities in the Renaissance* (q.v.), 57–71.

Cochrane, Eric. "Science and Humanism in the Italian Renaissance." *American Historical Review* 81 (1976): 1039–57.

Cohn, Norman. *Europe's Inner Demons: An Enquiry Inspired by the Great Witch-Hunt.* New York: Basic Books, 1975.

———. *The Pursuit of the Millennium.* Rev. ed. London and New York: Oxford Univ. Press, 1970.

Cole, Douglas. *Suffering and Evil in the Plays of Christopher Marlowe.* Princeton: Princeton Univ. Press, 1962.

Collins, Ardis B. *The Secular Is Sacred: Platonism and Thomism in Marsilio Ficino's "Platonic Theology."* The Hague: Nijhoff, 1974.

Comes, Natalis. *Mythologiae.* 1567. Reprint. The Renaissance and the Gods series, vol. 11. New York: Garland, 1976.

Cope, Jackson I. *The Theater and the Dream: From Metaphor to Form in Renaissance Drama.* Baltimore and London: Johns Hopkins Univ. Press, 1973.

Copenhaver, Brian P. "Scholastic Philosophy and Renaissance Magic in the *De vita* of Marsilio Ficino." *Renaissance Quarterly* 37 (1984): 523–54.

———. *Symphorien Champier and the Reception of the Occultist Tradition in Renaissance France.* The Hague and New York: Mouton, 1978.

Copleston, Frederick. *A History of Philosophy.* 8 vols. Rev. ed. London: Burns, Oates, and Washbourne, 1946–66. Especially helpful on the Platonic and Aristotelian traditions in the Middle Ages and the Renaissance.

Corfield, Cosmo. "Why Does Prospero Abjure His 'Rough Magic'?" *Shakespeare Quarterly* 36 (1985): 31–48.

Cornelius, R. M. *Christopher Marlowe's Use of the Bible.* Berne: Peter Lang, 1984.

Corpus Hermeticum. See Nock, A. D., ed.

Cowley, Abraham. *The English Writings of Abraham Cowley.* Ed. A. R. Waller. 2 vols. Cambridge: Cambridge Univ. Press, 1905–6.

Cox, Gerard H. "Apocalyptic Projection and the Comic Plot of *The Alchemist.*" *English Literary Renaissance* 13 (1983): 70–87.

Coxe, Francis. *A short treatise declaring the detestable wickednesse of magicall sciences.* [London: J. Alde, 1561.]

Craig, Hardin. "Magic in *The Tempest.*" *Philological Quarterly* 47 (1968): 8–15.

Craven, William G. *Giovanni Pico della Mirandola, Symbol of His Age: Modern Interpretations of a Renaissance Philosopher.* Travaux d'Humanisme et Renaissance, no. 185. Geneva: Librairie Droz, 1981.

Crombie, Alistair C. "Science and the Arts in the Renaissance: The Search for Truth and Certainty, Old and New." In Shirley and Hoeniger, *Science and the Arts in the Renaissance* (q.v.), 15–26. Considers the possible influence of Florentine Neoplatonism on the emergence of genuine science.

Cruttwell, Patrick. *The Shakespearean Moment.* London: Chatto and Windus, 1954. Important discussion of the disillusionment with Renaissance ideals in the late sixteenth and early seventeenth centuries.

Curry, Walter Clyde. *Shakespeare's Philosophical Patterns.* Baton Rouge: Louisiana State Univ. Press, 1937. Reprint. Gloucester, Mass.: Peter Smith, 1968.

D'Amico, John F. "Paolo Cortesi's Rehabilitation of Giovanni Pico della Mirandola." *Bibliothèque d'Humanisme et Renaissance* 44 (1982): 37–51. To those who wished to rehabilitate Pico, "it seemed necessary to disassociate Pico from the esoteric" (50).

Daneau, Lambert [Danaus, Lambertus]. *A Dialogue of Witches.* London: R. W., 1575.

———. *The wonderfull woorkmanship of the world: wherein is conteined an excellent discourse of Christian naturall philosophie, concernyng the fourme, knowledge, and use of all thinges created: specially gathered out of the fountains of Holy Scripture.* Trans. Thomas Twyne. London: Andrew Maunsell, 1578.

Danson, Lawrence. "Christopher Marlowe: The Questioner." *English Literary Renaissance* 12 (1982): 3–29.

———. "Jonsonian Comedy and the Discovery of the Social Self." *PMLA* 99 (1984): 179–93.

Davidson, Clifford. "Doctor Faustus of Wittenberg." *Studies in Philology* 59 (1962): 514–23.

Davies, Stevie. *The Feminine Reclaimed: The Idea of Woman in Spenser, Shakespeare, and Milton.* Lexington: Univ. Press of Kentucky, 1986. Includes discussion of Hermetic influences upon Shakespeare's romances, especially *Pericles* and *The Winter's Tale.*

Davies, Stevie, ed. *Renaissance Views of Man.* New York: Barnes and Noble, 1979.

Davis, J. C. *Utopia and the Ideal Society: A Study of English Utopian Writing, 1516–1700.* Cambridge: Cambridge Univ. Press, 1981.

Debus, Allen. *The Chemical Dream of the Renaissance.* Cambridge, Eng.: W. Heffer, 1968.

———. *The Chemical Philosophy: Paracelsian Science and Medicine in the Sixteenth and Seventeenth Centuries.* 2 vols. New York: Science History Publications, 1977.

———. *The English Paracelsians.* New York: Franklin Watts, 1965.

———. *Man and Nature in the Renaissance.* Cambridge and New York: Cambridge Univ. Press, 1978.

Dee, John. *Autobiographical Tracts of Dr. John Dee.* Ed. James Crossley. [Manchester, Eng.]: The Chetham Society, 1851. Includes Dee's *Compendious Rehearsal.*

———. *General and Rare Memorials Pertayning to the Paradoxal Cumpas.* London: John Daye, 1577.

———. *General and rare memorials pertayning to the Perfect Arte of Navigation.* London: John Day, 1587.

———. *John Dee on Astronomy: Propaedeumata Aphoristica (1558 and 1568), Latin and English.* Ed. and trans. Wayne Shumaker. Introd. J. L. Heilbron. Berkeley and Los Angeles: Univ. of California Press, 1978.

———. *A Letter, Containing a most briefe Discourse Apologeticall, with a plaine Demonstration, and fervent Protestation, for the lawfull, sincere, very faithfull and Christian course, of the Philosophicall studies and exercises, of a certaine studious Gentleman.* London: Peter Short, 1599. Originally composed c. 1594–95.

———. *The Mathematical Praeface to the Elements of Geometrie of Euclid of Megara, 1570.* Ed. Allen G. Debus. New York: Neale Watson Academic Publications, 1975.

———. *The Private Diary of Dr. John Dee, and the Catalogue of His Library of Manuscripts.* Ed. James Orchard Halliwell. London: Printed for the Camden Society by J. B. Nichols and Sons, 1842.

———. *To the Honorable Assemblie of the Commons in the present Parlament.* [London: n.p., 1604.] A poem requesting an act of Parliament declaring it unlawful to slander Dr. John Dee.

———. "A Translation of John Dee's 'Monas Hieroglyphica' (Antwerp, 1564), with an Introduction and Annotations." Ed. and trans. C. H. Josten. *Ambix* 12 (1964): 84–221.

———. *A True and Faithful Relation of What passed for many Yeers Be-*

tween Dr. John Dee . . . and Some Spirits. Ed. Meric Casaubon. London: D. Maxwell for T. Garthwait, 1659. Contains Dee's personal record of a number of seances, as well as letters and other documents. A modern edition appears in Shumaker, *Renaissance Curiosa* (q.v.).

Del Rio, Martin. *Disqvisitionum magicarum libri sex.* 3 vols. Louvain: Ex officina G. Rivii, 1599–1600.

Demetz, Peter; Thomas Greene; and Lowry Nelson, Jr., eds. *The Disciplines of Criticism: Essays in Literary Theory, Interpretation, and History.* New Haven: Yale Univ. Press, 1968. Includes essays by Thomas Greene and A. Bartlett Giamatti on the influence of Giovanni Pico's vision of human nature.

Dessen, Alan. *"The Alchemist,* Jonson's 'Estates' Play." *Renaissance Drama* 7 (1964): 35–54.

———. *Jonson's Moral Comedy.* Evanston, Ill.: Northwestern Univ. Press, 1971.

Dollimore, Jonathan. *Radical Tragedy: Religion, Ideology and Power in the Drama of Shakespeare and His Contemporaries.* Chicago: Univ. of Chicago Press, 1984.

Donne, John. *John Donne: The Anniversaries.* Ed. Frank Manley. Baltimore: Johns Hopkins Press, 1963.

Dop, Jan Albert. *Eliza's Knights: Soldiers, Poets, and Puritans in the Netherlands, 1572–1586.* Alblasserdam, Netherlands: Remak, 1981. Distributed by Kooyker International Booksellers, Leiden.

Du Chesne, Joseph [Quercetanus, Josephus]. See Tymme, Thomas, trans.; see also Hester, John, ed. and trans.

Duncan, Edgar Hill. "Jonson's *Alchemist* and the Literature of Alchemy." *PMLA* 61 (1946): 699–710.

Easlea, Brian. *Witch Hunting, Magic, and the New Philosophy: An Introduction to the Debates of the Scientific Revolution.* Brighton, Sussex: Harvester Press; Atlantic Highlands, N.J.: Humanities Press, 1980.

Eden, Richarde, and Richarde Willes, eds. and trans. *The History of Travayle in the West and East Indies, and other countreys lying eyther way.* London: Richarde Iugge, 1577. Often catalogued under "Anglerius, Petrus Martyr," or Peter Martyr, the author of the *Decades of the Newe Worlde,* a work incorporated into the *History.* See Carnicelli, "The Widow and the Phoenix" (q.v.), 422.

Edwards, Philip. "Shakespeare's Romances: 1900–1957." *Shakespeare Survey* 11 (1958): 1–18.

———. *Sir Walter Ralegh.* 1953. Reprint. Folcroft, Pa.: Folcroft Library Editions, 1976.

Egan, Robert. *Drama within Drama: Shakespeare's Sense of His Art in "King Lear," "The Winter's Tale," and "The Tempest."* New York: Columbia Univ. Press, 1975.

Ehrenpreis, Andreas, and Claus Felbinger. *Brotherly Community: The Highest Command of Love. Two Anabaptist Documents of 1650 and 1560.* Rifton, N.Y.: Plough Publishing House, 1978.

Eisenbichler, Konrad, and Olga Zorzi Pugliese, eds. *Ficino and Renaissance Neoplatonism.* Univ. of Toronto Italian Studies, no. 1. Ottawa: Dovehouse Editions Canada, 1986. Includes essays by Louis Valcke, Charles Trinkaus, and others on magic, cabala, and the ideal of human autonomy in Pico and Ficino.

Eliade, Mircea. *The Forge and the Crucible.* Trans. Stephen Corrin. New York: Harper and Row, 1962.

Eliot, T. S. *Essays on Elizabethan Drama.* 1932. Reprint. New York: Harcourt, Brace and World, 1960. Includes important and suggestive comparisons between the poetic styles of Marlowe and Jonson.

Ellis-Fermor, U[na] M[ary]. *Christopher Marlowe.* 1927. Reprint. Hamden, Conn.: Archon Books, 1967. Affirms a strong and immediate identification between Marlowe himself and the protagonist of *Dr. Faustus.*

Enck, John J. *Jonson and the Comic Truth.* Madison: Univ. of Wisconsin Press, 1957.

Erasmus, Desiderius. *Collected Works of Erasmus.* Ed. and trans. R.A.B. Mynors and others. Toronto: Univ. of Toronto Press, 1974–.

———. *The Correspondence of Erasmus.* Ed. and trans. R.A.B. Mynors and D.F.S. Thompson. Annotated by Wallace K. Ferguson, James K. McConica, and Peter G. Bietenholz. 6 vols. to date. In *Collected Works of Erasmus.* Toronto: Univ. of Toronto Press, 1974–.

———. *The Epistles of Erasmus.* Trans. Francis Morgan Nichols. 3 vols. New York: Longmans, Green, and Co., 1901–18.

———. *Opus Epistolarum Des. Erasmi Roterodami.* 12 vols. Ed. P. S. Allen and others. Oxford: Clarendon Press, 1906–58.

Erastus, Thomas. *Dispvtationvm de medicina nova Paracelsi, pars altera in qua philosophiae Paracelsiae principia et elementa explorantur.* [Basel: Apud Petrum Pernam, 1572–73?]

———. *Dispvtationvm de medicina nova Philippi Paracelsi pars prima: In qva, qvae de remediis svperstitiosis & magicis curationibus ille prodidit, praecipuè examinantur.* Basel: Apud Petrum Pernam, [1572].

Erikson, R. T. "Mnemonics and Giordano Bruno's Magical Art of Composition." *Cahiers Elisabethains* 20 (1981): 3–10. Endeavors to establish Giordano Bruno's direct influence on Marlowe's *Dr. Faustus.*

Ettin, Andrew V. "Magic into Art: The Magician's Renunciation of Magic in English Renaissance Drama." *Texas Studies in Literature and Language* 19 (1977): 268–93.

Evans, R.J.W. *Rudolf II and His World: A Study in Intellectual History, 1576–1612.* Oxford: Clarendon Press, 1973.

Feasey, Lynette, and Eveline Feasey. "Marlowe and the Homilies." *Notes and Queries* 195 (1950): 7–10. In their series of notes, the Feaseys argue that Marlowe was a theist who criticized such abuses of Christian doctrine as the "scourge of God" concept which, they believe, is satirized in *Tamburlaine.*

———. "Marlowe and the Prophetic Dooms." *Notes and Queries* 195 (1950): 356–59, 404–7, 419–21.

———. "The Validity of the Baines Document." *Notes and Queries* 194 (1949): 514–17.

Feingold, Mordechai. *The Mathematicians' Apprenticeship: Science, Universities and Society in England, 1560–1640.* Cambridge: Cambridge Univ. Press, 1984.

Ferguson, Wallace K. *The Renaissance in Historical Thought: Five Centuries of Interpretation.* Boston: Houghton Mifflin, 1948.

Festugière, A. J. *La Révélation d'Hermès Trismégiste.* 4 vols. Paris: Lecoffre, J. Gabalda et Cie., 1950–54.

Ficino, Marsilio. *De vita libri tres.* Ed. Martin Plessner. Hildesheim and New York: Georg Olms, 1978. Facsimile edition with variant readings listed; notes in German. References in the present study are to Paul Kristeller's facsimile edition of Ficino's *Opera* (q.v.).

———. *Marsilio Ficino and the Phaedrian Charioteer.* Ed. and trans. Michael J. B. Allen. Publications of the Center for Medieval and Renaissance Studies, UCLA, no. 14. Berkeley and Los Angeles:

Univ. of California Press, 1981. Contains several texts important for our understanding of Ficino's conception of the human soul's self-purification and spiritual ascent.

———. *Opera omnia.* Basel, 1576. Reprint edited by Paul Kristeller. 2 vols., paginated consecutively. Turin: Bottega d'Erasmo, 1962. Two sets of page numbers appear in this facsimile edition. References to the 1576 *Opera* in the present study are to the original page numbers, not those added at the bottom of the pages in the modern facsimile.

———. *Platonic Theology,* Book 3, Chapter 2; Book 13, Chapter 3; Book 14, Chapters 3 and 4. Trans. Josephine L. Burroughs. *Journal of the History of Ideas* 5 (1944): 227–39.

———. *Supplementum Ficinianum. Marsilii Ficini Florentini philosophi Platonici opuscula inedita et dispersa.* 2 vols. Ed. Paul Kristeller. Florence, Italy: L. S. Olschki, 1937.

———. *Théologie Platonicienne de l'immortalité des ames / Theologia Platonica de immortalitaté animorum.* Ed. and trans. Raymond Marcel. 3 vols. Paris: Société d'édition "Les Belles Lettres," 1964–70. Parallel-text edition in Latin and French.

Fioravante [Phioravante], Leonardo. See Hester, John, ed. and trans.

Firth, Katharine R. *The Apocalyptic Tradition in Reformation Britain, 1530–1645.* Oxford: Oxford Univ. Press, 1979. Documents the upsurge in apocalyptic prophecies in the 1580s and considers the possible influence of the Hermetic/Cabalist tradition.

Flachmann, Michael. "Ben Jonson and the Alchemy of Satire." *Studies in English Literature, 1500–1900* 17 (1977): 259–80.

Fludd, Robert. *Robert Fludd and His Philosophical Key, Being a Transcription of the MS at Trinity College, Cambridge.* Introd. Allen Debus. New York: Neale Watson, 1979.

Forester, James, ed. *The Pearle of Practise.* London: Richard Field, 1594. Paracelsian treatise compiled by John Hester and edited by Forester after Hester's death.

Foxe, John. *Actes and Monuments.* 2 vols. London: John Day, 1583.

Franck, Adolphe. *The Kabbalah: The Religious Philosophy of the Hebrews.* [New Hyde Park, N.Y.]: University Books, [1967].

Frazer, Sir James George. *The Golden Bough: A Study in Magic and Religion.* 3rd ed. 13 vols. 1911–36. Reprint. London: Macmillan; New York: St. Martin's Press, 1966. Especially pertinent to the present study is "Magic and Religion," 1:220–43.

French, Peter. *John Dee: The World of an Elizabethan Magus.* London: Routledge and Kegan Paul, 1972.

Fujita, Minoru. *Pageantry and Spectacle in Shakespeare.* Tokyo: Renaissance Institute, Sophia Univ., 1982. Includes a chapter entitled "'Wonder' in *The Tempest*," as well as commentary on spectacle in relation to Neoplatonic symbolism.

Garber, Marjorie. "'Infinite Riches in a Little Room': Closure and Enclosure in Marlowe." In Kernan, *Two Renaissance Mythmakers* (q.v.), 3–21.

Gardner, Helen. "Milton's 'Satan' and the Theme of Damnation in Elizabethan Tragedy." In *English Studies, 1948,* 46–66. English Association Essays and Studies, n.s. 1. Reprint. London: William Dawson and Sons, 1967. Includes commentary on *Dr. Faustus.*

Garin, Eugenio. *Astrology in the Renaissance: The Zodiac of Life.* Trans. Carolyn Jackson and June Allen; translation revised in conjunction with the author by Clare Robertson. London: Routledge and Kegan Paul, 1983.

———. *Giovanni Pico della Mirandola: Vita e dottrina.* Florence: F. Le Monnier, 1937.

———. *Italian Humanism: Philosophy and Civic Life in the Renaissance.* Trans. Peter Munz. New York: Harper and Row, 1965.

———. *Science and Civic Life in the Italian Renaissance.* Trans. Peter Munz. Garden City, N.Y.: Doubleday, Anchor Books, 1969.

The Geneva Bible: A Facsimile of the 1560 Edition. Introd. Lloyd E. Berry. Madison: Univ. of Wisconsin Press, 1969.

Gettings, Fred. *Dictionary of Occult, Hermetic, and Alchemical Sigils.* London: Routledge and Kegan Paul, 1981.

Giamatti, A. Bartlett. "Marlowe: The Arts of Illusion." *Yale Review* 61 (1972): 530–43.

———. "Proteus Unbound: Some Versions of the Sea God in the Renaissance." In Demetz, Greene, and Nelson, *The Disciplines of Criticism* (q.v.), 437–75.

Gianakaris, Constantine J. "The Humanism of Ben Jonson." *College Language Association Journal* 14 (1970): 115–26.

Gifford, George A. *A Dialogue Concerning Witches and Witchcraftes.* London: Iohn Windet for Tobie Cooke and Mihil Hart, 1593.

Gilmore, Myron P. *The World of Humanism, 1453–1517.* The Rise of

Modern Europe Series, vol. 2. New York: Harper and Row, 1952. Reprint. Westport, Conn.: Greenwood Press, 1983.

Giorgio, Francesco. *De harmonia mundi totius cantica tria.* Venice: in aedibus B. Vitalibus, 1525. A major source through which Cabalist ideas were disseminated in the sixteenth century.

Godshalk, W. L. *The Marlovian World Picture.* The Hague: Mouton, 1974.

Godwin, Joscelyn. *Athanasius Kircher: A Renaissance Man and the Quest for Lost Knowledge.* London and New York: Thames and Hudson, 1979.

Goldman, Michael. "Marlowe and the Histrionics of Ravishment." In Kernan, *Two Renaissance Mythmakers* (q.v.), 22–40.

Gombrich, E. H. "Botticelli's Mythologies: A Study in the Neoplatonic Symbolism of His Circle." *Journal of the Warburg and Courtauld Institutes* 8 (1945): 7–60.

———. "*Icones Symbolicae:* The Visual Image in Neo-Platonic Thought." *Journal of the Warburg and Courtauld Institutes* 11 (1948): 163–92.

———. "Renaissance and Golden Age." In Gombrich, *Norm and Form: Studies in the Art of the Renaissance,* 29–34. London: Phaidon, 1966.

Goodman, Paul. "Comic Plots." In Goodman, *The Structure of Literature.* Chicago: Univ. of Chicago Press, 1954; Phoenix Books, 1962. Reprinted in Barish, *Ben Jonson: A Collection of Critical Essays,* (q.v.). The first section of the chapter (pp. 82–103 of the Phoenix edition) discusses comic intrigue in *The Alchemist.*

Gordon, D. J. "*Hymenaei:* Ben Jonson's Masque of Union." *Journal of the Warburg and Courtauld Institutes* 8 (1945): 107–45.

———. "The Imagery of Ben Jonson's *The Masque of Blacknesse* and *The Masque of Beautie.*" *Journal of the Warburg and Courtauld Institutes* 6 (1943): 122–41.

Grant, Patrick. "The Magic of Charity: A Background to Prospero." *Review of English Studies* 27 (1976): 1–16.

Grant, R.A.D. "Providence, Authority, and the Moral Life in *The Tempest.*" *Shakespeare Studies* 16 (1983): 235–63.

Gray, Hanna. "Renaissance Humanism: The Pursuit of Eloquence." *Journal of the History of Ideas* 24 (1963): 497–514.

Greenblatt, Stephen. "Invisible Bullets: Renaissance Authority and

Its Subversion." *Glyph* 8 (1981): 40–61. Reprinted in revised form in *Political Shakespeare*, ed. Jonathan Dollimore and Alan Sinfield, 18–47. Ithaca: Cornell Univ. Press, 1985. The later version of the essay elaborates upon Greenblatt's interpretation of Shakespeare's history plays; the original version in *Glyph* includes some discussion of the possibility of "radical subversiveness" (41) in the Renaissance which is condensed in the later version.

———. *Renaissance Self-Fashioning from More to Shakespeare*. Chicago: Univ. of Chicago Press, 1980. Includes "Marlowe and the Will to Absolute Play," in which Greenblatt suggests that Marlowe is a nihilist whose plays "subvert his culture's metaphysical and ethical certainties" (220).

Greenburg, Sidney Thomas. *The Infinite in Giordano Bruno*. 1950. Reprint. New York: Farrar, Straus, and Giroux, 1978. Includes a translation of *Concerning the Cause, Principle, and One*.

Greene, Donald. "Augustinianism and Empiricism: A Note on Eighteenth-Century English Intellectual History." *Eighteenth-Century Studies* 1 (1967): 33–68.

Greene, Robert. *Greenes, Groatsworth of witte, bought with a million of Repentance*. London: William Wright, 1592. Reprint edited by G. B. Harrison. New York: Barnes and Noble, 1966.

Greene, Thomas M. "Ben Jonson and the Centered Self." *Studies in English Literature, 1500–1900* 10 (1970): 325–48.

———. "The Flexibility of the Self in Renaissance Literature." In Demetz, Greene, and Nelson, *The Disciplines of Criticism* (q.v.), 241–64.

Greg, W. W., ed. See Marlowe, Christopher.

Grene, Nicholas. *Shakespeare, Jonson, Molière: The Comic Contract*. Totowa, New Jersey: Barnes and Noble, 1980.

Guazzo, Francesco Maria. *Compendium maleficarum*. 1608. Trans. E. A. Ashwin, with notes by Montague Summers. London: John Rodker, 1929.

Haklvyt, Richard. *Voyages*. London: Everyman's Library, 1962.

Hall, Marie Boas. See Boas, Marie; see also Chastel, André.

Hall, Rupert A. "Science, Technology and Utopia in the Seventeenth Century." In Mathias, *Science and Society, 1600–1900* (q.v.), 33–53. Questions the relationships among science, technology, and utopianism.

Halli, Robert W., Jr. "Quack: The Writings and Career of Francis Anthony." *Renaissance Papers, 1986,* ed. Dale B. J. Randall and Joseph A. Porter, 97–110. Durham, N. C.: The Southeastern Renaissance Conference, 1986. Surveys the life (1550–1623) and writings of an Elizabethan alchemical physician, with emphasis upon his conflicts with the authoritarian Royal College of Physicians of London.

Hamilton, A. C. "Sidney and Agrippa." *Review of English Studies,* n.s. 7 (1956): 151–57.

Hamilton, Alistair. *The Family of Love.* Cambridge, Eng.: James Clark and Co., 1981.

Hardison, O. B. "The Orator and the Poet: The Dilemma of Humanist Literature." *Journal of Medieval and Renaissance Studies* 1 (1971): 33–44.

Hariot, Thomas. See Harriot.

Harrie, Jeanne. "Duplessis-Mornay, Foix-Candale, and the Hermetic Religion of the World." *Renaissance Quarterly* 31 (1978): 499–514.

Har[r]iot, Thomas. *A briefe and true report of the new found land of Virginia.* London: n.p., 1588. Reprint. Amsterdam: Theatrum Orbis Terrarum; New York: Da Capo Press, 1971.

Harris, Anthony. *Night's Black Agents: Witchcraft and Magic in Seventeenth-Century English Drama.* Manchester, Eng.: Manchester Univ. Press; Totowa, N.J.: Rowman and Littlefield, 1980.

Harrison, G. B., ed. *Shakespeare: The Complete Works.* New York: Harcourt, Brace and World, 1948.

———, ed. *Willobie his Avisa, 1594.* 1924. Reprint. New York: Barnes and Noble, 1966. Contains the depositions of witnesses at the Cerne Abbas inquiry into Sir Walter Ralegh's religious beliefs, as well as Professor Harrison's account of many other documents concerning Ralegh, Marlowe, and others.

Harrison, John Smith. *Platonism in English Poetry of the Sixteenth and Seventeenth Centuries.* New York: Columbia Univ. Press, 1903.

Harsnet, Samuel. *A Declaration of egregious Popish Impostures, to withdrawe the harts of her Maiesties subiects from their allegeance, and from the truth of Christian Religion professed in England, under the pretence of casting out devils.* London: James Roberts, 1603. A source for the names of devils mentioned in *King Lear* and *Macbeth,* Harsnet's treatise also includes some discussion of the Devil's claim to be "Prince and Monarch of the world" (47).

Hart, Jeffrey. "Prospero and Faustus." *Boston University Studies in English* 2 (1956–57): 197–206.

Hart, W. H. "Observations on Some Documents Relating to Magic in the Reign of Queen Elizabeth." *Archaeologia* 40 (1866): 389–97.

Hartwig, Joan. *Shakespeare's Analogical Scene: Parody as Structural Syntax.* Lincoln and London: Univ. of Nebraska Press, 1983. Includes "Cloten and Caliban: Parodic Villains."

———. *Shakespeare's Tragicomic Vision.* Baton Rouge: Louisiana State Univ. Press, 1972.

Harvey, Gabriel. *Pierces Supererogation; or, A New Prayse of the Old Asse.* London: John Wolfe, 1593. In vol. 2 of *The Works of Gabriel Harvey,* ed. Alexander B. Grosart. [London]: Printed for private circulation, 1884–85. For satirical references to alchemists, cabalists, etc., see the Grosart edition, 251.

Hatfield, Rab. "The Compagnia de' Magi." *Journal of the Warburg and Courtauld Institutes* 33 (1970): 107–61.

Haydn, Hiram. *The Counter-Renaissance.* 1950. Reprint. New York: Harcourt, Brace and World, n.d.

Hayes, T. Wilson. *Winstanley the Digger: A Literary Analysis of Radical Ideas in the English Revolution.* Cambridge: Harvard Univ. Press, 1979.

Heffner, Ray L., Jr. "Unifying Symbols in the Comedy of Ben Jonson." In *English Stage Comedy,* ed. W. K. Wimsatt, 74–97. English Institute Essays, 1954. New York: Columbia Univ. Press, 1955.

Helton, Tinsley, ed. *The Renaissance: A Reconsideration of the Theories and Interpretations of the Age.* Madison: Univ. of Wisconsin Press, 1961.

Heninger, S. K., Jr. *The Cosmographical Glass: Renaissance Diagrams of the Universe.* San Marino, Calif.: Huntington Library, 1977.

———. *"Touches of Sweet Harmony": Pythagorean Cosmology and Renaissance Poetics.* San Marino, Calif.: Huntington Library, 1974.

Henze, Richard. *"The Tempest:* Rejection of a Vanity." *Shakespeare Quarterly* 23 (1972): 420–34.

The Hermetic Museum, Restored and Enlarged. See Waite, Arthur Edward, ed.

Hermetica. See Scott, Walter, ed.

Hester, John, ed. and trans. *A Breefe Answere of Iosephus Quercetanus* [Joseph Du Chesne] *Armeniacus, Doctor of Phisick, to the exposition of Iacobus Aubertus Vindonis, concerning the original, and causes of mettalles, set foorth against Chimists . . . whereunto is added divers rare secretes, not heeretofore knowne of many.* London: n.p., 1591.

———, ed. and trans. *A Compendium of the rationall Secretes of . . . Leonardo Phioravante.* London: Imprinted by John Kyngston for George Pen, and I. H., 1582.

———, ed. and trans. *A Discourse upon Chyrurgery,* by Leonardo Phioravanti. London: Edward Allde, 1626.

———, ed. and trans. *An excellent Treatise teaching howe to cure the French Pockes . . . Drawne out of the Bookes of that learned Doctor and Prince of Phisitians, Theophrastus Paracelsus.* London: [John Charlwood], 1590.

———, ed. and trans. *The First Part of the Key of Philosophie.* London: Valentine Simmes, 1596. Reprint. English Experience Series, no. 605. Amsterdam: Theatrum Orbis Terrarum; New York: Da Capo Press, 1973.

———, ed. and trans. *The first part of the Key of philosophie. First written by T. Paraselsus* [sic]*, and now published by J. Hester.* London: R. Daye, 1580.

———, ed. and trans. *A Hundred and fourtene experiments and cures of the famous Phisition Philippus Aureolis Theophrastus Paracelsus.* London: [H. Middleton, 1583?] *STC* 19179.5 (formerly 19181). All references are to this edition. The copy of the 1596 edition (*STC* 19180) which I have examined is severely corrupted.

———. ed. and trans. *A Joyfull Jewell,* by Leonardo Fiorovantie. London: William Wright, [1579].

———, ed. and trans. *The Sclopotarie of Iosephus Quercetanus* [Joseph Du Chesne]*, phisition, or His booke containing the cure of wounds.* London: Printed by Roger Ward, for John Sheldrake, 1590.

———, ed. and trans. See Forester, James, ed.

Hexter, J. H. Introduction to *Utopia,* by Thomas More (q.v.).

Highfill, Philip, Jr., ed. *Shakespeare's Craft.* Carbondale and Edwardsville: Published for the George Washington University by the Southern Illinois Univ. Press, 1982. Includes commentary by Eugene Waith and Alvin Kernan on Shakespeare's romances.

Hill, Christopher. *Intellectual Origins of the English Revolution.* Oxford: Clarendon Press, 1965.

———. *The Religion of Gerrard Winstanley.* Oxford: Past and Present Society, 1978. Indicates the influence of the Family of Love and other sects which reacted against the traditional concept of original sin and regarded human nature as perfectible.

———. *The World Turned Upside Down: Radical Ideas during the English Revolution.* New York: Viking Press, 1972.

Hill, John Edward Christopher. See Hill, Christopher.

Hillman, Richard. "Chaucer's Franklin's Magician and *The Tempest*: An Influence beyond Appearances?" *Shakespeare Quarterly* 34 (1983): 426–32.

Hinman, Robert B. "The Apotheosis of Faust: Poetry and New Philosophy in the Seventeenth Century." In *Metaphysical Poetry,* ed. D. J. Palmer and Malcolm Bradbury, 148–79. Stratford-upon-Avon Studies, no. 11. London: Edward Arnold, 1970.

Hirsch, E. D., Jr. *The Aims of Interpretation.* Chicago and London: Univ. of Chicago Press, 1976.

———. *Validity in Interpretation.* New Haven: Yale Univ. Press, 1967.

The Historie of the damnable life, and deserued death of Doctor Iohn Faustus, newly imprinted and . . . amended. Trans. P. F. London: Thomas Orwin, 1592.

The History of the Damnable Life and Deserved Death of Doctor John Faustus, 1592. Ed. William Rose. London: G. Routledge and Sons, 1925. Reprint. South Bend, Ind.: n.p., 1963.

Hoeniger, F. David. "Shakespeare's Romances since 1958: A Retrospect." *Shakespeare Survey* 29 (1976): 1–10.

Holland, Henry. *A Treatise against Witchcraft.* Cambridge: John Legatt, Printer to the Univ. of Cambridge, 1590.

Holmyard, E. J. *Alchemy.* Harmondsworth: Penguin, 1957.

Homan, Sidney R. "Chapman and Marlowe: The Paradoxical Hero and the Divided Response." *Journal of English and Germanic Philology* 68 (1969): 391–406.

———. "*The Tempest* and Shakespeare's Last Plays: The Aesthetic Dimensions." *Shakespeare Quarterly* 24 (1973): 69–76. Argues in favor of ambivalence, rather than affirmation, in *The Tempest.*

Hondo, Masao. "The Meaning of Magic and Masque in *The Tempest.*" In *Poetry and Drama in the Age of Shakespeare,* ed. Peter Milward and Tetsuo Anzai, 167–83. Tokyo: Renaissance Institute, Sophia Univ., 1982.

Hooykaas, Reijer. *Religion and the Rise of Modern Science.* Edinburgh and London: Scottish Academic Press, 1973.

Howe, James Robinson. *Marlowe, Tamburlaine, and Magic.* Athens, Ohio: Ohio Univ. Press, 1976. Provides evidence for Giordano Bruno's influence on Marlowe.

Hoy, David Couzens. *The Critical Circle: Literature, History, and Philosophical Hermeneutics.* Berkeley and Los Angeles: Univ. of California Press, 1978.

Hyman, Stanley E. "Portraits of the Artist: Iago and Prospero." *Shenandoah* 21, no. 2 (Winter 1970): 18–42.

Jackson, Gabriele. *Vision and Judgment in Ben Jonson's Drama.* Yale Studies in English, no. 166. New Haven: Yale Univ. Press, 1968.

Jacquot, Jean. "Harriot, Hill, Warner, and the New Philosophy." In Shirley, *Thomas Harriot: Renaissance Scientist* (q.v.), 107–28. An important study of Giordano Bruno's influence upon the evolution of scientific and religious thought in England.

———. "Thomas Harriot's Reputation for Impiety." *Notes and Records of the Royal Society of London* 9 (1952): 164–87.

James, David Gwilym. *The Dream of Prospero.* Oxford: Clarendon Press, 1967.

James I of England. *Daemonologie.* Ed. G. B. Harrison. 1924. Reprint. New York: Barnes and Noble, 1966. Originally published in Edinburgh in 1597 and reprinted in London in 1603. Also contains *Newes from Scotland,* an account of a witchcraft trial in which James was personally involved.

Jantz, Harold. "An Elizabethan Statement on the Origin of the German Faust Book, with a Note on Marlowe's Sources." *Journal of English and Germanic Philology* 51 (1952): 137–53.

Jayne, Sears. "Ficino and the Platonism of the English Renaissance." *Comparative Literature* 4 (1952): 214–38.

Jensen, E. J., and L. A. Beaurline. "L. A. Beaurline and the Illusion of Completeness." *PMLA* 86 (1971): 121–27. Jensen's reply to Beaurline's "Ben Jonson and the Illusion of Completeness"(q.v.) and Beaurline's rejoinder.

Johnson, Francis R. "Marlowe's Astronomy and Renaissance Skepticism." *ELH* 13 (1946): 241–54.

Jonas, Hans. *The Gnostic Religion.* 2nd ed. Boston: Beacon Press, 1970.

Jonson, Ben. *The Alchemist.* Ed. Alvin Kernan. New Haven: Yale Univ. Press, 1974.

———. *The Alchemist.* Ed. Charles Montgomery Hathaway. New York: Holt, 1903.

———. *The Alchemist.* Ed. Douglas Brown. London: Ernest Benn, 1966.

———. *The Alchemist.* Ed. F. H. Mares. London: Methuen, 1967.

———. *The Alchemist.* Ed. S. Musgrove. Berkeley and Los Angeles: Univ. of California Press, 1968.

———. *Ben Jonson.* Ed. C. H. Herford and Percy Simpson. 11 vols. Oxford: Clarendon Press, 1925–52.

———. *Complete Masques.* Ed. Stephen Orgel. New Haven: Yale Univ. Press, 1969.

———. *Volpone.* Ed. Alvin Kernan. New Haven: Yale Univ. Press, 1962. Kernan's introduction includes a seminal discussion of metamorphosis in Jonson's plays and in Renaissance literature in general.

Josten, C. H. "An Unknown Chapter in the Life of John Dee." *Journal of the Warburg and Courtauld Institutes* 28 (1965): 223–57.

Jung, Carl Gustav. *Aion.* Trans. R.F.C. Hull. Vol. 9, pt. 2, of *The Collected Works of C. G. Jung.* Bollingen Series 20. New York: Pantheon, 1959.

———. "Introduction to the Religious and Psychological Problems of Alchemy." In *Basic Writings of C. G. Jung,* ed. Violet Staub de Laszlo. The Modern Library. New York: Random House, 1959.

———. *Psychology and Alchemy.* Trans. R.F.C. Hull. Vol. 12 of *The Collected Works of C. G. Jung.* Bollingen Series 20. New York: Pantheon Books, 1953.

Kay, Carol McGinnis, and Henry Jacobs, eds. *Shakespeare's Romances Reconsidered.* Lincoln and London: Univ. of Nebraska Press, 1978.

Kearney, Hugh F. *Science and Change, 1500–1700.* London: Weidenfeld and Nicolson, 1971.

Keefer, Michael H. "Verbal Magic and the Problem of the A and B Texts of *Doctor Faustus.*" *Journal of English and Germanic Philology* 82 (1983): 324–46.

Kermode, Frank. Introduction to *The Tempest,* by William Shakespeare. The New Arden Shakespeare. 6th ed. Cambridge: Harvard Univ. Press, 1958.

Kernan, Alvin. *The Cankered Muse.* New Haven: Yale Univ. Press, 1959.

———. *The Playwright as Magician.* New Haven: Yale Univ. Press, 1979.

———, ed. *Modern Shakespearean Criticism.* New York: Harcourt, Brace and World, 1970.

———, ed. *Two Renaissance Mythmakers: Christopher Marlowe and Ben Jonson.* Baltimore: Johns Hopkins Univ. Press, 1977.

———, ed. See also Jonson, Ben.

Kinsman, Robert S., ed. *The Darker Vision of the Renaissance: Beyond the Fields of Reason.* Berkeley and Los Angeles: Univ. of California Press, 1974.

Klibansky, Raymond. *The Continuity of the Platonic Tradition during the Middle Ages.* London: Warburg Institute, 1939.

Knight, G. Wilson. *The Crown of Life.* London: Oxford Univ. Press, 1947.

Knights, Lionel Charles. *Drama and Society in the Age of Jonson.* London: Chatto and Windus, 1937.

Knoll, Robert E. *Ben Jonson's Plays: An Introduction.* Lincoln: Univ. of Nebraska Press, 1964.

Knox, Ronald A. *Enthusiasm: A Chapter in the History of Religion.* New York: Oxford Univ. Press, 1950.

Kocher, Paul. *Christopher Marlowe: A Study of His Thought, Learning, and Character.* Chapel Hill: Univ. of North Carolina Press, 1946. Reprint. New York: Russell and Russell, 1962.

———. "John Hester, Paracelsian." In McManaway, Dawson, and Willoughby, *Joseph Quincy Adams Memorial Studies* (q.v.), 621–38.

———. "Paracelsian Medicine in England (ca. 1570–1600)." *Journal of the History of Medicine* 2 (1947): 451–80.

———. *Science and Religion in Elizabethan England.* San Marino, Calif.: Huntington Library, 1953.

Korkowski, Eugene. "Agrippa as Ironist." *Neophilologus* 60 (1976): 594–607.

Kramer, Heinrich, and James Sprenger. *Malleus maleficarum.* Trans. Montague Summers. London: John Rodker, 1928. Reprint. New York: Dover, 1971. An influential and revealing inquisitor's manual, widely used in witchcraft persecutions. Summers provides a bibliographical note on early editions.

Kristeller, Paul. *Eight Philosophers of the Italian Renaissance.* Stanford: Stanford Univ. Press, 1964.

———. *The Philosophy of Marsilio Ficino.* Trans. Virginia Conant. New York: Columbia Univ. Press, 1943.

———. *Renaissance Concepts of Man, and Other Essays.* New York: Harper and Row, 1972.

———. "Renaissance Platonism." In *Facets of the Renaissance,* ed. William Henry Werkmeister, 103–23. 1959. Reprint. Freeport, N.Y.: Books for Libraries Press, 1971.

———. *Renaissance Thought and Its Sources.* Ed. Michael Mooney. New York: Columbia Univ. Press, 1979. Major essays from Kristeller's previous studies, updated, with an introduction by the editor.

———. *Renaissance Thought: The Classic, Scholastic, and Humanistic Strains.* New York: Harper and Row, 1961. Revised and enlarged version of Kristeller's *The Classics and Renaissance Thought.*

———. *Renaissance Thought II: Papers on Humanism and the Arts.* New York: Harper and Row, 1965.

———. *Studies in Renaissance Thought and Letters.* Rome: Edizioni di storia e letteratura, 1956.

———, ed. See Ficino, *Opera omnia* and *Supplementum Ficinianum;* see also Cassirer, Kristeller, and Randall.

Kuntz, Marion L. D. *Guillaume Postel, Prophet of the Restitution of All Things: His Life and Thought.* Boston: Martinus Nijhoff, 1981.

Kuriyama, Constance Brown. "Dr. Greg and *Doctor Faustus:* The Supposed Originality of the 1616 Text." *English Literary Renaissance* 5 (1975): 171–97.

Larner, Christina. *Enemies of God: The Witch-Hunt in Scotland.* Baltimore: Johns Hopkins Univ. Press, 1981.

———. *Witchcraft and Religion: The Politics of Popular Belief.* New York: Blackwell, 1984.

Lea, Henry Charles, ed. *Materials toward a History of Witchcraft.* 3 vols. Philadelphia: Univ. of Pennsylvania Press, 1939.

Leggatt, Alexander. *Ben Jonson: His Vision and His Art.* London and New York: Methuen, 1981.

Levin, Harry. "Marlowe Today." *Tulane Drama Review* 8, no. 4 (Summer 1964): 22–31.

———. *The Myth of the Golden Age in the Renaissance.* Bloomington: Indiana Univ. Press, 1969.

———. *The Overreacher: A Study of Christopher Marlowe.* Cambridge: Harvard Univ. Press, 1952.

———. "Two Magian Comedies: *The Tempest* and *The Alchemist.*" *Shakespeare Survey* 22 (1969): 47–58.

Lewis, C. S. *English Literature in the Sixteenth Century, Excluding Drama.* Oxford: Clarendon Press, 1954.

Linden, Stanton J. "Francis Bacon and Alchemy: The Reformation of Vulcan." *Journal of the History of Ideas* 35 (1974): 547–60.

Lindley, David, "Music, Masque, and Meaning in *The Tempest.*" In Lindley, *The Court Masque* (q.v.), 47–59.

———, ed. *The Court Masque.* Manchester, Eng.: Manchester Univ. Press, 1984. Includes essays on Ben Jonson and Inigo Jones, as well as on *The Tempest.*

Lodge, Thomas. *The Anatomie of Alchymie.* Epistle 7 of *A Fig for Momus.* London: [J. Orwin] for C. Knight, 1595. Anti-alchemy satire.

Loewenstein, Joseph. *Responsive Readings: Versions of Echo in Pastoral, Epic, and the Jonsonian Masque.* New Haven: Yale Univ. Press, 1984. Includes some discussion of Jonson's ambivalence toward visual spectacle, theatricality, and hieroglyphics.

Logan, Terence P., and Denzell S. Smith, eds. *The Predecessors of Shakespeare: A Survey and Bibliography of Recent Studies in English Renaissance Drama.* Lincoln: Univ. of Nebraska Press, 1973. Includes a judicious essay on Marlowe, including evaluations of earlier studies of the text of *Doctor Faustus.*

Lovejoy, Arthur. *Essays in the History of Ideas.* Baltimore: Johns Hopkins Press, 1948.

Lovejoy, Arthur, and George Boas. *Primitivism and Related Ideas in Antiquity.* Baltimore: Johns Hopkins Press, 1935.

Luzzato, Moses Hayvim. *General Principles of the Kabbalah.* New York: Press of the Research Centre of Kabbalah, 1970.

McConica, J. K. *English Humanists and Reformation Politics.* Oxford: Clarendon Press, 1965.

Macfarlane, Alan. "A Tudor Anthropologist: George Gifford's *Discourse* and *Dialogue.*" In Anglo, *The Damned Art* (q.v.), 140–55.

———. *Witchcraft in Tudor and Stuart England.* London: Routledge and Kegan Paul; New York: Harper and Row, Torchbook, 1970.

McLean, Antonia. *Humanism and the Rise of Science in Tudor England.* New York: Neale Watson Academic Publications, 1972.

MacLure, Millar, ed. *Marlowe: The Critical Heritage, 1588–1896.* London: Routledge and Kegan Paul, 1979.

McManaway, James G.; Giles E. Dawson; and Edwin E. Willoughby, eds. *Joseph Quincy Adams Memorial Studies.* Washington, D.C.: Folger Shakespeare Library, 1948.

Madathanas, Henry. *The Golden Age Restored.* In Waite, *The Hermetic Museum* (q.v.).

Magnusson, A. Lynne. "Interruption in *The Tempest.*" *Shakespeare Quarterly* 37 (1986): 52–65.

Mahoney, Edward P., ed. *Philosophy and Humanism: Renaissance Essays in Honor of Paul Oskar Kristeller.* New York: Columbia Univ. Press, 1976.

Mahood, M. M. *Poetry and Humanism.* New Haven: Yale Univ. Press, 1950.

Maiorino, Giancarlo. "The Breaking of the Circle: Giordano Bruno and the Poetics of Immeasurable Abundance." *Journal of the History of Ideas* 38 (1977): 317–27.

———. "Voice of Its Own Birth: Bruno and the Foundation of Coleridge's Poetics." *Comparative Literature Studies* 19 (1982): 296–318.

Malland, A. George. "Roger Bacon as Magician." *Traditio* 30 (1974): 445–60.

Malleus maleficarum. See Kramer, Heinrich, and James Sprenger.

Mandel, Jerome. "Dream and Imagination in Shakespeare." *Shakespeare Quarterly* 24 (1973): 61–68.

Mandrou, Robert. *From Humanism to Science, 1480–1700.* Trans. Brian Pearce. Atlantic Highlands, N.J.: Humanities Press, 1979.

Manley, Frank. "The Nature of Faustus." *Modern Philology* 66 (1969): 218–31.

———, ed. See Donne, John.

Manuel, Frank E., and Fritzie P. Manuel. *Utopian Thought in the Western World.* Cambridge: Belknap Press of Harvard Univ. Press, 1979. Includes discussion of occult philosophers and radical Puritans in the Renaissance.

Marlowe, Christopher. *The Complete Works of Christopher Marlowe.* Ed. Fredson Bowers. 2 vols. Cambridge: Cambridge Univ. Press, 1973.

———. *Doctor Faustus.* Ed. John D. Jump. The Revels Plays. Cambridge: Harvard Univ. Press, 1962.

————. *Dr. Faustus: The A-Text.* Ed. David Ormerod and Christopher Wortham. Nedlands: Univ. of Western Australia Press, 1985.

————. *Marlowe's "Dr. Faustus," 1604–1616: Parallel Texts.* Ed. W. W. Greg. Oxford: Clarendon Press, 1950.

————. *The Tragical History of the Life and Death of Doctor Faustus: A Conjectural Reconstruction.* Ed. W. W. Greg. Oxford: Clarendon Press, 1950.

Masinton, Charles G. *Christopher Marlowe's Tragic Vision: A Study in Damnation.* Athens: Ohio Univ. Press, 1972.

Mason, James. *The Anatomie of Sorcery.* London: J. Legatte, 1612.

Massa, Daniel. "Giordano Bruno's Ideas in Seventeenth-Century England." *Journal of the History of Ideas* 38 (1977): 227–42.

Mathias, Peter, ed. *Science and Society, 1600–1900.* Cambridge and New York: Cambridge Univ. Press, 1972. Essays by P. M. Rattansi, Rupert Hall, and others on magic, science, and utopianism.

Maus, Katharine Eisaman. *Ben Jonson and the Roman Frame of Mind.* Princeton: Princeton Univ. Press, 1984.

Mazzeo, Joseph Anthony. *Renaissance and Revolution: Backgrounds to Seventeenth-Century English Literature.* New York: Random House, Pantheon Books, 1967. Important essays on Renaissance humanism, Machiavelli, Castiglione, Bacon, Hobbes, and "The Idea of Progress"; extensive bibliographical notes evaluating previous scholarship.

Mebane, John S. "Structure, Source, and Meaning in *A Midsummer Night's Dream.*" *Texas Studies in Literature and Language* 24 (1982): 255–70.

Milton, John. *The Works of John Milton.* Ed. Frank Allen Patterson and others. 20 vols. New York: Columbia Univ. Press, 1931–38.

Milward, Peter. *Shakespeare's Religious Background.* Bloomington: Indiana Univ. Press, 1973.

Montaigne, Michel de. *The essayes or morall, politike and militarie discourses.* Trans. J. Florio. London: V. Sims for E. Blount, 1603.

————. *The Essays of Montaigne. Done into English by John Florio, Anno 1603.* Introd. George Saintsbury. 1892–93. Reprint. New York: AMS Press, 1967.

Moore, Thomas. *The Planets Within: Marsilio Ficino's Astrological Psychology.* Studies in Jungian Thought. Lewisburg, Pa.: Bucknell

Univ. Press; London and Toronto: Associated Univ. Presses, 1982.

Moorin, Albert S. "The Sorcerer in Elizabethan and Jacobean Life and Drama." Ph.D. dissertation, University of Utah, 1972. For abstract, see *Dissertation Abstracts International* 33 (1972): 2335A.

More, Thomas. *Utopia.* Ed. J. H. Hexter and Edward Surtz. Vol. 4 of *The Yale Edition of the Complete Works of St. Thomas More.* New Haven: Yale Univ. Press, 1963.

———. *The Workes of Sir Thomas More.* London: John Cawod, John Waly, and Richarde Totell, 1557. Includes More's translation of a life of Giovanni Pico della Mirandola (1463–94) by the elder Pico's nephew, Gian Francesco Pico (1470–1533), as well as several of the elder Pico's devotional writings.

Mornay, Philippe de. *A Woorke concerning the trewnesse of the Christian Religion, written in French: Against Atheists, Epicures, Paynims, Iewes, Mahumetists, and other Infidels.* Trans. Philip Sidney and Arthur Golding. London: Imprinted for Thomas Cadman, 1587. Reprint edited by F. J. Sypher. Delmar, N.Y.: Scholars' Facsimiles and Reprints, 1976.

Moss, Jean Dietz. "The Family of Love and English Critics." *Sixteenth Century Journal* 6 (1975): 35–52.

———. *"Godded with God": Hendrik Niclaes and His Family of Love.* Philadelphia: American Philosophical Society, 1981.

———. "Variations on a Theme: The Family of Love in Renaissance England." *Renaissance Quarterly* 31 (1978): 186–95.

Mowat, Barbara. *The Dramaturgy of Shakespeare's Romances.* Athens: Univ. of Georgia Press, 1976.

———. "Prospero, Agrippa, and Hocus Pocus." *English Literary Renaissance* 11 (1981): 281–303.

Müller-Jahncke, Wolf Dieter. "The Attitude of Agrippa von Nettesheim (1486–1535) towards Alchemy." *Ambix* 22 (1975): 134–50.

Mullett, Michael A. *Radical Religious Movements in Early Modern Europe.* London and Boston: Allen and Unwin, 1980.

Mulryan, John. "The Occult Tradition and English Renaissance Literature." *Bucknell Review* 20, no. 3 (1972): 53–72.

Nashe, Thomas. *The Unfortunate Traveller.* In vol. 2 of *The Works of Thomas Nashe,* ed. Ronald B. McKerrow. 5 vols. London: Sidgwick and Jackson, 1904–10. Reprinted with corrections by F. P. Wilson. New York: Barnes and Noble, 1966.

Nauert, Charles. *Agrippa and the Crisis of Renaissance Thought.* Illinois Studies in the Social Sciences, no. 55. Urbana: Univ. of Illinois Press, 1965.

———. "Magic and Skepticism in Agrippa's Thought." *Journal of the History of Ideas* 18 (1957): 161–82.

Nelson, John Charles. *Renaissance Theory of Love: The Context of Giordano Bruno's "Eroici furori."* New York: Columbia Univ. Press, 1958.

The New Testament: Translated by William Tyndale, 1534. Ed. N. Hardy Wallis. Cambridge: Cambridge Univ. Press, 1938.

Newes from Scotland, Declaring the Damnable life and death of Doctor Fian, a notable Sorcerer, who was burned at Edenbrough in January last. London: William Wright, 1591. See James I, *Daemonologie.*

Nicholl, Charles. *The Chemical Theatre.* London: Routledge and Kegan Paul, 1980.

Nichols, John. *Progresses . . . of King James I.* 4 vols. London: J. B. Nichols, 1828.

Nicolson, Marjorie. *The Breaking of the Circle.* Rev. ed. New York: Columbia Univ. Press, 1960.

Noble, Richmond. *Shakespeare's Biblical Knowledge.* New York: Macmillan; London: Society for Promoting Christian Knowledge, 1935.

Nock, A. D., ed. *Corpus Hermeticum.* Trans. A. J. Festugière. 4 vols. Paris: Société d'édition "Les Belles Lettres," 1945–54. The standard edition of the Greek texts, with a parallel French translation; for a parallel-text edition with an English translation, see Scott, Walter, ed. and trans.

Norbrook, David. *Poetry and Politics in the English Renaissance.* London: Routledge and Kegan Paul, 1984.

Norton, Thomas. *Thomas Norton's "Ordinal of Alchemy."* Ed. John Reidy. Early English Text Society, no. 272. Oxford: Oxford Univ. Press, 1975.

O'Brien, Gordon Worth. *Renaissance Poetics and the Problem of Power.* Chicago: Institute of Elizabethan Studies, 1956. Important and stimulating study of Neoplatonism and related movements as sources of the affirmation of human power and nobility in Renaissance literature.

O'Malley, John W. "Man's Dignity, God's Love, and the Destiny of

Rome: A Text of Giles of Viterbo." *Viator: Medieval and Renaissance Studies* 3 (1972): 389–416.

Orgel, Stephen. *The Illusion of Power: Political Theater in the English Renaissance.* Berkeley and Los Angeles: Univ. of California Press, 1975.

———. *The Jonsonian Masque.* Cambridge: Harvard Univ. Press, 1967.

———, ed. See Jonson, Ben.

Ormerod, David, and Christopher Wortham, eds. See Marlowe, Christopher.

Ornstein, Robert. "The Comic Synthesis in *Doctor Faustus.*" *ELH* 22 (1955): 165–72.

———. "Marlowe and God: The Tragic Theology of *Dr. Faustus.*" *PMLA* 83 (1968): 1378–85.

Ortelius, Abraham. *Epitome of the Theater of the World.* Rev. M. Coignet. London: I. Shawe, 1603.

Ozment, Steven E. *Mysticism and Dissent: Religious Ideology and Social Protest in the Sixteenth Century.* New Haven and London: Yale Univ. Press, 1973.

Pagel, Walter. "Paracelsus and the Neoplatonic and Gnostic Tradition." *Ambix* 8 (1960): 125–66.

———. *Paracelsus: An Introduction to Philosophical Medicine in the Era of the Renaissance.* New York and Basel: S. Karger, 1958.

———. "The Prime Matter of Paraclesus." *Ambix* 9 (1961): 117–35.

———. "Recent Paracelsian Studies." *History of Science* 12 (1974): 200–211.

Palingenius, Marcellus. *The Zodiake of Life.* Trans. Barnabie Googe. London: Printed for Raufe Newberye, 1576. Facsimile reprint edited by Rosemond Tuve. New York: Scholars' Facsimiles and Reprints, 1947. See *STC* for various editions of this translation, as well as editions of the original Latin. Palingenius was a major source of spirit lore, cosmology, and moral and philosophical reflections for the Elizabethans; see Kocher's *Science and Religion,* 119, and Tuve's introduction.

Palmer, D. J. "Magic and Poetry in *Doctor Faustus.*" *Critical Quarterly* 6 (1964): 56–67.

Panofsky, Erwin. *Renaissance and Renascences in Western Art.* Stockholm: Almquist and Wiksell, 1960.

————. *Studies in Iconology: Humanistic Themes in the Art of the Renais-sance.* 2nd ed. New York: Harper and Row, 1962.

Paracelsus. *The Hermetic and Alchemical Writings of Aureolus Philippus Theophrastus Bombast, of Hohenheim, Called Paracelsus the Great.* Ed. and trans. Arthur Edward Waite. 2 vols. London: J. Elliott, 1894.

————. *Paracelsus: Selected Writings.* Ed. Jolande Jacobi. Trans. Norbert Guterman. 2nd ed. Bollingen Series, no. 28. Princeton: Princeton Univ. Press, 1958.

————. *Sämtliche Werke.* Part One. Ed. Karl Sudhoff and Wilhelm Matthiessen. Vols. 6–9, Munich: O. W. Barth, 1922–25. Vols. 1–5 and 10–14, Berlin: R. Oldenbourg, 1928–33. Part Two. Ed. Kurt Goldhammer and others. Vols. 1–7 and Supplement, Wiesbaden: Franz Steiner, 1955–[73].

————. See also Hester, John, ed. and trans.

Parks, George B. "Pico della Mirandola in Tudor Translation." In Mahoney, *Philosophy and Humanism* (q.v.), 352–69.

Parry, Graham. *The Golden Age Restored: The Culture of the Stuart Court, 1603–42.* New York: St. Martin's Press, 1981.

Parsons, Robert [Philopatris, pseud.]. *An Advertisement Written to a Secretarie of my L. Treasyrers of Ingland, by an Inglishe Intelligencer as he passed throughe Germanie towards Italie Concerninge An other booke newly written in Latin.* N.p., 1592. The frequently quoted passage on "Sir Walter Rauleys Schoole of Atheisme" appears on p. 18. (Some pages are misnumbered in the copy I have examined.) Somewhat more detail may be found in the Latin pamphlet listed below.

————. *Elizabethae, Angliae Reginae . . . edictum promulgatis . . . cum responsiae.* Lyons: Apud Ioannem Didier, 1592. This pamphlet was circulated in England during early 1592, and several translations appeared during the same year; the item above is the most widely read abridgment and translation.

Partridge, Edward Bellamy. *The Broken Compass: A Study of the Major Comedies of Ben Jonson.* New York: Columbia Univ. Press, 1958.

Paster, Gail Kern. "Ben Jonson's Comedy of Limitation." *Studies in Philology* 72 (1975): 51–71.

————. "Montaigne, Dido, and *The Tempest:* 'How Came That Widow in?'" *Shakespeare Quarterly* 35 (1984): 91–94.

Patterson, Annabel. *Censorship and Interpretation: The Conditions of Writing and Reading in Early Modern England.* Madison: Univ. of Wisconsin Press, 1984.

Pepper, Jon V. "A Letter from Nathaniel Torporley to Thomas Harriot." *British Journal for the History of Science* 3 (June 1967): 285–90.

———. "The Study of Thomas Harriott's Manuscripts: Harriott's Unpublished Papers." *History of Science* 6 (1967): 17–40.

Perkins, William. *A Discourse of the Damned Art of Witchcraft . . . Framed and Delivered by M. William Perkins, in his ordinarie course of Preaching, and now published by Tho. Pickering.* Printed by Cantrel Legge, Printer to the Universitie of Cambridge, 1608.

Peterson, Douglas L. *Time, Tide, and Tempest: A Study of Shakespeare's Romances.* San Marino, Calif.: Huntington Library, 1973.

Peterson, Richard S. "The Iconography of Jonson's *Pleasure Reconciled to Virtue.*" *Journal of Medieval and Renaissance Studies* 5 (1975): 123–53.

Philopatris, pseud. See Parsons, Robert.

Phioravante [Fioravante], Leonardo. See Hester, John, ed. and trans.

Pico della Mirandola, Gianfrancesco [Gian Francesco; also Giovanni Francesco] (1470–1533). *On the Imagination.* Trans. Harry Caplan. Cornell Studies in English, no. 16. New Haven: Yale Univ. Press (for Cornell University), 1930. See below the additional entries under the given name "Giovanni Francesco," which appears on the title pages of some Elizabethan translations of G. F. Pico's works.

Pico della Mirandola, Giovanni (1463–94). *Conclusiones.* Ed. Bohdan Kieszkowski. Geneva: Librairie Droz, 1973.

———. *De hominis dignitate, Heptaplus, De ente et uno, e scritti vari.* Ed. Eugenio Garin. Florence: Vallechi Editore, 1942.

———. *Heptaplus; or, Discourse on the Seven Days of Creation.* Translated with an introduction and glossary by Jessie Brewer McGaw. New York: Philosophical Library, 1977.

———. *On the Dignity of Man, On Being and the One, Heptaplus.* Trans. Charles Glenn Wallis, Paul J. W. Miller, and Douglas Carmichael. Indianapolis: Bobbs-Merrill, 1965.

———. *Opera omnia.* 2 vols. 1557. Reprint. Hildesheim: G. Olms, 1964.

———. *A Platonic Discourse on Love.* Trans. T. Stanley. 1651. Reprinted with an introduction by Edmund Gardner. Boston: Merrymount Press, 1914.

Pico della Mirandola, Giovanni Francesco [Gianfrancesco] (1470–1533). *Giovanni Pico della Mirandola: His Life by His Nephew Giovanni Francesco Pico.* Trans. Thomas More. Ed. J. M. Rigg. 1890. Reprint. London: D. Nutt, 1982. Also contains additional devotional works by Giovanni Pico (1463–94).

————. *Here is co[n]teyned the lyfe of Iohan Picus Erle of Mirandula.* Trans. Thomas More. London: J. Rastell, [1510?]. See *STC* for subsequent editions; this biography, as well as the collection of devotional treatises by Giovanni Pico, was also included in the 1557 edition of More's *Works.*

Plat[t], Hugh. *The Floures of Philosophie.* Woburn Abbey, Bedfordshire: H. Bynneman a. F. Coldocke, 1572.

————. *The Jewel House of Art and Nature.* London: P. Short, 1594.

Pollard, A. W.; G. R. Redgrave; W. A. Jackson; F. S. Ferguson; and Katharine F. Pantzer. *A Short-Title Catalogue of Books Printed in England, Scotland, and Ireland, and of English Books Printed Abroad, 1475–1640.* 2nd ed. 2 vols. London: The Bibliographical Society, 1976–86. In those instances in which numbers of the 2nd edition of the *STC* differ from those of the 1st edition, the original number is cited as part of the new entry. Unless stated otherwise, numbers cited in the present study are those of the 2nd edition.

Popkin, Richard. Introduction to *Opera,* by Heinrich Cornelius Agrippa von Nettesheim. See Agrippa.

Porta, Giovanni Battista della. *Magiae Natvralis, sive De Miraculis rerum naturalivm.* Naples: Apud M. Cancer, 1558.

————. *Natural Magick.* Anonymous translator. London: Printed for T. Young and S. Speed, 1658.

Pritchard, Alan. *Alchemy: A Bibliography of English–Language Writings.* London: Routledge and Kegan Paul, 1980.

Purnell, Frederick, Jr. "Francesco Partizi and the Critics of Hermes Trismegistus." *Journal of Medieval and Renaissance Studies* 6 (1976): 155–78.

————. "Hermes and the Sibyl: A Note on Ficino's *Pimander.*" *Renaissance Quarterly* 30 (1977): 305–10. See also Michael J. B. Allen's "The Sibyl in Ficino's Oaktree" (q.v.).

Quercetanus, Josephus [Du Chesne, Joseph]. See Hester, John, ed. and trans.; Tymme, Thomas, trans.

Quinn, David B., and John W. Shirley. "A Contemporary List of Hariot References." *Renaissance Quarterly* 22 (1969): 9–26. An analysis of Harriot's own list of references to himself, including many references to his alleged impiety.

Rabkin, Norman. *Shakespeare and the Problem of Meaning.* Chicago and London: Univ. of Chicago Press, 1981.

Rainold [Raynalde], Thomas. *A Compendious Declaration of the Excellent vertues of a certain lateli inventid oile.* Venice: Ioan. Gryphius, 1551.

Ralegh, Sir Walter. *Works of Sir Walter Ralegh.* Ed. William Oldys and Thomas Birch. 8 vols. 1829. Reprint. New York: Burt Franklin, n.d.

Randall, John Herman, Jr. *The Making of the Modern Mind.* Rev. ed. 1940. Reprint. New York: Columbia Univ. Press, 1976.

Rattansi, P. M. "Alchemy and Natural Magic in Raleigh's *History of the World.*" *Ambix* 13 (1966): 122–38.

———. "Art and Science: The Paracelsian Vision." In Shirley and Hoeniger, *Science and the Arts in the Renaissance* (q.v.), 50–58.

———. "Paracelsus and the Puritan Revolution." *Ambix* 11 (1963): 24–32.

———. "The Social Interpretation of Science in the Seventeenth Century." In Mathias, *Science and Society, 1600–1900* (q.v.), 1–32.

Ravetz, Jerome R. *Scientific Knowledge and Its Social Problems.* Oxford: Clarendon Press, 1971.

Raynalde, Thomas. See Rainold.

Read, John. *Prelude to Chemistry.* Cambridge: M.I.T. Press, 1966.

Record[e], Robert. *The Castle of Knowledge.* London: Reginald Wolfe, 1556.

———. *The Castle of Knowledge.* 2nd ed. London: Printed by Valentine Sims, assigned by Bonham Norton, 1596.

———. *The Ground of Artes[,] Teaching the worke and Practise of arithmetike.* London: R. Wolfe, 1543. See *STC* for the many subsequent editions.

———. *The Pathway to Knowledg[e].* London: R. Wolfe, 1551.

Redner, Harry. *In the Beginning Was the Deed: Reflections on the Passage of Faust.* Berkeley and Los Angeles: Univ. of California Press, 1982.

Redwine, James D., Jr. "Beyond Psychology: The Moral Basis of Jonson's Theory of Humour Characterization." *ELH* 28 (1961): 316–34.

Reed, Robert R. *The Occult on the Tudor and Stuart Stage.* Boston: Christopher, 1965.

Rees, Graham. "Francis Bacon's Semi-Paracelsian Cosmology." *Ambix* 22 (1975): 81–101.

The Renaissance: Essays in Interpretation. See Chastel, André.

Rice, Eugene F. *The Renaissance Idea of Wisdom.* Cambridge: Harvard Univ. Press, 1958.

Richmond, Velma Bourgeois. "The Humanist Rejection of Romance." *South Atlantic Quarterly* 77 (1978): 296–306.

Ripley, George. *The Compound of Alchymy.* Ed. Raph [*sic*] Rabbards. London: Thomas Orwin, 1591.

Robb, Nesca. *Neoplatonism of the Italian Renaissance.* London: G. Allen and Unwin, 1935.

Rose, Mark. *Heroic Love: Studies in Sidney and Spenser.* Cambridge: Harvard Univ. Press, 1968.

Rose, Paul Lawrence. *Bodin and the Great God of Nature: The Moral and Religious Universe of a Judaizer.* Geneva: Librairie Droz, 1980.

Rosenkreutz, Christian, pseud. See Allen, Paul, ed.

Rossi, Paolo. *Francis Bacon: From Magic to Science.* Trans. Sacha Rabinovich. Chicago: Univ. of Chicago Press, 1968.

———. "Hermeticism, Rationality, and the Scientific Revolution." In Bonelli and Shea, *Reason, Experiment, and Mysticism in the Scientific Revolution* (q.v.), 247–73.

Rossky, William. "Imagination in the English Renaissance: Psychology and Poetic." *Studies in the Renaissance* 5 (1958): 49–73.

Rowse, A. L. *Christopher Marlowe, His Life and Work.* New York: Harper and Row, 1964.

———. *The Expansion of Elizabethan England.* New York: St. Martin's Press, 1955.

———. *Sex and Society in Shakespeare's Age: Simon Forman the Astrologer.* New York: Scribner, 1974.

Ruderman, David B. "Giovanni Mercurio da Correggio's Appearance in Italy as Seen through the Eyes of an Italian Jew." *Renaissance Quarterly* 28 (1975): 309–22. Interesting account of a fifteenth-century Hermeticist who claimed to have experienced divine illumination and obtained prophetic and magical powers.

Rukeyser, Muriel. *The Traces of Thomas Hariot.* New York: Random House, 1971. An impressionistic and intriguing biography, based on a combination of wide reading and informed speculation.

Sadler, Lynn Veach. "Relations between Alchemy and Poetics in the Renaissance and Seventeenth Century." *Ambix* 24, pt. 2 (1977): 69–76.

Sanders, Wilbur. *The Dramatist and the Received Idea: Studies in the Plays of Marlowe and Shakespeare.* Cambridge: Cambridge Univ. Press, 1968.

Sargent, Ralph. *At the Court of Queen Elizabeth.* 1935. Reprinted as *The Life and Lyrics of Sir Edward Dyer.* London: Oxford Univ. Press, 1968.

Schmidgall, Gary. *Shakespeare and the Courtly Aesthetic.* Berkeley and Los Angeles: Univ. of California Press, 1981.

Schmitt, Charles B. *John Case and Aristotelianism in Renaissance England.* Kingston and Montreal: McGill-Queen's Univ. Press, 1983. Discusses the reaction against magic at Oxford in the late sixteenth century.

Scholem, Gershom. *Major Trends in Jewish Mysticism.* 3rd ed. New York: Schocken Books, 1967.

———. *On the Kabbalah and Its Symbolism.* Trans. Ralph Manheim. New York: Schocken Books, 1965.

———. *Sabbatai Sevi: The Mystical Messiah.* Princeton: Princeton Univ. Press, 1973.

Schuler, Robert M. *English Magical and Scientific Poems to 1700: An Annotated Bibliography.* New York: Garland, 1979.

———. "Some Spiritual Alchemies of Seventeenth-Century England." *Journal of the History of Ideas* 41 (1980): 293–318.

———. "William Blomfield, Elizabethan Alchemist." *Ambix* 20 (1973): 75–87.

Scot, Reginald. *The Discoverie of Witchcraft.* 1584. Ed. Montague Summers. London: John Rodker, 1930. Reprint. New York: Dover, 1972. Includes a bibliographical note on early editions.

Scott, Walter, ed. and trans. *Hermetica: The Ancient Greek and Latin Writings Which Contain Religious or Philosophic Teachings Ascribed to Hermes Trismegistus.* 4 vols. Oxford: Clarendon Press, 1924–36. Reprint. London: Dawson's, 1968. Parallel texts in Greek or

Latin and English. Because Scott has made rearrangements in some treatises, the Nock edition is considered standard.

Scoular, Kitty W. *Natural Magic: Studies in the Presentation of Nature in English Poetry from Spenser to Marvell.* Oxford: Clarendon Press, 1965.

Seligmann, Kurt. *Magic, Supernaturalism, and Religion.* New York: Random House, Pantheon Books, 1971. Originally published in 1948 as *The History of Magic,* this volume offers a broad survey of works on magic, alchemy, cabala, witchcraft, and related subjects from the ancient world through the eighteenth century. Although not fully documented, the work contains some notes and a "bibliographic resume."

Semon, Kenneth J. "Fantasy and Wonder in Shakespeare's Last Plays." *Shakespeare Quarterly* 25 (1974): 89–102.

Sewall, Richard B. *The Vision of Tragedy.* Rev. ed. New Haven: Yale Univ. Press, 1980.

Sewell, Elizabeth. "'As I was sometime Milan': Prospects for a Search for Giordano Bruno, through Prospero, Coleridge, and the Figure of Exile." *Mosaic: A Journal for the Comparative Study of Literature and Ideas* 8, no. 3 (Spring 1975): 127–37.

Shakespeare, William. *The Riverside Shakespeare.* Ed. G. Blakemore Evans and others. Boston: Houghton Mifflin, 1974.

———. See also Harrison, G. B., ed; and Kermode, Frank, ed.

Shapiro, Michael. "Role-Playing, Reflexivity, and Metadrama in Recent Shakespearean Criticism." *Renaissance Drama,* n.s. 12 (1981): 145–61.

Shea, William R. "Introduction: Trends in the Interpretation of Seventeenth-Century Science." In Bonelli and Shea, *Reason, Experiment, and Mysticism in the Scientific Revolution* (q.v.), 1–17.

Shepherd, Simon. *Marlowe and the Politics of Elizabethan Theatre.* New York: St. Martin's Press, 1986.

Shirley, John W. "The Scientific Experiments of Sir Walter Ralegh, the Wizard Earl, and the Three Magi in the Tower, 1603–1617." *Ambix* 4 (1949): 52–66.

———. *Thomas Harriot: A Biography.* Oxford: Clarendon Press, 1983.

———, ed. *Thomas Harriot: Renaissance Scientist.* Oxford: Clarendon Press, 1974.

Shirley, John W., and F. David Hoeniger, eds. *Science and the Arts in the Renaissance.* Cranbury, N.J.: Folger Books, for the Folger Shakespeare Library, Washington, D.C.; London and Toronto: Associated Univ. Presses, 1985. Includes essays on interrelationships among magic, humanism, and science.

Short-Title Catalogue. See Pollard, A. W., and others.

Shumaker, Wayne. *The Occult Sciences in the Renaissance: A Study in Intellectual Patterns.* Berkeley and Los Angeles: Univ. of California Press, 1972.

———, ed. *Renaissance Curiosa.* Binghamton, N.Y.: Center for Medieval and Early Renaissance Studies, 1982. Includes John Dee's *True and Faithful Relation* (q.v.).

Sidney, Philip. *A Defence of Poetry.* Ed. Jan Van Dorsten. 1966. Reprint. Oxford: Oxford Univ. Press, 1984.

Simon, Joan. *Education and Society in Tudor England.* Cambridge: Cambridge Univ. Press, 1966.

Singer, Dorothea Waley. *Giordano Bruno, His Life and Thought, with Annotated Translation of His Work, "On the Infinite Universe and Worlds."* New York: Abelard-Schuman, 1950.

Singleton, Charles S., ed. *Art, Science, and History in the Renaissance.* Baltimore: Johns Hopkins Press, 1967.

Sisson, C. J. "The Magic of Prospero." *Shakespeare Survey* 11 (1958): 70–77.

———. "A Topical Reference in *The Alchemist.*" In McManaway, Dawson, and Willoughby, *Joseph Quincy Adams Memorial Studies* (q.v.), 739–41.

Slights, William W. E. "A Source for *The Tempest* and the Context of the *Discorsi.*" *Shakespeare Quarterly* 36 (1985): 68–70. Sound evidence for a new source which emphasizes "the human agency through which providential forces reveal themselves in history" (69).

Southall, Raymond. "Ben Jonson and the Art of Living." In *Literature and the Rise of Capitalism: Critical Essays Mainly on the Sixteenth and Seventeenth Centuries,* 95–104. London: Laurence and Wishart, 1973.

Steane, J. B. *Marlowe: A Critical Study.* Cambridge: Cambridge Univ. Press, 1964.

Strathmann, Ernest A. *Sir Walter Ralegh: A Study in Elizabethan Skepticism.* New York: Columbia Univ. Press, 1951.

Szõnyi, Gy E. "The Quest for Omniscience: The Intellectual Background of Marlowe's *Dr. Faustus.*" *Acta Universitatis Szegediensis de Attila József Nominatae: Papers in English and American Studies* 1 (1980): 139–66.

Talbert, Ernest William. "The Interpretation of Jonson's Courtly Spectacles." *PMLA* 61 (1946): 454–73.

Taylor, Sherwood. *The Alchemists.* New York: H. Schuman, 1949.

Teall, John L. "Witchcraft and Calvinism in Elizabethan England: Divine Power and Human Agency." *Journal of the History of Ideas* 23 (1962): 21–36.

Tetzeli von Rosador, Kurt. *Magie im elisabethanischen Drama.* Braunschweig: Georg Westermann, 1970.

Thayer, Calvin Graham. *Ben Jonson: Studies in the Plays.* Norman: Univ. of Oklahoma Press, 1963.

———. "Theme and Structure in *The Alchemist.*" *ELH* 26 (1959): 23–35.

Theatricum Chemicum Britannicum. See Ashmole, Elias, ed.

Thomas, Keith. *Religion and the Decline of Magic.* New York: Charles Scribner's Sons, 1971.

Thomas Aquinas, Saint. *Basic Writings of Saint Thomas Aquinas.* Ed. Anton C. Pegis. 2 vols. New York: Random House, 1945. Vol. 2 includes *Contra Gentiles,* bk. 3, chaps. 101–110, on miracles, magic, and daemons.

———. *Summa Theologica.* Trans. Fathers of the English Dominican Province. 3 vols. 1920. Reprint. New York: Benziger Brothers, 1947–48.

Thoms, William John, ed. *Early English Prose Romances.* London: G. Routledge; New York: E. P. Dutton, 1906. Contains *The Famous Historie of Fryer Bacon,* a work rejecting magic as the epitome of excessive pride in human learning; and an edition of the English Faustbook.

Thorndike, Lynn. *A History of Magic and Experimental Science.* 8 vols. New York: Columbia Univ. Press, 1923–58.

———. "The Renaissance." *Encyclopaedia Britannica,* 1971 edition.

Tillyard, E.M.W. *Shakespeare's Last Plays.* New York: Barnes and Noble, 1964.

Traister, Barbara. *Heavenly Necromancers: The Magician in English Renaissance Drama.* Columbia: Univ. of Missouri Press, 1984.

Traversi, D[erek] A. "The Last Plays of Shakespeare." In Kernan, *Modern Shakespearean Criticism* (q.v.), 427–447. (First published in *The Age of Shakespeare*, ed. Boris Ford, 257–81. Vol. 2 of *A Guide to English Literature*. Rev. ed. Harmondsworth: Penguin, 1956.)

———. *Shakespeare: The Last Phase*. London: Hollis and Carter, 1954.

Trevor-Roper, Hugh. *The European Witch-Craze of the Sixteenth and Seventeenth Centuries*. 1956. Reprint. Harmondsworth: Penguin, 1978.

Trinkaus, Charles. *"In Our Image and Likeness": Humanity and Divinity in Italian Humanist Thought*. 2 vols., pages numbered consecutively. London: Constable; Chicago: Univ. of Chicago Press, 1970.

———. "Marsilio Ficino and the Ideal of Human Autonomy." In Eisenbichler and Pugliese, *Ficino and Renaissance Neoplatonism* (q.v.), 141–53.

Trout, Paul. "Magic and the Millennium: A Study of the Millenary Motifs in the Occult Milieu of Puritan England, 1640–1660." Ph.D. dissertation, Univ. of British Columbia, 1975. See *Dissertation Abstracts International* 36 (1976): 4520A.

———. "The Millenary Dream of Alchemy." Paper presented at the Modern Language Association convention, Chicago, December 29, 1973.

Tymme, Thomas. *The figure of Antichriste, with the tokens of the end of the World*. London: Imprinted for F. Coldocke, 1586.

———. *A preparation against the prognosticated dangers of this yeare, 1588*. London: I. Wolfe, 1588.

———, trans. *The Practise of Chymicall and Hermetical Physicke, for the preservation of health*, by Josephus Quersitanus. London: Thomas Creede, 1605. Tymme's "Forespeech to the Reader" affirms aggressively the importance of the advances in arts and sciences during the sixteenth century; Tymme emphasizes the Hermetic and Paracelsian traditions.

Uphaus, Robert W. *Beyond Tragedy: Structure and Experience in Shakespeare's Romances*. Lexington: Univ. Press of Kentucky, 1981.

———. "Virtue in Vengeance: Prospero's Rarer Action." *Bucknell Review* 18, no. 2 (Fall 1970): 34–51.

Valcke, Louis. "Magie et miracle chez Jean Pic de la Mirandole." In Eisenbichler and Pugliese, *Ficino and Renaissance Neoplatonism* (q.v.), 155–73.

Vickers, Brian, ed. *Occult and Scientific Mentalities in the Renaissance.* Cambridge and New York: Cambridge Univ. Press, 1984.

Waite, Arthur Edward. *The Real History of the Rosicrucians.* New York: J. W. Bouton, 1888. Although it must be updated and used with some caution, this work provides an interesting argument concerning the connection between the Rosicrucians and Paracelsus, as well as the utopian and apocalyptic elements of Rosicrucianism.

————, ed. *The Hermetic Museum, Restored and Enlarged.* 2 vols. London: James Elliott and Co., 1893. Reprint. London: John M. Watkins, 1953. A valuable collection of Renaissance and seventeenth-century Hermetic and alchemical treatises. Includes Henry Madathanas's *The Golden Age Restored.*

Waith, Eugene. *The Herculean Hero in Marlowe, Chapman, Shakespeare and Dryden.* New York: Columbia Univ. Press, 1962.

Walker, Daniel P. *The Ancient Theology: Studies in Christian Platonism from the Fifteenth to the Eighteenth Century.* Ithaca, N.Y.: Cornell Univ. Press, 1972.

————. *Spiritual and Demonic Magic from Ficino to Campanella.* London: Warburg Institute, 1958. Reprint. Nendeln: Kraus Reprint, 1969.

————. *Unclean Spirits: Possession and Exorcism in France and England in the Late Sixteenth and Early Seventeenth Centuries.* London: Scolar Press, 1981.

Wallace, John M. "'Examples Are Best Precepts': Readers and Meanings in Seventeenth-Century Poetry." *Critical Inquiry* 1 (1974–75): 273–90. Reveals the importance of "application" as a dominant mode of reading in the Renaissance; relevant to dramatic and nondramatic literature of the sixteenth and seventeenth centuries.

Wallis, R. T. *Neoplatonism.* London: Duckworth, 1972.

Walton, Michael T. "John Dee's 'Monas Hieroglyphica': Geometrical Cabala." *Ambix* 23 (1976): 116–23.

Ward, A. W., ed. *Marlowe: "Tragical History of Dr. Faustus." Greene: "Honourable History of Friar Bacon and Friar Bungay."* Oxford: Clarendon Press, 1887.

Ward, Robert. "What Is Forced by Fire: Concerning Some Influences of Chemical Thought and Practice upon English Poetry." *Ambix* 23 (1976): 80–95.

Warren, Michael J. "*Doctor Faustus:* The Old Man and the Text." *English Literary Renaissance* 11 (1981): 111–47.

Webster, Charles. *From Paracelsus to Newton: Magic and the Making of Modern Science.* Cambridge and New York: Cambridge Univ. Press, 1982.

Weil, Judith. *Christopher Marlowe: Merlin's Prophet.* London: Cambridge Univ. Press, 1977. Argues that Marlowe utilizes irony to reveal the folly of his boastful protagonists.

Weiner, Andrew D. "Expelling the Beast: Bruno's Adventures in England." *Modern Philology* 78 (1980–81): 1–13.

Weiss, Roberto. *Humanism in England during the Fifteenth Century.* 3rd ed. Oxford: Basil Blackwell, 1967.

Welsford, Enid. *The Court Masque.* 1927. Reprint. New York: Russell and Russell, 1962. Includes valuable discussion of the *The Tempest* as suggesting a mystery through concrete form.

West, Robert. "The Impatient Magic of *Doctor Faustus.*" *English Literary Renaissance* 4 (1974): 218–40.

———. *The Invisible World: A Study of Pneumatology in Elizabethan Drama.* Athens: Univ. of Georgia Press, 1939.

———. *Reginald Scot and Renaissance Writings on Witchcraft.* Boston: Twayne, 1984.

———. *Shakespeare and the Outer Mystery.* Lexington: Univ. of Kentucky Press, 1968.

Westcott, William Wynn. *The Study of the Kabbalah.* New York: Allied Publications, n.d.

Westman, Robert S., and J. E. McGuire. *Hermeticism and the Scientific Revolution.* Los Angeles: William Andrews Clark Memorial Library, UCLA: 1977.

Wier, Johann. *De Praestigiis Daemonum, et incantationibus ac veneficiis libri sex.* Basel: Ex officina Oporiniana, 1568.

———. *Histoires, disputes et discours des illusions et impostures des diables, des magiciens infames, sorcières et empoisonneurs.* [Paris]: Jacques Chouet, 1579.

Wightman, W.P.D. *Science in a Renaissance Society.* New York: Humanities Press, 1972.

Williams, George Huntston. *The Radical Reformation.* Philadelphia: Westminster Press, 1962.

Williams, Mary C. "Merlin and the Prince: *The Speeches at Prince Henry's Barriers.*" *Renaissance Drama,* n.s. 8 (1977): 221–30.

Williams, William Proctor. "Other Patterns of Stoicism, 1530–1670." *Modern Language Review* 69 (1974): 1–11.

Williamson, George. "The Restoration Revolt against Enthusiasm." *Studies in Philology* 30 (1933): 571–603.

Wind, Edgar. *Pagan Mysteries in the Renaissance*. Rev. ed. Harmondsworth: Penguin, 1967.

Wirszubski, Chaim. "Francesco Giorgio's Commentary on Giovanni Pico's Kabbalistic Theses." *Journal of the Warburg and Courtauld Institutes* 37 (1974): 145–56.

Witt, Ronald. "Medieval 'Ars Dictaminis' and the Beginnings of Humanism: A New Construction of the Problem." *Renaissance Quarterly* 35 (1982): 1–35.

Woodhouse, A.S.P. "Nature and Grace in *The Faerie Queene*." *ELH* 16 (1949): 194–228.

Woodman, David. *White Magic and English Renaissance Drama*. Rutherford, N.J.: Fairleigh Dickinson Univ. Press, 1973.

Wraight, A. D. *In Search of Christopher Marlowe: A Pictorial Biography*. New York: Vanguard Press, 1965.

Wyrick, Deborah Baker. "The Ass Motif in *The Comedy of Errors* and *A Midsummer Night's Dream*." *Shakespeare Quarterly* 33 (1982): 432–48.

Yates, Frances. *The Art of Memory*. Chicago: Univ. of Chicago Press, 1966.

———. *Astraea: The Imperial Theme in the Sixteenth Century*. London: Routledge and Kegan Paul, 1975.

———. *Giordano Bruno and the Hermetic Tradition*. Chicago: Univ. of Chicago Press, 1964. Reprint. New York: Random House, Vintage, 1969.

———. "A Great Magus." Review of *John Dee*, by Peter French, and *The Occult Sciences in the Renaissance*, by Wayne Shumaker. *New York Review of Books*, January 25, 1973, 39–42.

———. *Lull and Bruno: Collected Essays*. London: Routledge and Kegan Paul, 1982. Includes "Renaissance Philosophers in Elizabethan England: John Dee and Giordano Bruno."

———. *Majesty and Magic in Shakespeare's Last Plays*. Boulder, Colo.: Shambhala, 1978. Reprint, with altered title, of *Shakespeare's Last Plays: A New Approach*.

———. *The Occult Philosophy in the Elizabethan Age*. London: Routledge and Kegan Paul, 1979.

———. "Queen Elizabeth as Astraea." *Journal of the Warburg and Courtauld Institutes* 10 (1947): 27–82. A fundamental contribution to our understanding of Elizabethan iconography in relation to mystical imperialism. Reprinted in *Astraea.*

———. *The Rosicrucian Enlightenment.* London: Routledge and Kegan Paul, 1972.

———. *Shakespeare's Last Plays: A New Approach.* London: Routledge and Kegan Paul, 1975.

———. *A Study of "Love's Labor's Lost."* Cambridge: Cambridge Univ. Press, 1936.

———. *Theatre of the World.* Chicago: Univ. of Chicago Press, 1969.

Young, David. *The Heart's Forest: A Study of Shakespeare's Pastoral Plays.* New Haven: Yale Univ. Press, 1972.

———. "Where the Bee Sucks: A Triangular Study of *Doctor Faustus, The Alchemist,* and *The Tempest.*" In Kay and Jacobs, *Shakespeare's Romances Reconsidered* (q.v.), 149–66. Argues that Shakespeare responds in *The Tempest* to the aesthetic of both *Doctor Faustus* and *The Tempest.*

Zambelli, Paola. "Magic and Radical Reformation in Agrippa of Nettesheim." *Journal of the Warburg and Courtauld Institutes* 39 (1976): 69–103.

Zetterburg, J. Peter. "The Mistaking of 'the Mathematicks' for Magic in Tudor and Stuart England." *Sixteenth-Century Journal* 11 (1980): 83–97.

Zika, Charles. "Reuchlin and Erasmus: Humanism and the Occult Philosophy." *Journal of Religious History* (Sydney) 9 (1977): 223–46.

———. "Reuchlin's *De verbo mirifico* and the Magic Debate of the Late Fifteenth Century." *Journal of the Warburg and Courtauld Institutes* 39 (1976): 104–38.

Index

Adam Kadmon: in Cabala, 47–49, 83–84

Agrippa, Cornelius: *De occulta philosophia,* 53–61, 62; *De vanitate,* 61–71, 90, 100–101, 110; and humanistic education, 20; and Jonson, 144; magical procedures in works of, 53–61, 61–72 passim; and Marlowe, 72, 122, 123; and occult tradition, 2, 20, 38, 53–72, 73; and Shakespeare, 180; and traditional authorities, 53, 58, 62–72, 73, 90, 97, 98, 100, 105; view of human nature, 7, 53–72 passim

Alchemist, The: and "enthusiasm" (divine inspiration), xiii, 137, 140–42, 148–53, 159–61, 171–73; and occult tradition, 3–4, 137–55, 159–61; and reform movements, 137–55; and return of the Golden Age, 139–40, 145, 151–52, 155, 200; and scientific objectivity, xiii, 159–61, 171–73; and traditional authorities, xiii, 97, 137–55 passim, 156–57, 171–73; vision of human nature in, 3–4, 87, 137–57, 160–61, 171–73

Alchemy (*see also* Occult tradition; Paracelsians; Paracelsus): in Agrippa von Nettesheim, 65; in Ficino, 25–26; and Jonson, 137–55, 162–63, 172; in Pico della Mirandola, Giovanni, 46; and reform movements, 6, 15, 75, 91–96; and *The Tempest,* 181

Altman, Joel, 235n.6

Anabaptists (*see also* Reform movements; Reformation, Protestant), 15, 96, 240–41n.6; satirized by Jonson, 140–42, 146, 148, 152–53, 157

Angels (*see also* Daemons; Sephiroth): in Agrippa von Nettesheim, 58–60, 65; in Dee, John, 85; in Ficino, 26, 31–34; in Pico della Mirandola, Giovanni, 39, 42, 44–50; in Ralegh, 81

Application as a principle of interpretation, xiii

Archetypes. *See* Adam Kadmon; Ideas, Platonic; Universals

Aristotle: as authority figure, 7, 9,

esp. 33–35; and Paracelsus, 102;
in Pico della Mirandola, Giovanni, 39–52; and reform movements, 15–21 passim, 84
God
—relation to created world: in
Agrippa von Nettesheim, 53–72;
in Bacon, 170–71; in *Dr. Faustus,*
113; in Ficino, 17, 22–35; in Jonson, 170–71; in Paracelsus and
Paracelsians, 90–96; in Pico
della Mirandola, Giovanni, 39–
52; in Renaissance Neoplatonism, 17
—relation to humankind, 4, 6–7,
11–21, 75; in Agrippa von Nettesheim, 53–72; in Dee, John,
84–87; and *Dr. Faustus,* 122, 129;
in Ficino, 22–35; in Paracelsus
and Paracelsians, 90–96; in Pico
della Mirandola, Giovanni, 39–
52; in Ralegh, 80–81; in Scot,
Reginald, 109–10; in *The Tempest,* 176–90
Godshalk, W. L., 235n.6
Goetia. See Magic; Witchcraft, accusations of
Golden Age (*see also* Reform movements; Utopianism), 12–21, 83–
96 passim, 200; in *The Alchemist,*
139–40, 145, 151–52, 155; in
Jonson's masques, 13, 157, 161–
62; and *The Tempest,* 197
Goldman, Michael, 235n.6
Greenblatt, Stephen, 119, 227n.11
Greene, Donald, 169–70
Greene, Robert, 117, 120
Greene, Thomas M., 241n.9
Greg, W. W., 233–34n.2

Hacket, William, 141
Hakluyt, Richard, 77
Hall, Marie Boas, 207n.6
Harriot, Thomas: and the evolution
of science, 77, 78–79; heretical
beliefs of, 78–80, 89; and Mar-
lowe, 78–79, 113, 120, 129,
227n.10
Harris, Anthony, 206n.4, 207n.5
Harrison, G. B., 107
Hartwig, Joan, 248n.14
Harvey, Gabriel, 109
Hatton, Christopher, 73, 86
Haydn, Hiram, 20, 241n.12
Hermeticism (*see also* Alchemy;
Gnosticism; Magic; Neoplatonism; Occult Tradition): in
Agrippa von Nettesheim, 53–72
passim; in Ficino, 24–35 passim;
and Jonson, 139–73 passim; and
magic, 34; and Marlowe, 113–36;
in occult tradition, 11, 17–21, 38,
73–112 passim, 210–11n.27; in
Pico della Mirandola, Giovanni,
38–52 passim; in sixteenth-
century England, 6–8, 38, 75–
112 passim; in *The Tempest,* 176–
99 passim
Hester, John, 92–93
Hierarchy, social. *See* Authority,
challenges to; Reform movements
Hill, Christopher, 2, 209n.22,
231n.47
Hill, Nicholas, 78, 80
Hippocrates, 94
Hirsch, E. D.: on authorial intention, xii, 203n.1; on evaluation of
texts, xiii

39–52; in Postel, Guillaume, 84; satirized in *The Alchemist*, 137–55; skepticism regarding, 110; in *The Tempest*, 180, 181, 186, 190
—of the individual, 10–21 passim; in Agrippa von Nettesheim, 55–56, 57–58, 60–61, 68–70; in Bacon, Francis, 111; in Bruno, Giordano, 87–89; in Dee, John, 85–87; in *Dr. Faustus*, 123–29, 135; in Ficino, 23–35; in Pico della Mirandola, Giovanni, 39–52; satirized in *The Alchemist*, 137–38, 141–48, 149–55 passim; in *The Tempest*, 176–77, 180–81, 183–86, 194–96, 199
Renaissance (*see also* Art; Authority, challenges to; Golden Age; Humanism; Humankind; Reactionary forces; Reform movements): and Agrippa von Nettesheim, 69–72; and Jonson, 171–73; and occult tradition, 1–21, 200–201; and Shakespeare, 174–76, 190–99; twentieth century interpretations of, 1–6, 36
Reuchlin, Johannes, 10, 20, 38, 97, 207n.8
Revelation, divine: in Agrippa von Nettesheim, 55–56, 57–58, 60–66, 68–70; Bacon's critique of, 111; in Dee, John, 85–86; and *Dr. Faustus*, 132; in Ficino, 23–35; and Jonson, xiii, 137, 140–42, 148–53, 156–73; and magic, 6, 20–21, 37, 42–52 passim; and Paracelsianism, 90–96 passim, 101; in Pico della Mirandola,

Giovanni, 39–52 passim; and reform movements, 15–21, 64–66, 68–70, 91–92; and *The Tempest*, 181, 184, 189–90, 199
Rosicrucians, 138, 139, 162, 163
Rossi, Paolo, on science and the occult tradition, 2, 3, 38, 217n.2
Rowley, Samuel, 119, 233n.2
Rudolf II (Holy Roman Emperor), 87, 138

Sanders, Wilbur, 119, 234n.5
Sanford, James, 62
Scholasticism (*see also* Thomas Aquinas, Saint): and occult tradition, 16–17, 43, 97
Scholem, Gershom, 48
Science (*see also* Empiricism): contrasted with magic, 3, 7, 37–38; and humanism, 8–10, 111, 207n.6; and Marlowe, 113–15, 136; and neoclassicism, 169–73; and occult tradition, 2–3, 6–8, 24–25, 35, 36–38, 73–96, 97–108 passim, 109–12, 217–18n.2
Scot, Reginald, 109–11
Self-determination. *See* Humankind; Metamorphosis of the self
Seneca, 156
Sephiroth (*see also* Angels; Daemons): in Agrippa von Nettesheim, 59; in Pico della Mirandola, Giovanni, 47–50, 59
Sewall, Richard, 235n.5
Shakespeare, William (see also *The Tempest*): and humanism, 20; and Jonson, xiii–xiv, 173, 177; and Marlowe, xiii–xiv, 173, 177; and occult tradition, xi, 3–4, 17, 20,

55; in *The Tempest,* 197

Valcke, Louis, 219n.6
Vickers, Brian, 2, 3, 217n.2
Virgil, 156

Walker, D. P., 31, 33, 211n.1
Wallace, John, xiii
Wallis, R. T., 33
Ward, A. W., 6
Warner, Walter, 78, 79, 80
Warren, Michael J., 234n.2
Weiner, Andrew, 2, 88, 205n.3
West, Robert, 121, 122, 177–78,
    179, 180, 182, 206n.4
Westman, Robert, 217–18n.2
Wier, Johann, 110
Wightman, Edward, 141
Witchcraft, accusations of (*see also*
    Reactionary forces), 4, 6, 7, 31–
    33, 44–45, 53, 61–72, 73–74, 76,
    96–108; and Agrippa von Net-

tesheim, 53, 54–58, 61–72; and
Dr. Faustus, 114, 115, 121–22;
skepticism concerning, 109–11;
and *The Tempest,* 181–82, 194
Woodman, David, 206n.4, 207n.5
Wortham, Christopher, 234

Yates, Frances: on Agrippa von Net-
    tesheim, 62; on British imperial-
    ism, 84; on Dee, John, 87; on Fi-
    cino, 211n.1; on humanism, 2,
    19–20, 97, 156; on magic and
    science, 2, 36–37; on occult tra-
    dition, 1–3, 19–20, 84, 97; on
    Pico della Mirandola, Giovanni,
    36–37, 45; on sixteenth-century
    English literature, 2; on witch-
    craft persecution as reactionary
    force, 97

Zambelli, Paolo, 71
Zika, Charles, 20, 207n.8